discover
SPAIN

ANTHONY HAM
DAMIEN SIMONIS, SARAH ANDREWS, STUART BUTLER,
JOHN NOBLE, JOSEPHINE QUINTERO, MILES RODDIS,
ARPI ARMENAKIAN SHIVELY

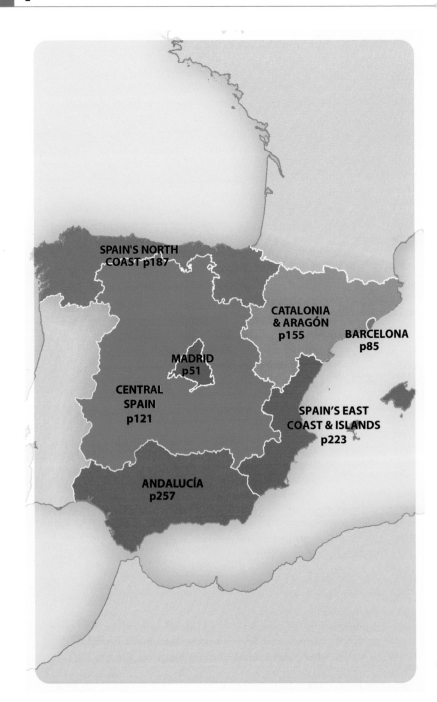

DISCOVER SPAIN

Madrid (p51) World-class art galleries, beautiful plazas, terrific restaurants and pulsating nightlife are Madrid specialities.

Barcelona (p85) Barcelona has extraordinary Gaudí architecture and is the epicentre of Spain's gastronomic revolution.

Central Spain (p121) The Spanish interior boasts beguiling cities, timeless villages, and even fine Roman ruins in Mérida.

Catalonia & Aragón (p155) This region combines the striking Pyrenees with lovely villages and monument-studded cities.

Spain's North Coast (p187) The country's north offers the Guggenheim, a magnificent coastline, and Spain's culinary capital.

Spain's East Coast & Islands (p223) Mediterranean Spain in microcosm, from great architecture to idyllic beaches.

Andalucía (p257) The Spain you dreamed of, with stunning scenery, exquisite Islamic-era architecture and passionate flamenco.

↘ CONTENTS

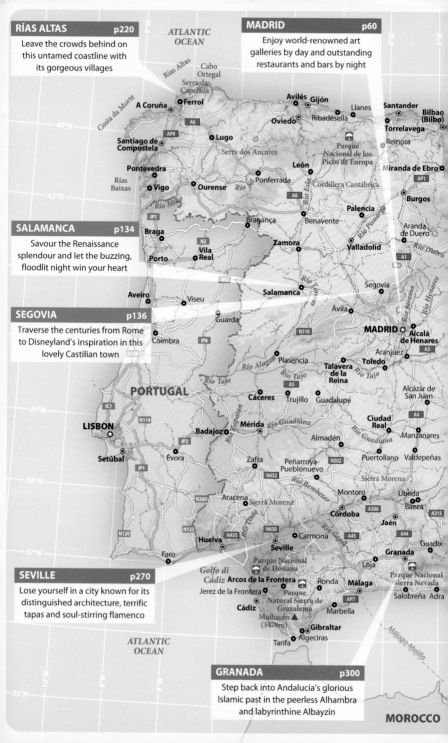

ATLANTIC OCEAN

Rías Altas

Costa da Morte

Cabo Ortegal

Serra da Capelada

A Coruña   Ferrol

Avilés   Gijón

Oviedo   Ribadesella

Llanes   Santander   Bilbao (Bilbo)

Torrelavega

Reinosa

Santiago de Compostela

Lugo

Serra dos Ancares

Parque Nacional de los Picos de Europa

Miranda de Ebro

Pontevedra

León

Cordillera Cantábrica

Vigo   Ourense   Río

Ponferrada

Río Esla

Rías Baixas

Río Miño

Bragança

Benavente

Palencia

Río Pisuerga

Burgos

Aranda de Duero

Braga

Zamora

Valladolid

Río Duero

N2

Vila Real

Porto

IP1

IP2

Salamanca

Río Tormes

Segovia

Río Arlanza

Río Henares

Aveiro

Viseu

Ávila

MADRID   Alcalá de Henares

A3

Coimbra

Guarda

N110

IP6

Plasencia

Aranjuez   Toledo

PORTUGAL

Río Alagón

Río Tajo

Talavera de la Reina

Río Tajo

Alcázar de San Juan

A4

IC1

N119

Cáceres

Trujillo

Guadalupe

LISBON

Badajoz

Mérida

Río Guadiana

Ciudad Real

Manzanares

Río Guadiana

Setúbal

IP2

Almadén

Puertollano

Valdepeñas

IP1

Évora

Zafra

Peñarroya-Pueblonuevo

N502

N432

Sierra Morena

Río Bembezar

Montoro

Úbeda

Baeza

A306

A315

N260

Aracena

Sierra Morena

Córdoba

Jaén

A44

N120

N122

N435

Río Tinto

N630

Carmona

Río Genil

A45

Guadix

Huelva

Seville

Granada

Faro

Parque Nacional de Doñana

Golfo di Cádiz

Arcos de la Frontera

Loja

Parque Nacional Sierra Nevada

Jerez de la Frontera

Ronda

Málaga

Salobreña   Adra

Parque Natural Sierra de Grazalema

Cádiz

Mulhacén (3478m)

Marbella

AP7

Málaga-Melilla

Gibraltar

Tarifa   Algeciras

ATLANTIC OCEAN

MOROCCO

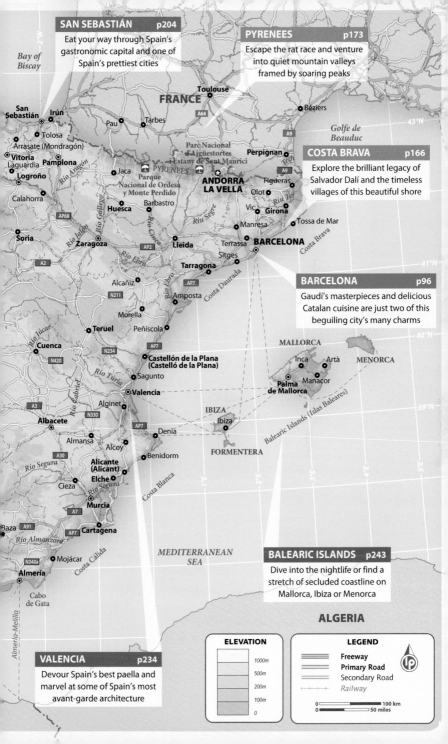

SAN SEBASTIÁN p204
Eat your way through Spain's gastronomic capital and one of Spain's prettiest cities

PYRENEES p173
Escape the rat race and venture into quiet mountain valleys framed by soaring peaks

COSTA BRAVA p166
Explore the brilliant legacy of Salvador Dalí and the timeless villages of this beautiful shore

BARCELONA p96
Gaudí's masterpieces and delicious Catalan cuisine are just two of this beguiling city's many charms

BALEARIC ISLANDS p243
Dive into the nightlife or find a stretch of secluded coastline on Mallorca, Ibiza or Menorca

VALENCIA p234
Devour Spain's best paella and marvel at some of Spain's most avant-garde architecture

Bay of Biscay

FRANCE

San Sebastián
Irún
Tolosa
Arrasate (Mondragón)
Vitoria
Laguardia Pamplona
Logroño
Calahorra
Soria
Pau
Tarbes
Toulouse
Béziers
Golfe de Beauduc

Jaca
Parque Nacional de Ordesa y Monte Perdido
PYRENEES
Parc Nacional d'Aigüestortes i Estany de Sant Maurici
ANDORRA LA VELLA
Perpignan
Figueras
Olot
Vic Girona
Tossa de Mar

Huesca
Barbastro
Zaragoza
Lleida
Manresa
Terrassa
BARCELONA
Sitges
Tarragona
Alcañiz
Amposta
Costa Brava
Costa Daurada

Río Aragón
Río Gállego
Río Jalón
Río Ebro
Riu Segre
Riu Cinca
Riu Ter

Cuenca
Teruel
Morella
Peñíscola
MALLORCA
MENORCA
Inca
Artà
Manacor
Palma de Mallorca

Castellón de la Plana (Castelló de la Plana)
Sagunto
Valencia
Alginet
Albacete
Almansa
Alcoy
Benidorm
Denia
IBIZA
Ibiza
FORMENTERA

Balearic Islands (Islas Baleares)

Río Júcar
Río Cabriel
Río Turia
Río Segura

Alicante (Alicant)
Elche
Cieza
Murcia
Cartagena
Baza
Mojácar
Almería
Cabo de Gata
Costa Blanca
Costa Cálida

Río Almanzora

MEDITERRANEAN SEA

ALGERIA

ELEVATION
1000m
500m
200m
100m
0

LEGEND
Freeway
Primary Road
Secondary Road
Railway

0 — 100 km
0 — 50 miles

⇘ THIS IS SPAIN

Spain could be Europe's most exotic country. From soulful flamenco and delicious food, to avant-garde architecture and cities, Spain is a beguiling mix of stirring and often curious traditions, live-for-the-moment hedonism and a willingness to embrace the future with a relentlessly adventurous spirit.

But let's begin with the drama and diversity of the Spanish landscape. Some of Europe's most beautiful mountain ranges – the Pyrenees and Picos de Europa in the north and the Sierra Nevada in the south – are found here, and often close to coastlines of singular beauty, particularly in Asturias, Galicia and Almería in Andalucía.

Adding personality to Spain's natural splendour, villages of rare and timeless beauty have colonised the most improbable locations. Whether in the postcard-perfect *pueblos blancos* (white villages) of Andalucía or the stone-and-timber architecture of hamlets across Central Spain and Aragón, these are vestiges of Old Spain that still cling to traditions like nowhere else in Europe.

A world away, Spain's dynamic cities are temples to all that is modern and cool. Madrid, Barcelona, Valencia and Seville have become bywords for that peculiarly Spanish talent for living the good life, and for doing so at full volume and all night. At the same time, most cities promise a daytime feast of more sedate but nonetheless exceptional sites, from world-class art galleries to graceful Islamic-era monuments, from *barrios* (neighbourhoods) overflowing with medieval charm to zany Gaudí flights of fancy.

'Spain's dynamic cities are temples to all that is modern and cool'

And yet, for all of Spain's obvious appeal, some visitors feel as though visiting the country is akin to standing outside a riotous party with your nose pressed up against the glass. Spain is perhaps the best-known, least-understood country in Europe, but it's also one of the most welcoming and accessible. By demystifying the central pillars of Spanish life – such as flamenco, Spanish cuisine and eating customs – this guide takes you inside that party, where having a good time is almost guaranteed.

↘ SPAIN'S TOP
25 EXPERIENCES

`1`

↘ LA SAGRADA FAMÍLIA, BARCELONA

The strangely fluid towers of La Sagrada Família (p105) can be seen from any vantage point in the city, but you need to get close to it to understand the scale of Gaudí's ever-evolving masterpiece, and final gift to the city. Get there early enough and you'll get to experience the forest-like interior in relative peace.

Joanna Potts, Lonely Planet staff

↘ DIVE INTO MADRID'S NIGHTLIFE

2

If the culture of Madrid is its heart, then the nightlife is its soul. You could be forgiven for thinking that sunset is the time when the city comes to life. The tapestry of vivid colours, the roar of conversation flowing out of the bars (p76), and the intoxicating aromas of tapas are just the beginning.

Damien Bown, Australia

3

↘ MARVEL AT GRANADA'S ALHAMBRA

Not even soaring temperatures could keep us from marvelling at the intricately designed peristyles of the Alhambra (p303) and looking out to the glittering landscape of Granada below.

Suzi Stanicic, traveller

1 DALE BUCKTON; 2 KRZYSZTOF DYDYNSKI; 3 JOHN ELK III

1 La Sagrada Família (p105), Barcelona; 2 Night out in Madrid (p76); 3 Alhambra (p303), Granada

↘ CIUDAD DE LAS ARTES Y LAS CIENCIAS

A harp, its tip stabbing the sky, a whale skeleton, Darth Vader's helmet and a giant, never-blinking eye: such are the images that the brain throws up as it struggles to take in the wondrous forms of Valencia city's **Ciudad de las Artes y las Ciencias** (City of Arts and Sciences; p234).

Miles Roddis, Lonely Planet author

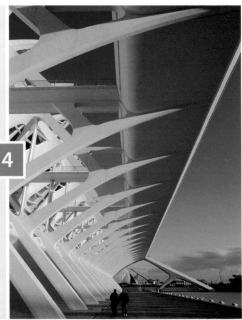

↘ LA MEZQUITA DE CÓRDOBA

The **Mezquita** (p297) hints at a refined age when Muslims, Jews and Christians lived side by side and enriched their city with an interaction of diverse and vibrant cultures. It's likely, however, that a less glamorous reality prevailed, with medieval Córdoba brimming with racial and class-based tension.

Vesna Maric, Lonely Planet author

↘ SAVOUR SAN SEBASTIÁN PINTXOS

Pintxos in San Sebastián (p208) are like ice to the Eskimos. No matter which bar you wander into you're guaranteed an assorted swarm of *pintxos* platters covering the entire bar, leaving little room to rest a drink. For the Basque people of San Sebastián, enjoying *pintxos* is beyond a religion.

Mark Adams, Lonely Planet staff

4 GREG ELMS; 5 KARL BLACKWELL; 6 DALLAS STRIBLEY

4 Promenade beside Museo de las Ciencias Príncipe Felipe, Ciudad de las Artes y las Ciencias (p234), Valencia; 5 Mezquita interior (p297), Córdoba; 6 *Pintxos* on bar counter, San Sebastián (p208)

↘ WANDER THROUGH GRANADA'S ALBAYZÍN

Go to Plaza Nueva to enjoy a glass of *tinto de verano* (summer wine), walk the streets of the **Albayzín** (p305), where you can go to take an Arabic tea or eat a *shawarma*. Walk up to the Iglesia Sant Pedro and take a drink where you will have a nice view to the Alhambra.

Robert T, traveller

7

SPAIN'S TOP 25 EXPERIENCES

8

CELEBRATE EASTER IN SEVILLE

Return to Spain's medieval Christian roots and join Seville's masses for the dramatic Easter celebration of Semana Santa (see the boxed text, p276). Religious fraternities parade elaborate *pasos* (sculptural representations) of Christ around the city to the acclamation of the populace.

Damien Simonis, Lonely Planet author

LINGER IN RENAISSANCE SALAMANCA

The elegant central square of Salamanca, Plaza Mayor (p134), is possibly the most comely in all of Spain. Nearby, the Catedral Nueva (p134) is an extraordinary melding of late-Gothic and Renaissance art.

Damien Simonis, Lonely Planet author

9

7 ALFREDO MAIQUEZ; 8 RICHARD ROSS; 9 BETHUNE CARMICHAEL

7 View of the Albayzín (p305) from the Alhambra, Granada; 8 Semana Santa (Easter Week) festivities (p276), Seville; 9 Catedral Nueva (p134), Salamanca

SPAIN'S TOP 25 EXPERIENCES

10 DRIVE THE ASTURIAN COAST

The **Asturian Coast** (p214) between Llanes and Ribadesella is wild and beautiful. The coastline is punctuated by sandy beaches and framed by the backdrop of the Picos, which creep almost to the coast. The best beach is the most inaccessible, the Playa de Torimbia, close to the village of Niembro.

Neil Manders, Lonely Planet staff

11 MADRID'S GOLDEN ART TRIANGLE

The grand holy trinity of Madrid's art galleries form a triangle around Paseo del Prado. For an A to Z of Western art head to the **Thyssen-Bornemisza** (p65). If you like the Spanish masters, visit the **Prado** (p63). Or if modern art tickles your palate, the **Reina Sofía** (p63) and its haunting highlight, Picasso's *Guernica*, are worth the airfare to Madrid on their own.

Clifton Wilkinson, Lonely Planet staff

↘ PARQUE NACIONAL SIERRA NEVADA

12

A short drive southeast of Granada, the area known as Los Cahorros in the **Sierra Nevada** (p308) is good for short walks, with trails running alongside the Río Monachil. The most popular route – the Cahorros Altos, heading upstream – passes over a high suspension bridge and alongside waterfalls.

Zora O'Neill, Lonely Planet author

13

↘ FLAMENCO IN ANDALUCÍA

Flamenco (p316) performers who successfully communicate their passion will have you on the edge of your seat. The gift of sparking this kind of response is known as *duende* (spirit).

Damien Simonis, Lonely Planet author

10 MATTHEW SCHOENFELDER; 11 GUY MOBERLY; 12 ALFREDO MAIQUEZ; 13 PAUL BERNHARDT

10 Coastline near Llanes, Asturias (p214); 11 Gallery in Museo del Prado (p63), Madrid; 12 Sierra Nevada Ski Station (p309); 13 Flamenco dancer, Cádiz (p280)

14

⬦ PICOS DE EUROPA

For a unique experience, venture into the **Picos** (p215) beyond Sotres. The area was depopulated during the 1970s and '80s, but fortunately a paved road halted the exodus and brought intrepid day visitors to this bucolic paradise.

Neil Manders, Lonely Planet staff

↘ STROLL BARCELONA'S LA RAMBLA

Always a conductor of Barcelona's energy, La Rambla (p101) surges with revellers on New Year's Eve. Headed towards Plaça de Catalunya, they count down to midnight – *cava* in one hand, 12 grapes in the other – eventually dispersing across town to party until dawn.

Debra Herrmann, Lonely Planet staff

15

14 MATTHEW SCHOENFELDER; 15 ALEX SEGRE/ALAMY

14 Picos de Europa (p215), Asturias; 15 La Rambla (p101), Barcelona

↘ SLEEP IN LUXURIOUS PARADORES

Spain's state-owned *paradores* are far more than a place to sleep. From former palaces to one-time castles and convents, *paradores* offer nights of grandeur and historical charm. Most are also magnificently sited, none more so than in **Ronda** (p296) or **Granada** (p306).

Anthony Ham, Lonely Planet author

16

17

↘ VILLAGES IN ARAGÓN

East of Zaragoza, the Monegros Desert is a pretty desolate place. On a tired late drive, we decided to stop over, hoping to find a homely village welcome. The village we chose was in the full throes of their village fiesta. See p186 for more on Aragón's villages.

Neil Manders, Lonely Planet staff

↗ TOUR LA RIOJA WINE COUNTRY

We stayed in **Laguardia** (p210) and drove around to the wineries of Marques de Riscal, Ysios and Ramirez de Ganuza, both for the wines as well as the architecture (Gehry for Riscal, Calatrava for Ysios). We booked for tours and the people were very friendly.

Peech, traveller

18

16 DAVID TOMLINSON; 17 JOHN BANAGAN; 18 ROBERTO GEROMETTA

16 Parador de Ronda (p296); 17 Village of Alquézar (p186), Aragón; 18 Frank Gehry–designed Bodegas Marqués de Riscal (p211), La Rioja

↘ SANTIAGO DE COMPOSTELA

The Galician capital, **Santiago de Compostela** (p216), is known for its rain as much as its stunning cathedral, but even the continuous drizzle couldn't detract from the city's beauty. In fact, the misty atmosphere only added to my enjoyment of the place.

Clifton Wilkinson, Lonely Planet staff

19

SPAIN'S TOP 25 EXPERIENCES

20

↘ DISCOVER THE COSTA BRAVA

After the heat and crowds of Barcelona, it was a relief to hop off the bus in the quaint little village of Tossa de Mar on the **Costa Brava** (p166). A whitewashed room in a hotel right on the beach, swimming in the ocean, siestas in the afternoons, late dinners of paella and creme caramel – perfecto!

Jessica Boland, Lonely Planet staff

19 WAYNE WALTON; 20 PETER ADAMS PHOTOGRAPHY LTD/ALAMY

19 Catedral de Santiago de Compostela (p217); 20 Seaside village, Costa Brava (p166)

21

↘ LAZE ON MENORCA BEACHES

Menorca (p251) is a Unesco Biosphere Reserve with beaches that defy description. Some assert that reaching them by sea is the height of pleasure, but happening upon them from the interior brings equal joy. Among the best are Cala Macarelleta and Cala en Turqueta.

Damien Simonis, Lonely Planet author

↘ SAMPLE THE BEST JAMÓN

One restaurant we went to in Andalucía had a particularly complicated menu. Sensing our befuddlement the waiter offered a suggestion: *'jamón?' 'Si.'* We nodded gratefully. He deftly carved slices of rosy, translucent **ham** (p345) from a leg and served it to us with olive oil, fresh bread and shavings of parmesan cheese. It was salty, melt-in-the-mouth perfection.

Joanna Potts, Lonely Planet staff

22

⬎ SHOP IN BARCELONA

No trip to Barcelona is complete without a spot of shopping on **Passeig de Gracia** (p117). A shopper's paradise, I love this street as it caters to those interested in both designer goods and the latest high-street trends. When your credit card is maxed out, there's nothing better than relaxing with a coffee in one of the numerous cafes or bars – heaven!

Becky Rangecroft, Lonely Planet staff

23

24

⬎ TOLEDO OF THREE FAITHS

Toledo (p142) is a gorgeous place, like a city-sized version of a medieval Spanish hill-town with just the right combination of grand monuments and twisting narrow lanes in which to get lost. It's also like walking through a history book written in stone with churches, mosques and synagogues.

Anthony Ham, Lonely Planet author

21 GUY MOBERLY; 22 KRZYSZTOF DYDYNSKI; 23 NEIL SETCHFIELD; 24 CHRISTOPHER GROENHOUT

21 North coast beach (p253), Menorca; 22 *Jamón* in the Mercat de la Boqueria (p101), Barcelona; 23 Custo Barcelona (p117); 24 View of Toledo (p142) from across Rio Tajo

↘ SEGOVIA

We came from Madrid to **Segovia** (p136) and stayed there a night. My memory is of a town all gold: honey stone under sun. Wandering the cobbled lanes and peering into a guitar shop. Lazily drinking thick hot chocolate. And who would have thought that an aqueduct could be so impressive?

Rose Mulready, Lonely Planet staff

25

STEPHEN SAKS

Segovia cathedal (p137)

SPAIN'S TOP ITINERARIES

THE BIG THREE

THE BIG THREE

FIVE DAYS BARCELONA TO GRANADA

Even in five days, you can get a taste for what makes Spain special. Spend a couple of days in Barcelona, take a high-speed train to Madrid for one night, then a train (four to five hours) or flight to Granada for two more nights.

❶ BARCELONA

There's no better introduction to Spain than strolling along **La Rambla** (p101), then branching out into the 15th-century **Barri Gòtic** (p100) with its fine monuments, lovely plazas and medieval streetscape. You could pause in the **Museu Picasso** (p104), but make sure you leave time for the city's astonishing collection of works left by Antoni Gaudí: **La Sagrada Família** (p105) is one of Spain's most extraordinary buildings, followed closely by **Casa Batlló** (p105), **La Pedrera** (p105) and **Park Güell** (p107). There's also some terrific **shopping** (p116), and this is one of the best places in Spain to sample innovative Spanish (and Catalan) food.

❷ MADRID

With just a day in the Spanish capital, head for the **Museo del Prado** (p63) with its masterpieces by Velázquez, Goya and a host of European masters, followed by a visit to the nearby **Centro de Arte Reina Sofía** (p63) for a dose of Salvador Dalí and Picasso's peerless *Guernica*. For some quiet down time, immerse yourself in the oasis that is the **Parque del Buen Retiro** (p71). After dark, pass through

LEFT: KRZYSZTOF DYDYNSKI; RIGHT: JOHN ELK III

Left: Casa Battló (p105), Barcelona; Right: Cathedral walkway, Barri Gòtic (p100), Barcelona

MEDITERRANEAN SEA

the **Plaza Mayor** (p62), then skip from bar to bar in **La Latina** (see the boxed text, p75), a *barrio* famous for its delicious tapas varieties. Dip into Madrid's legendary nightlife and you may not emerge until dawn.

❸ GRANADA

It's a four- to five-hour train journey to Granada, but consider flying to save time. Spend your first day exploring **Albayzín** (p305), Granada's one-time Islamic quarter, with its whitewashed tangle of laneways that tumble down the hillside. Also don't miss the gilded **La Capilla Real** (p304), the city's extravagant Christian counterpoint to the dominant Islamic splendour. For food, Granada has some of Spain's most generous **tapas** (p306) and there are excellent places for **flamenco** (p307). But it's the **Alhambra** (p303), arguably Spain's most beautiful collection of buildings, that you came so far to see, so get an early start and plan to spend as much of your second day here as you can.

SPAIN'S TOP ITINERARIES

SPAIN'S BEGUILING NORTH

SPAIN'S BEGUILING NORTH

10 DAYS SEGOVIA TO SANTIAGO DE COMPOSTELA

If your vacation extends to 10 days, you can, with your own wheels, range through Spain's Castilian heartland, visit San Sebastián, then follow the stunning northern coast to Galicia. Your starting point, Segovia, is a 35-minute train journey from Madrid.

❶ SEGOVIA

One of Spain's most engaging inland towns, Segovia has the splendid Roman-era **aqueduct** (p136) and the whimsical **Alcázar** (p138). In between are delightful streets, fine restaurants, sweeping views and a host of other architectural highlights. A day here is enough, but only just.

❷ SALAMANCA

Salamanca's Renaissance and plateresque sandstone architecture finds its most glorious expression in the **Plaza Mayor** (p134), arguably Spain's most beautiful square, and the **Catedral Nueva** (p134). Salamanca is at its best floodlit at night, with energy flowing through the streets.

❸ LEÓN

Nothing can prepare you for the first time you step inside Leon's **cathedral** (p139) where stained glass windows bathe the interior in ethereal light. The **Real Basílica de San Isidro** (p139) is also splendid, while the charming old quarter, Barrio Húmedo, is very much alive.

❹ SAN SEBASTIÁN

Two nights in San Sebastián is a minimum. Graceful architecture and the postcard-perfect **Playa de la Concha** (p205) are a stunning

Playa de la Concha (p205), San Sebastián

DALLAS STRIBLEY

combination best viewed from atop Monte Igueldo (p205). But San Sebastián is a world culinary capital, known for its mind-blowing tapas and Michelin-starred restaurants, such as Arzak (p208).

❺ SANTILLANA DEL MAR
All along the coast of Cantabria and Asturias, isolated coves conceal picturesque fishing villages, but if you can linger in just one place, pass the night in Santillana del Mar (p212), a timeless village set back from the coast with an idyllic setting and medieval architecture.

❻ RÍAS ALTAS
Driving Galicia's coast, especially the Rías Altas, ranks among Spain's best journeys. Cabo Ortegal (p221), Serra de Capelada (p220) and Betanzos (p220) are highlights, while the vertiginous cliffs and deserted beaches will leave you gasping at the wild beauty. Allow two days.

❼ SANTIAGO DE COMPOSTELA
Santiago de Compostela, with its echoes of the sacred, is a suitably epic last stop on your journey through northern Spain. Its cathedral (p217) is the city's soaring centrepiece, but the city radiating out from here is a microcosm of urban Spain.

SPAIN'S TOP ITINERARIES

SPAIN'S BEGUILING NORTH

ANDALUCÍA & THE MEDITERRANEAN

TWO WEEKS SEVILLE TO MALLORCA

Two weeks in Spain enables you to see the best of Andalucía, including magnificent cities and hilltop villages, and get a taste of the Spanish Mediterranean. You'll need a car for Andalucía. Consider flying from Granada to Valencia and taking a catamaran to the islands.

❶ SEVILLE

Seville is Andalucía in a nutshell. The **Barrio de Santa Cruz** (p275) is all dressed in white, there are exquisite Islamic monuments such as the **Alcázar** (p271), and the **Cathedral and Giralda** (p274) are superb. Throw in some of Spain's best tapas and a thriving **flamenco** (p279) scene, and you'll find two days here barely enough.

❷ CÁDIZ

Surrounded on three sides by water, Cádiz' lovely buildings have a languid waterfront atmosphere, while its tightly packed white-walled streets pulse with life. Highlights include the **cathedral** (p280) with stunning views from its tower and signposts to what may be Europe's oldest continuously inhabited city. Above all, though, this is a city that just loves to have fun.

❸ ARCOS DE LA FRONTERA

You've seen the pictures of brilliantly white villages clinging precariously to an Andalucian hilltop. There are many candidates throughout

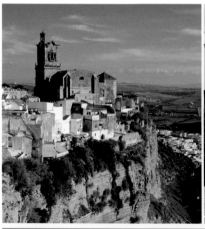

LEFT: PATRICK SYDER; RIGHT: DIANA MAYFIELD

Left: Arcos de la Frontera (p285); Right: Cafe in Barrio de Santa Cruz (p275), Seville

the region, but none surpass **Arcos de la Frontera** (p285). Breathtaking from a distance and enchanting within, this is one place where the reality is every bit as beautiful as you imagined.

❹ RONDA

Clifftop Ronda is another dreamy Andalucian *pueblo blanco* (white village). The views from the **Puente Nuevo** (p295) are exceptional, but turn around to explore the town and you'll unearth **Arab-era baths** (p295), fine churches, Spain's most beautiful **bullring** (p295) and ancient **walls** (p295). Terrific accommodation and outstanding restaurants are other Ronda specialities.

❺ CÓRDOBA

One of the most celebrated landmarks of world Islamic architecture, Córdoba's **Mezquita** (p297) should not be missed; its forest of striped horseshoe arches are aesthetic harmony wrought in stone. The **Judería** (p296), gardens of the **Alcázar** (p299) and **Arab baths** (p299) are other highlights, as are Córdoba's **restaurants** (p300) and **festivals** (p299). It deserves at least two nights.

❻ GRANADA

If Córdoba represents Andalucía's early glories, Granada is its glittering highpoint. The **Alhambra** (p303), arguably the most important cultural site in Spain, is blessed with the **Palacio Nazaríes** (p303) and **Generalife gardens** (p304). There are fine views of the Alhambra and the Sierra Nevada from across the valley in the **Albayzín** (p305). For more on Granada, see p300.

❼ LAS ALPUJARRAS

Separated from Granada by the Sierra Nevada mountains, **Las Alpujarras** (p309) is an altogether different world. White villages cling to arid slopes and preside over deep crags, and the further you explore the more you encounter all the timeless charm of rural Andalucía. This is prime walking country and deserves at least two days.

❽ VALENCIA

Valencia has many strings to its bow. Its most eye-catching attraction is the futuristic **Ciudad de las Artes y las Ciencias** (p234), but the **Cathedral** (p235), home to the Holy Grail, **Lonja** (p236) and beachside restaurants will more than fill your day here. The night belongs to the historic **Barrio del Carmen** (p239).

❾ MALLORCA

A couple of days on Mallorca offer the ideal combination of clamour and calm to finish your journey. Palma de Mallorca's gorgeous old town includes the landmark **cathedral** (p246), while the **old Palma houses** (p244) and fine restaurants are real treats. Along the northwestern coast, villages like **Estellencs** (p247) are at once beautiful and a world away.

GREG ELMS

Barrio del Carmen (p239), Valencia

↘ PLANNING YOUR TRIP

SPAIN'S BEST...

ART GALLERIES

- **Museo del Prado, Madrid** (p63) World-class gallery with Goya, Velázquez and the pick of European masters.
- **Centro de Arte Reina Sofía, Madrid** (p63) Stunning contemporary art that includes Dalí, Miró, and Picasso's *Guernica*.
- **Museo Picasso Málaga** (p289) Over 200 Picasso works in a stunningly converted palace in the city of his birth.
- **Teatre-Museu Dalí** (p172) Dalí's weird-and-wonderful legacy that's so much more than a museum.

PLACES FOR SPANISH FOOD

- **Old town, San Sebastián** (p208) Spain's culinary capital with more Michelin stars than Paris (!) and the country's best *pintxos* (tapas).

- **Barcelona** (p112) Home city for Catalonia's legendary cooking, blending tradition with innovation.
- **La Latina, Madrid** (p75) The best tapas from around Spain in one medieval, central neighbourhood.
- **Valencia** (p238) The birthplace of paella and still the place for the most authentic version.

PLACES FOR ISLAMIC SPLENDOUR

- **Alhambra, Granada** (p303) The priceless jewel in Andalucía's crown and symbol of Al-Andalus.
- **Mezquita, Córdoba** (p297) Perfection and harmony in this glorious early-Islamic mosque.
- **Alcázar, Seville** (p271) Pleasure palace with exquisite architecture and gardens.
- **Aljafería, Zaragoza** (p182) A rare, glittering outpost of Al-Andalus in the north.

BILL WASSMAN

D'Alt Vila (p248), Ibiza

⇘ UNSPOILED COASTLINES

- **Rías Altas, Galicia** (p220) Spain's most breathtaking coast with cliffs and isolated beaches.
- **Costa da Morte, Galicia** (p221) Wild and windswept Atlantic shore with beautiful, quiet villages.
- **Menorca's North Coast** (p252) The Balearic Islands before the tourists arrived, and an insight into why they did.
- **Cabo de Gata, Andalucía** (p311) Andalucía's most dramatic and remote Mediterranean corner.

⇘ AREAS FOR HIKING

- **Sierra Nevada, Andalucía** (p308) Extraordinary scenery, wildlife, and mainland Spain's highest terrain.
- **Parc Nacional D'Aigüestortes i Estany De Sant Maurici, Catalonia** (p173) Magnificent mountain scenery and walking trails in the Catalan Pyrenees.
- **Las Alpujarras** (p309) Rural Andalucía at its best amid gorgeous valleys.
- **Picos de Europa, Asturias** (p215) Jagged mountain range close to the Asturian coast.

⇘ VILLAGE ESCAPES

- **Santillana del Mar, Cantabria** (p212) Possibly the country's most picturesque village.
- **Aïnsa, Aragón** (p184) Medieval stone village in the Pyrenean foothills.

- **Arcos de la Frontera, Andalucía** (p285) The poster child for Andalucía's white hill villages.
- **Sierra de Francia, Castilla y León** (p136) One of Spain's forgotten, enchanted corners.

⇘ POST-ISLAMIC ARCHITECTURAL WONDERS

- **La Sagrada Família, Barcelona** (p105) Gaudí's masterpiece and icon of Barcelona and its Modernista splendour.
- **Museo Guggenheim, Bilbao** (p203) The astonishing Frank Gehry–designed symbol of the new Bilbao.
- **Ciudad de las Artes y las Ciencias, Valencia** (p234) Valencia's showpiece avant-garde complex by world-renowned local architect Santiago Calatrava.
- **Baeza, Andalucía** (p309) Andalucía's finest Renaissance collection tucked away in little-visited Jaén province.

⇘ NIGHTLIFE

- **Ibiza** (p250) Europe's after-dark club and chill-out capital.
- **Madrid** (p76) Nights that never seem to end with bars, clubs and great live music.
- **Valencia** (p239) Barrio del Carmen nights are famous throughout Spain.
- **Salamanca, Castilla y León** (p135) Feel-good nights beneath floodlit Renaissance buildings.

THINGS YOU NEED TO KNOW

AT A GLANCE

- **ATMs** Linked to international networks and on every street corner
- **Credit Cards** Visa and MasterCard more widely accepted than other brands
- **Currency** Euro
- **Language** English widely spoken in tourist areas, less so elsewhere; Galician, Basque and Catalan spellings used on many signs
- **Tipping** Small change, more if you wish
- **Visas** Not required for most nationalities; see also p365

ACCOMMODATION

- **Hostales** Budget accommodation, often with private bathroom; see p349.
- **Hotels** Wide range of midrange and top-end hotels; see p349.
- **Paradores** State-run hotels, usually in sumptuously converted historic buildings; see p349.
- **Casas Rurales** Charming and usually family-run rural accommodation; see p348.

ADVANCE PLANNING

- **Three months before** Start shopping for your flight (p366), car hire (p369) and, in summer, reserve your accommodation (p348).
- **One month before** Reserve your entry ticket to Granada's Alhambra (p303) and book any long-distance train journeys (p371).

- **One week before** Confirm your reservation with your hotel.

BE FOREWARNED

- **Museums** Most major museums close on Mondays.
- **Restaurants** Most restaurants open from 1.30pm to 4pm and from 9pm to 11.30pm.
- **Shops** Many smaller shops close from 2pm to 5pm.

COSTS

- **Up to €100 per day** Decent budget accommodation, eating the *menú del día* (p343), and not much long-haul travel; goes further away from major tourist areas.
- **€100–200 per day** Comfortable (and sometimes semi-luxurious) accommodation, good restaurants and train travel.
- **More than €200** Luxury hotels (including Paradores; see p349) and fine dining.

EMERGENCY NUMBERS

- **Ambulance** ☎061
- **EU standard emergency number** ☎112
- **Fire** Bomberos; ☎080
- **Local Police** Policía Municipal; ☎092
- **National Police** Policía Nacional; ☎091

⬊ GETTING AROUND

- **Air** Numerous internal flights, including with low-cost companies; some flights require a change in Madrid. See p367.
- **Boat** Ferries connect the Balearic Islands with each other and with Valencia and Barcelona; see p368.
- **Bus** Private companies cover the whole country, more cheaply and more slowly than trains, often going where the rails don't; see p368.
- **Train** Extensive and extremely modern network with the high-speed AVE trains connecting Madrid with many cities in around two hours; see p371.

⬊ GETTING THERE & AWAY

- **Air** Direct flights to Spanish cities from across Europe and North America. Major international airports include Madrid, Barcelona, Málaga and Palma de Mallorca. Charter flights also operate in summer. See p366.
- **Train** Direct trains to Madrid and Barcelona from Paris and (in the case of Barcelona) elsewhere in Europe; see p366.

⬊ TECH STUFF

- **Wi-fi** Becoming more common in midrange and top-end hotels, cafes and some public areas; see p358.

LEFT: HOLGER LEUE; RIGHT: OLIVER STREWE

Left: Ferry boats, Mallorca (p243); Right: Museo Guggenheim (p203), Bilbao

- **Mobile phones (cell phones)** Operate on GSM 900/1800, hence compatible with wider European and Australian phones, generally not with those from the USA and Japan, but can be rented; see p362.

WHAT TO BRING

- **Passport or EU ID Card** You'll need it to enter the country and for credit card transactions.
- **Money belt** Petty theft is a small but significant risk in some cities and tourist areas; see p352.
- **Travel Insurance** See p358.
- **National and/or International Driving Licence** Essential if you plan to rent a car; see p369.

WHEN TO GO

- **Summer** Almost guaranteed sun, but masses of other travellers along the coast.
- **Spring and Autumn** The nicest time to visit with milder temperatures and generally fewer tourists.
- **Winter** Bitterly cold inland and in mountain areas (although good for skiing); Andalucía and the Mediterranean Coast quite mild and quieter.
- **Festivals** To be enjoyed or avoided, depending on your inclination. Either way you need to know when they are; see p46 for major festivals and the relevant regional chapters for local affairs.

KARL BLACKWELL

Courtyard of a Spanish *parador* (p349), Andalucía

GET INSPIRED

⇲ BOOKS

- **The Ornament of the World** (2003) Maria Rosa Menocal's fascinating look at Andalucía's Islamic centuries.
- **Ghosts of Spain** (2007) Giles Tremlett's take on contemporary Spain and its tumultuous past.
- **Getting to Mañana** (2004) Miranda Innes's terrific take on starting a new life in an Andalucian farmhouse.
- **A Late Dinner** (2007) Paul Richardson's beautifully written journey through Spanish food.
- **A Handbook for Travellers** (1845) Richard's Ford's sometimes irascible, always enlightening window on 19th-century Spain.
- **Sacred Sierra: A Year on a Spanish Mountain** (2009) Jason Webster's alternative to the expat-renovates-a-farmhouse genre.

⇲ FILMS

- **Vicky Cristina Barcelona** (2008) Barcelona plays a starring role with a brief cameo from Oviedo in this Woody Allen film.
- **Volver** (2006) Pedro Almodóvar's most beautiful recent film.
- **Todo Sobre Mi Madre** (All About My Mother; 1999) Considered by many to be Almodóvar's finest.
- **Mar Adentro** (2004) Alejandro Amenábar's touching movie filmed in Galicia.
- **Jamón Jamón** (1992) Launched the careers of Javier Bardem and Penélope Cruz.

⇲ MUSIC

- **Paco de Lucía Antología** (1995) Collected works by Spain's most celebrated flamenco guitarist.
- **Una Leyenda Flamenca** (1993) Camarón de la Isla, flamenco's late, all-time singing legend.
- **Lagrimas Negras** (2003) Bebo Valdés and Diego El Cigala in stunning flamenco-Cuban fusion.
- **Sueña La Alhambra** (2005) Enrique Morente, one of flamenco's most enduring and creative voices.
- **La Luna en el Río** (2003) Carmen Linares, flamenco's foremost female voice in the second half of the 20th century.
- **Pokito a Poko** (2005) Chambao's beguiling brand of *nuevo flamenco* (new flamenco).

⇲ WEBSITES

- **Welcome to Spain** (www.spain.info) Useful official tourist office site.
- **Lonely Planet** (www.lonelyplanet.com) Country information, build your own itinerary and the Thorn Tree Forum.
- **Paradores** (www.parador.es) Start planning that special night in Spain.
- **Vayafiestas.com** (www.vayafiestas.com) Spanish-only site with month-by-month info on fiestas around the country.
- **Spain Travel Guide** (www.spanishfiestas.com) Detailed tourist information for most Spanish regions.

CALENDAR

JAN   FEB   MAR   APR

Sevillana dancing during the Feria de Abril

FEBRUARY–MARCH

CARNAVAL
Carnaval's true home is Cádiz (p280) with 10 irreverent days of fancy-dress parades and general merriment. The other Carnaval epicentre is Sitges (p118). It ends on the Tuesday 47 days before Easter Sunday.

SEMANA SANTA (HOLY WEEK)
The week leading up to Easter Sunday entails parades of *pasos* (holy figures) and big crowds. It is most extravagantly celebrated in Seville, Ávila, Cuenca, Toledo, Málaga, Córdoba and Lorca.

FESTIVAL DE JEREZ
This two-week festival in Jerez de la Frontera (p283) has flamenco as the centrepiece of a music-and-dance-dominated program, drawing many of the biggest flamenco stars. See www .festivaldejerez.es for more details.

MARCH

LAS FALLAS   12–19 MAR
This festival consists of energetic all-night dancing and drinking, first-class fireworks, and processions. Its principal stage is Valencia city (p234) and it culminates in the ritual burning of effigies in the streets. See www.fallas .es (in Spanish).

APRIL

MOROS Y CRISTIANOS
22–24 APR
Colourful parades and mock battles between Christian and Muslim 'armies' in Alcoy (p238), near Alicante, make this one of the most spectacular of several similar events around Valencia and Alicante provinces.

FERIA DE ABRIL

This week-long party held in late April in Seville (p270) sees *Sevillanos* ride around on horseback and in elaborate horse-drawn carriages by day and, dressed up in their best traditional finery, dance late into the night. See http://feriadesevilla.andalunet.com (in Spanish).

◥ MAY

FERIA DEL CABALLO

The Feria del Caballo held in early May in Jerez de la Frontera (p283) is one of Andalucía's biggest festivals. It features equestrian contests, parades, bullfights, music and dance, with colourful processions of horses and horse-drawn carriages.

Cordoban courtyard, Concurso de Patios

CONCURSO DE PATIOS CORDOBESES

Scores of beautiful private courtyards, usually bedecked with flowers, are opened to the public for two weeks in Córdoba (p296) in early to mid-May. It's a rare window on one of Andalucía's most distinctive architectural traditions. See www.patiosdecordoba.net (in Spanish).

ES FIRÓ   AROUND 11 MAY

Sóller, in northern Mallorca, is 'invaded' by Muslim pirates around the 11th of May. This gives rise to a 'battle' between townsfolk and invaders. This event recreates an infamous 1561 assault in which Ses Valentes Dones (Valiant Women) played a key part in victory.

Semana Santa procession, Seville

PLANNING YOUR TRIP

CALENDAR

CALENDAR

| JAN | FEB | MAR | APR |

FIESTA DE SAN ISIDRO　15 MAY

The most important annual festival in **Madrid** (p71) celebrates the city's patron saint with bullfights, parades, locals in traditional dress, concerts and more. Some of the events, such as the bullfighting season, last for a month.

MAY–JUNE

CORPUS CRISTI

On the Thursday in the ninth week after Easter, religious celebrations take place. Those in Toledo (www.corpuschristi toledo.es) are the most impressive, while Seville also puts on its finest.

JUNE

HOGUERAS DE SAN JUAN　23 JUN

Midsummer bonfires and fireworks feature on the eve of the Fiesta de San Juan (24 June) along the Mediterranean coast. It's celebrated with particular gusto in Menorca's **Ciutadella** (p251). See www.santjoanweb.com.

JUNE–JULY

FESTIVAL INTERNACIONAL DE LA GUITARRA

Flamenco is the focus of this two-week guitar festival in **Córdoba** (p296) in late June or early July; you'll also hear live classical, rock and blues performances. See www.guitarracordoba.com.

JULY

DÍA DE SANTIAGO　25 JUL

The Feast of St James is spectacularly celebrated in **Santiago de Compostela** (p216), the site of St James' tomb, with fireworks (on 24 July) and two weeks

SIMON GREENWOOD

La Tomatina, Buñol

MAY	JUN	JUL	AUG	SEP	OCT	NOV	DEC

PLANNING YOUR TRIP

CALENDAR

of revelry and homage. This is also Galicia's national day.

JULY–AUGUST

FESTIVAL DE TEATRO CLÁSICO

The Roman theatre and amphitheatre in Mérida (p152) become the perfect stage for the classics of ancient Greece and Rome, as well as William Shakespeare. Performances are held most nights during July and August.

AUGUST

FERIA DE MÁLAGA

The pick of Andalucía's summer ferias, this nine-day version in Málaga (p289) in mid-August, has it all: fireworks, concerts and round-the-clock music, dancing and horse parades in the city centre by day and the feria grounds by night.

SEMANA GRANDE OR ASTE NAGUSIA

Bilbao (p200) is touched by a little summer madness for about 10 days surrounding 15 August with processions, cultural events, music and much partying. Similar events take place in various towns along the Bay of Biscay coast.

LA TOMATINA

Tens of thousands of people launch about 100 tonnes of tomatoes at one another in just an hour or so in Buñol (p238) It happens on the penultimate or last Wednesday in August.

Traditional dress worn for Las Fallas (p46)

HANNAH LEVY

SEPTEMBER

BIENAL DE FLAMENCO

Spain's biggest flamenco festival, the Bienal in Seville (p270), draws the biggest names in the genre. It's held only in even-numbered years and the Alcázar provides the wonderful backdrop for many of the performances. See www.bienal-flamenco.org.

FESTES DE LA MERCÈ AROUND 24 SEP

The biggest annual party in Barcelona (p110) marks the end of summer with four days of parades, concerts, theatre, *castellers* (human-castle builders), fireworks synchronised with the Montjuïc fountains, spitting dragons and devils from across Catalonia, fire running and more.

↘ MADRID

KRZYSZTOF DYDYNSKI

Palacio de Cristal, Parque del Buen Retiro (p71)

GREATER MADRID

INFORMATION
Japanese Embassy.....................**1** C4
Netherlands Embassy.............**2** C2
Torre Espacio (Australian
& UK embassies)....................**3** C1

SIGHTS & ACTIVITIES
Cooking Club.............................**4** B2

SLEEPING
Hotel Puerta América...............**5** D3

ENTERTAINMENT
Estadio Santiago
Bernabéu......................**6** C3
Plaza de Toros
Monumental de las
Ventas.......................................**7** D4

TRANSPORT
Chamartín train station...........**8** C1

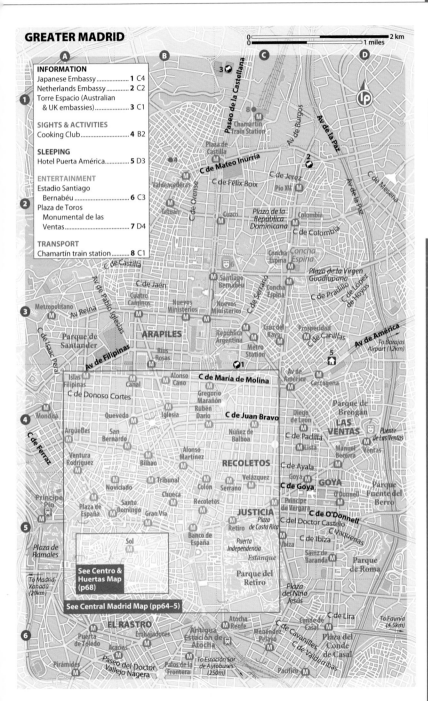

MADRID HIGHLIGHTS

MADRID

1 MUSEO DEL PRADO

BY LEONARDO HERNÁNDEZ, MEMBER OF FRIENDS OF THE PRADO AND REGULAR PRADO VISITOR

Founded in 1819 by Fernando VII (depicted in a frieze above the Puerta de Velázquez as protector of the Arts with gods behind his throne), El Prado ranks among the world's best museums and is the key to understanding painters such as Hieronymus Bosch (El Bosco), El Greco, Velázquez and Goya. One visit is never enough.

⬆ LEONARDO HERNÁNDEZ' DON'T MISS LIST

❶ LA RENDICIÓN DE BREDA (LAS LANZAS), BY DIEGO VELÁZQUEZ

Velázquez's masterpiece shows the moment in 1625 in which Ambrosio Spinola, a Spanish general, accepts the surrender of the Dutch town of Breda after a long siege. The Spanish novelist Arturo Pérez-Reverte mixed fantasy and reality in his novel *The Sun over Breda,* claiming that his character Captain Alatriste appeared in the painting but was later mysteriously erased by Velázquez.

❷ EDIFICIO JERÓNIMOS

The museum's extension, designed by Spanish architect Rafael Moneo, is worth visiting on its own. Highlights include the Sala de las Musas (Room of the Muses), the giant doors by Cristina Iglesias, the upper garden, and El Claustro de los Jerónimos (Jerónimos' Cloister).

❸ LA FAMÍLIA DE CARLOS IV, BY FRANCISCO DE GOYA

This painting is a small fragment of Spanish history transferred to canvas.

Clockwise from top: Visitors admire *La Família de Carlos IV;* Statue of Diego Velázquez; Exterior of Museo del Prado; Museum interior; Jerónimos entrance to the Museo del Prado

It shows the royal family in 1800 with Fernando (later Fernando VII) dressed in blue on the left. His fiancée has not yet been chosen, which may be why Goya depicts her with no facial definition. Goya portrayed himself in the background just as Velazquez did in *Las Meninas*.

❹ *EL DESCENDIMIENTO*, BY ROGER VAN DER WEYDEN

This 1435 painting is unusual, both for its size and for the recurring crossbow shapes in the painting's upper corners, which are echoed in the bodies of Mary and Christ (the painting was commissioned by a crossbow manufacturers brotherhood). Once the central part of a triptych, the painting is filled with drama and luminous colours.

❺ *LA CONDESA DE VILCHES*, BY FEDERICO MADRAZO

The painter was a friend of the model, which may be why he is able to transmit all her grace and sensuality. The light blue dress, the tone of her skin, the brightness in her eyes and the slightly pointed smile suggest a timeless sympathy that endures through the centuries.

⬤ THINGS YOU NEED TO KNOW

Admission €8 **Free entry** 6pm to 8pm Tuesday to Saturday and 5pm to 8pm Sunday **Self-guided tours** The Museo del Prado's website (www.museodelprado.es/coleccion/que-ver/) has selections of paintings aimed at one- to three-hour visits **See the author's review, p63**

MADRID

MADRID HIGHLIGHTS

2

⬈ IMMERSE YOURSELF IN ART

Within a mile of each other, Madrid's three world-class art galleries – the **Museo del Prado** (p63), **Museo Thyssen-Bornemisza** (p65) and **Centro de Arte Reina Sofía** (p63) – have made the city one of Europe's most important artistic capitals. Here, Spanish icons such as Goya, Velázquez, Picasso and Dalí share wall space with a host of European masters.

3

⬈ EXPLORE OLD MADRID

One of the most beautiful city squares in the world, **Plaza Mayor** (p62) also serves as a gateway to the old-world elegance of Madrid's oldest *barrios* (neighbourhoods). The grandeur of the **Palacio Real** (p62) is offset by the tangle of medieval lanes in La Latina, punctuated by some of Madrid's most intimate and charming little plazas, among them **Plaza de la Villa** (p63) and **Plaza de la Paja** (p63).

⬆ RELAX IN PARQUE DEL BUEN RETIRO

Once a royal playground, the **Parque del Buen Retiro** (p71) is a haven from city life in the heart of one of Europe's noisiest cities. On Sundays it positively throngs with people, musicians and a happy buzz, while during the rest of the week it's quiet and ideal for tracking down its elegant if quirky collection of monuments.

⬆ TAKE A TAPAS TOUR

Madrid's La Latina district ranks among Spain's best *barrios* for **tapas** (p75). Here you'll find culinary influences from all over the country that spans the full spectrum of tapas philosophies, from the traditional to the brave new world. Calle de la Cava Baja is the hub, but it spills over into surrounding streets, and then echoes out across the city.

⬆ LISTEN TO LIVE MUSIC

A diverse **live music scene** (p80) is one of the many attractions of the long Madrid night. Venues serve up a nightly feast of flamenco, jazz and a host of other live music, drawing a mix of big local and international names, emerging groups and alternative acts. This being Madrid, many don't take the stage until close to midnight.

2 KRZYSZTOF DYDYNSKI; 3 RICHARD NEBESKY; 4 KRZYSZTOF DYDYNSKI; 5 OLIVER STREWE; 6 GUY MOBERLY

2 Centro de Arte Reina Sofía (p63); 3 Plaza de Oriente (p63) and Palacio Real (p62); 4 Monument to Alfonso XII, Parque del Buen Retiro (p 71); 5 Selection of tapas (p75); 6 Live music at Populart (p81)

MADRID

MADRID'S BEST...

⬇ OFF-THE-RADAR GALLERIES

- **Real Academia de Bellas Artes de San Fernando** (p67) Little-known gallery with big-name masterpieces.
- **Ermita de San Antonio de la Florida** (p67) Exquisite collection of Goya frescoes.

⬇ WAYS TO WORK UP AN APPETITE

- **El Rastro** (p62) Dive into the madness of Madrid's massive Sunday market.
- **Hammam Medina Mayrit** (p70) Submit to a scrub and massage in Islamic-style surrounds.
- **Parque del Buen Retiro** (p71) Stroll through Madrid's monumental public gardens.
- **Palacio Real** (p62) Follow the trail of royalty through this expansive palace's 50 rooms.

⬇ TAPAS BARS

- **Almendro 13** (p75) Traditional tapas in La Latina.
- **Casa Alberto** (p75) One of Madrid's longest-standing and most traditional *tabernas*.
- **Taberna Txacoli** (p75) An icon of Basque tapas.
- **Casa Lucas** (p75) The marriage of innovation with tradition.
- **Sula Madrid** (p76) Innovative tapas and a sleek and sophisticated atmosphere.

⬇ PRETTY PLAZAS

- **Plaza Mayor** (p62) Elegant focal point of downtown.
- **Plaza de la Villa** (p63) Cosy square surrounded by beautiful architecture.
- **Plaza de Santa Ana** (p63) Heartbeat of Huertas.
- **Plaza de la Paja** (p63) Village-like intimacy of Old Madrid.

Sunday flea market at El Rastro (p62)

KRZYSZTOF DYDYNSKI

MADRID'S BEST...

THINGS YOU NEED TO KNOW

VITAL STATISTICS

- **Population** 3.5 million
- **Area** 505 sq km
- **Best time to visit** April/May and September/October

NEIGHBOURHOODS IN A NUTSHELL

- **Los Austrias, Sol & Centro** (p62) The oldest corner of Madrid.
- **La Latina & Lavapiés** (p62) Lively tapas scene and multicultural melting pot.
- **Huertas & Atocha** (p63) Vibrant inner-city *barrio*.
- **Paseo del Prado & El Retiro** (p63) Fine art galleries and the Parque del Buen Retiro.
- **Salamanca** (p69) Upscale neighbourhood with Madrid's best shopping.
- **Malasaña & Chueca** (p69) Gay Chueca and hard-rocking Malasaña lend much life to the city.
- **Chamberí & Argüelles** (p69) Quieter *barrios* north of the centre.

RESOURCES

- **Centro de Turismo de Madrid** (Map p68; ☎ 91 429 49 51; www.es madrid.com; Plaza Mayor 27; ⏰ 9.30am-8.30pm; Ⓜ Sol) Further information points at Plaza de la Cibeles, Plaza de Colón, Plaza de Callao and elsewhere.
- **Regional tourist office** (☎ 91 429 49 51, 902 10 00 07; www.turismomadrid .es; Calle del Duque de Medinaceli 2; ⏰ 8am-8pm Mon-Sat, 9am-2pm Sun; Ⓜ Banco de España)

EMERGENCY NUMBERS

- **Emergency** (☎ 112)
- **Policía Nacional** (☎ 091)
- **Servicio de Atención al Turista Extranjero** (Foreign Tourist Assistance Service; Map pp64-5; ☎ 91 548 85 37, 91 548 80 08; satemadrid@munimadrid .es; Calle de Leganitos 19; ⏰ 9am-10pm; Ⓜ Plaza de España or Santo Domingo) To report thefts or other crime-related matters.

GETTING AROUND

- **Air** (p83) Madrid's Barajas Airport (www.aena.es) has excellent connections with Europe and beyond.
- **Metro** (p84) Best for getting anywhere in town, including the airport.
- **Taxis** (p84) Some of the cheapest in Europe.

BE FOREWARNED

- **Most museums and galleries** Close on Monday.
- **Centro de Arte Reina Sofía** Opens Monday, closes Tuesday.
- **Many restaurants** Close in August.

MADRID

DISCOVER MADRID

No city on earth is more alive than Madrid, a beguiling place whose sheer energy carries a simple message: this city knows how to live. It's true Madrid doesn't have the immediate cachet of Paris, the monumental history of Rome or the reputation for cool of that other city up the road. But it's a city that becomes truly great once you're under its skin and get to know its *barrios* (districts). There you'll discover a diverse city whose contradictory impulses are legion, the perfect expression of Europe's most passionate country writ large.

This city has transformed itself into Spain's premier style centre and its calling cards are many: astonishing art galleries, relentless nightlife, an exceptional live music scene, a feast of fine restaurants and tapas bars, and a population that's mastered the art of the good life. It's not that other cities don't have these things. It's just that Madrid has all of them in bucket-loads.

DISCOVER MADRID

MADRID IN...

Two Days

You've a hectic day ahead of you so plan it around the best places (and plazas) to relax en route. Begin in **Plaza Mayor** (p62), with its architectural beauty, fine *terrazas* (terraces) and endlessly fascinating passing parade. Wander down Calle Mayor, passing the delightful **Plaza de la Villa** (p63), and head for the **Palacio Real** (p62). By then you'll be ready for a coffee or something stronger, and there's no finer place to rest than in **Plaza de Oriente** (p63). Double back up towards the Puerta del Sol, and then on to **Plaza de Santa Ana** (p63), the ideal place for a long, liquid lunch. Time for some high culture, so stroll down the hill to the incomparable **Museo del Prado** (p63), the home of a grand collection of predominantly Spanish old masters and one of the best art galleries in Europe. In anticipation of a long night ahead, catch your breath in the **Parque del Buen Retiro** (p71) before heading into **Chueca** or **Malasaña** for great restaurants (p76), followed by some terrific live music (p80).

On day two, cram in everything you didn't have time for on day one. Choose between the **Centro de Arte Reina Sofía** (p63) and the **Museo Thyssen-Bornemisza** (p65), then jump on the metro for a quick ride across town to the astonishing Goya frescoes in the **Ermita de San Antonio de la Florida** (p67). Finish off with tapas in **La Latina** (see the boxed text, p75) and end up with drinks at **Museo Chicote** (p79).

ORIENTATION

In Spain, all roads lead to Madrid's Plaza de la Puerta del Sol, kilometre zero, the physical and emotional heart of the city.

South of the Puerta del Sol is the oldest part of the city, with Plaza Mayor and Los Austrias to the southwest and the busy streets of the Huertas *barrio* to the southeast. Also to the south lie La Latina and Lavapiés.

North of Plaza de la Puerta del Sol is a modern shopping district and, beyond that, the east–west thoroughfare Gran Vía and the gay *barrio* Chueca, gritty Malasaña, then Chamberí and Argüelles. East of the Puerta del Sol, across the Paseo del Prado and Paseo de los Recoletos, lie El Retiro park and Salamanca.

INFORMATION

Centro de Turismo de Madrid (Map p68; ☎ 91 429 49 51; www.esmadrid.com; Plaza Mayor 27; ⏱ 9.30am-8.30pm; Ⓜ Sol) The *ayuntamiento* (town hall) also runs bright-orange information points at Plaza de la Cibeles, at Plaza de Callao, outside the Centro de Arte Reina Sofía and at the T4 terminal at Barajas airport. There's another tourist office underneath Plaza de Colón.

Regional tourist office (Map pp64-5; ☎ 91 429 49 51, 902 10 00 07; www.turismomadrid .es; Calle del Duque de Medinaceli 2; ⏱ 8am-8pm Mon-Sat, 9am-2pm Sun; Ⓜ Banco de España) There are also offices at Barajas airport (T1 and T4), and Chamartín and Atocha train stations.

MADRID

ORIENTATION

CLOCKWISE FROM TOP LEFT: GUY MOBERLY; KRZYSZTOF DYDYNSKI; KRZYSZTOF DYDYNSKI; GUY MOBERLY

Clockwise from top: Artworks in the Museo del Prado (p63); Parque del Buen Retiro (p71); Open-air cafes in Plaza Mayor (p62); El Ángel Caído, Parque del Buen Retiro (p71)

MADRID

SIGHTS

LOS AUSTRIAS, SOL & CENTRO

PLAZA MAYOR

The stunningly beautiful **Plaza Mayor** (Map p68; **M** Sol) is a highlight of any visit to Madrid. Designed in 1619 by Juan Gómez de Mora, the plaza's first public ceremony was the beatification of San Isidro Labrador, Madrid's patron saint. Thereafter, bullfights watched by 50,000 spectators were a recurring spectacle until 1878, while the autos-da-fé (the ritual condemnation of heretics) of the Spanish Inquisition also took place here. Today, among the uniformly ochre apartments with wrought-iron balconies, you can still see the exquisite frescoes of the 17th-century **Real Casa de la Panadería** (Royal Bakery).

PALACIO REAL

Spain's lavish **Palacio Real** (Royal Palace; Map p68; ☎ 91 542 69 47; www.patrimonionacional.es; Calle de Bailén s/n; adult/child, student & EU senior €10/3.50, adult without guide €8, EU citizens free Wed; 🕑 9am-6pm Mon-Sat, 9am-3pm Sun & holidays Apr-Sep, 9.30am-5pm Mon-Sat, 9am-2pm Sun & holidays Oct-Mar; **M** Ópera) is a jewel box of a palace, although it's used only occasionally for royal ceremonies; the royal family moved to the modest Palacio de la Zarzuela years ago.

The official tour leads through 50 of the palace rooms, which hold a good selection of Goyas, 215 absurdly ornate clocks and five Stradivarius violins still used for concerts and balls.

CONVENTO DE LAS DESCALZAS REALES

The grim, prisonlike walls of the **Convento de las Descalzas Reales** (Convent of the Barefoot Royals; Map p68; ☎ 91 542 69 47; www .patrimonionacional.es; Plaza de las Descalzas 3; adult/child €5/2.50, EU citizens free Wed, incl Convento de la Encarnación €6/3.40; 🕑 10.30am-12.45pm & 4-5.45pm Tue-Thu & Sat, 10.30am-12.45pm Fri, 11am-1.45pm Sun; **M** Ópera or Sol) offer no hint that behind the plateresque facade lies a sumptuous stronghold of the faith.

LA LATINA & LAVAPIÉS

EL RASTRO

A Sunday morning at **El Rastro** (Map pp64-5; 🕑 8am-3pm Sun; **M** La Latina), Europe's largest flea market, is a Madrid institution. It's been an open-air market for half a millennium.

MADRID CARD

If you intend to do some intensive sightseeing and travelling on public transport, it might be worth looking at the **Madrid Card** (☎ 91 360 47 72; www.madrid card.com). It includes free entry to more than 40 museums in and around Madrid (including the Museo del Prado, Museo Thyssen-Bornemisza, Centro de Arte Reina Sofía, Estadio Santiago Bernabéu and Palacio Real) and free Descubre Madrid walking tours, as well as discounts on public transport, on the Madrid Visión tourist bus and in certain shops and restaurants. The ticket is available for one/two/three days (€42/55/68). There's also a cheaper version (€28/32/36), which just covers cultural sights. The Madrid Card can be bought online, over the phone, or in person at the tourist offices on Plaza Mayor and in Calle del Duque de Medinaceli, and in some tobacconists and hotels – a list of major sales outlets can be found on the website.

MADRID

The madness begins at Plaza de Cascorro, near La Latina metro stop, and you could easily spend an entire morning inching your way down Calle de la Ribera de Curtidores and the maze of streets branching off it. For many *madrileños,* the best of El Rastro comes after the stalls have shut down and everyone crowds into nearby bars for an *aperitivo* (aperitif) of vermouth and tapas, turning the *barrio* into the site of a spontaneous Sunday fiesta.

HUERTAS & ATOCHA
CENTRO DE ARTE REINA SOFÍA
Adapted from the shell of an 18th-century hospital, the **Centro de Arte Reina Sofía** (off Map p64-5; ☎ 91 774 10 00; www .reinasofia.es; Calle de Santa Isabel 52; adult/child & senior/student €6/free/4, 2.30-9pm Sat & Sun free, audioguide €3; ⏱ 10am-9pm Mon & Wed-Sat, 10am-2.30pm Sun; Ⓜ Atocha) houses the best in modern (predominantly) Spanish art, principally spanning the 20th century up to the 1980s.

The big attraction for most visitors is Picasso's *Guernica* in Room 6 on the 2nd floor, which alone is worth the entrance price.

Primary among the other stars in residence is the work of Joan Miró (1893–1983), which adorns Room 12, a long gallery adjacent to the Picasso collection. Amid his often delightfully bright primary-colour efforts are some of his equally odd sculptures. You'll also want to rush to Room 10 to view the 20 or so canvases by Salvador Dalí (1904–89), especially the surrealist extravaganza *El Gran Masturbador* (1929).

PASEO DEL PRADO & EL RETIRO
MUSEO DEL PRADO
One of the world's top museums, the **Museo del Prado** (Map pp64-5; ☎ 91 330 28

Plaza de la Villa
CHRISTOPHER WOOD

SIGHTS

⬎ IF YOU LIKE...
If you like the **Plaza Mayor** (p62), we think you'll easily fall in love with these other central Madrid plazas (squares):

- **Plaza de la Villa** (Map p68; Ⓜ Ópera) Intimate square enclosed on three sides by 17th-century barroco madrileño (Madrid-style baroque architecture: a pleasing amalgam of brick, exposed stone and wrought iron).
- **Plaza de Santa Ana** (Map p68; Ⓜ Sol, Sevilla or Antón Martín) A delightful confluence of elegant architecture and irresistible energy, and the focal point of Huertas' intellectual life.
- **Plaza de Oriente** (Map pp64-5; Ⓜ Ópera) An elegant and gloriously alive monument to imperial Madrid.
- **Plaza de la Paja** (Map p68; Ⓜ La Latina) Feels like you've stumbled upon a village square in the heart of the city.

00; http://museoprado.mcu.es; Paseo del Prado; adult/under 18yr & over 65yr/student €8/free/4, Sun free, audioguide €3.50; ⏱ 9am-8pm Tue-Sun; Ⓜ Banco de España) has a peerless collection of Spanish and European art. Spend as long as you can here or, better still, plan

CENTRAL MADRID

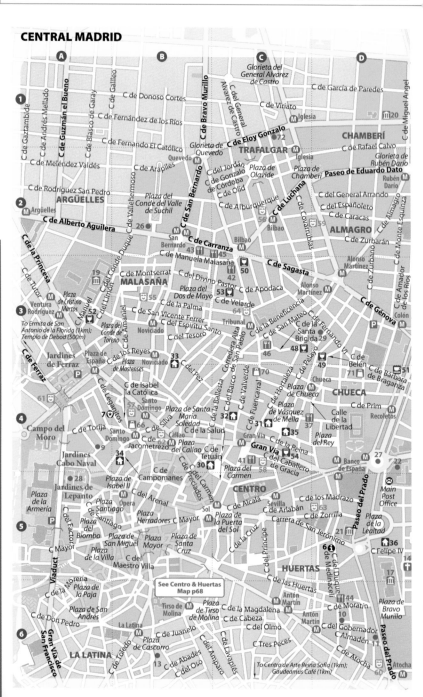

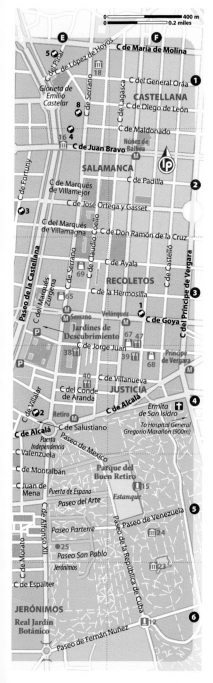

to make a couple of visits because it can be a little overwhelming if you try to take it all in at once.

The more than 7000 paintings held in the Museo del Prado's impressive collection (just over half are currently on display) are like a window on the historical vagaries of the Spanish soul: grand and imperious in the royal paintings of Velázquez; darkly tumultuous in the Pinturas Negras (Black Paintings) of Goya; and outward-looking in the collection of sophisticated works of art from all across Europe.

The building in which the Prado is housed is itself an architectural masterpiece. Completed in 1785, the neoclassical Palacio de Villanueva served, somewhat ignominiously, as a cavalry barracks for Napoleon's troops during their occupation of Madrid between 1808 and 1813. In 1814, King Fernando VII decided to use the palace as a museum. Five years later the Museo del Prado opened with 311 Spanish paintings on display, and it's never looked back. In late 2007 the long-awaited extension of the Prado opened to critical acclaim.

Entrance to the Prado is via the western Puerta de Velázquez (in the old part of the Prado) or the eastern Puerta de los Jerónimos (the extension), but first, tickets must be purchased from the ticket office at the northern end of the building, opposite the Hotel Ritz.

MUSEO THYSSEN-BORNEMISZA

The favourite art gallery of many visitors to Madrid, the Museo Thyssen-Bornemisza (Map pp64-5; ☎ 91 369 01 51; www.museothyssen.org; Paseo del Prado 8; adult/concession €6/4; ⏰ 10am-7pm Tue-Sun; Ⓜ Banco de España) has something for everyone, with a breathtaking breadth of artistic styles, from the masters of medieval art to the zany world of contemporary painting. All the big names are represented here, sometimes with just a single painting, but the Thyssens' gift to Madrid and the art-loving public is to have them all under one roof.

CAIXA FORUM
The extraordinary **Caixa Forum** (Map pp64–5; ☎ 91 330 73 00; www.fundacio.lacaixa .es in Spanish; Paseo del Prado 36; admission free; ☼ 10am-10pm; Ⓜ Atocha), which opened in early 2008 at the southern end of the Paseo del Prado, is one of the most exciting architectural innovations to emerge in Madrid in recent years. Seeming to hover above the ground, this brick edifice is topped by an intriguing summit of rusted iron. On an adjacent wall is the *jardín colgante* (hanging garden), a lush verti-

cal wall of greenery almost four storeys high. Inside are four floors of exhibition and performance space awash in stainless steel and with soaring ceilings.

PLAZA DE LA CIBELES
Of all the grand roundabouts that punctuate the elegant boulevard of Paseo del Prado, **Plaza de la Cibeles** (Map pp64–5; Ⓜ Banco de España) most evokes the splendour of Imperial Madrid.

The jewel in the crown is the astonishing **Palacio de Comunicaciones**. Completed in 1917, it combines elements of the North American monumental style of the period with Gothic and Renaissance touches.

The spectacular fountain of the goddess Cybele at the centre of the plaza is also one of Madrid's most beautiful.

MADRID

Garden of the Museo Sorolla

KRZYSZTOF DYDYNSKI

SIGHTS

↘ IF YOU LIKE...

If you like the **Museo del Prado** (p63), **Centro de Arte Reina Sofía** (p63) and **Museo Thyssen-Bornemisza** (p65), Madrid has numerous other homes to artistic masterpieces that would be world-famous in any other city:

- **Real Academia de Bellas Artes de San Fernando** (Map p68; ☎ 91 524 08 64; http://rabasf.insde.es in Spanish; Calle de Alcalá 13; adult/senior & under 18yr/student €3/free/1.50, Wed free to all; ☽ 9am-5pm Tue-Sat, 9am-2.30pm Sun Sep-Jun, varied hours summer; Ⓜ Sevilla) Home to works by Zurbarán, El Greco, Rubens, Tintoretto, Goya, Sorolla and Juan Gris, and some 'minor' works by Velázquez and Picasso.

- **Ermita de San Antonio de la Florida** (off Map pp64-5; ☎ 91 542 07 22; Glorieta de San Antonio de la Florida 5; ☽ 9.30am-8pm Tue-Fri, 10am-2pm Sat & Sun; Ⓜ Príncipe Pío) Stunning frescoes by Goya fill the ceiling of this small hermitage.

- **Museo de la Escultura Abstracta** (Map pp64-5; Paseo de la Castellana; Ⓜ Rubén Dario) Fascinating open-air collection of 17 abstract sculptures, including works by Eduardo Chillida, Joan Miró, Eusebio Sempere and Alberto Sánchez.

- **Museo Sorolla** (Map pp64-5; ☎ 91 310 15 84; http://museosorolla.mcu.es in Spanish; Paseo del General Martínez Campos 37; adult/child/student €2.40/free/1.20; ☽ 9.30am-3pm Tue-Sat, 10am-3pm Sun; Ⓜ Iglesia or Gregorio Marañón) The former home of renowned Valencian artist Joaquín Sorolla contains many of his works.

- **Museo Municipal de Arte Contemporáneo de Madrid** (Map pp64-5; ☎ 91 588 29 28; www.munimadrid.es/museoartecontemporaneo in Spanish; Calle del Conde Duque 9; admission free; ☽ 10am-2pm & 5.30-9pm Tue-Sat, 10.30am-2.30pm Sun; Ⓜ Plaza de España) Houses contemporary Spanish and international paintings, sculpture, photography and graphic art.

MADRID

CENTRO & HUERTAS

CENTRO & HUERTAS

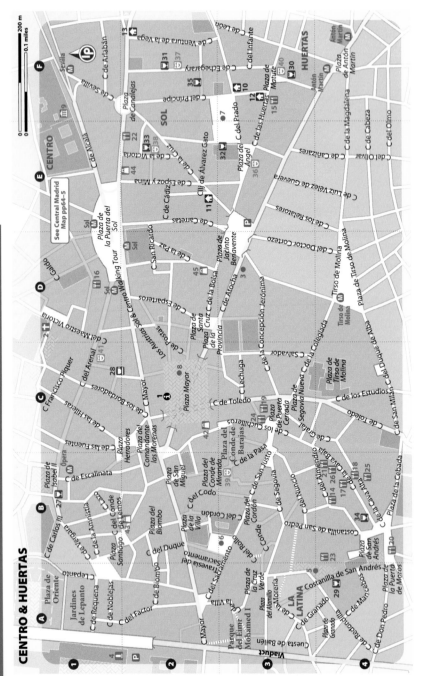

IGLESIA DE SAN JERÓNIMO EL REAL

Tucked away behind the Museo del Prado, the lavish Iglesia de San Jerónimo el Real (Map pp64-5; ☎ 91 420 35 78; Calle de Ruiz de Alarcón 19; ☽ 10am-1pm & 5-8pm Mon-Sat; Ⓜ Atocha or Banco de España) was largely destroyed during the Peninsular War. The interior was reconstructed during the 19th century, however, and is just exquisite. The chapel was traditionally favoured by the Spanish royal family and it was here, amid the mock-Isabelline splendour, that King Juan Carlos I was crowned in 1975 upon the death of Franco.

SALAMANCA
MUSEO LÁZARO GALDIANO

In an imposing early 20th-century Italianate stone mansion, the Museo Lázaro Galdiano (Map pp64-5; ☎ 91 561 60 84; www.flg.es in Spanish; Calle de Serrano 122; adult/student €4/3, Sun free; ☽ 10am-4.30pm Wed-Mon; Ⓜ Gregorio Marañón) has some 13,000 works of art and objets d'art. Apart from works by van Eyck, Bosch, Zurbarán, Ribera, Goya, Claudio Coello, El Greco, Gainsborough and Constable, this is a rather oddball assembly of all sorts of collectables.

MALASAÑA & CHUECA
SOCIEDAD GENERAL DE AUTORES Y EDITORES

The swirling, melting wedding cake of a building that is the Sociedad General de Autores y Editores (General Society of Authors & Editors; Map pp64-5; Calle de Fernando VI 4; Ⓜ Alonso Martínez) is as close as Madrid comes to the work of Antoni Gaudí. It's a joyously self-indulgent ode to Modernisme and one of a kind in Madrid.

CHAMBERÍ & ARGÜELLES
TEMPLO DE DEBOD

Remarkably, this authentic 4th-century-BC Egyptian temple sits in the heart of Madrid, in the Parque de la Montaña. The Templo de Debod (off Map pp64-5; ☎ 91 366 74 15; www.munimadrid.es/templodebod in Spanish; Paseo del Pintor Rosales; admission free; ☽ 10am-2pm & 6-8pm Tue-Fri, 10am-2pm Sat & Sun Apr-Sep, 9.45am-1.45pm & 4.15-6.15pm Tue-Fri, 10am-2pm Sat & Sun Oct-Mar; Ⓜ Ventura Rodríguez) was saved from the rising waters of Lake Nasser, formed by the Aswan High Dam, and sent block by block to Spain in 1968. The views from the surrounding gardens towards the Palacio Real are quite special.

MADRID

SIGHTS

MADRID

ACTIVITIES

ACTIVITIES

Hammam Medina Mayrit (Map p68; ☎ 902 33 33 34; www.medinamayrit.com; Calle de Atocha 14; ⏱ 10am-midnight; Ⓜ Sol) A traditional Arab bath; bookings required.

COURSES

Alambique (Map pp64-5; ☎ 91 547 42 20; www.alambique.com; Plaza de la Encarnación 2; Ⓜ Ópera or Santo Domingo) Cooking classes start from around €50, with English-language courses from €70.

Cooking Club (Map p53; ☎ 91 323 29 58; www.club-cooking.com in Spanish; Calle de Veza 33; Ⓜ Valdeacederas) Regular classes encompassing a range of cooking styles.

MADRID FOR CHILDREN

Madrid has plenty to keep the little ones entertained. A good place to start is **Casa de Campo** (Ⓜ Batán), where there are swimming pools, the Zoo Aquarium de Madrid and the Parque de Atracciones, which has a 'Zona Infantil' with sedate rides for the really young. To get to Casa de Campo, take the *teleférico,* one of the world's most horizontal cable cars, which putters for 2.5km out from the slopes of La Rosaleda.

Another possibility is **Faunia** (off Map 53; ☎ 91 301 62 35; www.faunia.es in Spanish; Avenida de las Comunidades 28; adult/under 12yr €23/17; Ⓜ Valdebernardo), a modern animal theme park with an 'Amazon jungle' and 'Polar Ecosystem'. Opening hours vary.

At the mammoth indoor playground **Parque Secreto** (Map pp64-5; ☎ 91 593 14 80; www.parquesecreto.com in Spanish; Plaza del Conde del Valle de Suchil 3; admission per 30min from €2.50; ⏱ 5-9pm Mon-Fri, 11.30am-2pm & 4.30-9pm Sat & Sun; Ⓜ San Bernardo), you'll find 800 sq metres of indoor playgrounds (labyrinths, floating castles, pits filled with plastic balls, toboggans etc) for kids aged up to 11.

Other possibilities include seeing Real Madrid play at the **Estadio Santiago Bernabéu** (p81), wandering through the soothing greenery of the **Parque del Buen Retiro** (p71), where in summer there are puppet shows and boat rides, or skiing at **Madrid Xanadú** (off Map 53; ☎ 902 36 13 09; www.madridsnowzone.com in Spanish; Calle Puerto de Navacerrada, Arroyomolinos; ⏱ 10am-10pm Sun-Thu, 10am-midnight Fri & Sat).

TOURS

The Centro de Turismo de Madrid (p59) offers dozens of guided walking, cycling and bus itineraries through its **Descubre Madrid** (Discover Madrid; ☎ 91 588 29 06; www.esmadrid.com; walking tours adult/concession €3.30/2.70, bus tours €6.45/5.05, bicycle tours €3.30/2.70 plus €6 bike rental) program.

The privately run **Adventurous Appetites** (☎ 639 331073; www.adventurous appetites.com; 4hr tours €50) organises tapas tours through central Madrid from the bear statue in Puerta del Sol. Prices include the first drink but exclude food.

FESTIVALS & EVENTS
FEBRUARY
Festival Flamenco A combination of big names and rising talent comes together for five days of fine flamenco music in one of the city's theatres.

MARCH–APRIL
Jazz es Primavera (www.sanjuanevange lista.org) Three weeks of jazz in the leading jazz venues across the city.

MAY
Suma Flamenca (www.madrid.org/suma flamenca in Spanish) Another soul-filled flamenco festival that draws some of the biggest names in the genre.
Dos de Mayo On 2 May 1808, Napoleon's troops put down an uprising in

KRZYSZTOF DYDYNSKI

Parque del Buen Retiro

MADRID

FESTIVALS & EVENTS

↘ **PARQUE DEL BUEN RETIRO**

A Sunday walk in El Retiro is as much a Madrid tradition as tapas and terrace cafes. Littered with marble monuments, landscaped lawns, the occasional elegant building and abundant greenery, it's quiet and contemplative during the week, but comes alive on weekends. Apart from strolling, people come here to read the Sunday papers in the shade, take a boat ride (€4 for 45 minutes) or enjoy a cool drink at the numerous outdoor *terrazas*.

The *estanque* (lake) is watched over by the massive structure of the Monument to Alfonso XII on the eastern side, complete with marble lions.

Other highlights include the 1887 Palacio de Cristal, a charming metal-and-glass structure south of the lake, which hosts temporary exhibitions; the 1883 Palacio de Velázquez, which was closed for renovations at the time of research; and, at the southern end of the park, a statue of El Ángel Caído (the Fallen Angel, aka Lucifer), one of the world's few statues to the devil.

Things you need to know: Parque del Buen Retiro (Map pp64-5; ☽ 6am-midnight May-Sep, 6am-11pm Oct-Apr; Ⓜ Retiro, Príncipe de Vergara, Ibiza or Atocha); Palacio de Cristal (☎ 91 574 66 14; ☽ 11am-8pm Mon-Sat, 11am-6pm Sun & holidays May-Sep, 10am-6pm Mon-Sat, 10am-4pm Sun & holidays Oct-Apr)

Madrid, and commemoration of the day has become an opportunity for much festivity, often called the Fiesta de la Comunidad de Madrid.

Fiesta de San Isidro Around 15 May, Madrid's patron saint is honoured with a week of nonstop processions, parties and bullfights.

JUNE

Día del Orgullo de Gays, Lesbianas y Transexuales The colourful Gay Pride Parade sets out from the Puerta de Alcalá in the early evening, and winds its way around the city in an explosion of music and energy, ending up at the Puerta del Sol.

MADRID

SLEEPING

JULY–AUGUST
Veranos de la Villa Madrid's town hall stages a series of cultural events, shows and exhibitions, known as Summers in the City.

AUGUST–SEPTEMBER
La Noche en Blanco On September's White Night, first held in 2006, Madrid stays open all night with a citywide extravaganza of concerts and general revelry in 120 venues.

OCTOBER–NOVEMBER
Fiesta de Otoño Music, dance and theatre take over Madrid from mid-October to mid-November, during the fantastically cultural weeks of the Autumn Festival.

KRZYSZTOF DYDYNSKI
Hotel Urban

Emociona Jazz Madrid loves its jazz too much to be confined to just one festival. In November, groups from far and wide converge on the capital for concerts across town.

SLEEPING
Having undergone something of a hotel revolution, the city now has high-quality accommodation across all price ranges and caters to every taste.

LOS AUSTRIAS, SOL & CENTRO
Hostal Acapulco (Map pp64–5; ☎ 91 531 19 45; www.hostalacapulco.com; 4th fl, Calle de la Salud 13; s/d/tr €52/62/79; Ⓜ Gran Vía; 🔾 💻) This immaculate little *hostal* (budget hotel) is a cut above many in Madrid, with marble floors, recently renovated bathrooms, double-glazed windows and comfortable beds. Street-facing rooms have balconies overlooking sunny Plaza del Carmen.

Hotel Meninas (Map pp64–5; ☎ 91 541 28 05; www.hotelmeninas.com; Calle de Campomanes 7; s/d from €109/129; Ⓜ Ópera; 💻) Opened in 2005, this is the sort of place where an interior designer licked his or her lips and created a masterwork of minimalist luxury. The colour scheme is blacks, whites and greys, with dark-wood floors and splashes of fuchsia and lime-green.

HUERTAS & ATOCHA
Hostal Adriano (Map p68; ☎ 91 521 13 39; www.hostaladriano.com; 4th fl, Calle de la Cruz 26; s/d/tr €49/63/83; Ⓜ Sol) They don't come any better than this bright and cheerful *hostal* wedged in the streets that mark the boundary between Sol and Huertas. Most rooms are well sized and each has its own colour scheme.

Alicia Room Mate (Map p68; ☎ 91 389 60 95; www.room-matehoteles.com; Calle del Prado 2; d €90-200; Ⓜ Sol or Antón Martín; 💻) One of the landmark properties of the designer Room Mate chain of hotels, Hotel Alicia overlooks Plaza de Santa Ana with beautiful, spacious rooms. The style (the work of Pascua Ortega) is a touch more muted than in other Room Mate hotels, but the supermodern look remains intact, the downstairs bar is oh-so-cool, and the service young and switched on.

Hotel Miau (Map p68; ☎ 91 369 71 20; www.hotelmiau.com; Calle del Príncipe 26; s/d incl breakfast €85/95; Ⓜ Sol or Antón Martín; ⊠ 🖵) If you want to be close to the nightlife of Huertas or you can't tear yourself away from the beautiful Plaza de Santa Ana, then this is your place. Light tones, splashes of colour and elegant modern art adorn the rooms, which are large and well equipped.

OUR PICK Hotel Urban (Map p68; ☎ 91 787 77 70; www.derbyhotels.com; Carrera de San Jerónimo 34; d €200-350; Ⓜ Sevilla; ⊠ 🖵 🏊) The towering glass edifice of Hotel Urban is the epitome of art-inspired, superstylish designer cool. With its clean lines, modern art and antiques from around the world, it's a wonderful antidote to the more classic charm of Madrid's five-star hotels of longer standing. The rooftop swimming pool is Madrid's best and the gorgeous terrace is heaven on a candlelit summer's evening.

PASEO DEL PRADO & EL RETIRO

Hotel Ritz (Map pp64-5; ☎ 91 701 67 67; www.ritzmadrid.com; Plaza de la Lealtad 5; d €562-675; Ⓜ Banco de España; ⊠ 🖵) The grand old lady of Madrid, the Hotel Ritz is the height of exclusivity. One of the most lavish buildings in the city, its classic style and impeccable service are second to none. Not surprisingly, it's the hotel of choice for presidents, kings and celebrities. The public areas are palatial and awash with antiques, while the rooms are extravagantly large, opulent and supremely comfortable.

MALASAÑA & CHUECA

Hostal Don Juan (Map pp64-5; ☎ 91 522 31 01; 2nd fl, Plaza de Vázquez de Mella 1; s/d/tr €38/53/71; Ⓜ Gran Vía) This elegant two-storey *hostal* is filled with art (each room has original works) and antique furniture that could grace a royal palace. Rooms are simple but luminous and large, and most have a balcony facing out onto the street.

Hostal La Zona (Map pp64-5; ☎ 91 521 99 04; www.hostallazona.com; 1st fl, Calle de Valverde 7; s/d/tr €50/60/85; Ⓜ Gran Vía; 🖵) Catering primarily to a gay clientele, the stylish Hostal La Zona has exposed brickwork, wooden pillars and a subtle colour scheme. Other highlights include free internet, helpful staff and air-conditioning/heating in every room.

OUR PICK Hotel Óscar (Map pp64-5; ☎ 91 701 11 73; www.room-matehoteles.com; Plaza de Vázquez de Mella 12; d €90-200, ste €150-280; Ⓜ Gran Vía) Simply outstanding. Hotel Óscar's designer rooms ooze style and sophistication. Some have floor-to-ceiling murals, the lighting is always funky and the colour scheme is awash with pinks, lime-greens, oranges or a more minimalist black-and-white.

OUR PICK Hotel Abalú (Map pp64-5; ☎ 91 531 47 44; www.hotelabalu.com; Calle del Pez 19; s/d from €74/105, ste €140-200; Ⓜ Noviciado) At last, Malasaña has its own boutique hotel, an oasis of style amid the *barrio*'s time-worn feel. Each room has its own design drawn from the imagination of Luis Delgado, from retro chintz to Zen, baroque to pure white, and most aesthetics in between.

BEYOND THE CENTRE

OUR PICK Hotel Puerta América (Map p53; ☎ 91 744 54 00; www.hoteles-silken.com/hpam; Avenida de América 41; d from €239; Ⓜ Cartagena; 🅿 ⊠ 🖵) Take some of world architecture's most innovative names and give

Casa Alberto
KRZYSZTOF DYDYNSKI

them a floor each to design. The result? An extravagant pastiche of styles, from curvy minimalism and zany montages of 1980s chic to bright-red bathrooms that feel like a movie star's dressing room.

EATING

After holding fast to its rather unexciting local cuisine for centuries (aided, it must be said, by loyal locals who never saw the need for anything else), Madrid has finally become one of Europe's culinary capitals.

LOS AUSTRIAS, SOL & CENTRO

La Gloria de Montera (Map pp64-5; ☎ 91 523 44 07; Calle del Caballero de Gracia 10; meals €20-25; Ⓜ Gran Vía) La Gloria de Montera combines classy decor with eminently reasonable prices. The food's not especially creative, but the tastes are fresh, the surroundings are sophisticated and you'll get a good initiation into Spanish cooking without paying over the odds.

Restaurante Sobrino de Botín (Map p68; ☎ 91 366 42 17; www.botin.es; Calle de los Cuchilleros 17; meals €35-45; Ⓜ La Latina or Sol) It's not every day that you can eat in the oldest restaurant in the world (1725), which also appears in many novels about Madrid, most notably Hemingway's *The Sun Also Rises*. The secret of its staying power is fine *cochinillo* (suckling pig; €21) and *cordero asado* (roast lamb; €21) cooked in wood-fired ovens. Eating in the vaulted cellar is a treat.

LA LATINA & LAVAPIÉS

Naïa Restaurante (Map p68; ☎ 91 366 27 83; www.naiarestaurante.com in Spanish; Plaza de la Paja 3; meals €25-30; Ⓨ lunch & dinner Mon-Sat; Ⓜ La Latina) On the lovely Plaza de la Paja, Naïa has a real buzz about it, with a cooking laboratory overseen by Carlos López Reyes, delightful modern Spanish food and a chill-out lounge downstairs.

Casa Lucio (Map p68; ☎ 91 365 32 52; www.casalucio.es in Spanish; Calle de la Cava Baja 35; meals €35-45; Ⓨ lunch & dinner Sun-Fri, dinner Sat, closed Aug; Ⓜ La Latina) Lucio has been wowing *madrileños* with his light touch, quality ingredients and home-style local cooking for ages – think seafood, roasted meats and eggs (a Lucio speciality) in abundance.

HUERTAS & ATOCHA

Maceiras (Map pp64-5; ☎ 91 429 15 84; Calle de las Huertas 66; meals €20-25; ☾ lunch & dinner Tue-Sun, dinner Mon; Ⓜ Antón Martín) Galician tapas (think octopus, green peppers etc) never tasted so good as in this agreeably rustic bar down the bottom of the Huertas hill, especially when washed down with a crisp white Ribeiro.

Casa Alberto (Map p68; ☎ 91 429 93 56; www.casaalberto.es in Spanish; Calle de las Huertas 18; meals €20-25; ☾ noon-1.30am Tue-Sat, noon-4pm Sun; Ⓜ Antón Martín) One of the most atmospheric old *tabernas* of Madrid, Casa Alberto has been around since 1827. The secret to its staying power is vermouth on tap, excellent tapas and fine sit-down meals; *rabo de toro* (bull's tail) is a good order.

Lhardy (Map p68; ☎ 91 522 22 07; www.lhardy.com; Carrera de San Jerónimo 8; meals €50-60; ☾ lunch & dinner Mon-Sat, lunch Sun; Ⓜ Sol or

MADRID

EATING

A TAPAS TOUR OF MADRID

Madrid's home of tapas is La Latina, especially along Calle de la Cava Baja and the surrounding streets. **Almendro 13** (Map p68; ☎ 91 365 42 52; Calle de Almendro 13; meals €15-25; Ⓜ La Latina) is regularly voted among the top tapas bars in Madrid for traditional Spanish tapas, with an emphasis on quality rather than frilly elaborations. Down on Calle de la Cava Baja, **Taberna Txacoli** (Map p68; ☎ 91 366 48 77; Calle de la Cava Baja 26; meals €15-20; ☾ lunch & dinner Tue & Thu-Sat, lunch Sun, dinner Wed; Ⓜ La Latina) does Basque 'high cuisine in miniature', although these are some of the biggest *pintxos* (Basque tapas) you'll find. On the same street, **Casa Lucas** (Map p68; ☎ 91 365 08 04; Calle de la Cava Baja 30; meals €20-25; ☾ lunch & dinner Thu-Tue, dinner Wed; Ⓜ La Latina) and **La Chata** (Map p68; ☎ 91 366 14 58; Calle de la Cava Baja 24; meals €25-30; ☾ lunch & dinner Thu-Mon, dinner Wed; Ⓜ La Latina) are also hugely popular. Not far away, **Juanalaloca** (Map p68; ☎ 91 364 05 25; Plaza de la Puerta de Moros 4; meals €30-35; ☾ lunch & dinner Tue-Sun, dinner Mon; Ⓜ La Latina) does a magnificent *tortilla de patatas* (potato and onion omelette), and **Taberna Matritum** (Map p68; ☎ 91 365 82 37; Calle de la Cava Alta 17; meals €20-30; ☾ lunch Mon-Fri, lunch & dinner Sat & Sun; Ⓜ La Latina) serves great *tostas* (toasts) and other tapas.

Most famous for *bacalao* (cod) is **Casa Labra** (Map p68; ☎ 91 531 00 81; Calle de Tetuán 11; meals €15-20; ☾ 11am-3.30pm & 6-11pm; Ⓜ Sol), which has been around since 1860 and was a favourite of the poet Federico García Lorca. However, many *madrileños* wouldn't eat *bacalao* anywhere except **Casa Revuelta** (Map p68; ☎ 91 366 33 32; Calle de Latoneros 3; meals €10-15; ☾ lunch & dinner Tue-Sat, lunch Sun; Ⓜ La Latina or Sol), clinched by the fact that the owner painstakingly extracts every fish bone in the morning.

Away to the east in Salamanca, **Biotza** (Map pp64-5; ☎ 91 781 03 13; Calle de Claudio Coello 27; ☾ 9am-midnight Mon-Thu, 9am-2am Fri & Sat; Ⓜ Serrano) offers creative Basque *pintxos* in stylish surrounds, while **La Colonial de Goya** (Map pp64-5; ☎ 91 575 63 06; Calle de Jorge Juan 34; meals €20; ☾ 8am-midnight Mon-Fri, 8am-1am Sat; Ⓜ Velázquez) serves up 68 different varieties of *pintxos*.

Sevilla) This Madrid landmark (since 1839) is an elegant treasure-trove of takeaway gourmet tapas. Upstairs is the upscale preserve of house specialities such as *callos*, *cocido*, pheasant in grape juice and lemon soufflé.

SALAMANCA

La Galette (Map pp64-5; ☎ 91 576 06 41; Calle del Conde de Aranda 11; meals €30-35; ✆ lunch & dinner Mon-Sat, lunch Sun; Ⓜ Retiro; Ⓥ) This lovely little restaurant combines an intimate dining area with checked tablecloths and cooking that the owner describes as 'baroque vegetarian'.

Sula Madrid (Map pp64-5; ☎ 91 781 61 97; www.sula.es; Calle de Jorge Juan 33; meals €70-80; ✆ lunch & dinner Mon-Sat; Ⓜ Velázquez) If you want to catch Salamanca's happening vibe, head for Sula, a gourmet food store, superstylish tapas bar and clean-lined restaurant where gastronomic wunderkind Quique Dacosta (voted Spain's best chef in 2005) serves up a range of Mediterranean dishes that you won't find anywhere else.

MALASAÑA & CHUECA

Ribeira Do Miño (Map pp64-5; ☎ 91 521 98 54; Calle de la Santa Brígida 1; meals €20-25; ✆ lunch & dinner Tue-Sat; Ⓜ Tribunal) This riotously popular seafood bar and restaurant is where *madrileños* with a love for seafood indulge their fantasies. The *mariscada de la casa* (€30 for two) is a platter of seafood so large that even the hungriest of visitors will leave satisfied.

ourpick La Musa (Map pp64-5; ☎ 91 448 75 58; www.lamusa.com.es; Calle de Manuela Malasaña 18; meals €25-30; Ⓜ San Bernardo) A local favourite of Malasaña's hip, young crowd, La Musa has designer decor, lounge music and food that will live long in the memory. They don't take reservations, so put your name on the waiting list at the bar.

Bazaar (Map pp64-5; ☎ 91 523 39 05; www .restaurantbazaar.com; Calle de la Libertad 21; meals €25-30; Ⓜ Chueca) Bazaar's popularity among the well-heeled and often-famous shows no sign of abating. Its pristine white interior design with theatre lighting may draw a crowd that looks like it stepped out of the pages of *Hola!* magazine, but the food is extremely well priced and innovative.

ourpick La Isla del Tesoro (Map pp64-5; ☎ 91 593 14 40; Calle de Manuela Malasaña 3; meals €30; Ⓜ Bilbao; Ⓥ) La Isla del Tesoro is loaded with quirky charm – the dining area is like someone's fantasy of a secret garden come to life. The cooking here is assured and wide-ranging in its influences; the jungle burger is typical in a menu that's full of surprises.

ourpick Nina (Map pp64-5; ☎ 91 591 00 46; Calle de Manuela Malasaña 10; meals €30-35; Ⓜ Bilbao) This is one of our favourite restaurants in Madrid, with fantastic food, great service and a stylish dining area.

DRINKING

To get an idea of how much *madrileños* like to go out and have a good time, consider one simple statistic: Madrid has more bars than any city in the world – six, in fact, for every 100 inhabitants.

LOS AUSTRIAS, SOL & CENTRO

Chocolatería de San Ginés (Map p68; ☎ 91 365 65 46; Pasadizo de San Ginés 5; ✆ 9am-7am Wed-Sun, 6pm-7am Mon & Tue; Ⓜ Sol) Perhaps the best-known of Madrid's *chocolate con churros* vendors, this Madrid institution is at its most popular from 3am to 6am as clubbers make a last stop for sustenance on their way home. Only in Madrid.

Café del Real (Map p68; ☎ 91 547 21 24; Plaza de Isabel II 2; ✆ 9am-1am Sun-Thu, 10am-2am Fri & Sat; Ⓜ Ópera) One of the nicest cafes in central Madrid, this place serves a rich variety of creative coffees and a few cocktails to a soundtrack of chill-out music. The best seats are upstairs.

LA LATINA & LAVAPIÉS

Delic (Map p68; ☎ 91 364 54 50; Costanilla de San Andrés 14; ☺ 11am-2am Tue-Sun, 8pm-2am Mon; Ⓜ La Latina) We could go on for hours about this long-standing cafe-bar, but we'll reduce it to its most basic elements: nursing an exceptionally good mojito or three on a warm summer's evening at an outdoor table on one of Madrid's prettiest plazas is one of life's great pleasures. Bliss.

Gaudeamus Café (off Map pp64-5; ☎ 91 528 25 94; www.gaudeamuscafe.com in Spanish; 4th fl, Calle de Tribulete 14; ☺ 3.30pm-midnight Mon-Fri, 8pm-midnight Sat; Ⓜ Lavapiés) Decoration that's light and airy, with pop-art posters of Audrey Hepburn and James Bond. A large terrace with views over the Lavapiés rooftops. A stunning backdrop of a ruined church atop which the cafe sits. With so much else going for it, it almost seems incidental that this cafe serves great teas, coffees and snacks.

Taberna Tempranillo (Map p68; ☎ 91 364 15 32; Calle de la Cava Baja 38; ☺ 1-4pm & 8pm-midnight; Ⓜ La Latina) You could come here for the tapas, but we are recommending Taberna Tempranillo primarily for its wines, of which there is a selection that puts most other Spanish bars to shame.

HUERTAS & ATOCHA

El Imperfecto (Map p68; Plaza de Matute 2; ☺ 3pm-2am Sun-Thu, 3pm-3am Fri & Sat; Ⓜ Antón Martín) Its name notwithstanding, the 'Imperfect One' is our ideal Huertas bar, with live jazz on Tuesdays (and sometimes other nights) and a drinks menu as long as a saxophone, ranging from cocktails (€6.50) and spirits to milkshakes, teas and creative coffees.

Sula Madrid

KRZYSZTOF DYDYNSKI

La Venencia (Map p68; ☎ 91 429 73 13; Calle de Echegaray 7; ☺ 1-3.30pm & 7.30pm-1.30am Sun-Thu, 1-3.30pm & 7.30pm-2.30am Fri & Sat; Ⓜ Sol) This is how sherry bars should be – old-world, drinks poured straight from the dusty wooden barrels and none of the frenetic activity for which Huertas is famous.

Taberna Alhambra (Map p68; ☎ 91 521 07 08; Calle de la Victoria 9; ☺ 10am-2am; Ⓜ Sol) There can be a certain sameness about the bars between Sol and Huertas, which is why this fine old *taberna* stands out. The striking facade and exquisite tilework of the interior are quite beautiful; however, this place is anything but stuffy and the vibe is cool, casual and busy.

Penthouse (Map p68; ☎ 91 701 60 20; 7th fl, Plaza de Santa Ana 14; ☺ 9pm-4am Wed-Sat,

MADRID

DRINKING

5pm-midnight Sun; Ⓜ Antón Martín or Sol) High above the clamour of Huertas, this exclusive cocktail bar has a delightful terrace overlooking Plaza de Santa Ana and the rooftops of downtown Madrid. It's a place for sophisticates, with chill-out areas strewn with cushions, funky DJs and a dress policy designed to sort out the classy from the wannabes.

Viva Madrid (Map p68; ☎ 91 429 36 40; www .barvivamadrid.com; Calle de Manuel Fernández y González 7; ☽ 1pm-2am Sun-Thu, 1pm-3am Fri & Sat; Ⓜ Antón Martín or Sol) A beautifully tiled bar, some of the best mojitos in town, a friendly atmosphere, a mixed crowd and scattered tables – what more could a *madrileño* want?

SALAMANCA

Café-Restaurante El Espejo (Map pp64-5; ☎ 91 308 23 47; Paseo de los Recoletos 31; ☽ 10.30am-1am Sun-Thu, 10.30am-2am Fri & Sat; Ⓜ Colón) Once a haunt of writers and intellectuals, this Modernista gem could well overwhelm you with its mirrors, chandeliers and bow-tied service of another

era; it's quiet and refined, although the outdoor tables are hugely popular in summer.

MALASAÑA & CHUECA

Areia (Map pp64-5; ☎ 91 310 03 07; www .areiachillout.com in Spanish; Calle de Hortaleza 92; ☽ 12.30pm-3am Mon-Thu, 12.30pm-3.30am Fri-Sun; Ⓜ Chueca or Alonso Martínez) The ultimate lounge bar by day (cushions, chill-out music and dark, secluded corners where you can hear yourself talk, or even snog quietly), this place is equally enjoyable by night. It's cool, funky and low-key all at once, although the cocktails can be pricey.

La Vía Láctea (Map pp64-5; ☎ 91 446 75 81; Calle de Velarde 18; ☽ 7.30pm-3am; Ⓜ Bilbao or Tribunal) A living, breathing and somewhat grungy relic of *la movida*, La Vía Láctea remains a Malasaña favourite for a mixed, informal crowd who seem to live for the 1980s – eyeshadow for boys and girls is a recurring theme. There are plenty of drinks to choose from and by early on Sunday morning anything goes.

KRZYSZTOF DYDYNSKI

Kapital nightclub

Café Belén (Map pp64-5; ☎ 91 308 24 47; Calle de Belén 5; 🕑 3.30pm-3am; Ⓜ Chueca) Café Belén is cool in all the right places – lounge and chill-out music, dim lighting, a great range of drinks (the mojitos are as good as you'll find in Madrid and that's saying something) and a low-key crowd that's the height of casual sophistication.

El Jardín Secreto (Map pp64-5; ☎ 91 541 80 23; Calle de Conde Duque 2; 🕑 5.30pm-12.30am Mon-Thu & Sun, 6.30pm-2.30am Fri & Sat; Ⓜ Plaza de España) 'The Secret Garden' is all about intimacy and romance in a *barrio* that's one of Madrid's best-kept secrets. Lit by Spanish designer candles, draped in organza from India and serving up chocolates from the Caribbean, it's at its best on a summer's evening, but the atmosphere never misses a beat.

Café Comercial (Map pp64-5; ☎ 91 521 56 55; Glorieta de Bilbao 7; 🕑 7.30am-midnight Mon, 7.30am-1am Tue-Thu, 7.30am-2am Fri, 8.30am-2am Sat, 9am-midnight Sun; Ⓜ Bilbao) This glorious old Madrid cafe proudly fights a rearguard action against progress with heavy leather seats, abundant marble and old-style waiters. Though it's as close as Madrid came to the intellectual cafes of Paris' Left Bank, Café Comercial now has a clientele that has broadened to include just about anyone.

Museo Chicote (Map pp64-5; ☎ 91 532 67 37; www.museo-chicote.com; Gran Vía 12; 🕑 8am-4am Mon-Sat; Ⓜ Gran Vía) The founder of this Madrid landmark is said to have invented more than a hundred cocktails, which the likes of Hemingway, Sophia Loren and Frank Sinatra all enjoyed at one time or another. It's still frequented by film stars and socialites, and it's at its best after midnight when a lounge atmosphere takes over, couples cuddle on the curved benches and some of the city's best DJs do their stuff.

ENTERTAINMENT

CLUBS

LOS AUSTRIAS, SOL & CENTRO

Cool (Map pp64-5; ☎ 902 499 994; Calle de Isabel la Católica 6; 🕑 11pm-6am Thu-Sat; Ⓜ Santo Domingo) Cool by name, cool by nature: think gorgeous people, gorgeous clothes and a strict entry policy. One of the hottest clubs in the city, it features curvy white lines, discreet lounge chairs in dark corners and a pulsating dance floor.

Costello Café & Niteclub (Map pp64-5; www.costelloclub.com; Calle del Caballero de Gracia 10; 🕑 6pm-3am; Ⓜ Gran Vía) Costello Café & Niteclub has an innovative mix of pop, rock and fusion in smooth-as-silk, Warholesque surrounds. It may close earlier than we'd like, but we still think this is one of the coolest places in town.

Oba Oba (Map pp64-5; Calle de Jacometrezo 4; 🕑 11pm-5.30am Sun-Thu, 11pm-6am Fri & Sat; Ⓜ Callao) This nightclub is Brazilian down to its G-strings, with live music some nights and dancing 'til dawn every night of the week. You'll find plenty of Brazilians in residence, which is the best recommendation we can give for the music and the authenticity of its caipirinhas.

Teatro Joy Eslava (Map p68; ☎ 91 366 54 39; www.joy-eslava.com in Spanish; Calle del Arenal 11; 🕑 11.30pm-6am; Ⓜ Sol) The only things guaranteed at this grand old Madrid dance club (housed in a 19th-century theatre) are a crowd and the fact that it will be open. (The club claims to have opened every single day for the past 27 years.) The music and the crowd are a mixed bag, but queues are long and invariably include locals and tourists, and even the occasional *famoso*.

HUERTAS & ATOCHA

Kapital (Map pp64-5; ☎ 91 420 29 06; www.grupo-kapital.com in Spanish; Calle de Atocha 125; 🕑 6-10pm & midnight-6am Thu-Sun; Ⓜ Atocha)

RICHARD NEBESKY

Bullfighting poster at Plaza de Toros

One of the most famous megaclubs in Madrid, this massive seven-storey nightclub has something for everyone: from cocktail bars and dance music to karaoke, salsa, hip hop and more chilled spaces for R&B and soul. The crowd is sexy, well heeled and up for a good time.

MALASAÑA & CHUECA

Tupperware (Map pp64-5; ☎ 91 446 42 04; Corredera Alta de San Pablo 26; ⏰ 8pm-3.30am Sun-Wed, 9pm-3.30am Thu-Sat; Ⓜ Tribunal) A Malasaña stalwart, Tupperware draws a 30-something crowd, spins indie rock with a bit of soul and classics from the '60s and '70s, and generally revels in its kitsch (eyeballs stuck to the ceiling, and plastic TVs with action-figure dioramas lined up behind the bar).

THEATRE & DANCE

Teatro de la Zarzuela (Map pp64-5; ☎ 91 524 54 00; http://teatrodelazarzuela.mcu.es; Calle de Jovellanos 4; Ⓜ Banco de España) This theatre, built in 1856, is the premier place to see *zarzuela*. It also hosts a smattering of classical music and opera, as well as the cutting-edge Compañía Nacional de Danza.

LIVE MUSIC
FLAMENCO

Las Carboneras (Map p68; ☎ 91 542 86 77; www.tablaolascarboneras.com in Spanish; Plaza del Conde de Miranda 1; admission from €33; ⏰ shows 9pm & 11.30pm Mon-Thu, 8.30pm & 11pm Fri & Sat; Ⓜ Sol or La Latina) Like most of the *tablaos* around town, this place sees far more tourists than locals, but the quality is top-notch. It's not the place for gritty, soul-moving spontaneity, but it's still an excellent introduction and one of the few places that flamenco aficionados seem to have no complaints about.

Las Tablas (Map pp64-5; ☎ 91 542 05 20; www.lastablasmadrid.com in Spanish; Plaza de España 9; admission €10-30; ⏰ shows 10.30pm; Ⓜ Plaza de España) Las Tablas has quickly earned a reputation for quality flamenco. Most nights you'll see a classic flamenco show, with plenty of throaty singing and soul-baring dancing.

JAZZ

Café Central (Map p68; ☎ 91 369 41 43; www.cafecentralmadrid.com in Spanish; Plaza del Angel 10; admission €9-15; ⏰ 1pm-2.30am Sun-Thu, 1pm-4am Fri & Sat; Ⓜ Antón Martín or Sol) This art-deco bar has consistently been voted one of the best jazz venues in the world by leading jazz magazines, and with more than 8000 gigs under its belt, it rarely misses a beat. There's everything from Latin jazz and fusion to tango and classic jazz; shows start at 10pm and tickets go on sale an hour before the set starts.

Populart (Map p68; ☎ 91 429 84 07; www .populart.es in Spanish; Calle de las Huertas 22; admission free; ☺ 6pm-2.30am Mon-Thu, 6pm-3.30am Fri & Sat; Ⓜ Antón Martín or Sol) One of Madrid's classic jazz clubs, this place offers a low-key atmosphere and top-quality music – mostly jazz, but with occasional blues, swing and even flamenco thrown into the mix. Shows start at 11pm, but if you want a seat get here early.

El Berlín Jazz Club (Map pp64-5; ☎ 91 521 57 52; www.cafeberlin.es in Spanish; Calle de Jacometrezo 4; admission €6-12; ☺ 7pm-2.30am Tue-Sun; Ⓜ Callao or Santo Domingo) El Berlín is a Madrid jazz stalwart and the kind of place that some serious jazz fans rave about as the most authentic in town.

OTHER LIVE MUSIC

Café La Palma (Map pp64-5; ☎ 91 522 50 31; www.cafelapalma.com in Spanish; Calle de la Palma 62; admission free-€6; ☺ 4pm-2am Sun-Thu, 4pm-3.30am Fri & Sat; Ⓜ Noviciado) It's amazing how much variety Café La Palma has packed into its labyrinth of rooms. Live shows featuring hot local bands are held at the back, while DJs mix up the front.

Clamores (Map pp64-5; ☎ 91 445 79 38; www .clamores.es in Spanish; Calle de Alburquerque 14; admission €5-20; ☺ 6pm-3am Sun-Thu, 6pm-4am Fri & Sat; Ⓜ Bilbao) This one-time classic jazz cafe has morphed into one of the most diverse live music stages in Madrid. Jazz is still a staple, but world music, flamenco, soul fusion, singer-songwriter, pop and rock all make regular appearances.

Honky Tonk (Map pp64-5; ☎ 91 445 61 91; www.clubhonky.com in Spanish; Calle de Covarrubias 24; admission free; ☺ 9pm-5am; Ⓜ Alonso Martínez) Despite the name, this is a great place to see local rock 'n' roll, though many acts have a little country or blues thrown into the mix too. It's a fun vibe in a smallish club that's been around since the heady 1980s.

La Boca del Lobo (Map p68; ☎ 91 429 70 13; Calle de Echegaray 11; admission free-€10; ☺ 9.30pm-3am Tue-Thu & Sun, 9.30pm-3.30am Fri & Sat; Ⓜ Sevilla) Known for offering mostly rock and alternative concerts, La Boca del Lobo (The Wolf's Mouth) is as dark as its name suggests.

SPORT
BULLFIGHTING

From the Fiesta de San Isidro in mid-May until the end of October, Spain's top bullfighters come to swing their capes at **Plaza de Toros Monumental de las Ventas** (Map p53; ☎ 91 356 22 00; www .las-ventas.com in Spanish; Calle de Alcalá 237; Ⓜ Ventas), one of the largest rings in the bullfighting world.

Ticket sales begin a few days before the fight, at the Las Ventas **ticket office** (☺ 10am-2pm & 5-8pm). You can also buy tickets at the authorised **La Central Bullfight Ticket Office** (Map p68; Calle de la Victoria; Ⓜ Sol).

FOOTBALL

The Estadio Santiago Bernabéu, home of Real Madrid, is a temple to football and one of the world's great sporting arenas; watching a game here is akin to a pilgrimage for sports fans.

Named after the club's long-time president, the **stadium** (Map p53; ☎ 91 398 43 00; www.realmadrid.com; Avenida de Concha Espina 1; tour adult/under 14yr €10/8; ☺ 10am-7pm Mon-Sat, 10.30am-6.30pm Sun; Ⓜ Santiago Bernabéu) is a mecca for *madridistas* (Real Madrid football fans) worldwide. For a self-guided tour of the stadium, buy your ticket at ticket window 10 (next to gate 7).

Tickets for matches start at around €15 and run up to the rafters for major matches. Unless you book through a ticket agency, turn up at the ticket office at Gate 42 on Avenida de Concha Espina early in

Café Central (p80)

KRZYSZTOF DYDYNSKI

the week before a scheduled game. The all-important telephone number for booking tickets (which you later pick up at Gate 42) is ☎ 902 32 43 24, which only works if you're calling from within Spain.

SHOPPING

FASHION & SHOES

Mercado de Fuencarral (Map pp64-5; ☎ 91 521 41 52; Calle de Fuencarral 45; 11am-9pm Mon-Sat; Ⓜ Tribunal) Madrid's home of alternative club-cool revels in reverse snobbery. It's funky, grungy and filled with more torn T-shirts, black leather and silver studs than you'll ever need.

Agatha Ruiz de la Prada (Map pp64-5; ☎ 91 319 05 01; Calle de Serrano 27; 10am-8.30pm Mon-Sat; Ⓜ Serrano) This boutique has to be seen to be believed, with pinks, yellows and oranges everywhere you turn. It's fun and exuberant, but it's not just for kids: it's also serious and highly original fashion.

Davidelfín (Map pp64-5; ☎ 91 700 04 53; www.davidelfin.com; Calle de Jorge Juan 31; 10.30am-2.30pm & 4.30-8.30pm Mon-Sat;

Ⓜ Velázquez) This young Spanish designer combines catwalk fashions with a rebellious spirit. The look is young, sometimes edgy and an enthusiastic nod to the avant garde.

Gallery (Map pp64-5; ☎ 91 576 79 31; www .gallerymadrid.com; Calle de Jorge Juan 38; 10.30am-8.30pm Mon-Sat; Ⓜ Príncipe de Vergara or Velázquez) This stunning showpiece of men's fashions and accessories (shoes, bags, belts and the like) is the new Madrid in a nutshell – stylish, brand-conscious and all about having the right look. With an interior designed by Thomas Alia, it's one of the city's coolest shops for men.

FOOD & DRINK

Mantequería Bravo (Map pp64-5; ☎ 91 576 76 41; Calle de Ayala 24; 9.30am-2.30pm & 5.30-8.30pm Mon-Fri, 9.30am-2.30pm Sat; Ⓜ Serrano) Behind the attractive old facade lies a connoisseur's paradise, filled with local cheeses, sausages, wines and coffees. Mantequería Bravo won the 2007 prize for Madrid's best gourmet food shop or delicatessen – it's as simple as that.

Reserva y Cata (Map pp64-5; ☎ 91 319 04 01; www.reservaycata.com in Spanish; Calle del Conde de Xiquena 13; ⏱ 11am-2.30pm & 5-9pm Mon-Fri, 11am-2.30pm Sat; Ⓜ Colón or Chueca) This old-style wine shop stocks an excellent range of local wines, and the knowledgeable staff can help you pick out a great one for your next dinner party or a gift for a friend back home.

HANDICRAFTS

Antigua Casa Talavera (Map pp64-5; ☎ 91 547 34 17; Calle de Isabel la Católica 2; ⏱ 10am-1.30pm & 5-8pm Mon-Fri, 10am-1.30pm Sat; Ⓜ Santo Domingo) The extraordinary tiled facade of this wonderful shop conceals an Aladdin's Cave of ceramics from all over Spain. This is not the mass-produced stuff aimed at the tourist market, but comes from the small family potters of Andalucía and Toledo, and ranges from the decorative (tiles) to the useful (plates, jugs and other kitchen items).

El Arco Artesanía (Map p68; ☎ 91 365 26 80; www.elarcoartesania.com; Plaza Mayor 9; ⏱ 11am-9pm; Ⓜ Sol or La Latina) This superstylish shop in the southwestern corner of Plaza Mayor sells an outstanding array of homemade designer souvenirs, from stone and glasswork to jewellery and home fittings.

José Ramírez (Map p68; ☎ 91 531 42 29; www.guitarrasramirez.com; Calle de la Paz 8; ⏱ 10am-2pm & 4.30-8pm; Ⓜ Sol) José Ramírez is one of Spain's best guitar makers and his guitars have been strummed by a host of flamenco greats and international musicians (even the Beatles).

El Flamenco Vive (Map p68; ☎ 91 547 39 17; www.elflamencovive.es; Calle del Conde de Lemos 7; ⏱ 10am-2pm & 5-9pm Mon-Sat; Ⓜ Ópera) This temple to flamenco has it all, from guitars, songbooks and well-priced CDs, to polka-dotted dancing costumes, shoes, colourful plastic jewellery and literature about flamenco.

Gil (Map p68; ☎ 91 521 25 49; Carrera de San Jerónimo 2; ⏱ 9.30am-1.30pm & 4.30-8pm Mon-Fri, 9.30am-1.30pm Sat; Ⓜ Sol) You don't see them much these days, but the exquisite fringed and embroidered *mantones* and *mantoncillos* (traditional Spanish shawls worn by women on grand occasions) and delicate *mantillas* (Spanish veils) are stunning and uniquely Spanish gifts. Gil also sells *abanicos* (Spanish fans).

GETTING THERE & AWAY
AIR

Madrid's **Barajas airport** (Aeropuerto de Barajas; off Map p53; ☎ 902 40 47 04; www.aena.es) lies 15km northeast of the city.

For a full list of which airlines operate from which terminals, visit www.esmadrid.com – click on 'Services' then 'Transport'.

BUS

Estación Sur de Autobuses (off Map p53; ☎ 91 468 42 00; www.estaciondeautobuses.com in Spanish; Calle de Méndez Álvaro 83; Ⓜ Méndez Álvaro), just south of the M30 ring road, is the city's principal bus station. It serves most destinations to the south and many in other parts of the country.

TRAIN

Madrid is served by two main train stations. The bigger of the two is **Atocha train station** (Antigua Estación de Atocha; Map p53; Ⓜ Atocha Renfe), at the southern end of the city centre. **Chamartín train station** (Map p53; Ⓜ Chamartín) lies in the north of the city. For bookings, contact **Renfe** (☎ 902 24 02 02; www.renfe.es) at either train station.

High-speed Tren de Alta Velocidad Española (AVE) services connect Madrid to Seville (via Córdoba), Valladolid (via Segovia), Toledo, Málaga and Barcelona (via Zaragoza).

MADRID

GETTING AROUND

Agatha Ruiz de la Prada (p82)
KRZYSZTOF DYDYNSKI

GETTING AROUND

Madrid is well served by an excellent and rapidly expanding underground rail system (metro) and an extensive bus service. In addition, you can get from the north to the south of the city quickly by using *cercanías* (local trains) between Chamartín and Atocha train stations. Taxis are also a reasonably priced option.

TO/FROM THE AIRPORT

The easiest way into town from the airport is line 8 of the metro (entrances in T2 and T4) to the Nuevos Ministerios transport interchange, which connects with lines 10 and 6. It operates from 6.05am to 2am. The journey to Nuevos Ministerios takes around 20 minutes from T2 and around 30 minutes from T4.

A taxi to the centre will cost you around €25 (up to €35 from T4), depending on traffic and where you're going; in addition to what the meter says, you pay a €5.25 supplement.

METRO

Madrid's modern **metro** (☎ **902 44 44 03; www.metromadrid.es**) is a fast and safe way to navigate the city, and generally easier than getting to grips with bus routes.

There are 11 colour-coded lines in central Madrid, in addition to the modern southern suburban MetroSur system, as well as lines heading east to the major population centres of Pozuelo and Boadilla del Monte. The metro operates from 6.05am to 2am. A single ticket costs €1; a 10-ride Metrobús ticket is €7.

GREATER BARCELONA

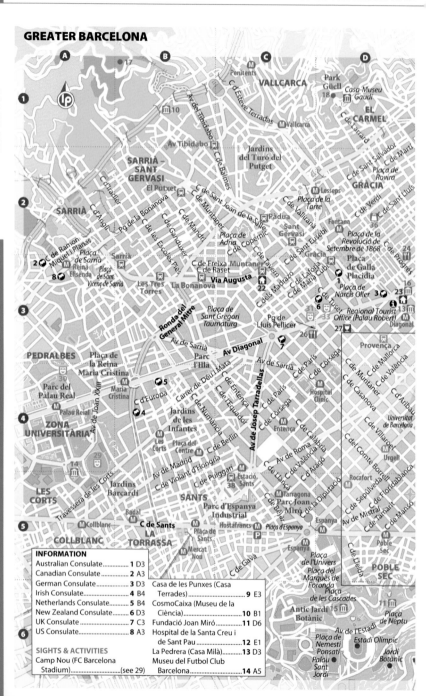

INFORMATION

Australian Consulate	**1** D3
Canadian Consulate	**2** A3
German Consulate	**3** D3
Irish Consulate	**4** B4
Netherlands Consulate	**5** B4
New Zealand Consulate	**6** D3
UK Consulate	**7** C3
US Consulate	**8** A3

SIGHTS & ACTIVITIES

Camp Nou (FC Barcelona Stadium)	(see 29)
Casa de les Punxes (Casa Terrades)	**9** E3
CosmoCaixa (Museu de la Ciència)	**10** B1
Fundació Joan Miró	**11** D6
Hospital de la Santa Creu i de Sant Pau	**12** E1
La Pedrera (Casa Milà)	**13** D3
Museu del Futbol Club Barcelona	**14** A5

BARCELONA

GREATER BARCELONA

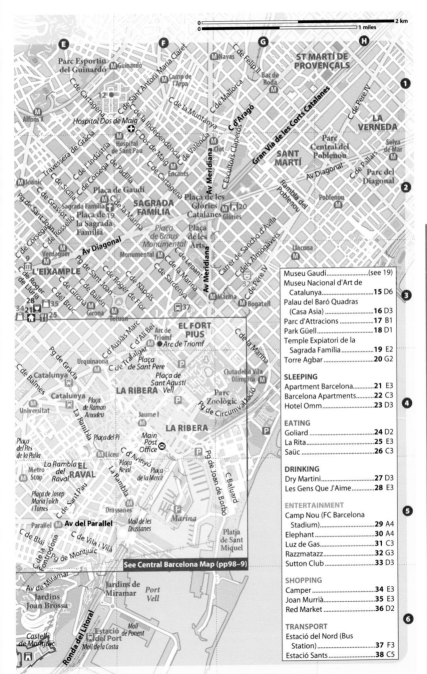

Museu Gaudí..........................(see 19)
Museu Nacional d'Art de
  Catalunya................................**15** D6
Palau del Baró Quadras
  (Casa Asia) **16** D3
Parc d'Attraccions **17** B1
Park Güell **18** D1
Temple Expiatori de la
  Sagrada Família....................**19** E2
Torre Agbar **20** G2

SLEEPING
Apartment Barcelona.............**21** E3
Barcelona Apartments............**22** C3
Hotel Omm................................**23** D3

EATING
Goliard......................................**24** D2
La Rita......................................**25** E3
Saüc...**26** C3

DRINKING
Dry Martini...............................**27** D3
Les Gens Que J'Aime..............**28** E3

ENTERTAINMENT
Camp Nou (FC Barcelona
  Stadium).................................**29** A4
Elephant...................................**30** A4
Luz de Gas...............................**31** C3
Razzmatazz..............................**32** G3
Sutton Club..............................**33** D3

SHOPPING
Camper.....................................**34** E3
Joan Murrià...............................**35** E3
Red Market **36** D2

TRANSPORT
Estació del Nord (Bus
  Station)..................................**37** F3
Estació Sants...........................**38** C5

BARCELONA HIGHLIGHTS

1　LA SAGRADA FAMÍLIA

BY JORDI FAULÍ, DEPUTY ARCHITECTURAL DIRECTOR FOR LA SAGRADA FAMÍLIA

The Temple Expiatori de la Sagrada Família is Antoni Gaudí's masterpiece, on which he worked for 43 years. It's a slender structure devoted to geometric perfection and sacred symbolism. It's also a work-in-progress spanning the generations but never losing Gaudí's breathtaking originality and architectural synthesis of natural forms.

⤵ JORDI FAULÍ'S DON'T MISS LIST

❶ PASSION FACADE

Among the Fachada de la Pasión's stand-out features are the angled columns, scenes from Jesus' last hours, an extraordinary rendering of the Last Supper and a bronze door that reads like a sculptured book. But the most surprising view is from inside the door on the extreme right (especially in the afternoon with the sun in the west).

❷ MAIN NAVE

The majestic Nave Principal showcases Gaudí's use of tree motifs for columns to support the domes: he described this space as a forest. But it's the skylights that give the nave its luminous quality, even more so once the scaffolding is removed in 2010 and light will flood down onto the apse and main altar from the skylight 75m above the floor.

❸ SIDE NAVE AND NATIVITY TRANSEPT

Although beautiful in its own right, with windows that project light into the interior, this is the perfect place

Clockwise from top: Construction work continues; Passion facade; Script on bronze door in the Passion Facade; Sculpted figures on the Nativity Facade; Towers of La Sagrada Família

BARCELONA

BARCELONA HIGHLIGHTS

to view the sculpted tree-like columns and get an overall perspective of the main nave. Turn around and you're confronted with the inside of the Nativity Facade, an alternative view that most visitors miss; the stained-glass windows are superb.

❹ NATIVITY FACADE

The Fachada del Nacimiento is Gaudí's grand hymn to Creation. Begin by viewing it front-on from a distance, then draw close enough (but to one side) to make out the details of its sculpted figures. The complement to the finely wrought detail is the majesty of the four parabolic towers that reach for the sky and are topped by Venetian stained glass.

❺ THE MODEL OF COLÒNIA GÜELL

Among the many original models used by Gaudí in the Museu Gaudí (situated beneath the cathedral), the most interesting is the church at Colònia Güell. From the side you can visualise the harmony and beauty of the interior. It's upside-down because that's how Gaudí worked to best study the building's form and structural balance.

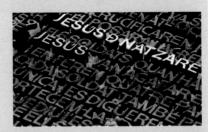

⬎ THINGS YOU NEED TO KNOW

How it's done Gaudí spent the last 12 years of his life preparing plans for how the building was to be finished Expected completion date 2020 to 2040 Best photo op Take a lift (€2) up one of the towers Admission €8 Guided tours €3.50, up to four daily See our author's review, p105

BARCELONA HIGHLIGHTS

2 | EAT LIKE A LOCAL

BY BEGO SANCHIS, OWNER OF COOK & TASTE COOKING SCHOOL

Eating in Barcelona means getting a taste of genuine Catalan culture and understanding how the people here pass their day. Barcelona is a crossroad of cultures rich in historical influences, where the secret has always been exploration and experimentation from a solid base of traditional cooking in a bid to satisfy the five senses.

⌇ BEGO SANCHIS' DON'T MISS LIST

❶ BREAKFAST IN MERCAT DE LA BOQUERIA

Mercat de la Boqueria (p101) is the largest of Barcelona's 40 markets and is an obligatory stop for breakfast. Lose yourself in the passageways and let yourself be carried along by the uproar of stallholders and buyers. But your visit is not complete until you've finished with *un desayuno de cuchara* (breakfast eaten with a spoon or fork) from one of the food stalls.

❷ PRE-LUNCH SNACK

Stop for a light snack accompanied by a cava (sparkling wine) or *vermut* (vermouth) – two local drinks of which Catalans are rightfully proud – at a sunny outdoor table. Where else in the world can you see elegant señoras enjoying their *bocadillo* (filled roll) with a glass of sparkling wine before lunch?

❸ LUNCH IN THE BARRIO OF FISHERMEN

For lunch you just have to try a seafood rice dish in any bar in the Barrio

Clockwise from top: Mercat de la Boqueria (p101); *Bocadillo* with *jamón;* Tapas in a local *taberna;* Dining at Plaça Reial (p103); Hot chocolate and *churros*

de Pescadores (Barrio of Fishermen), otherwise known as La Barceloneta (p105). Wander the streets, study the various options and, above all, choose a place where there are far more locals than tourists – this is the best guarantee of authenticity!

❹ AFTERNOON TEA

Between lunch and dinner, pause for one of Barcelona's three traditional pastries – a *chocolate con churros* (deep-fried donuts dipped in thick chocolate), *melindro* (a small baked cake) or *ensaimada* (another sweet, baked pastry). The best places are the chocolaterías along Carrer del Pi or, even better, Carrer dels Banys Nous, close to Plaça Sant Josep Oriol in the Barri Gòtic.

❺ A TAPAS DINNER

The best way to sample so many different recipes is to base your dinner around tapas until your stomach says enough. You could enjoy the whole meal in one bar, but most locals hop from one bar to the next, trying the various house specialities in each one.

↘ THINGS YOU NEED TO KNOW

Cooking Courses Cook and Taste (p109) **Top survival tip** Pace yourself and don't eat too much at each stop **Best photo op** Mercat de la Boqueria (p101) or eating *churros* dripping with chocolate **See our author's coverage of eating in Barcelona, p112**

BARCELONA HIGHLIGHTS

3

⤵ EXPLORE GAUDÍ'S BARCELONA

Few architects have come to define a city quite like Gaudí. La Sagrada Família (p105) is the master architect's showpiece and is quite simply the most imaginative cathedral in the world. In the stately streets of L'Eixample, Casa Batlló (p105) is his most beautiful secular creation, closely followed by La Pedrera (p105). Park Güell (p107) has the aspect of a fairytale alongside a museum to the great man.

4

⤵ PARADE DOWN LA RAMBLA

La Rambla (p101) connects the Plaça de Catalunya with the waterfront, passing en route numerous distinguished buildings (we especially love the Mercat de la Boqueria). But it's the life coursing along this pedestrian boulevard that makes La Rambla special, an endless procession of street performers, flower sellers, and what can seem like a representative cross-section of the world's peoples.

BARCELONA

BARCELONA HIGHLIGHTS

5

↘ WANDER THE BARRI GÒTIC

You'll spend many happy hours in Barcelona getting lost in the Barri Gòtic (p100), Barcelona's oldest quarter. There are landmark public buildings (including the cathedral) and some lovely squares to provide breathing space, but what the 'Gothic Quarter' is all about is meandering with neither plan nor pace.

6

↘ MUSEU PICASSO

Pablo Picasso spent a decade in Barcelona before he decamped to Paris, and the Museu Picasso (p104) is a fitting tribute to his connection with the city. Don't come expecting his cubist works, for the gallery focuses on his early years. As long as you have that understanding, you'll enjoy this priceless insight into one of the towering figures of 20th-century art.

7

↘ SAMPLE NOUVEAU CATALAN CUISINE

The innovation and studied experimentation that has revolutionised Spanish cuisine finds its true home in Barcelona. In the city's bars (p114) and restaurants (p112), you'll find Catalonia's celebrated local staples alongside taste combinations that you never imagined in your wildest dreams.

3 KRZYSZTOF DYDYNSKI; 4 CHRIS MELLOR; 5 ALFREDO MAIQUEZ; 6 NEIL SETCHFIELD; 7 PASCALE BEROUJON

3 Interior of the Casa Batlló (p105); 4 La Rambla (p101); 5 Barri Gòtic (p100); 6 Museu Picasso exterior; 7 Typical Barcelona tapas

BARCELONA

BARCELONA'S BEST...

BARCELONA'S BEST...

⬆ PLACES FOR ART

- **Museu Picasso** (p104) Picasso's early, pre-Cubist works.
- **Fundació Joan Miró** (p108) Showcases one of Spain's finest 20th-century artists.
- **Museu Nacional D'Art de Catalunya** (p108) Titian, Canaletto, Rubens and Gainsborough.
- **Museu d'Art Contemporani de Barcelona** (p103) Avant-garde contemporary art.

⬆ PLACES FOR A VIEW

- **La Sagrada Família** (p105) Stirring views from the cathedral's towers.
- **Monument A Colom** (p100) Sweeping coastal and La Rambla views.
- **Casa Batlló** (p105) A swirling facade and a zany rooftop.
- **Montserrat** (p119) On a clear day, you'll see the Pyrenees and Mallorca.

⬆ PLACES FOR INNOVATIVE CATALAN COOKING

- **Suquet de l'Almirall** (p113) Seafood from a Ferran Adrià–trained chef.
- **Inopia** (p113) Gourmet tapas from Ferran Adrià's brother.
- **Saüc** (p113) Emerging reputation for designer cooking.
- **Pla** (p112) New-style cooking in the old-style Barri Gòtic.
- **Cal Pep** (p112) One of Barcelona's most celebrated tapas bars.

⬆ PLAÇAS IN THE CIUTAT VELLA

- **Plaça Reial** (p103) Neoclassical square with Gaudí fountains.
- **Passeig del Born** (p104) Historic square with Barcelona's grandest Gothic church.
- **Plaça del Rei** (p102) Former royal courtyard within sight of the cathedral.

KRZYSZTOF DYDYNSKI

Plaça Reial (p103)

THINGS YOU NEED TO KNOW

↘ VITAL STATISTICS

- **Population** 1.59 million
- **Area** 477 sq km
- **Best time to visit** Year-round.

↘ NEIGHBOURHOODS IN A NUTSHELL

- **La Rambla** (p101) Barcelona's iconic thoroughfare.
- **Barri Gòtic** (p100) The city's oldest quarter, east of La Rambla.
- **El Raval** (p103) Slightly seedy inner-city neighbourhood west of La Rambla.
- **La Ribera** (p104) Another old quarter northeast of the Barri Gòtic; includes hip El Born.
- **La Barceloneta** (p105) Coastal neighbourhood with beaches, northeast of Port Vell.
- **L'Eixample** (p105) Nineteenth-century *barrio* near Plaça de Catalunya, with Barcelona's best Modernista architecture.

↘ RESOURCES

- **Oficina d'Informació de Turisme de Barcelona** (Map pp98-9; ☎ 93 285 38 32; www.barcelonaturisme.com; Plaça de Catalunya 17-S underground; ⏰9am-9pm) Branch offices around the city.
- **Le Cool** (www.lecool.com) Subscribe for free to this site for weekly events listings.
- **Ruta del Modernisme** (www.rutadelmodernisme.com) Routes, monuments and events related to Modernisme.

- **BCN Nightlife** (www.bcn-nightlife.com) Info on bars, clubs and parties across town.

↘ EMERGENCY NUMBERS

- **Mossos d'Esquadra** (Map pp98-9; ☎ 088; Carrer Nou de la Rambla 80) Catalan police, for reporting thefts.
- **Guàrdia Urbana** (Local Police; Map pp98-9; ☎ 092; La Rambla 43) Also for theft-related matters.
- **Ambulance** (☎ 061)
- **Emergency** (☎ 112)
- **Policía Nacional** (☎ 091)

↘ GETTING AROUND

- **Air** (p117) Barcelona's Aeroport del Prat (www.aena.es) has excellent connections with Europe and beyond.
- **Metro** (p118) The best way for getting around town with six lines.
- **Train** (p117) Rail links with the rest of Spain and Europe.

↘ BE FOREWARNED

- **Most museums and galleries** Close on Monday (although most Gaudí sites open seven days).
- **Football** Tickets to Barcelona games (p116) must be booked 15 days before match day.

DISCOVER BARCELONA

Set on a plain rising gently from the sea to a range of wooded hills, Barcelona is Spain's most cosmopolitan city and one of the Mediterranean's busiest ports. Restaurants, bars and clubs are always packed, as is the seaside in summer.

It regards its long past with pride. From Roman town it passed to medieval trade juggernaut, and its old centre constitutes one of the greatest concentrations of Gothic architecture in Europe. Beyond this core are some of the world's more bizarre buildings: surreal spectacles capped by Antoni Gaudí's La Sagrada Família church.

Barcelona has been breaking ground in art, architecture and style since the late 19th century. From the marvels of Modernisme to the modern wonders of today, the racing heart of Barcelona has barely skipped a beat. The city's avant-garde chefs whip up a storm that has even the French reaching for superlatives. The city itself could keep you occupied for weeks but just outside are sandy beaches, Sitges and the Montserrat mountain range.

BARCELONA IN...

Two Days

Start with the Barri Gòtic (p100). After a stroll along La Rambla (p101), wade into the labyrinth to admire La Catedral (p101) and surrounding monuments, including the fascinating Plaça del Rei, now part of the Museu d'Història de la Ciutat (p102). Cross Via Laietana into La Ribera (p104) to square up to the city's favourite and most beautiful church, the Església de Santa Maria del Mar (p104), and the nearby Museu Picasso (p104). To round off, plunge into the warren of bars and restaurants in the funky El Born area, in the lower end of La Ribera, for a meal and cocktails.

The following day, start off at Gaudí's Park Güell (p107), conceived as a residential hideaway for the well-off and now a joyous public park laced with the architect's singular creations. After a picnic lunch in the park, head for Gaudí's extraordinary work in progress, La Sagrada Família (p105).

Four Days

You could start the third day with another round of Gaudí, visiting Casa Batlló (p105) and La Pedrera (p105). Day four should be dedicated to Montjuïc (p108), with its museums, galleries, fortress, gardens and Olympic stadium.

BARCELONA

HISTORY

It is thought that Barcelona may have been founded by the Carthaginians in about 230 BC, taking the surname of Hamilcar Barca, Hannibal's father.

Under Ramon Berenguer III (1082–1131), Catalonia launched its own fleet and sea trade developed.

In 1137 Ramon Berenguer IV married Petronilla, heiress of Aragón, creating a joint state and setting the scene for Catalonia's golden age.

The accession of the Aragonese noble Fernando to the throne in 1479 augured ill for Barcelona, and his marriage to Queen Isabel of Castilla more still. Catalonia effectively became a subordinate part of the Castilian state. In the War of the Spanish Succession (1702–13), Barcelona backed the wrong horse, was abandoned by its European allies and fell to Felipe V in September 1714. Felipe abolished the Generalitat (Parliament), built a huge fort, the Ciutadella, to watch over Barcelona, and banned the writing and teaching of Catalan.

The 19th century brought economic resurgence. The flourishing bourgeoisie paid for lavish buildings, many of them in the unique Modernisme style, whose leading exponent was Antoni Gaudí (seven of his buildings in Barcelona together form a World Heritage site).

Modernisme was the most visible aspect of the Catalan Renaixença, a movement for the revival of Catalan language and culture in the late 19th century. By the turn of the 20th century, Barcelona

HISTORY

CLOCKWISE FROM LEFT: KRZYSZTOF DYDYNSKI; ALFREDO MAIQUEZ; GUY MOBERLY

Clockwise from left: Església de Santa Maria del Mar (p104); Mosaic lizard in Gaudí's Park Güell (p107); Marble heads displayed in the Museu d'Història de la Ciutat (p102)

CENTRAL BARCELONA

BARCELONA

CENTRAL BARCELONA

INFORMATION
French Consulate **1** D2
Guàrdia Urbana (Local
   Police) **2** E4
Mossos d'Esquadra
   (Catalan Police)................... **3** D5
Oficina d'Informació de
   Turisme de Barcelona....... **4** F3
Oficina d'Informació de
   Turisme de Barcelona........ **5** D2

SIGHTS & ACTIVITIES
Ajuntament............................... **6** E3
Antic Hospital de la Santa
   Creu **7** D4
Barcelona Walking Tours.....(see 5)
Casa Amatller........................... **8** C1
Casa Batlló................................ **9** C1
Casa Lleó Morera..................... **10** C1
Casa Padellàs.......................(see 24)
Castell dels Tres Dragons....... **11** G2
Catedral.................................... **12** E3
Cook & Taste............................ **13** E4
Església de Santa Maria
   del Mar................................ **14** F3
Església de Santa Maria
   del Pi.................................... **15** E3
Fundació Antoni Tàpies........... **16** C1
Gran Teatre del Liceu.............. **17** E4
L'Aquàrium............................... **18** G5
Mercat de la Boqueria............. **19** D3
Monument a Colom.................. **20** F5
Mosaïc de Miró......................... **21** E4
Museu d'Art
   Contemporani de
   Barcelona............................ **22** C3
Museu de Cera **23** E5
Museu d'Història de la
   Ciutat.................................. **24** F3
Museu Picasso **25** F3
Palau de la Generalitat **26** E3
Palau de la Música
   Catalana.............................. **27** E2
Palau de la Virreina................. **28** D3
Palau Güell............................... **29** E4
Parc de la Ciutadella............... **30** H2
Roman Wall............................... **31** F3
Roman Wall............................... **32** F3
Saló del Tinell......................... **33** E3
Sinagoga Major........................ **34** F3
Temple Romà d'Augustí........... **35** E3

SLEEPING
Casa Camper............................ **36** D3
Chic & Basic.............................. **37** G2
Hostal Campi............................ **38** D3
Hostal Gat Raval...................... **39** C3
Hostal Gat Xino **40** C4
Hostal Girona........................... **41** E1
Hostal Goya.............................. **42** D1
Hotel Banys Orientals.............. **43** F3
Hotel Continental..................... **44** D3

Hotel Costanza......................... **45** E1
Hotel Neri.................................. **46** E3

EATING
Agut **47** F4
Cal Pep **48** G3
Can Majó **49** H5
Cerveseria Catalana................. **50** B1
Organic **51** D4
Orígen **52** G3
Pla... **53** F3
Pla de la Garsa......................... **54** F2
Restaurant Elche...................... **55** D6
Suquet de l'Almirall **56** H5

DRINKING
Bar Marsella.............................. **57** D4
Boadas....................................... **58** D3
Club Soul **59** E4
La Fianna................................... **60** F3
La Vinya del Senyor **61** F3
Manchester................................ **62** F4
Premier...................................... **63** A1

ENTERTAINMENT
Harlem Jazz Club...................... **64** F4
Jamboree................................... **65** E4
Sala Tarantos............................ **66** E4

SHOPPING
Antonio Miró............................. **67** C1
Custo Barcelona........................ **68** G3

To Xampany (100m);
Farmàcia Torres
(330m)

To A1 Aerobús
(400m)

To Inopia
(700m)

75

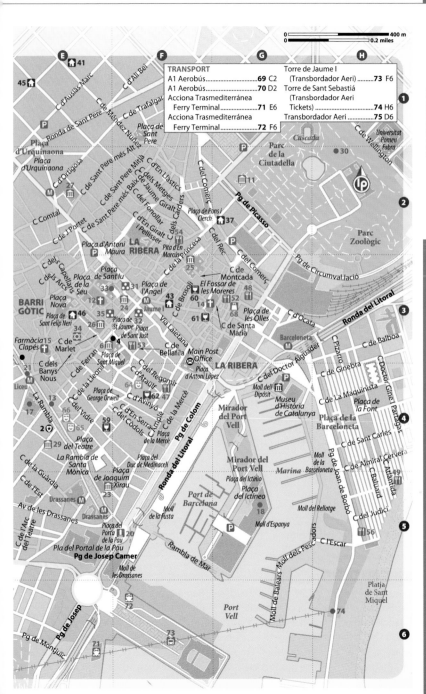

BARCELONA

CENTRAL BARCELONA

was also Spain's hotbed of avant-garde art, with close ties to Paris.

The big social change under Franco was the flood of immigrants, chiefly from Andalucía, attracted by economic growth in Catalonia. Some 750,000 people came to Barcelona in the '50s and '60s, and almost as many to the rest of Catalonia. Many of these new immigrants lived in appalling conditions.

The 1992 Olympics spurred a burst of public works, bringing new life to areas such as Montjuïc, where the major events were held, and the once-shabby waterfront. The impetus has barely let up.

ORIENTATION

The focal axis is La Rambla, a 1.25km boulevard running northwest, and slightly uphill, from Port Vell (Old Harbour) to Plaça de Catalunya. The latter marks the boundary between Ciutat Vella (Old City) and L'Eixample, the grid extension into which Barcelona grew from the late 19th century.

Ciutat Vella, a warren of streets, hotels, centuries-old buildings, restaurants and bars, spreads either side of La Rambla. Its heart is the lower half of the section east of La Rambla, called the Barri Gòtic (Gothic Quarter). West of La Rambla is somewhat edgier El Raval.

You will find most of Barcelona's singular Modernista architecture, including La Sagrada Família, in L'Eixample.

INFORMATION

In addition to the following listed tourist offices, information booths operate at Estació Nord bus station, Portal de la Pau and at the foot of the Monument a Colom (Map pp98–9). At least three others are set up at various points around the city centre in summer.

Oficina d'Informació de Turisme de Barcelona Main Branch (Map pp98-9; ☎ 93 285 38 32; www.barcelonaturisme.com; Plaça de Catalunya 17-S underground; 🕑 9am-9pm); Aeroport del Prat (🕑 9am-9pm); Estació Sants (🕑 8am-8pm Jun-Sep, 8am-8pm Mon-Fri, 8am-2pm Sat, Sun & holidays Oct-May); Town Hall (Map pp98-9; Carrer de la Ciutat 2; 🕑 9am-8pm Mon-Fri, 10am-8pm Sat, 10am-2pm Sun & holidays)

SIGHTS
GRAN TEATRE DEL LICEU

Barcelona's grand opera house (Map pp98-9; ☎ 93 485 99 00; www.liceubarcelona .com; La Rambla dels Caputxins 51-59; admission with/without guide €8.50/4; 🕑 guided tours 10am, unguided visits 11.30am, noon, 12.30pm & 1pm; Ⓜ Liceu) was built in 1847, largely destroyed by fire in 1994 and reopened better than ever in 1999. The Liceu can seat up to 2300 opera fans.

MONUMENT A COLOM

The bottom end of La Rambla, and the harbour beyond, lie under the supervision of this late-19th-century monument (Map pp98-9; ☎ 93 302 52 24; Plaça del Portal de la Pau; lift adult/under 4yr/senior & 4-12yr €2.50/free/1.50; 🕑 9am-8.30pm Jun-Sep, 10am-6.30pm Oct-May; Ⓜ Drassanes; ♿) to the glory of Christopher Columbus (who some Catalan historians insist came from Barcelona rather than Genoa in Italy). Take the lift to the top for spectacular views over the city.

BARRI GÒTIC

Barcelona's 'Gothic Quarter', east of La Rambla, is a medieval warren of narrow, winding streets, quaint *plaças* (plazas), and grand mansions and monuments from the city's golden age. Many of its great buildings date from the 15th century or earlier.

BARCELONA

BILL WASSMAN

Mercat de la Boqueria

SIGHTS

⇘ LA RAMBLA

Head to Spain's most famous street for that first taste of Barcelona's vibrant atmosphere. Flanked by narrow traffic lanes, La Rambla is a broad pedestrian boulevard, lined with cafes and restaurants, and crowded deep into the night with a cross-section of Barcelona's permanent and transient populace. A visit to Barcelona wouldn't be right without at least one wander along La Rambla.

The Palau de la Virreina is a grand 18th-century rococo mansion housing a municipal arts-entertainment information and ticket office. Next is the Mercat de la Boqueria, one of the best-stocked and most colourful produce markets in Europe. Plaça de la Boqueria, where four side streets meet just north of Liceu metro station, is your chance to walk all over a Miró – the colourful Mosaïc de Miró in the pavement, with one tile signed by the artist.

Things you need to know: La Rambla (Map pp98–9); Palau de la Virreina (**Map pp98–9; La Rambla de Sant Josep 99;** Ⓜ **Liceu)**

PLAÇA DE SANT JAUME

It's hard to imagine that on this very spot, a couple of thousand years ago, folk in togas would discuss the day's events and Roman politics. For hereabouts lay the Roman-era Forum, and the square as you see it today has again been Barcelona's political hub since at least the 15th century. Facing each other across it are the Palau de la Generalitat (the seat of Catalonia's government; Map pp98–9) on the north side, and the *ajuntament* (Map pp98–9) on the south side. Both have fine Gothic interiors.

CATEDRAL & AROUND

You can reach Barcelona's catedral (Map pp98–9; ☎ 93 342 82 60; Plaça de la Seu; admission free, special visit €5; ⏰ 8am-12.45pm & 5.15-8pm, special visit 1-5pm Mon-Sat, 2-5pm Sun & holidays; Ⓜ Jaume I), one of its most magnificent Gothic structures, by following Carrer del Bisbe northwest from Plaça de Sant Jaume.

SIGHTS

WARNING! KEEP AN EYE ON YOUR VALUABLES

Every year aggrieved readers write in with tales of woe from Barcelona. Petty crime and theft, with tourists as the prey of choice, is a problem, so you need to take a few common-sense precautions to avoid joining this regrettable list. Nine times out of 10 it is easy enough to avoid.

Thieves and pickpockets operate on airport trains and the metro, especially around stops popular with tourists (such as La Sagrada Família). The Old City (Ciutat Vella) is the pickpockets' and bag-snatchers' prime hunting ground. Take special care on and around La Rambla. Prostitutes working the lower (waterfront) end often do a double trade in wallet snatching. Also, stay well clear of the ball-and-three-cups (*trileros*) brigades on La Rambla. This is always a set-up and you will lose your money (and maybe have your pockets emptied as you watch the game).

For a bird's-eye (mind the poop) view of medieval Barcelona, visit the cathedral's **roof and tower** (admission €2.20) by a lift from the Capella de les Animes del Purgatori, near the northeast transept.

From the southwest transept, exit to the lovely **claustre** (cloister), with its trees, fountains and geese (there have been geese here for centuries).

PLAÇA DEL REI

A stone's throw east of the cathedral, Plaça del Rei is the courtyard of the former Palau Reial Major, the palace of the Counts of Barcelona and monarchs of Aragón.

Most of the tall, centuries-old buildings surrounding Plaça del Rei are now open to visitors as the **Museu d'Història de la Ciutat** (City History Museum; Map pp98-9; ☎ 93 256 21 00; www.museuhistoria.bcn.cat; Carrer del Veguer; adult/under 7yr/senior & student €6/free/4, admission free from 4pm 1st Sat of month; ☽ 10am-2pm & 4-7pm Tue-Sat, 10am-3pm Sun Oct-Mar, 10am-8pm Tue-Sat, 10am-3pm Sun Apr-Sep; Ⓜ Jaume I). This is one of Barcelona's most fascinating sights, combining large sections of the former palace with a subterranean walk through Roman and Visigothic Barcelona.

The entrance to the museum is through 16th-century **Casa Padellàs** (Map pp98-9), just south of Plaça del Rei. Casa Padellàs, with its courtyard typical of Barcelona's late-Gothic and baroque mansions, was moved here in the 1930s because of roadworks. The external courtyard staircase now leads to a restored Roman tower. Below ground awaits a remarkable walk through excavated Roman and Visigothic **ruins** – complete with sections of a Roman street, baths and shops, along with remains of a Visigothic basilica.

The **Saló del Tinell** (Map pp98-9) was the royal palace's throne hall, a masterpiece of strong, unfussy Catalan Gothic architecture, built in the mid-14th century with wide, rounded arches holding up a wooden roof.

PLAÇA DE SANT JOSEP ORIOL & AROUND

This small plaza is the prettiest in the Barri Gòtic. The plaza is dominated by the Gothic **Església de Santa Maria del Pi** (Map pp98-9; ☽ 8.30am-1pm & 4.30-9pm Mon-Sat, 9am-2pm & 5-9pm Sun & holidays; Ⓜ Liceu), completed in the 16th century. The beautiful rose window above its entrance on

Plaça del Pi is claimed to be the world's biggest.

SINAGOGA MAJOR

The area between Carrer dels Banys Nous, to the east of the church, and Plaça de Sant Jaume is known as the Call, and was Barcelona's **Jewish quarter** – and centre of learning – from at least the 11th century until anti-Semitism saw the Jews expelled from it in 1424. Here the sparse remains of what is purported to be the medieval **Sinagoga Major** (Main Synagogue; Map pp98-9; ☎ 93 317 07 90; www.calldebarcelona.org; Carrer de Marlet 5; admission €2 donation; ⏲ 11am-6pm Mon-Sat, 11am-3pm Sun; Ⓜ Liceu) have been revealed and returned to occasional use as a functioning temple.

PLAÇA REIAL & AROUND

Just south of Carrer de Ferran, **Plaça Reial** (Map pp98–9) is an elegant shady square surrounded by eateries, nightspots and budget accommodation. Its 19th-century neoclassical architecture (which replaced a centuries-old monastery) looks as if it would be at home in some Parisian quarter (but the palm trees wouldn't). The lampposts next to the central fountain are Gaudí's first known works.

EL RAVAL

MUSEU D'ART CONTEMPORANI & AROUND

The vast, glossy white **Museu d'Art Contemporani de Barcelona** (Macba; Map pp98-9; ☎ 93 412 08 10; www.macba.es; Plaça dels Àngels 1; adult/concession €7.50/6, Wed €3.50; ⏲ 11am-8pm Mon & Wed, 11am-midnight Thu-Fri, 10am-8pm Sat, 11am-3pm Sun & holidays late Jun-late Sep, 11am-7.30pm Mon & Wed-Fri, 10am-8pm Sat, 10am-3pm Sun & holidays late Sep-late Jun; Ⓜ Universitat) is a temple to contemporary art. Artists frequently on show include Antoni Tàpies, Miquel Barceló and a host of very now installation artists.

Two blocks southeast of Plaça dels Àngels is an architectural masterpiece from another age. Founded in the early 15th century as the city's main hospital, the **Antic Hospital de la Santa Creu** (Map pp98-9; ☎ 93 270 23 00; Carrer de l'Hospital 56;

BARCELONA

SIGHTS

GAVIN GOUGH

Giant chimneypots of Gaudí's La Pedrera (p105)

Temple Romà d'Augustí

↘ IF YOU LIKE...

If you like the signposts to Roman Barcelona in the **Museu d'Història de la Ciutat** (p102), we think your imagination will also be stirred by the following:

- **Roman Walls** (Map pp98-9) Third- and 4th-century walls rebuilt after the first attacks by Germanic tribes from the north. One section is on the southwest side of Plaça de Ramon Berenguer el Gran, and the other is by the north end of Carrer del Sotstinent Navarro.
- **Temple Romà d'Augustí** (Roman Temple of Augustus; Map pp98-9; Carrer de Paradis 10; admission free; ⏱ 10am-2pm Mon-Sat) Four mighty, 1st-century AD columns from the temple stand just beyond the southeast end of the cathedral.

admission free; ⏱ library 9am-8pm Mon-Fri, 9am-2pm Sat) today houses the **Biblioteca de Catalunya** (Catalonia's national library). Take a look inside to admire some fine Catalan Gothic construction.

LA RIBERA
PALAU DE LA MÚSICA CATALANA
The **Palau de la Música Catalana** (Palace of Catalan Music; Map pp98-9; ☎ 902 47 54 85; www.palaumusica.org; Carrer de Sant Francesc

de Paula 2; adult/child/student incl guided tour €10/free/9; ⏱ 50min tours every 30min 10am-6pm Easter & Aug, 10am-3.30pm Sep-Jul; Ⓜ Urquinaona) is a Modernista high point and World Heritage site. It's not exactly a symphony, more a series of crescendos in tile, brick, sculptured stone and stained glass. Built between 1905 and 1908 by Lluís Domènech i Montaner for the Orfeo Català musical society, it was conceived as a temple for the Catalan Renaixença.

MUSEU PICASSO
Barcelona's most visited **museum** (Map pp98-9; ☎ 93 256 30 00; www.museupicasso.bcn.es; Carrer de Montcada 15-23; adult/senior & under 16yr/student €9/free/3, temporary exhibitions adult €5.80, admission free 1st Sun of month; ⏱ 10am-8pm Tue-Sun & holidays; Ⓜ Jaume I) occupies five of the many fine medieval stone mansions (worth wandering into for their courtyards and galleries) on narrow Carrer de Montcada. This collection is unique in giving such insight into the early period of his life but those interested primarily in cubism may not be satisfied.

ESGLÉSIA DE SANTA MARIA DEL MAR
Carrer de Montcada opens at its southeast end into **Passeig del Born**, a plaza that once rang to the cheers and jeers of medieval jousting tournaments, today replaced at night by animated carousing. At its southwest tip rises Barcelona's finest Gothic church, the **Església de Santa Maria del Mar** (Map pp98-9; ☎ 93 319 05 16; Plaça de Santa Maria del Mar; admission free; ⏱ 9am-1.30pm & 4.30-8pm; Ⓜ Jaume I).

PARC DE LA CIUTADELLA
East from La Ribera and north of La Barceloneta, the gentle **Parc de la Ciutadella** (Map pp98-9; ⏱ 8am-6pm Nov-Feb, 8am-8pm Oct & Mar, 8am-9pm Apr-Sep; ♿)

makes a fine antidote to the noise and bustle of the city.

LA BARCELONETA & THE COAST

Barcelona's small fishing fleet ties up along the Moll del Rellotge, south of the museum. On La Barceloneta's seaward side are the first of Barcelona's **beaches**, which are popular on summer weekends.

L'EIXAMPLE

Stretching north, east and west of Plaça de Catalunya, L'Eixample (the Extension) was Barcelona's 19th-century answer to overcrowding in the medieval city.

LA SAGRADA FAMÍLIA

If you only have time for one sightseeing outing, this should be it. The **Temple Expiatori de la Sagrada Família** (Expiatory Temple of the Holy Family; Map pp86-7; ☎ 93 207 30 31; www.sagradafamilia.org; Carrer de Mallorca 401; adult/senior & student €8/5, incl Casa-Museu Gaudí in Park Güell €9/6; ☻ 9am-8pm Apr-Sep, 9am-6pm Oct-Mar; Ⓜ Sagrada Família) inspires awe with its sheer verticality and, in the true manner of the great medieval cathedrals it emulates, it's still not finished after more than 100 years. Work is proceeding apace, however, and it might be done by anything between the 2020s and 2040s.

The church was the project to which Antoni Gaudí dedicated the latter part of his life. He stuck to a basic Gothic cross-shaped ground plan, but devised a temple 95m long and 60m wide, which was able to seat 13,000 people.

The northeast, or **Nativity Facade**, is the Sagrada Família's artistic pinnacle, and was mostly done under Gaudí's personal supervision. You can climb high up inside some of the four towers by a combination of lifts and narrow spiral staircases – a vertiginous experience. Beneath the tow-ers is a tall, three-part portal on the theme of Christ's birth and childhood.

The semicircular **apse** was the first part to be finished (in 1894). The interior of the church remains a building site but the nave has been roofed over, and a forest of extraordinary angled pillars is in place.

Open the same times as the church, the **Museu Gaudí** (Map pp86-7), below ground level, includes material on Gaudí's life and other work, as well as models and photos of La Sagrada Família. Gaudí is interred in the simple crypt at the far end.

CASA BATLLÓ

If La Sagrada Família is his master symphony, the **Casa Batlló** (Map pp98-9; ☎ 93 216 03 66; www.casabatllo.es; Passeig de Gràcia 43; adult/student & senior €16.50/13.20; ☻ 9am-8pm; Ⓜ Passeig de Gràcia) is Gaudí's whimsical waltz. The facade, sprinkled with bits of blue, mauve and green tiles, and studded with wave-shaped window frames and balconies, rises to an uneven blue-tiled roof with a solitary tower. The roof represents Sant Jordi (St George) and the dragon, and if you stare long enough at the building, it almost seems a living being. Inside the main salon overlooking Passeig de Gràcia everything swirls. The roof, with its twisting chimneypots, is equally astonishing, and provides a chance for a close-up look at the St George-and-the-dragon motif that dominates the view from the street.

LA PEDRERA

Back on Passeig de Gràcia is another Gaudí masterpiece, built between 1905 and 1910 as a combined apartment and office block. Formally called the Casa Milà, after the businessman who commissioned it, it's better known as **La Pedrera** (The Quarry; Map pp86-7; ☎ 902 40 09 73; www.fundaciocaixacatalunya.es; Carrer de Provença

BARCELONA

SIGHTS

BARCELONA

NEIL SETCHFIELD

Detail of chimney on Palau Güell

SIGHTS

↘ IF YOU LIKE...

If you like Gaudí's **Casa Batlló** (p105), we're sure that you'll also like the following Modernista gems (including another couple by Gaudí) that are scattered around Barcelona:

- **Palau Güell** (Map pp98-9; www.palauguell.cat; Carrer Nou de la Rambla 3-5) The only major Modernista building in Ciutat Vella, it lacks some of Gaudí's later playfulness but is still a characteristic riot of styles (art nouveau, Gothic, Islamic) and materials.
- **Colònia Güell** (www.coloniaguellbarcelona.com) Apart from La Sagrada Família, this Utopian textile-workers' complex was the last grand project Gaudí turned his hand to, outside Barcelona at Santa Coloma de Cervelló; his main role was to erect the colony's church.
- **Casa Lleó Morera** (Map pp98-9; Passeig de Gràcia 35) On the same block as Casa Batlló, this house is swathed in art nouveau carving on the outside and has a bright, tiled lobby; it's the work of master Catalan architect, Lluís Domènech i Montaner.
- **Casa Amatller** (Map pp98-9; www.amatller.org; Passeig de Gràcia 41) Also in the same block, Josep Puig i Cadafalch's signature work has Gothic-style window frames and a stepped gable with all sorts of unlikely sculptures and busts jutting out.
- **Fundació Antoni Tàpies** (Map pp98-9; www.fundaciotapies.org; Carrer d'Aragó 255) Around the corner from Casa Batlló, this is a pioneering Modernista building of the early 1880s and a homage to, and by, the eponymous leading 20th-century Catalan artist.
- **CosmoCaixa (Museo del Ciència)** (Map pp86-7; www.fundacio.lacaixa.es; Carrer de Teodor Roviralta 47-51, Zona Alta) Up the Tibidabo hill overlooking Barcelona, this fine Modernista building has been converted into a mind-blowing science museum, complete with an expansive chunk of Amazonian rainforest.

261-265; adult/student & EU senior €8/4.50; 🕑 9am-8pm Mar-Oct, 9am-6.30pm Nov-Feb; Ⓜ Diagonal) because of its uneven grey-stone facade, which ripples around the corner of Carrer de Provença.

Visit the lavish top-floor flat, attic and roof, together known as the **Espai Gaudí** (Gaudí Space). The roof is the most extraordinary element, with its giant chimneypots looking like multicoloured medieval knights.

PALAU DEL BARÓ QUADRAS & CASA DE LES PUNXES

A few blocks north and east of La Pedrera are two of Puig i Cadafalch's major buildings. **Palau del Baró Quadras** (Casa Asia; Map pp86-7; ☎ 93 238 73 37; www.casaasia.es; Avinguda Diagonal 373; 🕑 10am-8pm Mon-Sat, 10am-2pm Sun; Ⓜ Diagonal) was built between 1902 and 1904 with fantastical neo-Gothic carvings on the facade and a fine stained-glass gallery.

Nearby Casa Terrades is better known as **Casa de les Punxes** (House of Spikes; Map pp86-7; Avinguda Diagonal 420) because of its pointed, witch's-hat turrets.

HOSPITAL DE LA SANTA CREU I DE SANT PAU

Domènech i Montaner excelled himself as architect and philanthropist with the Modernista masterpiece **Hospital de la Santa Creu i de Sant Pau** (Map pp86-7; ☎ 902 07 66 21; www.santpau.es; Carrer de Cartagena; Ⓜ Hospital de Sant Pau), long one of the city's most important hospitals. The whole complex (a World Heritage site), including 16 pavilions, is lavishly decorated and each pavilion is unique.

TORRE AGBAR

Jean Nouvel's glimmering cucumber-shaped **tower** (Map pp86-7; ☎ 93 342 21 29; www.torreagbar.com; Avinguda Diagonal 225; 🕑 10am-7pm Mon-Sat, 10am-2pm Sun; Ⓜ Glòries) has come to share the skyline limelight with La Sagrada Família, and it is now the most visible landmark in the city.

PARK GÜELL

North of Gràcia, **Park Güell** (Map pp86-7; ☎ 93 413 24 00; Carrer d'Olot 7; admission free; 🕑 10am-9pm Jun-Sep, 10am-8pm Apr, May & Oct, 10am-7pm Mar & Nov, 10am-6pm Dec-Feb; Ⓜ Lesseps or Vallcarca; 🚌 24; ♿) is where Gaudí turned his hand to landscape gardening and the artificial almost seems more natural than the natural.

Just inside the main entrance on Carrer d'Olot, visit the park's **Centre d'Interpretació** (☎ 93 285 68 99; adult/under 16yr/student €2/free/1.50; 🕑 11am-3pm) in the **Pavelló de Consergeria**, the typically curvaceous, Gaudían former porter's home that hosts a display on Gaudí's building methods and the history of the park. There are nice views from the top floor.

CAMP NOU

One of Barcelona's most visited museums is the **Museu del Futbol Club Barcelona** (Map pp86-7; ☎ 93 496 36 00; www.fcbarcelona.es; Carrer d'Aristides Maillol; adult/child €8.50/6.80; 🕑 10am-8pm Mon-Sat, 10am-2.30pm Sun & holidays mid-Apr–mid-Oct, 10am-6.30pm Mon-Sat, 10am-2.30pm Sun & holidays mid-Oct–mid-Apr; Ⓜ Collblanc), next to the club's giant Camp Nou stadium. Barça is one of Europe's top football clubs and its museum is a hit with fans the world over.

Camp Nou, built in 1957, is one of the world's biggest stadiums, holding 100,000 people, and the club has a world-record membership of 156,000. Guided **tours** (adult/child €13/10.40) are available.

On match days there are no tours and the museum opens from 10am to 1pm.

BARCELONA

SIGHTS

THE MODERNISTAS' MISSION

Antoni Gaudí (1852–1926), known above all for La Sagrada Família (p105), was just one, albeit the most spectacular, of a generation of inventive architects who left an indelible mark on Barcelona between 1880 and the 1920s. They were called the Modernistas.

The local offshoot of the Europe-wide phenomenon of art nouveau, Modernisme was characterised by its taste for sinuous, flowing lines and (for the time) adventurous combinations of materials like tile, glass, brick, iron and steel. But Barcelona's Modernistas were also inspired by an astonishing variety of other styles too: Gothic and Islamic, Renaissance and Romanesque, Byzantine and baroque.

Gaudí and co were trying to create a specifically Catalan architecture, often looking back to Catalonia's medieval golden age for inspiration. It is no co-incidence that Gaudí and the two other leading Modernista architects, Lluís Domènech i Montaner (1850–1923) and Josep Puig i Cadafalch (1867–1957), were prominent Catalan nationalists.

L'Eixample, where most of Barcelona's new building was happening at the time, is home to the bulk of the Modernistas' creations. Others in the city include Gaudí's Palau Güell (p106) and Park Güell (p107); Domènech i Montaner's Palau de la Música Catalana (p104); Castell dels Tres Dragons (Map pp98–9) and the Hotel España restaurant (Carrer de Sant Pau 9-11, El Raval); and Puig i Cadafalch's Els Quatre Gats restaurant (Carrer de Montsió 3bis, Barri Gòtic).

MONTJUÏC

Montjuïc, the hill overlooking the city centre from the southwest, is dotted with museums, soothing gardens and the main group of 1992 Olympic sites, along with a handful of theatres and clubs.

MUSEU NACIONAL D'ART DE CATALUNYA

The pompous-looking **Palau Nacional**, built in the 1920s for World Exhibition displays and designed to be a temporary structure, houses one of the city's most important **museums** (Map pp86-7; ☎ 93 622 03 76; www.mnac.es; Mirador del Palau Nacional; adult/senior & under 15yr/student €8.50/free/6, admission free 1st Sun of month; ☻ 10am-7pm Tue-Sat, 10am-2.30pm Sun & holidays; Ⓜ Espanya).

Works by the Venetian Renaissance masters Veronese (1528–88), Titian (1490–1557) and Canaletto (1697–1768), along with Rubens (1577–1640) and even England's Gainsborough (1727–88), feature in this museum.

FUNDACIÓ JOAN MIRÓ

Dedicated to one of the greatest artists to emerge in Barcelona in the 20th century, Joan Miró, the **Fundació Joan Miró** (Map pp86-7; ☎ 93 443 94 70; www.bcn.fjmiro.es; Plaça de Neptu; adult/senior & child €8/6, temporary exhibitions €4/3; ☻ 10am-8pm Tue-Wed, Fri & Sat, 10am-9.30pm Thu, 10am-2.30pm Sun & holidays Jul-Sep, 10am-7pm Tue-Wed, Fri & Sat, 10am-9.30pm Thu, 10am-2.30pm Sun & holidays Oct-Jun; ☐ 50, 55, PM or Funicular) is a must-see gallery.

The collections include some 450 paintings, sculptures and textile works, and more than 7000 drawings, but only a selection is shown at any one time.

GETTING THERE & AWAY

You *could* walk from Ciutat Vella (the foot of La Rambla is 700m from the eastern end of Montjuïc). Escalators run up to the Palau Nacional from Avinguda de Rius i Taulet and Passeig de les Cascades. They continue as far as Avinguda de l'Estadi.

Take the metro (lines 2 and 3) to Parallel station and get on the **funicular railway** (🕙 9am-10pm Apr-Oct, 9am-8pm Nov-Mar) from there to Estació Parc Montjuïc.

COURSES

Cook and Taste (Map pp98-9; ☎ 93 302 13 20; www.cookandtaste.net; La Rambla 58; half-day workshop €60) Learn to whip up a paella or stir a gazpacho in this Spanish cookery school.

BARCELONA FOR CHILDREN

An initial stroll along La Rambla is full of potential distractions and wonders, from the bird stands to the living statues and buskers, and the **Museu de Cera** (Wax Museum; Map pp98-9; ☎ 93 317 26 49; www.museocerabcn.com; Passatge de la Banca 7; adult/under 5yr/senior & 5-11yr €7.50/free/4.50; 🕙 10am-10pm daily Jun-Sep, 10am-1.30pm & 4-7.30pm Mon-Fri, 11am-2pm & 4.30-8.30pm Sat, Sun & holidays; Ⓜ Drassanes) is a classic diversion.

At the bottom end of La Rambla, more options present themselves: a ride up to the top of the **Monument a Colom** (p100) or seeing sharks at **L'Aquàrium** (Map pp98-9; ☎ 93 221 74 74; www.aquariumbcn .com; Moll d'Espanya; adult/under 4yr/4-12yr/over 60yr €16/free/11/12.50; 🕙 9.30am-11pm Jul & Aug, 9.30am-9.30pm Jun & Sep, 9.30am-9pm Mon-Fri & 9.30am-9.30pm Sat & Sun Oct-May; Ⓜ Drassanes).

The **Transbordador Aeri** (Cable Car; Map pp98-9; one way/return €9/12.50; 🕙 11am-8pm mid-Jun–mid-Sep, 10.45am-7pm daily Mar–mid-Jun & mid-Sep–late Oct, 10.30am-5.45pm late Oct-Feb; Ⓜ Barceloneta), strung across the harbour between La Barceloneta and Montjuïc, is an irresistible ride. Or scare the willies out of them with a ride in the Hotel Krueger horror house at Tibidabo's **Parc d'Atraccions** (Map p86-7; ☎ 93 211 79 42; www.tibidabo.es; Plaça de Tibidabo 3-4; adult/child shorter than 1.2m €24/9; 🕙 noon-10pm or 11pm Wed-Sun Jul-early Sep, other closing times vary) amusement park!

TOURS

Barcelona Walking Tours (Map pp98-9; ☎ 93 285 38 34; Plaça de Catalunya 17-S) The Oficina d'Informació de Turisme de Barcelona organises guided walking tours. All tours last two hours and start at the tourist office.

ALFREDO MAIQUEZ

Museu de Cera (Wax Museum)

FESTIVALS & EVENTS

Dia de Sant Jordi This is the day of Catalonia's patron saint (George) and also the Day of the Book: men give women a rose, women give men a book, publishers launch new titles; La Rambla and Plaça de Sant Jaume are filled with book and flower stalls. Celebrated on 23 April.

Dia de Sant Joan This is a colourful midsummer celebration on 24 June with bonfires, even in the squares of L'Eixample, and fireworks marking the evening preceding this holiday.

Dia per l'Alliberament Lesbià i Gai The city's big gay and lesbian festival and parade on the Saturday nearest 28 June.

Festa Major de Gràcia (www.festamajordegracia.org) This is a madcap local festival held in Gràcia around 15 August, with decorated streets, dancing and concerts.

La Diada Catalonia's national day on 11 September, marking the fall of Barcelona in 1714, is a fairly solemn holiday in Barcelona.

Festes de la Mercè (www.bcn.cat/merce) The city's biggest party involves around four days of concerts, dancing, *castellers* (human-castle builders), a fireworks display synchronised with the Montjuïc fountains, dances of giants on the Saturday, and *correfocs* – a parade of fireworks – spitting dragons and devils from all over Catalonia, on the Sunday. Held around 24 September.

SLEEPING

There is no shortage of hotels (with new ones opening seemingly every five minutes) in Barcelona, but its continuing status as one of Europe's city-break getaway flavours-of-the-month and its busy trade fair calendar mean that it is often a good idea to book in advance.

LA RAMBLA

Hotel Continental (Map pp98-9; ☎ 93 301 25 70; www.hotelcontinental.com; La Rambla 138; s/d €82/92; ✹ 🖳) Rooms in this classic old Barcelona hotel (where George Orwell stayed during the Civil War) are spare but have romantic touches such as ceiling fans. Try for a double with balcony over La Rambla (for which you pay €20 extra).

BARRI GÒTIC

Hostal Campi (Map pp98-9; ☎ 93 301 35 45; hcampi@terra.es; Carrer de la Canuda 4; d €62, s/d without bathroom €31/54) An excellent lower-end deal. The best rooms are the doubles with their own loo and shower. Although basic, they are extremely roomy and bright.

Hotel Neri (Map pp98-9; ☎ 93 304 06 55; www.hotelneri.com; Carrer de Sant Sever 5; d from €248; ✹ 🖳) Occupying a beautifully adapted, centuries-old building, this stunningly renovated medieval mansion combines historic stone walls with sexy plasma TVs. Downstairs is a fine restaurant and you can take a drink and catch some rays on the roof deck.

EL RAVAL

Hostal Gat Raval (Map pp98-9; ☎ 93 481 66 70; www.gataccommodation.com; Carrer de Joaquín Costa 44; d €80, s/d without bathroom €50/70; ✹ 🖳) There's a pea-green and lemon-lime colour scheme in this hip, young, 2nd-floor *hostal* deep in El Raval. Rooms are pleasant, secure and each is behind a green door, but only some have private bathroom. Across the road you have a choice of busy bars to while away the evenings.

Hostal Gat Xino (Map pp98-9; ☎ 93 324 88 33; www.gataccommodation.com; Carrer de l'Hospital 149-155; s/d €66/84, ste with terrace €130; ✹ 🖳) Better still than Gat Raval is this newer version. The lime-green theme

KRZYSZTOF DYDYNSKI

Auditorium of the Palau de la Música Catalana (p104)

continues but rooms are more spacious and all have bathroom. The suite has views to Montjuïc.

Casa Camper (Map pp98-9; ☎ 93 342 62 80; www.camper.es; Carrer d'Elisabets 11; s/d €240/284; ✕ 🖳 ✕) Run by the Mallorcan shoe people in the better end of El Raval, these designer digs offer rooms with a few surprises, like the Vinçon furniture.

LA RIBERA

Chic & Basic (Map pp98-9; ☎ 93 295 46 52; www.chicandbasic.com; Carrer de la Princesa 50; d €96-171; ✕ 🖳) In a completely renovated building with high vaults in the facade are 31 spotlessly white rooms. There are high ceilings, enormous beds (room types are classed as M, L and XL!) and lots of detailed touches (LED lighting, TFT TV screens and the retention of many beautiful old features of the original building, such as the marble staircase).

ourpick Hotel Banys Orientals (Map pp98-9; ☎ 93 268 84 60; www.hotelbanysorientals.com; Carrer de l'Argenteria 37; s/d €89/107; ✕ 🖳) Cool blues and aquamarines combine with

dark-hued parquet floors to lend this boutique beauty an understated charm. All rooms – admittedly on the small side but impeccably presented – look onto the street or back lanes.

L'EIXAMPLE

Hostal Girona (Map pp98-9; ☎ 93 265 02 59; www.hostalgirona.com; Carrer de Girona 24; r up to €66) A 2nd-floor, family-run *hostal*, the Girona is a basic but clean and friendly spot. Rooms range from poky singles with communal bathroom to airy doubles with balcony (beware of traffic noise in summer when you'll have to keep the windows open).

Hostal Goya (Map pp98-9; ☎ 93 302 25 65; www.hostalgoya.com; Carrer de Pau Claris 74; s €70, d €96-113; ✕) The Goya is a gem of a spot on the chichi side of l'Eixample and a short stroll from Plaça de Catalunya. Rooms have parquet floors and a light colour scheme that varies from room to room.

Hotel Constanza (Map pp98-9; ☎ 93 270 19 10; www.hotelconstanza.com; Carrer del Bruc 33;

s/d €90/120; ⌘ ⌨) Constanza is a boutique belle that has stolen the heart of many a visitor to Barcelona. Even smaller singles are made to feel special with broad mirrors and strong colours (reds and yellows, with black furniture).

Hotel Omm (Map pp86-7; ☎ 93 445 40 00; www.hotelomm.es; Carrer de Rosselló 265; d from €257; ⌘ ⌨) The balconies look like strips of metallic skin peeled back from the shiny surface of the hotel – the sort of idea a latter-day Modernista might have had! Light, clear tones dominate in the ultramodern rooms, and the sprawling foyer bar is a popular evening meeting point for guests and outsiders alike.

APARTMENTS

Apartment Barcelona (Map pp86-7; ☎ 93 215 79 34; www.apartmentbarcelona.com; Carrer de València 286)

Barcelona Apartments (Map pp86-7; ☎ 93 414 55 28; www.barcelonapartments.com; Via Augusta 173)

EATING

Barcelona was always a good place to eat but in recent years it has evolved into something of a foodies' paradise on earth, combining rich Catalan cooking traditions with a new wave of cutting-edge chefs at the vanguard of what has been dubbed *nueva cocina española*. The city has taken on quite a cosmopolitan hue too.

Cartas (menus) may be in Catalan, Spanish or both; some establishments also have foreign- language menus.

BARRI GÒTIC

Agut (Map pp98-9; ☎ 93 315 17 09; Carrer d'En Gignàs 16; meals €35; ⌚ lunch & dinner Tue-Sat, lunch Sun; ⌘) Contemporary paintings on the walls contrast with the fine traditional Catalan dishes offered in this timeless restaurant.

Pla (Map pp98-9; ☎ 93 412 65 52; www .pla-repla.com; Carrer de Bellafila 5; meals €45-50; ⌚ dinner daily; ⌘) In this modern den of inventive cooking with music worthy of a club, the chefs present deliciously strange combinations such as *bacallà amb salsa de pomes verdes* (cod in a green apple sauce).

EL RAVAL

Organic (Map pp98-9; ☎ 93 301 09 02; www .antoniaorganickitchen.com; Carrer de la Junta de Comerç 11; meals €14-20; ⌚ noon-midnight; ⌘ Ⓥ) A long sprawl of a vegetarian diner, Organic is always full. Choose from a limited range of options that change from day to day, and tuck into the all-you-can-eat salad bar in the middle of the restaurant. At night prices go up a tad and a full waiting service operates.

LA RIBERA

Orígen (Map pp98-9; ☎ 93 310 75 31; www.origen 99.com; Carrer de la Vidrieria 6-8; meals €15-20; ⌚ 12.30pm-1am; ⌘) With a treasure chest of Catalan regional products for sale, this place also has a long menu of bite-sized dishes (mostly around €5 to €8), such as *ànec amb naps* (duck and turnip) or *civet de senglar* (jugged boar), which you can mix and match over wine by the glass.

Pla de la Garsa (Map pp98-9; ☎ 93 315 24 13; Carrer dels Assaonadors 13; meals €25; ⌚ dinner daily; ⌘) This 17th-century house is ideal for a romantic dinner. Timber beams, a peppering of tables around the dining area and soft ambient music combine to make an enchanting setting for traditional Catalan cooking.

Cal Pep (Map pp98-9; ☎ 93 310 79 61; www .calpep.com; Plaça de les Olles 8; meals €45; ⌚ lunch & dinner Tue-Fri, dinner Mon, lunch Sat Sep-Jul; ⌘) This gourmet tapas bar is one of the most popular in town and it can be difficult to snaffle a spot here.

LA BARCELONETA & THE COAST

Can Majó (Map pp98-9; ☎ 93 221 58 18; Carrer del Almirall Aixada 23; meals €30-40; ☾ lunch & dinner Tue-Sat, lunch Sun) Virtually on the beach (with tables outside in summer), Can Majó has a long and steady reputation for fine seafood, particularly its rice dishes (€14 to €20).

Suquet de l'Almirall (Map pp98-9; ☎ 93 221 62 33; Passeig de Joan de Borbó 65; meals €45-50; ☾ lunch & dinner Tue-Sat, lunch Sun; ☒) A family business run by one of the acolytes of Ferran Adrià's El Bulli restaurant (see the boxed text, p177), the order of the day is top-class seafood.

L'EIXAMPLE

La Rita (Map pp86-7; ☎ 93 487 23 76; Carrer d'Aragó 279; meals €20; ☒) Locals line up to dine here, if only because the price-quality rapport is excellent. So join the queue to get inside this boisterous restaurant. You have a broad choice between classic local cooking and some more inventive dishes.

Cerveseria Catalana (Map pp98-9; ☎ 93 216 03 68; Carrer de Mallorca 236; meals €25; ☒) This 'Catalan brewery' is great for its cornucopia of tapas (€3 to €7) and *montaditos* (canapés, €1.80 to €3.50). The variety of hot tapas, mouth-watering salads and other snacks draws a well-dressed crowd.

Inopia (off Map pp98-9; ☎ 93 424 52 31; www .barinopia.com; Carrer de Tamarit 104; meals €25-30; ☾ dinner Tue-Fri, lunch & dinner Sat) Albert Adrià, brother of star chef Ferran, has his hands full with this busy gourmet-tapas temple.

Saüc (Map pp86-7; ☎ 93 321 01 89; www .saucrestaurant.com; Passatge de Lluís Pellicer 12; meals €70-80; ☾ Tue-Sat; ☒) Pop down into this back-lane basement place and enter an upcoming gourmet landmark. The decor is sober but the dishes are sins for the senses.

GRÀCIA

Goliard (Map pp86-7; ☎ 93 207 31 75; Carrer de Progrés 6; meals €30-35; ☾ lunch & dinner Mon-Fri, dinner Sat & Sun; ☒) This quiet diner is a haven of exquisite designer cooking at modest prices. Book ahead.

ALFREDO MAIQUEZ

Hotel Omm

MONTJUÏC & POBLE SEC

Restaurant Elche (Map pp98-9; ☎ 93 441 30 89; Carrer de Vila i Vilà 71; meals €30) With tables spreading over two floors, and old-world style in service and settings, this spot has been doing some of Barcelona's best paella (of various types) and *fideuá* (vaguely similar to paella, but made with vermicelli noodles) since the 1960s.

DRINKING

Barcelona's bars run the gamut from wood-panelled wine cellars to bright waterfront places and trendy designer bars. Most are at their liveliest from about 10pm to 2am or 3am.

A word of warning on La Rambla: while it can be pleasant enough to tipple here, few locals would even think about it and bar prices tend to be exorbitant – €25 for a carafe of sangria is not unheard of.

BARRI GÒTIC

Club Soul (Map pp98-9; ☎ 93 302 70 26; www .barceloca.com; Carrer Nou de Sant Francesc 7; ☾ 10pm-2.30am Mon-Thu, 10pm-3am Fri & Sat, 8pm-2.30am Sun) One of the hippest club-style hang-outs in this part of town. Each night the DJs change the musical theme, ranging from deep funk to deeper house.

Manchester (Map pp98-9; ☎ 663 071748; www.manchesterbar.com; Carrer de Milans 5; ☾ 7pm-2.30am Sun-Thu, 7pm-3am Fri & Sat) Settle in for a beer and the sounds of great Manchester bands, from Depeche Mode to Oasis. It has a pleasing rough-and-tumble feel, with tables jammed in every which way.

EL RAVAL

Bar Marsella (Map pp98-9; Carrer de Sant Pau 65; ☾ 10pm-2am Mon-Thu, 10pm-3am Fri & Sat) In business since 1820, the Marsella specialises in *absenta* (absinthe), a beverage known for its supposed narcotic qualities.

Nothing much has changed here since the 19th century and the local tipple certainly has a kick.

Boadas (Map pp98-9; ☎ 93 318 88 26; Carrer dels Tallers 1; ☾ noon-2am Mon-Thu, noon-3am Fri & Sat) Inside the unprepossessing entrance is one of the city's oldest cocktail bars (famed for its daiquiris). The bow-tied waiters have been serving up their poison since 1933, and both Joan Miró and Hemingway tippled here.

LA RIBERA

La Fianna (Map pp98-9; ☎ 93 315 18 10; www.lafianna.com; Carrer dels Banys Vells 15; ☾ 6pm-1.30am Sun-Wed, 6pm-2.30am Thu-Sat) There is something medieval-Asian about this bar, with its bare stone walls, forged-iron candelabras and cushion-covered lounges. This place heaves and as the night wears on it's elbow room only.

La Vinya Del Senyor (Map pp98-9; ☎ 93 310 33 79; Plaça de Santa Maria del Mar 5; ☾ noon-1am Tue-Sun) The wine list is as long as *War & Peace,* and the terrace lies in the shadow of Santa Maria del Mar. You can crowd inside the tiny wine bar itself or take a bottle upstairs to the one available table.

PORT VELL & THE COAST

The Barcelona beach scene, apart from the roasting of countless bodies, warms up to dance sounds in the summer months. In addition to waterfront restaurants and bars (especially on and near Port Olímpic), a string of *chiringuitos* (provisional bars) sets up along the beaches. Most are strung along from Platja de Bogatell to Platja de Nova Mar Bella.

L'EIXAMPLE & AROUND

There are three main concentrations for carousers in L'Eixample, although bars are dotted about all over. The top end of Carrer d'Aribau and the area where it crosses Avinguda Diagonal attracts a heterogenous and mostly local crowd to its many bars and clubs. Carrer de Balmes is lined with clubs for a mostly teen 'n' twenties crowd. The city's gay-and-lesbian circuit is concentrated around Carrer del Consell de Cent.

Dry Martini (Map pp86-7; ☎ 93 217 50 72; Carrer d'Aribau 162-166; ☽ 1pm-2am Sun-Thu, 1pm-3am Fri & Sat) Waiters serve up the best dry martini in town, or whatever else your heart desires, in this classic cocktail lounge. Sink into a leather lounge and nurse a huge G&T.

Les Gens Que J'aime (Map pp86-7; ☎ 93 215 68 79; Carrer de València 286; ☽ 6pm-2.30am Sun-Thu, 6pm-3am Fri & Sat) This intimate relic of the 1960s offers jazz music in the background and a cosy scattering of velvet-backed lounges around tiny dark tables.

Premier (Map pp98-9; ☎ 93 532 16 50; Carrer de Provença 236; ☽ 6pm-2.30am Mon-Thu, 6pm-3am Fri & Sat) Relax at the bar or in a lounge in this funky little French-run wine bar.

ENTERTAINMENT
CLUBS
Elephant (Map pp86-7; ☎ 93 334 02 58; www .elephantbcn.com; Passeig dels Tillers 1; admission Fri & Sat €15, Wed, Thu & Sun free; ☽ 11pm-3am Wed, 11pm-5am Thu-Sun) Getting in here is like being invited to some Beverly Hills private party. Models and wannabes mix freely, as do the drinks. A big tent-like dance space is the focus but mingle around the various garden bars too.

Luz De Gas (Map pp86-7; ☎ 93 209 77 11; www.luzdegas.com; Carrer de Muntaner 244-246; admission up to €15; ☽ 11.30pm-6am) Set in a grand theatre that is frequently the scene of live acts, this club attracts a crowd of well-dressed beautiful people, whose tastes in music vary according to the night.

Razzmatazz (Map pp86-7; ☎ 93 272 09 10; www.salarazzmatazz.com; Carrer dels Almogàvers 122 or Carrer de Pamplona 88; admission €15; ☽ 1-6am Fri & Sat) A half-dozen blocks back from Port Olímpic is this stalwart of Barcelona's club and concert scene, with five different clubs in one huge space.

Sutton Club (Map pp86-7; ☎ 93 414 42 17; www.thesuttonclub.com; Carrer de Tuset 13; admission €15; ☽ 11.30pm-6am Tue-Sat) A classic club with mainstream sounds, this place inevitably attracts just about everyone pouring in and out of the nearby bars at some stage in the evening – if the bouncers let them in, that is.

DAMIEN SIMONIS

Festes de la Mercè (p110) finery at Mar Bella beach

Young football fans at Camp Nou

KRZYSZTOF DYDYNSKI

LIVE MUSIC

Harlem Jazz Club (Map pp98-9; ☎ 93 310 07 55; Carrer de la Comtessa de Sobradiel 8; admission up to €10; ☒ 8pm-4am Tue-Thu & Sun, 8pm-5am Fri & Sat) This narrow, smoky, old-town dive is one of the best spots in town for jazz. Every now and then it mixes it up with a little rock, Latin or blues. There are usually two sessions in an evening.

Jamboree (Map pp98-9; ☎ 93 319 17 89; www.masimas.com/jamboree; Plaça Reial 17; admission €9; ☒ 9.30pm-6am) Concerts start at 11pm and proceed until about 2am at the latest, at which point attentive jazz fans convert themselves into clubbers. Some of the great names of jazz and blues have filled the air with their sono-rous contributions.

Sala Tarantos (Map pp98-9; ☎ 93 319 17 89; http://masimas.com/tarantos; Plaça Reial 17; admis-sion from €6; ☒ performances 8.30pm, 9.30pm & 10.30pm daily) This basement locale is the stage for some of the best flamenco to pass through Barcelona. You have to keep an eye out for quality acts, otherwise you can pop by for the more pedestrian regu-lar performances.

SPORT

FC Barcelona (Barça for aficionados) has one of the best stadiums in Europe – the 100,000-capacity **Camp Nou** (Map pp86-7; ☎ 902 18 99 00, from abroad +34 93 496 36 00; www.fcbarcelona.com; ☒ tickets 9am-1.30pm & 3.30-6pm Mon-Fri) in the west of the city. Tickets for national-league games are available at the stadium, by phone or online. For the latter two options, non-members must book 15 days before the match. You can also obtain them through the ServiCaixa.

SHOPPING

All of Barcelona seems to be lined with unending ranks of fashion boutiques and design stores.

Most of the mainstream fashion and design stores can be found on a shop-ping 'axis' that looks like the hands of a clock set at about 20 to five. From Plaça de Catalunya it heads along Passeig de Gràcia, turning left into Avinguda Diagonal. From here as far as Plaça de la Reina Maria Cristina, the Diagonal is jammed with shopping options.

A squadron of antiques stores is scattered about Carrer dels Banys Nous in the Barri Gòtic, in whose labyrinthine lanes you can find all sorts of curious stores.

FASHION

Antonio Miró (Map pp98-9; ☎ 93 487 06 70; www.antoniomiro.es; Carrer del Consell de Cent 349) Mr Miró is one of Barcelona's haute-couture kings. He concentrates on light, natural fibres to produce smart, unpretentious men's and women's fashion.

Custo Barcelona (Map pp98-9; ☎ 93 268 78 93; www.custo-barcelona.com; Plaça de les Olles 7) Custo bewitches people the world over with a youthful, psychedelic panoply of women's and men's fashion. It has several branches around town.

Red Market (Map pp86-7; ☎ 93 218 63 33; Carrer de Verdi 20) Several funky fashion boutiques dot themselves along this street. Here you'll run into bright, uninhibited urban wear and accessories.

FOOD & DRINK

Joan Murrià (Map pp86-7; ☎ 93 215 57 89; Carrer de Roger de Llúria 85) Ramon Casas designed the Modernista shop-front ads for this delicious delicatessen, where the shelves groan under the weight of speciality food from around Catalonia and beyond.

Xampany (off Map pp98-9; ☎ 610 845011; Carrer de València 200; ☽ 4.30-10pm Mon-Fri, 10am-2pm Sat) Since 1981 this 'Cathedral of Cava' has been a veritable Aladdin's cave of *cava*, with bottles of the stuff crammed high and into every possible chaotic corner of this dimly lit locale.

SHOES

Camper (Map pp86-7; ☎ 93 215 63 90; www.camper.com; Carrer de València 249) This Mallorcan success story is the Clarks of Spain. Its shoes range from the eminently sensible to the stylishly fashionable. It has stores all over town.

GETTING THERE & AWAY
AIR
Aeroport del Prat (☎ 902 40 47 04; www.aena.es) is 12km southwest of the centre at El Prat de Llobregat. Barcelona is a big international and domestic destination, with direct flights from North America as well as many European cities.

BOAT
Regular passenger and vehicular ferries to/from the Balearic Islands, operated by **Acciona Trasmediterránea** (Map pp98-9; ☎ 902 45 46 45; www.trasmediterranea.es), dock along both sides of the Moll de Barcelona wharf in Port Vell.

BUS
Long-distance buses for destinations throughout Spain leave from the **Estació del Nord** (Map pp86-7; ☎ 902 30 32 22; www.barcelonanord.com; Carrer d'Ali Bei 80).

CAR & MOTORCYCLE
Avis, Europcar, Hertz and several other big companies have desks at the airport, Estació Sants train station and Estació del Nord bus terminus.

TRAIN
The main international and domestic station is **Estació Sants** (Map pp86-7; Plaça dels Països Catalans), 2.5km west of La Rambla.

Since early 2008 the high-speed AVE train between Barcelona and Madrid has provided some serious competition for that air route.

GETTING AROUND

The metro is the easiest way of getting around and reaches most places you're likely to visit (although not the airport).

For public transport information, make a call to ☎ 010.

TO/FROM THE AIRPORT

The **A1 Aerobús** (off Map pp98-9, Map pp98-9; ☎ 93 415 60 20; one-way €4.05; 30-40min) runs from the airport to Plaça de Catalunya via Plaça d'Espanya, Gran Via de les Corts Catalanes (on the corner of Carrer del Comte d'Urgell) and Plaça de la Universitat (six to 15 minutes depending on the time of day) from 6am to 1am. Considerably slower local buses also operate.

Renfe's *rodalies* line 10 runs between the airport and Estació de França in Barcelona (about 35 minutes), stopping at Estació Sants and Passeig de Gràcia.

A taxi to/from the centre, about a half-hour ride depending on traffic, costs between €18 and €22.

Sagalés (☎ 902 13 00 14; www.sagales .com) runs direct Barcelona Bus services between Girona-Costa Brava Airport and Estació del Nord bus station in Barcelona (one way/return €12/21, 70 minutes), connecting with flights.

CAR & MOTORCYCLE

Limited parking in the Ciutat Vella is virtually all for residents only, with some metered parking. Parking stations are also scattered all over L'Eixample, with a few in the old centre too.

METRO & FGC

The **Transports Metropolitans de Barcelona (TMB) metro** (☎ 010; www .tmb.net) has six numbered and colour-coded lines.

Suburban trains run by the **Ferrocarrils de la Generalitat de Catalunya** (**FGC**; ☎ 93 205 15 15; www.fgc.net) include a couple of useful city lines. One heads north from Plaça de Catalunya. A branch of it will get you to Tibidabo and another within spitting distance of the Monestir de Pedralbes.

The other FGC line heads to Manresa from Plaça d'Espanya, and is handy for the trip to Montserrat (opposite).

TICKETS & TARGETAS

Targeta T-10 (€7.20) 10 rides (each valid for 1¼ hours) on the metro, buses and FGC trains. You can change between metro, FGC, *rodalies* and buses.

Targeta T-DIA (€5.50) Unlimited travel on all transport for one day.

AROUND BARCELONA

SITGES

pop 26,200

Sitges attracts everyone from jet-setters to young travellers, honeymooners to week-ending families, and from Barcelona's night owls to an international gay crowd. The beach is long and sandy, the nightlife thumps until breakfast and there are lots of groovy boutiques if you need to spruce up your wardrobe.

INFORMATION

Main tourist office (☎ 93 810 93 40; www .sitgestur.com; Carrer de Sínia Morera 1; ⏰ 9am-8pm mid-Jun–mid-Sep, 9am-2pm & 4-6.30pm Mon-Fri Oct–mid-Jun)

FESTIVALS & EVENTS

Carnaval (Around February; dates change from year to year) in Sitges is a week-long riot just made for the extrovert, the ambiguous and the exhibitionist, capped by an extravagant gay parade that's held on the last night.

EATING

La Nansa (☎ 93 894 94 19 27; Carrer de la Carreta 24; meals €35; ⏲ lunch & dinner Thu-Mon Feb-Dec) Cast just back from the waterfront up a little lane in a fine old house is this seafood specialist that does a good line in paella and other rice dishes.

Pic Nic (☎ 93 811 00 40; Passeig de la Ribera s/n; meals €35-40; ⏲ lunch Sun-Thu, lunch & dinner Fri & Sat) With views straight out over the sea, this good-natured, rowdy seafood eatery is perfect for a group lunch. Fish and seafood rice dishes (paella and company) are the speciality here.

DRINKING & ENTERTAINMENT

Much of Sitges' nightlife happens on one short pedestrian strip packed with humanity right through the night in summer: Carrer del 1er de Maig. Also known as Calle del Pecado (Sin Street), it vibrates to the volume of 10 or so disco-bars, all trying to outdo each other in decibels. That said, virtually all bars shut by 3.30am.

GETTING THERE & AWAY

From about 6am to 10pm, four *rodalies* per hour run from Passeig de Gràcia and Estació Sants in Barcelona to Sitges (€2.60, 38 to 46 minutes from Passeig de Gràcia depending on intermediate stops).

MONTSERRAT

Montserrat (Serrated Mountain), 50km northwest of Barcelona, is a 1236m-high mountain of truly weird rock pillars, shaped by wind, rain and frost from a conglomeration of limestone, pebbles and sand that once lay under the sea. With the historic Benedictine Monestir de Montserrat, one of Catalonia's most important shrines, cradled at 725m on its side, it makes a great outing from Barcelona.

ORIENTATION & INFORMATION

The **information office** (☎ 93 877 77 01; www.abadiamontserrat.net; ⏲ 9am-6pm) has information on the complex and walking trails.

SIGHTS & ACTIVITIES
MONESTIR DE MONTSERRAT

The monastery was founded in 1025 to commemorate a 'vision' of the Virgin on the mountain. Wrecked by Napoleon's troops in 1811, then abandoned as a result of anticlerical legislation in the 1830s, it was rebuilt from 1858. Today a community of about 80 monks resides here. Pilgrims come from far and wide to venerate *La Moreneta* (The Black Virgin), a 12th-century Romanesque wooden sculpture

Carnaval mask

ALFREDO MAIQUEZ

Monestir de Montserrat (p119)

DAMIEN SIMONIS

of Mary with the infant Jesus, which has been Catalonia's patron since 1881.

The two-part **Museu de Montserrat** (☎ 93 877 77 77; Plaça de Santa Maria; adult/student €6.50/5.50; ☖ 10am-6pm) has an excellent collection, ranging from an Egyptian mummy and Gothic altarpieces to art by El Greco, Monet, Degas and Picasso.

From Plaça de Santa Maria you enter the courtyard of the 16th-century **basilica** (admission incl La Moreneta €5; ☖ 9am-8.15pm Jul-Sep, earlier closing rest of yr), the monastery's church.

If you're around the basilica at the right time, you'll catch a brief performance by the **Montserrat Boys' Choir** (Escolania; www.escolania.net; admission free; ☖ performances 1pm & 6.45pm Mon-Fri, 11am & 6.45pm Sun Sep-Jun), reckoned to be Europe's oldest music school.

You can explore the mountain above the monastery on a web of paths leading to some of the peaks and to 13 empty and rather dilapidated hermitages. The

Funicular de Sant Joan (one way/return €4.15/6.60; ☖ every 20min 10am-5.40pm Apr-Oct, to 7pm mid-Jul–Aug, 11am-4.30pm Nov-Mar) will carry you up the first 250m from the monastery.

From the Sant Joan top station, it's a 20-minute stroll (signposted) to the **Sant Joan chapel**, with fine westward views. More exciting is the one-hour walk northwest, along a path marked with occasional blobs of yellow paint, to Montserrat's highest peak, **Sant Jeroni**, from where there's an awesome sheer drop on the north face.

GETTING THERE & AWAY

The R5 line trains operated by **FGC** (☎ 93 205 15 15) run from Plaça d'Espanya station in Barcelona to Monistrol de Montserrat up to 18 times daily starting at 5.24am. They connect with the rack-and-pinion train, or **cremallera** (☎ 902 31 20 20; www .cremallerademontserrat.com), which takes 17 minutes to make the upwards journey and costs €4.10/6.50 one way/return.

CENTRAL SPAIN

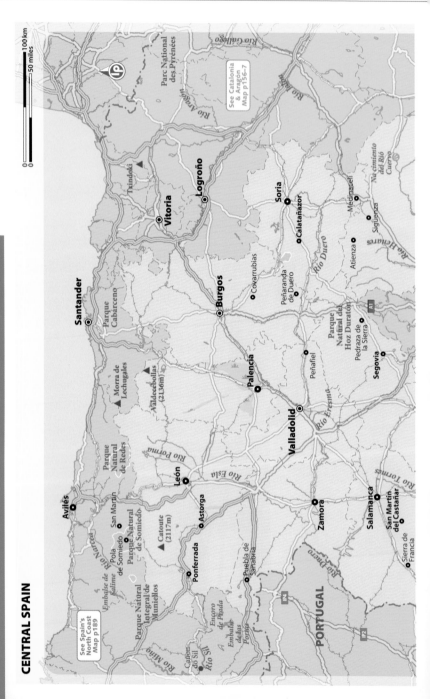

100 km
50 miles

Rio Gállego

Parc National
des Pyrénées

Rio Aragón

See Catalonia
& Aragón
Map p156–7

Txindoki

Vitoria

Logroño

Rio Duero

Nacimiento
del Rió
Cuervo

Soria

Calatañazor

Medinaceli

Sigüenza

Santander

Parque
Cabárceno

Burgos

Covarrubias

Peñaranda
de Duero

Rio Duero

Atienza

Rio Henares

A1

Morra de
Lechugales

Valdecebollas
(2136m)

Palencia

Parque
Natural del
Hoz Duratón

Pedraza de
la Sierra

Peñafiel

Segovia

Parque
Natural
de Redes

Valladolid

Rio Eresma

Rio Porma

León

Rio Esla

Avilés

Parque Natural
de Somiedo

San Martín
de Somiedo

Pola
de
Somiedo

Catoute
(2117m)

Astorga

Rio Tormes

Zamora

Salamanca

San Martín
del Castañar

Sierra de
Francia

Embalse de
Valdime

See Spain's
North Coast
Map p189

Parque Natural
Integral de
Muniellos

Ponferrada

Puebla de
Sanabria

Cañón
do Sil

Rio Sil

Rio Miño

Encoro
de Prada

Embalse
de las
Portas

PORTUGAL

IP4

IP2

Rio Douro

Rio Narcea

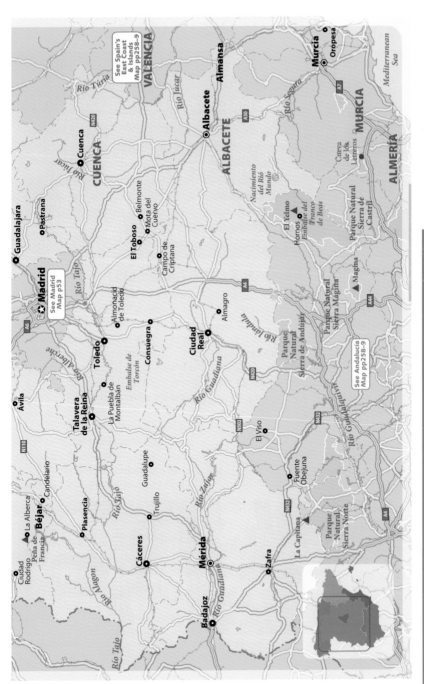

CENTRAL SPAIN

See Spain's East Coast & Islands Map pp258–9

VALENCIA

Rio Túria

Rio Júcar

Almansa

Murcia

Oropesa

Mediterranean Sea

MURCIA

A7

CUENCA

Cuenca

Pastrana

Rio Júcar

Belmonte

Mota del Cuervo

El Toboso

Campo de Criptana

N320

ALBACETE

Albacete

N301

N30

Rio Segura

Cueva de los Letreros

ALMERÍA

Nacimiento del Rió Mundo

El Yelmo

Hornos

Embalse del Tranco de Beas

Parque Natural Sierra de Castril

Magina

Guadalajara

Madrid

See Madrid Map p53

Almonacid de Toledo

A6

Toledo

Rio Tajo

Embalse de Torcón

Consuegra

Almagro

Ciudad Real

Rio Jandula

Parque Natural Sierra de Andújar

Parque Natural Sierra Mágina

Rio Guadalquivir

A44

N322

A4

See Andalucia Map pp258–9

Ávila

N110

Candelario

Béjar

La Alberca

Peña de Francia

Ciudad Rodrigo

Rio Alagón

Plasencia

Rio Tajo

Rio Alberche

La Puebla de Montalbán

Talavera de la Reina

Guadalupe

Trujillo

Cáceres

Rio Tajo

Rio Guadiana

Mérida

Badajoz

Rio Guadiana

Rio Zújar

N502

El Viso

N420

Fuente Obejuna

La Capitana

Parque Natural Sierra Norte

Zafra

N432

A4

CENTRAL SPAIN HIGHLIGHTS

1 SALAMANCA

BY BEATRIZ CASTAÑO & JUAN OLAZABAL, ADOPTED *CHARROS* (SALAMANCA NATIVES)

Salamanca is monumental (as recognised by Unesco) and very cultural (it was Europe's Capital of Culture in 2002), but the full Salamanca experience requires a little local knowledge. Behind the grand facades, it's all about discovering secret corners that locals love and learning new ways to look at its well-known sights.

◥ BEATRIZ' AND JUAN'S DON'T MISS LIST

❶ LA PLAZA MAYOR

By all means admire the plaza's 88 arches adorned with busts, and the way the sun turns the plaza's local sandstone to gold. But the essence of Salamanca, where life is performance, is to take up residence at one of the outdoor tables and watch all the life of Salamanca flow through the plaza.

❷ THE CATHEDRALS & PLAZA ANAYA

Apart from the cathedrals' landmark architectural features, look for the astronaut mischievously carved into the Catedral Nueva's northern door during restorations, and the cracks and broken stained-glass windows from the 1755 earthquake. Right outside, students pass the afternoon, sometimes in song, in Plaza Anaya, one of Salamanca's most charming corners.

❸ THE UNIVERSITY FACADE

The facade of Salamanca's prestigious university is a plateresque masterpiece. But the devil lies in the detail. Trying to find the famous frog of Salamanca

Clockwise from top: La Plaza Mayor at night; Catedral Nueva main entrance; Grounds of Salamanca University; Enjoying tapas and a drink

is a local rite of passage: according to local legend, the student who fails to find it will fail in their studies. But its origins probably lie in lust – it's actually a symbol of female sexuality…

❹ TAPAS ALONG CALLE VAN DYCK

Tapas is a Salamanca passion and Calle de Van Dyck, north of the old town, is the most emblematic tapas street, where it's all about Salamanca's famous pork products, especially *embutidos* (cured meats). Hop from bar to bar and try the *pincho moruno* (marinated kebab), *lomo* (cured pork sausage), *jamón* and *chanfaina* (a paella accompanied with various pork cuts).

❺ STAYING OUT AS LONG AS YOUR BODY LASTS

A quarter of the people in Salamanca are students, which means that the city never sleeps. The most famous drink is '*el garrafón*' (any alcohol of low quality), which suits a student's budget, but be warned – the hangovers can last for days.

↘ THINGS YOU NEED TO KNOW

Location 2½ hours northwest of Madrid **Best photo op** Out over the old town from Puerta de la Torre in the Catedral Nueva **Top survival tip** Take a siesta after lunch **Frog-spotting tip** Look for one of the skulls **See our author's coverage of Salamanca, p134**

CENTRAL SPAIN HIGHLIGHTS

2

⬊ DISCOVER DISNEYLAND IN SEGOVIA

North of the mountains that encircle Madrid, the old town of **Segovia** (p136) has monuments that span Spanish history. At one end stands one of Europe's best-preserved Roman aqueducts, while at the other is the fairytale-yet-fortress-like Alcázar, which inspired the designers of Disneyland's famous castle. In between, stunning buildings and fine restaurants stand watch over the lively streets.

3

⬊ EXPLORE RENAISSANCE SALAMANCA

Beautiful and brimful of life, **Salamanca** (p134) always ranks high on travellers' favourite small cities lists. The exquisite Plaza Mayor, floodlit to magical effect at night, may be the centrepiece, but the Renaissance and plateresque sandstone architecture is also magnificent. Salamanca's large student population adds life to the elegance with an almost incessant yet agreeable buzz.

4

⬐ EXPERIENCE VILLAGES TIME FORGOT

Away from tourist routes, Central Spain's stone-and-timber villages are one of its best-kept secrets. From La Alberca (p136) and Puebla de Sanabria (p137) to Medinaceli (p137) and Atienza (p137), these villages are Old Spain hidden away from the frenetic pace of the 21st century.

5

⬐ MARVEL AT LEÓN'S CATHEDRAL

Few churchs combine delicacy and grandeur to such sublime effect as León's cathedral (p139). Prettily proportioned on the outside, a riot of colour within, the cathedral's 128 stained-glass windows will leave you breathless. The slap of sandals on flagstones is also a reminder that this is a staging post for pilgrims along the Camino de Santiago.

6

⬐ WANDER THROUGH MONUMENTAL TOLEDO

Picturesque Toledo (p142) is like a window on the Spanish soul. So many are the monuments to the city's polyglot Christian, Jewish and Muslim past that it has the quality of a living museum: this is one place where comparisons to the great cities of North Africa and the Middle East are not misplaced.

2 DAVID TOMLINSON; 3 WAYNE WALTON; 4 DIEGO LEZAMA; 5 ALDO PAVAN; 6 VISIONS OF AMERICA, LLC/ALAMY

2 Alcázar (p138), Segovia; 3 Sandstone architecture in Salamanca (p134); 4 Cobblestone lane in La Alberca (p136); 5 León Cathedral (p139); 6 Historic Toledo (p142)

CENTRAL SPAIN'S BEST...

⇘ SIGNPOSTS TO THE PAST

- **León Cathedral** (p139) Soaring monument to Catholic Spain.
- **Burgos Cathedral** (p141) Breathtaking cathedral in the Castilian heartland.
- **Mérida** (p152) Spain's most impressive Roman ruins.
- **Toledo** (p142) Synagogues, churches and mosques.
- **El Acueducto, Segovia** (p136) Astonishing feat of Roman engineering.

⇘ ESCAPES FROM MODERN SPAIN

- **Ciudad Monumental, Cáceres** (p148) Central Spain's best preserved old town.
- **Sierra de Francia** (p136) Time-worn mountain villages.
- **Puebla de Sanabria** (p137) Castle-village far from Spain's beating heart.
- **Old-world villages** (p137) Central Spain's most charming hamlets.

⇘ PLACES WITH A VIEW

- **Trujillo's castle** (p150) Panoramic views of Extremadura.
- **Puente de San Pablo, Cuenca** (p147) Cuenca in all its glory.
- **Iglesia de San Ildefonso, Toledo** (p143) Sweeping views over the Toledo rooftops.
- **Plaza Mayor at night, Salamanca** (p134) One of Spain's most beautiful squares.
- **Windmills of Consuegra** (p146) Don Quijote's famous windmills in all their glory.

⇘ HILLTOP CASTLES

- **Alcázar, Segovia** (p138) Clifftop castle that inspired a fairytale.
- **Peñafiel** (p152) Long, narrow battlements with a wine museum.
- **Belmonte** (p152) The way castles should be, in Don Quijote country.

ALDO PAVAN

Segovia's El Acueducto (p136)

THINGS YOU NEED TO KNOW

⭧ VITAL STATISTICS

- **Population** 5.3 million
- **Area** 215,120 sq km (almost half of Spain)
- **Best time to visit** April/May and September/October.

⭧ LOCALITIES IN A NUTSHELL

- **Castilla y León** (p132) The Castilian heartland north of Madrid is home to lively, monument-rich cities (such as Ávila, Salamanca, Segovia, León and Burgos) and charming medieval villages.
- **Castilla-La Mancha** (p142) This vast high plateau running south and east from Madrid is a land of sweeping horizons, isolated villages and the beautiful towns of Toledo and Cuenca.
- **Extremadura** (p148) Another inland region running along the Portuguese border, Extremadura is steeped in history with Cáceres, Trujillo and the Roman city of Mérida among the highlights.

⭧ ADVANCE PLANNING

- **One month before** Book your accommodation (earlier if you're planning to come during Semana Santa, p46).
- **Two weeks before** Book long-distance train journeys (www.renfe.es) and car hire (p371).

⭧ RESOURCES

- **Castilla y León** (www.turismocastilla yleon.com) Informative site for north-central Spain.
- **Castilla-La Mancha** (www.turismo castillalamancha.com) Castilla-La Mancha's tourism portal.
- **Extremadura** (www.turismoextre madura.com in Spanish) Website run by regional tourist board of Extremadura.

⭧ EMERGENCY NUMBERS

- **Emergency** (☎ 112)
- **Policía Nacional** (☎ 091)

⭧ GETTING AROUND

- **Air** International airport in Valladolid, but best connections from Madrid.
- **Train** Extensive rail system connecting most of Central Spain.
- **Bus** Wherever trains don't go.
- **Road** Good network of motorways, with smaller connecting roads.

⭧ BE FOREWARNED

- **Most museums** Close on Monday.
- **Many restaurants** Close on Sunday night and all day Monday.
- **Semana Santa** Accommodation during Holy Week is scarce and expensive – book weeks, even months in advance.

CENTRAL SPAIN ITINERARIES

CITIES OF THE NORTH Three Days

Vibrant urban life set against the backdrop of monumental architecture is something of a speciality in Central Spain. The three cities covered here are each worth at least a day – they're easily accessible from Madrid and they're close enough to each other to ensure you don't lose too much time en route.

For centuries, **(1) Toledo** (p142) was Spain's capital-in-waiting and a world-renowned centre for learning and tolerance among its Muslim, Jewish and Christian population – Toledo's grand public buildings from all three communities are almost without peer. Stay overnight to fully appreciate the city once the day-trippers have headed elsewhere. Away to the northeast (you may have to go via Madrid), **(2) Salamanca** (p134) is one of Spain's most uniformly magnificent provincial towns, a showpiece of soothing Renaissance sandstone architecture with student life coursing through its streets. Finish up in **(3) Segovia** (p136), home to a castle that seems to have sprung from a child's imagination, a Roman aqueduct, a litter of distinguished churches and a nightly soundtrack that never seems to abate.

SOUTHERN ESCAPES Five Days

Extremadura is Spain's least-visited corner and its many attractions add a whole new dimension to your Spanish experience. Extremadura makes for a good detour en route to Andalucía.

The old quarter of **(1) Cáceres** (p148) is like stepping back into a quietly forgotten medieval world, even as the roar of nearby nightlife fills the air like the clamour of a distant war. Off to the east, **(2) Trujillo** (p150) has an agreeable village-like atmosphere and more grand monuments than many larger cities. East again (you'll need to detour south, then northeast), **(3) Guadalupe** (p151) is dominated by its stunning monastery (where you can sleep), and is the perfect retreat from life on the road. Visit during the week as weekend bar activity drowns out the solitude. **(4) Mérida** (p152) promises an escape of a different kind as you step back into the splendour of Ancient Rome. Your last port of call, whitewashed **(5) Zafra** (p153) strongly evokes nearby Andalucía.

CATHEDRALS & VILLAGES One Week

From the quiet murmuring of pilgrims shuffling through the cathedrals of the north to the even quieter villages in the rolling hill country deep in the Spanish interior, this itinerary traverses the heart and soul of Central Spain.

Rising up from the plains of central Castilla y León, the city of **(1) Burgos** (p140) is dominated by its glorious cathedral. South, in the

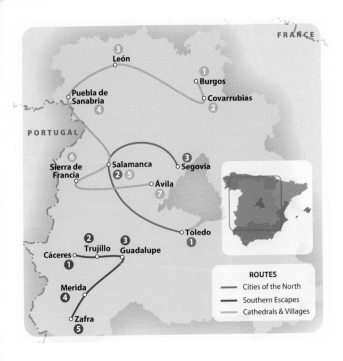

ROUTES
— Cities of the North
— Southern Escapes
— Cathedrals & Villages

Burgos hinterland, (2) Covarrubias (p137) promises one of Spain's most intimate village experiences and is serenity itself, especially after dark. The splendid cathedral in (3) León (p139) has stained-glass windows without rival in Spain. As you meander south, (4) Puebla de Sanabria (p137) perfectly captures rural Castilla y León's delightfully somnambulant air. A night in (5) Salamanca (p134) is rarely enough, but it should allow you to explore its exquisite twin cathedrals and Plaza Mayor. Salamanca also serves as the gateway to the (6) Sierra de Francia (p136), a pretty mountain region of quiet back roads and stone-and-timber villages. Your last stop is in the walled city of (7) Ávila (p132), a cathedral city par excellence.

DISCOVER CENTRAL SPAIN

Spain's Castilian heartland is a world away from the glamour of the *costas* and the clamour of the big cities. As such, it's a fascinating insight into what makes the country tick away from well-travelled tourist trails and offers Spain without the stereotypes.

The endless horizons of Central Spain's thinly populated high *meseta* (plateau) are where you'll find some of Spain's most engaging towns. Renaissance Salamanca, walled Ávila, lovely little Segovia, and Toledo and Cáceres where history seems written on every stone are the standout attractions, but the cathedral cities of León and Burgos and Merida's impressive Roman ruins are also as beautiful as they are soul-stirring. Another speciality of the area is its medieval villages, often isolated outposts of tradition and old-world architecture.

Central Spain is divided into three main regions: Castilla y León in the north, Castilla-La Mancha in the south and Extremadura in the southeast.

CASTILLA Y LEÓN

ÁVILA

pop 53,800 / elev 1130m

Ávila's old city, surrounded by imposing city walls comprising eight monumental gates, 88 watchtowers and more than 2500 turrets, is one of the best-preserved medieval bastions in all Spain.

Within the walls, Ávila can appear caught in a time warp. It's a deeply religious city that for centuries has drawn pilgrims to the cult of Santa Teresa de Ávila, with many churches, convents and high-walled palaces. As such, Ávila is the essence of Castilla, the epitome of Old Spain.

INFORMATION

Centro de Recepción de Visitantes (tourist office; ☎ 902 10 21 21; www.avilaturismo .com; Avenida de Madrid 39; ☼ 10am-6pm Nov-Mar, 9am-8pm Apr-Oct)

SIGHTS

Ávila's 12th-century **catedral** (☎ 920 21 16 41; Plaza de la Catedral; admission €4; ☼ 10am-7pm

Mon-Fri, 10am-8pm Sat, noon-6pm Sun Jun-Sep, shorter hours rest of year) is not just a house of worship, but also an ingenious fortress: its stout granite apse forms the central bulwark in the heavily fortified eastern wall of the town. Although the main fa-cade hints at the cathedral's 12th-century, Romanesque origins, the church was fin-ished 400 years later in a predominantly Gothic style, making it the first Gothic church in Spain.

Ávila's splendid **12th-century walls** (murallas; ☎ 920 21 13 87; adult/child €4/2.50) rank among the world's best-preserved medieval defensive perimeters. Raised to a height of 12m between the 11th and 12th centuries, the walls stretch for 2.5km atop the remains of earlier battlements of the Muslims and Romans.

The two access points are at the **Puerta del Alcázar** (☼ 11am-6pm Tue-Sun Oct-Apr, 11am-8pm Tue-Sun May-Sep) and the **Puerta de los Leales** (Casa de las Carnicerias; ☼ 10am-6pm Tue-Sun Oct-Apr, 10am-8pm Tue-Sun May-Sep), which allow walks of 300m and 800m, respectively.

Commissioned by the Reyes Católicos (Catholic Monarchs), Fernando and Isabel, and completed in 1492, **El Monasterio de Santo Tomás** (☎ 920 22 04 00; Plaza de Granada 1; admission €3; ☺ 10am-1pm & 4-8pm) is an exquisite example of Isabelline architecture and is rich in historical resonance.

The **Convento de Santa Teresa** (☎ 920 21 10 30; Plaza de la Santa; admission free; ☺ 8.45am-1.30pm & 3.30-9pm Tue-Sun), built in 1636 over the saint's birthplace, is the epicentre of the cult surrounding Teresa.

FESTIVALS & EVENTS

Ávila's principal festival, **Fiesta de Santa Teresa**, honours the city's patron saint with processions, concerts and fireworks in the second week of October.

Ávila is one of the best places in Castilla y León to watch the solemn processions of **Semana Santa** (Easter Holy Week).

SLEEPING

Hostal Arco San Vicente (☎ 920 22 24 98; www.arcosanvicente.com; Calle de López Núñez 6; s €45-50, d €60-70) A terrific option, this en-

gaging *hostal* (budget hotel) has lovely, brightly painted rooms and friendly owners. The rooms at the back are quieter and have a private terrace.

ourpick **Hotel Las Leyendas** (☎ 920 35 20 42; www.lasleyendas.es; Calle de Francisco Gallego 3; s €55-67, d €67-85; ❄) Occupying the house of 16th-century Ávila nobility just outside the city walls, this beautiful, intimate hotel overflows with period touches (original wooden beams, exposed brick and stonework) wedded to modern amenities.

EATING

ourpick **Restaurante Reyes Católicos** (☎ 920 25 56 27; www.restaurante-reyescatolicos .com in Spanish; Calle de los Reyes Católicos 6; menú del día from €17, meals €25-35) Most *asadores* (restaurants specialising in roasted meats) in Ávila are old-school, with dark, wood-panelled dining areas. This slick, modern restaurant is a refreshing change.

Mesón del Rastro (☎ 920 21 12 19; Plaza del Rastro 1; menú del día €20; ☺ lunch & dinner Thu-Sat, lunch only Sun-Wed) The dining room at Mesón del Rastro, with its dark-wood

CENTRAL SPAIN

CASTILLA Y LEÓN

OLIVER STREWE

Celebrating Semana Santa (Holy Week) in Ávila

beams, announces immediately that this is a bastion of Castilian cooking. Expect hearty, delicious mainstays such as *chuleton de Ávila* (€13), *judías del barco de Ávila* (€7) and *cordero asado* (roast lamb; €15).

GETTING THERE & AWAY

From the **train station** (☎ 902 24 02 02; Paseo de la Estación), more than 30 trains run daily to Madrid (from €6.50, 1¼ to two hours) and a handful to Salamanca (€8.40, one to 1½ hours).

SALAMANCA

pop 156,000

Whether floodlit by night or bathed in midday sun, there's something magical about Salamanca. This is a city of rare architectural splendour, awash with sandstone overlaid with Latin inscriptions in ochre, and with an extraordinary virtuosity of plateresque and Renaissance styles. But this is also Castilla's liveliest city, home to a massive Spanish and international student population who throng the streets at night and provide the city with so much life.

INFORMATION

Municipal tourist office (☎ 923 21 83 42; www.salamanca.es; Plaza Mayor 14; ⏱ 9am-2pm & 4.30-8pm Mon-Fri, 10am-8pm Sat, 10am-2pm Sun)

Regional tourist office (☎ 923 26 85 71; Casa de las Conchas, Rúa Mayor s/n; ⏱ 9am-2pm & 5-8pm daily mid-Sep–Jun, 9am-8pm Sun-Thu, 9am-9pm Fri & Sat Jul–mid-Sep)

SIGHTS

PLAZA MAYOR

Built between 1729 and 1755, Salamanca's exceptional grand square is widely considered Spain's most beautiful central plaza, particularly at night when it's illuminated (until midnight) to magical effect. Designed by Alberto Churriguera, it's a remarkably harmonious and controlled baroque display.

CATEDRAL NUEVA

The tower of the late-Gothic **Catedral Nueva** (☎ 923 21 74 76; Plaza Anaya; ⏱ 9am-8pm) lords over the centre of Salamanca, its compelling *churrigueresco* dome visible from almost every angle. It is, however, the magnificent Renaissance doorways, particularly the Puerta del Nacimiento on the western face, that stand out as one of several miracles worked in the city's sandstone facades.

For fine views over Salamanca, head to the **Puerta de la Torre** (Ieronimus; Plaza de Juan XXIII; admission €3.25; ⏱ 10am-7.15pm), at the southwestern corner of the cathedral's facade.

CATEDRAL VIEJA

The Catedral Nueva's largely Romanesque predecessor, the **Catedral Vieja** (adult/student €4.25/2; ⏱ 10am-7.30pm) is adorned with an exquisite 15th-century altarpiece, with 53 panels depicting scenes from the lives of Christ and Mary, topped by a representation of the Final Judgment – it's one of the most beautiful Renaissance altarpieces beyond Italy's shores.

UNIVERSIDAD CIVIL

The visual feast of the entrance facade to Salamanca's **university** (☎ 923 29 44 00; Calle de los Libreros; adult/student €4/2, free Mon morning; ⏱ 9.30am-1pm & 4-7pm Mon-Fri, 9.30am-1pm & 4-6.30pm Sat, 10am-1pm Sun) is a tapestry in sandstone, bursting with images of mythical heroes, religious scenes and coats of arms.

SLEEPING

ourpick **Hostal Catedral** (☎ 923 27 06 14; Rúa Mayor 46; s/d €30/48; ❄) Just across from the cathedrals, this lovely *hostal* has a few

WAYNE WALTON

Plaza Mayor, Salamanca

extremely pretty, clean-as-a-whistle, bright bedrooms with showers.

Hostal Concejo (☎ 923 21 47 37; www .hconcejo.com in Spanish; Plaza de la Libertad 1; s €45-54, d €56-69, tr €79-92; P ⊠ 🖳) A cut above your average drab and functional Spanish *hostal,* the stylish Concejo has polished wood floors, and some rooms, although small, have balconies overlooking a pretty square.

our pick **Microtel Placentinos** (☎ 923 28 15 31; www.microtelplacentinos.com; Calle de Placentinos 9; s €54-80, d €67-92; ⊠) One of Salamanca's most charming boutique hotels, Microtel Placentinos is tucked away on a quiet street and has rooms with exposed stone walls and wooden beams.

EATING

our pick **Mandala Café** (☎ 923 12 33 42; Calle de Serranos 9-11; meals €15-20; V) Cool, casual and deservedly popular, Mandala specialises in a wide range of *platos combinados* (combination plates; €4.20 to €9). There are also salads and plenty of vegetarian choices.

our pick **Mesón Cervantes** (☎ 923 21 72 13; Plaza Mayor 15; meals €25-30; ⏰ 10am-midnight) This is another great place where you can eat at the outdoor tables on the plaza, but the dark wooden beams and atmospheric buzz of the Spanish crowd on the 1st floor should be experienced at least once.

El Pecado (☎ 923 26 65 58; Plaza de Poeta Iglesias 12; meals €40, menú de degustación €45) One of the trendy places to regularly attract Spanish celebrities (such as Pedro Almodóvar and Ferran Adrià) in recent times, El Pecado (The Sin) has an intimate dining room and quirky, creative menu.

DRINKING

Taberna La Rayuela (Rúa Mayor 19; ⏰ 6pm-1am Sun-Thu, 6pm-2am Fri & Sat) This low-lit upstairs bar buzzes with a 20-something crowd and is probably our favourite spot in town for first drinks.

Tío Vivo (Calle del Clavel 3; ⏰ 4pm-late) Here you can sip drinks by flickering candle-light. It's in the must-visit category, not least to peek at the whimsical decor of carousel horses and oddball antiquities.

GETTING THERE & AWAY

Up to eight trains depart daily for Madrid's Chamartín station (€16.50, 2½ hours) via Ávila (€8.40, one hour).

SIERRA DE FRANCIA

Hidden away in a remote corner of south-western Castilla y León, this mountainous region with wooded hillsides and pretty stone-and-timber villages is among Castilla y León's best-kept secrets. Quiet mountain roads connect villages that you could easily spend days exploring and where the pace of life remains untouched by the modern world.

LA ALBERCA

pop 1160 / elev 1048m

La Alberca is one of the largest and most beautifully preserved of the Sierra de Francia's villages, a historic and harmonious huddle of narrow alleys flanked by gloriously ramshackle houses built of stone, wood beams and plaster.

La Alberca's classiest hotel, **Hotel Doña Teresa** (☎ 923 41 53 08; www.hoteldeteresa.com in Spanish; Carretera Mogarraz; s/d from €60/80) is a perfect fit for the village's old-world charm and is just a short stroll from Plaza Mayor. It also has a good restaurant.

Buses travel between La Alberca and Salamanca (€4.75, around 30 minutes) twice daily on weekdays and once a day on weekends.

SEGOVIA

pop 56,100 / elev 1002m

Unesco World Heritage–listed Segovia has always had a whiff of legend about it, not least in the myths that Segovia was founded by Hercules or by the son of Noah. It may also have something to do with the fact that nowhere else in Spain has such a stunning monument to Roman grandeur (the soaring aqueduct) survived in the heart of a vibrant modern city. Or maybe it's because art really has imitated life Segovia-style – Walt Disney is said to have modelled Sleeping Beauty's castle in California's Disneyland on Segovia's Alcázar. Whatever it is, the effect is stunning: a city of warm terracotta and sandstone hues set amid the rolling hills of Castilla and against the backdrop of the Sierra de Guadarrama.

INFORMATION

Centro de Recepción de Visitantes (tourist office; ☎ 921 46 67 20; www.turismo desegovia.com; Plaza del Azoguejo 1; ☼ 10am-7pm Sun-Fri, 10am-8pm Sat)

SIGHTS

Segovia's most recognisable symbol is **El Acueducto** (Roman aqueduct), an 894m-long engineering wonder that looks like an enormous comb plunged into Segovia. First raised here by the Romans in the 1st century AD, the aqueduct was built with not a drop of mortar to hold the more than 20,000 uneven granite blocks together. It's made up of 163 arches and, at its highest point in Plaza del Azoguejo, rises 28m high.

From Plaza del Azoguejo, beside the aqueduct, Calle Real winds up into the heart of Segovia.

A little further on you reach **Plaza de San Martín**, one of the most captivating little squares in Segovia. The square is presided over by a statue of Juan Bravo and the 14th-century **Torreón de Lozoya** (☎ 921 46 24 61; admission free; ☼ 5-9pm Tue-Fri, noon-2pm & 5-9pm Sat & Sun), a tower that was once an armoury and now houses exhibitions. The pièce de résistance, however, is the Romanesque **Iglesia de San Martín**, with the segoviano touch of a Mudéjar tower and arched gallery. The interior boasts a Flemish Gothic chapel.

ALBERTO PAREDES/ALAMY

Traditional wooden door in Candelario

⤵ IF YOU LIKE...

If you like **La Alberca** (opposite), Central Spain is home to scores of equally captivating villages:

- **San Martín del Castañar** Half-timbered, agreeably ramshackle stone village close to La Alberca.
- **Puebla de Sanabria** Ancient alleyways unfolding around a 15th-century castle in northwestern Castilla y León.
- **Candelario** Dramatic stone-and-wood village high in the Sierra de Béjar in southwestern Castilla y León.
- **Pedraza de la Sierra** Captivating walled village with an evocative castle northeast of Segovia.
- **Covarrubias** Charming riverside hamlet fanning out from cobblestone squares southeast of Burgos.
- **Peñaranda de Duero** Fortress-village with stately Plaza Mayor and a grand Renaissance palace along the Río Duero.
- **Calatañazor** Tiny and romantic hilltop village with crooked, cobbled lanes, terracotta roofs and a medieval air west of Soria.
- **Pastrana** An unspoiled village with honey-coloured stone buildings and a Tuscany feel in northern Castilla-La Mancha.
- **Atienza** A postcard-perfect walled medieval village crowned by a ruined castle close to Sigüenza.
- **Medinaceli** Stone-built village high on a hill with Roman ruins south of Soria.

Started in 1525 after its Romanesque predecessor had burned to the ground in the War of the Communities, the **catedral** (☎ 921 46 22 05; Plaza Mayor; adult/concession €3/2, 9.30am-1.15pm Sun free; ⏱ 9.30am-5.30pm Oct-Mar, 9.30am-6.30pm Apr-Sep) is a final, powerful expression of Gothic architecture in Spain that took almost 200 years to complete; the cathedral was completed and consecrated in 1768.

CENTRAL SPAIN

CASTILLA Y LEÓN

SEGOVIA

Rapunzel towers, turrets topped with slate witches' hats and a *deep* moat at its base make the **Alcázar** (☎ 921 46 07 59; www.alcazardesegovia.com; Plaza de la Reina Victoria Eugenia; adult/concession €4/3, tower €2, EU citizens free 3rd Tue of month; ☉ 10am-6pm Oct-Mar, 10am-7pm Apr-Sep) a prototype fairy-tale castle, so much so that its design inspired Walt Disney's vision of Sleeping Beauty's castle. Fortified since Roman days, the site takes its name from the Arabic *al-qasr* (fortress). It was rebuilt and expanded in the 13th and 14th centuries, but the whole lot burned down in 1862. What you see today is an evocative, over-the-top reconstruction of the original.

Highlights include the **Sala de las Piñas** and the **Sala de Reyes**. The views from the summit of the **Torre de Juan II** are truly exceptional, and put the old town's hilltop location into full context.

SLEEPING

our pick Hostal Juan Bravo (☎ 921 46 34 13; Calle de Juan Bravo 12; d with washbasin/bathroom €35/43) An excellent choice with sparkling rooms, Hostal Juan Bravo has rooms at the back with stunning views of the Sierra de Guadarrama. The friendly owners round out a great package.

our pick Hospedería La Gran Casa Mudéjar (☎ 921 46 62 50; www.lacasamudejar.com; Calle de Isabel La Católica 8; d €60-160; ⊠ 🖳) Spread over two buildings, this place has been magnificently renovated, blending genuine, 15th-century Mudéjar ceilings in some rooms with modern amenities.

EATING

Casa Duque (☎ 921 46 24 87; www.restauranteduque.es; Calle de Cervantes 12; menús del día €21-40) They've been serving *cochinillo asado*

(€19) here since the 1890s and long ago mastered the art. For the uninitiated, try the *menú segoviano* (€31), which includes *cochinillo,* or the *menú gastronómico* (€40), which gives a taste of many local specialities.

ourpick Restaurante El Fogón Sefardí (☎ 921 46 62 50; www.lacasamudejar.com; Calle de Isabel La Católica 8; meals €30-40) This is one of the most original places in town, serving Sephardic cuisine in a restaurant with an intimate patio or a splendid dining hall with original, 15th-century Mudéjar flourishes.

GETTING THERE & AWAY

Up to nine normal trains run daily from Madrid to Segovia (€5.90 one way, two hours), leaving you at the main train station 2.5km from the aqueduct. The faster option is the high-speed AVE (€9 one-way, 35 minutes), which deposits you at the new Segovia-Guiomar station, 5km from the aqueduct.

LEÓN

pop 135,100 / elev 527m

León is one of our favourite cities in the region, combining stunning historical architecture with an irresistible energy. Its standout attraction is the cathedral, one of the most beautiful in all of Spain. By night León is taken over by its large student population, who provide it with a deep-into-the-night soundtrack of revelry that floods the narrow streets and plazas of the picturesque old quarter, the Barrio Húmedo.

INFORMATION

Tourist office (☎ 987 23 70 82; Plaza de la Regla; ⏰ 9am-2pm & 5-8pm Mon-Fri, 10am-2pm & 5-8pm Sat & Sun Oct-Jun, 9am-8pm daily Jul-Sep) The tourist office also organises guided city tours.

ALDO PAVAN

León Cathedral

⯈ CATEDRAL

León's 13th-century cathedral, with its soaring towers, flying buttresses and truly breathtaking interior, is the city's spiritual heart.

After going through the main entrance, lorded over by the scene of the Last Supper, an extraordinary gallery of *vidrieras* (stained-glass windows) awaits. French in inspiration and mostly executed from the 13th to the 16th centuries, the windows evoke an atmosphere unlike that of any other cathedral in Spain; the kaleidoscope of coloured light is offset by the otherwise gloomy interior.

Things you need to know: ☎ 987 87 57 70; www.catedraldeleon.org in Spanish; ⏰ 8.30am-1.30pm & 4-7pm Mon-Sat, 8.30am-2.30pm & 5-7pm Sun Oct-Jun, 8.30am-1.30pm & 4-8pm Mon-Sat, 8.30am-2.30pm & 5-8pm Sun Jul-Sep

SIGHTS

REAL BASÍLICA DE SAN ISIDORO

Older even than the cathedral, the Real Basílica de San Isidoro provides a stunning Romanesque counterpoint to the former's Gothic strains.

The attached **Panteón Real** (☎ 987 87 61 61; admission €4, free Thu afternoon; ⏰ 10am-1.30pm & 4-6.30pm Mon-Sat, 10am-1.30pm Sun

CENTRAL SPAIN

CASTILLA Y LEÓN

WAYNE WALTON
Cathedral exterior, Astorga

⤷ IF YOU LIKE...

If you like the cathedrals in **León** (p139) and **Burgos** (p141), the cathedrals in the following towns will also appeal:

- **Palencia** One of the largest Castilian cathedrals, with a treasure trove of religious art and ornate chapels.
- **Plasencia** Two cathedrals in one: Gothic and plateresque from the 16th century, and Romanesque from the 13th century.
- **Astorga** Plateresque on the outside and Gothic on the inside with a stunning altarpiece.

Sep-Jun, 9am-8pm Mon-Sat, 9am-2pm Sun Jul & Aug) houses the remaining sarcophagi, which rest with quiet dignity beneath a canopy of some of the finest Romanesque frescoes in Spain.

SLEEPING

Hostal Albany (☎ 987 26 46 00; www.albany leon.com; Calle de la Paloma 13; s/d €35/50; 🖳) The sort of place you'd expect to find in Barcelona or Madrid, Hostal Albany is a high-class *hostal* with a designer touch. Clean lines, plasma TVs, great bathrooms and cheerful colour schemes abound.

ourpick **La Posada Regia** (☎ 987 21 31 73; www.regialeon.com in Spanish; Calle de Regidores 9-11; s €55-65, d €90-120) You won't find many

places better than this in northern Spain. The secret is a 14th-century building, magnificently restored (wooden beams, exposed brick and understated antique furniture), with individually styled rooms, character that overflows into the public areas and supremely comfortable beds and bathrooms.

Hostal de San Marcos (☎ 987 23 73 00; www.parador.es; Plaza de San Marcos 7; d from €198; 🗙 🖳) León's sumptuous *parador* is one of the finest hotels in Spain. With charming, palatial rooms fit for royalty, this is one of the *parador* chain's flagship properties.

EATING

ourpick **El Tizón** (☎ 987 25 60 49; Plaza de San Martín 1; menú del día €13, meals €25-30; 🕒 lunch & dinner Mon-Wed, Fri & Sat, lunch only Sun) The tapas are good here, but the small sit-down restaurant, with an abundant set lunch, is even better. No wonder it's always full.

Restaurante Artesano (☎ 987 21 53 22; www.palaciojabalquinto.com in Spanish; Calle de Juan de Arfe 2; menú del día €18, meals €35) One of the classier places to eat in León, Restaurante Artesano combines creative food, modern art and the renovated 17th-century Palacio Jabal Quinto.

GETTING THERE & AWAY

Regular daily trains travel to Valladolid (from €9.60, two hours), Burgos (from €17.90, two hours), Oviedo (from €7.15, two hours), Madrid (from €22.40, 4¼ hours) and Barcelona (from €43.20, 10 hours).

BURGOS

pop 174,100 / elev 861m

The extraordinary Gothic cathedral of Burgos is one of Spain's glittering jewels of religious architecture. But this is a city that rewards deeper exploration: below the surface lies vibrant nightlife, good restaurants and, when the sun's shining, pretty streetscapes that extend far beyond the landmark cathedral. There's even a whiff of legend about the place: beneath the majestic spires of the cathedral lies Burgos' favourite and most roguish son, El Cid.

INFORMATION

Municipal tourist office (☎ 947 28 88 74; www.aytoburgos.es in Spanish; Plaza del Rey Fernando 2; ✆ 10am-2pm & 4.30-7.30pm Mon-Fri, 10am-1.30pm & 4-7.30pm Sat & Sun mid-Sep-Jun, 10am-8pm daily Jul-mid-Sep)

SIGHTS

The Unesco World Heritage–listed **cat-edral** (☎ 947 20 47 12; Plaza del Rey Fernando; adult/child/pilgrim & student/senior €4/1/2.50/3; ✆ 9.30am-7.30pm 19 Mar-Oct, 10am-7pm Nov-18 Mar) is a masterpiece that's probably worth the trip to Burgos on its own. It had humble origins as a modest Romanesque church, but work began on a grander scale in 1221. Remarkably, within 40 years most of the

French Gothic structure that you see today had been completed. The twin towers, which went up later in the 15th century, each represent 84m of richly decorated Gothic fantasy and they're surrounded by a sea of similarly intricate spires.

The main altar is a typically overwhelming piece of gold-encrusted extravagance, while directly beneath the star-vaulted central dome lies the **tomb of El Cid**.

SLEEPING

ourpick **Hotel Norte y Londres** (☎ 947 26 41 25; www.hotelnorteylondres.com; Plaza de Alonso Martínez 10; s €46-75, d €55-120; P ⌨) Set in a former 16th-century palace and with understated period charm, this fine hotel promises spacious rooms with antique furnishings, polished wooden floors and pretty balconies; those on the 4th floor are more modern.

Hotel La Puebla (☎ 947 20 00 11; www .hotellapuebla.com; Calle de la Puebla 20; s €58-70, d €73-106; P ✖ ⌨) This boutique hotel adds a touch of style to the Burgos hotel scene, with professional service. The

Hostal de San Marcos, León

rooms aren't huge and most don't have views, but they're softly lit and supremely comfortable.

EATING

ourpick **Cervecería Morito** (☎ 947 26 75 55; Calle de la Sombrerería; ☾ 1-3.30pm & 7.30pm-midnight) Cervecería Morito is the undisputed king of Burgos tapas bars and it's always crowded, even on the quietest of nights; if it's full downstairs, there's more room on the 1st floor.

ourpick **Casa Ojeda** (☎ 947 20 90 52; www.grupojeda.com in Spanish; Calle de Vitoria 5; meals €30-40; ☾ lunch & dinner Mon-Sat, lunch only Sun) This Burgos institution, all sheathed in dark wood, is one of the best places in town to try *cordero asado* (€21).

DRINKING

There are two main hubs of Burgos nightlife. The first is along Calle de San Juan and Calle de la Puebla, with plenty of bars to get your night started.

For later nights on weekends, Calle del Huerto del Rey, just northeast of the cathedral and known locally as Las Llanas, is the sort of street you'd hate to live above, with literally dozens of bars.

SHOPPING

Casa Quintanilla (Calle de la Paloma 22; ☾ 10am-8.30pm Mon-Sat, 10am-2pm Sun) This is the pick of many stores around the centre offering local produce that's ideal for a picnic or a gift for back home.

GETTING THERE & AWAY

Burgos is connected with Madrid (from €23.10, four hours, up to seven daily), Bilbao (from €16.60, three hours, five daily), León (from €17.90, two hours, four daily), Valladolid (from €8.20, 1¼ hours, up to 13 daily) and Salamanca (from €20.10, 2½ hours, three daily).

CASTILLA-LA MANCHA

TOLEDO
pop 55,100 / elev 655m

Toledo is Spain's equivalent of a downsized Rome. You don't need a metro to cover the city's sights, only a pair of sturdy shoes. Toledo's labyrinth of narrow streets, plazas and inner patios is also reminiscent of the *medinas* (towns) of Damascus, Cairo or Morocco's Fez, although the historic diversity of Romans, Jews and Muslims equals an intriguing combination of synagogues and churches, as well as mosques. Add to this a lofty setting, high above Río Tajo, and it's no surprise that Toledo is one of Spain's most-visited cities.

INFORMATION

Main tourist office (☎ 925 25 40 30; www.toledoturismo.com; Plaza del Ayuntamiento s/n; ☾ 10.30am-2.30pm Mon, 10.30am-2.30pm & 4.30-7pm Tue-Sun) Located across from the cathedral.

SIGHTS

In summer, many sights open for up to three hours longer than the times cited.

CATEDRAL DE TOLEDO

Toledo's **catedral** (Plaza del Ayuntamiento; adult/under 12yr €7/free; ☾ 10.30am-6.30pm Mon-Sat, 2-6.30pm Sun) dominates the skyline, reflecting the city's historical significance as the heart of Catholic Spain.

During the three centuries of Muslim rule it contained Toledo's central mosque, which was subsequently destroyed in 1085. The construction of the cathedral dates from the 13th century.

Mudéjar elements are visible in the interior decoration, and the Spanish Renaissance is evident in the many chapels that line the church naves.

Sinagoga de Santa María La Blanca, Toledo

ALBERTO PAREDES/ALAMY

IGLESIA DE SAN ILDEFONSO

The main attraction of this pretty 18th-century **church** (Plaza Juan de Mariana 1; admission €1.90; ☺ 10am-6.45pm), also known as the Iglesia de los Jesuítas, is the view from the top of the twin towers.

JEWISH QUARTER

Toledo's former *judería* (Jewish quarter) was once home to 11 synagogues.

Of the two synagogues remaining, don't miss **Sinagoga del Tránsito**, which was built in 1355 by special permission of Pedro I (construction of synagogues was by then prohibited in Christian Spain). The synagogue now houses the **Museo Sefardi** (☎ 925 22 36 65; www.museosefardi .net in Spanish; Calle Samuel Leví s/n; adult/under 12yr/12-25yr €2.40/free/1.20, audioguide €3; ☺ 10am-6pm Tue-Sat, 10am-2pm Sun).

Nearby, **Sinagoga de Santa María La Blanca** (☎ 925 22 72 57; Calle de los Reyes Católicos 4; admission €2.30; ☺ 10am-6pm) is characterised by the horseshoe arches that delineate the five naves – classic Almohad architecture.

North of the synagogues lies the Franciscan monastery and church of **San Juan de los Reyes** (☎ 925 22 38 02; Calle San Juan de los Reyes 2; admission €1.90; ☺ 10am-6pm), notable for its delightful cloisters.

ISLAMIC TOLEDO

On the northern slopes of town you'll find the **Mezquita del Cristo de la Luz** (Cuesta de Carmelitas Descalzos 10; adult/under 12yr/12-25yr €1.90/free/1.40; ☺ 10am-6pm), a modest mosque that is nonetheless quite beautiful.

SLEEPING

La Posada de Manolo (☎ 925 28 22 50; www .laposadademanolo.com; Calle de Sixto Ramón Parro 8; s/d incl breakfast from €42/66) This boutique-style hotel has themed each floor with furnishings and decor reflecting one of the three cultures of Toledo: Christian, Islamic and Jewish. There are stunning views of the old town and cathedral from the terrace.

ourpick **Hostal Casa de Cisneros** (☎ 925 22 88 28; www.hostal-casa-de-cisneros.com;

TOLEDO

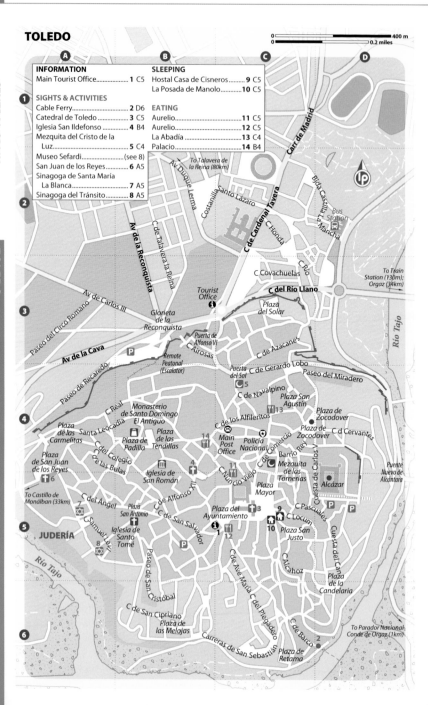

INFORMATION
Main Tourist Office...................**1** C5

SIGHTS & ACTIVITIES
Cable Ferry.............................**2** D6
Catedral de Toledo **3** C5
Iglesia San Ildefonso **4** B4
Mezquita del Cristo de la
  Luz..................................**5** C4
Museo Sefardi.........................(see 8)
San Juan de los Reyes **6** A5
Sinagoga de Santa María
  La Blanca............................**7** A5
Sinagoga del Tránsito **8** A5

SLEEPING
Hostal Casa de Cisneros **9** C5
La Posada de Manolo.............**10** C5

EATING
Aurelio...................................**11** C5
Aurelio...................................**12** C5
La Abadía **13** C4
Palacio..................................**14** B4

0 ———————— 400 m
0 ———————— 0.2 miles

To Talavera de
la Reina (80km)

To Train
Station (130m);
Orgaz (34km)

JUDERÍA

To Castillo de
Monálban (33km)

To Parador Nacional
Conde de Orgaz (1km)

Calle del Cardenal Cisneros; s/d €50/80; 🖫) Across from the cathedral, this seductive *hostal* is built on the site of an 11th-century Islamic palace, parts of which can be spied via a glass porthole in the lobby floor. In comparison, this building is a 16th-century youngster with pretty stone-and-wood-beamed rooms and exceptionally voguish en suite bathrooms.

Parador Nacional Conde de Orgaz (☎ 925 22 18 50; www.parador.es; Cerro del Emperador s/n; s/d €114/159; P 🖫 🖲) High above the southern bank of Río Tajo, Toledo's *parador* (luxurious state-owned hotel) boasts a classy interior and breathtaking city views. However, current renovation works could be a distraction; call first to ensure you are not sleeping within earshot of a pneumatic drill.

EATING

ourpick Palacio (☎ 925 21 59 72; Calle Alfonso X el Sabio 3; menú €13.90, meals €14-18) An unpretentious place where stained glass, beams and efficient old-fashioned service combine with traditional no-nonsense cuisine. Hungry? Try a gut-busting bowl of *judías con perdiz* (white beans with partridge) for starters.

La Abadía (☎ 925 25 11 40; Plaza de San Nicolás 3; meals €25-30, menú €28; V) In a former 16th-century palace, this atmospheric bar and restaurant is ideal for romancing couples. The menu includes meat and fish plates, as well as lightweight dishes like goat's cheese salad with pumpkin and sunflower seeds – perfect for small (distracted) appetites.

Aurelio (☎ 925 22 13 92; Plaza del Ayuntamiento 4; meals from €35; 🕙 closed dinner Sun) The three restaurants under this name are among the best of Toledo's top-end eateries (the other locations are Calle de la Sinagoga 1 and 6). Game, fresh produce and traditional Toledan dishes are prepared with panache.

GETTING THERE & AWAY
The N401 connects Toledo with Madrid.

The high-speed AVE service runs every hour or so to Madrid's Atocha station (€9, 30 minutes).

ALMAGRO
pop 9100

The jewel in Almagro's crown is the extraordinary Plaza Mayor with its wavy tiled roofs, stumpy columns and faded bottle-green porticoes. Although it looks quasi-oriental, the 16th-century plaza has Germanic roots, dating back to the reign of Carlos I. The town is a delight to wander around, the relatively traffic-free cobbled streets flanked by Renaissance palaces, churches and shops selling local cheeses, embroidery and basketware.

INFORMATION
Tourist office (☎ 926 86 07 17; www.ciudad-almagro.com in Spanish; Plaza Mayor 1; 🕙 10am-2pm & 5-8pm Tue-Fri, 10am-2pm & 5-7pm Sat, 11am-2pm Sun)

SIGHTS
Opening onto the plaza is the oldest theatre in Spain: the 17th-century **Corral de Comedias** (☎ 926 88 24 58; Plaza Mayor 18; adult/under 12yr/12-25yr incl audioguide in English €2.50/free/2; 🕙 10am-2pm & 5-7pm Tue-Sat, 11am-2pm & 5-7pm Sun Sep-Jun, 10am-2pm & 6-9pm Tue-Fri, 10am-2pm & 6-8pm Sat, 11am-2pm & 6-8pm Sun Jul & Aug), an evocative tribute to the Golden Age of Spanish theatre with rows of wooden balconies facing the original stage, complete with dressing rooms. It's still used for performances, especially during July's **Festival Internacional de Teatro Clásico** (www.festivaldealmagro.com in Spanish).

SLEEPING

La Posada de Almagro (☎/fax 926 26 12 01; www.laposadadealmagro.es; Calle de Gran Maestre 5; s/d from €35/55; ☒) This 16th-century former coaching inn has retained its original character with open galleries, rustic beamed rooms and courtyards. The downstairs bar-restaurant is popular (and noisy).

Retiro del Maestre (☎ 926 26 11 85; www.retirodelmaestre.com in Spanish; Calle San Bartolomé 5; s/d incl breakfast €70/87; P ☒ 🖳) Enjoy five-star treatment and style here without the hurly-burly of a big hotel. The rooms are spacious and washed in warm yellow and blue; go for those on the upper floor with private balconies.

EATING

Bar Las Nieves (☎ 926 86 12 90; Plaza Mayor 52; snacks from €5, paella €5) One of the better Plaza Mayor bars, featuring chairs on the square and less-expensive light eats, plus paella on Sundays.

El Corregidor (☎ 926 86 06 48; Calle de Jerónimo Ceballos 2; menú €30, meals €35-40; ☽ closed Mon except Jul) The town's best eating and drinking place, with several lively bars flanking a leafy central courtyard and a hotchpotch decor that somehow works. The upstairs restaurant features high-quality Manchegan cooking; check out the wall of culinary awards.

GETTING THERE & AWAY

Two trains go daily to Madrid (€13.65, 2¾ hours), with up to six to Ciudad Real (€2.30, 15 minutes) and two to Valencia (€25.20, 4¼ hours); for destinations to the south, change in Ciudad Real.

CONSUEGRA

This is *the* place for the novice windmill-spotter, where you can get that classic shot of a dozen *molinos de vientos* (windmills) flanking the 13th-century **castle** (admission €2; ☽ 9.30am-1.30pm & 3.30-5.30pm; ♿).

The **tourist office** (☎ 925 47 57 31; ☽ 9am-2pm & 4.30-7pm Mon-Fri, from 10.30am Sat & Sun) is in the Bolero mill (they all have names), which is the first you come to as the road winds up from the town.

DAVID TOMLINSON

'Hanging House', Cuenca

There are regular weekday buses (three on weekends) running between Consuegra and Toledo (€4.34, one hour), and up to seven buses daily to Madrid (€7, two hours).

CAMPO DE CRIPTANA

Ten windmills straddle the town's summit, and their proximity to the surrounding houses makes an interesting contrast with Consuegra. The town is pleasant, if unexceptional. The **tourist office** (☎ 926 56 22 31; 🕗 10am-2pm & 5-8pm Tue-Sat, 10am-2pm Sun) is in the Poyatos mill.

If you want to stay overnight, lovely **Hospedería Casa de la Torrecilla** (☎ 926 58 91 30; www.casadelatorrecilla.com; Calle Cardenal Monescillo 17; s/d €35/53) has a vividly patterned and tiled interior patio. Housed in an early-20th-century nobleman's house, the rooms have parquet floors and are spacious and atmospheric; several have original stone fireplaces and balconies.

CUENCA

pop 53,000

A World Heritage site, Cuenca is one of Spain's most enchanting cities, its old centre a stage set of evocative medieval buildings. Most emblematic are the *casas colgadas,* the hanging houses, which perch above the deep gorges that surround the town. As in so many Spanish cities, the surrounding new town is modern and forgettable, so keep the blinkers on during the approach – up the hill lies another world.

INFORMATION

Main tourist office (☎ 969 32 31 19; www.aytocuenca.org in Spanish; Plaza Mayor s/n; 🕗 9am-9pm Mon-Sat, 9am-2.30pm Sun May-Sep, 9am-2pm & 5-8pm Mon-Sat, 9am-2pm Sun Oct-Apr) In the historic centre.

CHRISTOPHER GROENHOUT

Islamic architecture, Toledo (p142)

CENTRAL SPAIN

CASTILLA-LA MANCHA

SIGHTS & ACTIVITIES

The most striking element of medieval Cuenca, the *casas colgadas* jut out precariously over the steep defile of Río Huécar. Dating from the 16th century, the houses with their layers of wooden balconies seem to emerge from the rock as if an extension of the cliffs. For the best views of the *casas colgadas,* cross the **Puente de San Pablo** footbridge, or walk to the northernmost tip of the old town, where a **mirador** offers unparalleled views.

FESTIVALS & EVENTS

Cuenca's **Semana Santa** celebrations are renowned throughout Spain, particularly for the eerie, silent processions through the streets of the old town.

IN SEARCH OF DON QUIJOTE

Part of the charm of a visit to Castilla-La Mancha is the chance to track down the real-life locations into which Miguel de Cervantes placed his picaresque hero. These days it requires less puzzling over maps than previously: to celebrate the fourth centenary of this epic tale in 2007, the 250km Route of Don Quijote was created, with signposts that direct you along tracks, cattle paths and historic routes throughout the region.

Out of all the places and sights you can ponder along the way, the *molinos de vientos* (windmills) are the most obvious, for it was these 'monstrous giants' that so haunted El Quijote and with which he tried to battle. Although Consuegra's are the most attractive, those that are specifically mentioned in Cervantes' novel are the windmills of Campo de Criptana (p147) and Mota del Cuervo. Other highlights on the trail include the castle of Belmonte (p152) and El Toboso, where the knight discovered the lovely Dulcinea.

SLEEPING

Posada de San José (☎ 969 21 13 00; www .posadasanjose.com; Ronda de Julián Romero 4; s/d without bathroom from €25/38, with views from €55/86) Owned by Antonio and his Canadian wife, Jennifer, this 17th-century former choir school retains an extraordinary monastic charm with its crumbling portal, uneven floors and original tiles.

Parador (☎ 969 23 23 20; www.parador .es; Calle de Hoz de Huécar; d €143; P) This majestic former convent commands stunning views of the *casas colgadas*. The aesthetically revamped rooms have a luxury corporate feel, while the public areas are headily historic with giant tapestries and antiques.

EATING

ourpick **La Bodeguilla de Basilio** (☎ 969 23 52 74; Calle Fray Luis de León 3; raciones €10-13) Arrive here with an appetite, as you're presented with a complimentary plate of tapas when you order a drink, and not just a slice of dried-up cheese – typical freebies are a combo of quail eggs, ham, fried potatoes, lettuce hearts and courgettes.

Mesón Casas Colgadas (☎ 969 22 35 52; Calle de los Canónigos 3; meals €25-35, menú €28) Housed in one of the *casas colgadas*, Cuenca's gourmet pride and joy fuses an amazing location with delicious traditional food, such as venison stew.

GETTING THERE & AWAY

Cuenca lies on the train line connecting Madrid and Valencia.

GETTING AROUND

Local buses 1 and 2 do the circuit from the new town to Plaza Mayor (€0.70, every 30 minutes) with numerous stops, including outside the train station.

EXTREMADURA

CÁCERES

pop 89,000

The Ciudad Monumental (old town) here is truly extraordinary. The narrow cobbled streets twist and climb among ancient stone walls lined with palaces and mansions while the skyline is decorated with turrets, spires, gargoyles and enormous storks' nests. Protected by defensive walls, it has survived almost intact from its 16th-century heyday. Stretching at its feet, arcaded Plaza Mayor is one of Spain's finest public squares.

INFORMATION

Municipal tourist office (☎ 927 24 71 72; Calle Ancha 7; ☻ 10am-2pm & 4.30-7.30pm or 5.30-8.30pm Tue-Sun)

SIGHTS

Enter the Ciudad Monumental from Plaza Mayor through the 18th-century **Arco de la Estrella**, built this wide for the passage of carriages. The **Concatedral de Santa María** (Plaza de Santa María; ☻ 10am-1pm & 5-8pm Mon-Sat, 9.30am-2pm & 5-8pm Sun), a 15th-century Gothic cathedral, creates an impressive opening scene.

Also on the plaza are the **Palacio Episcopal** (Bishop's Palace), the **Palacio de Mayoralgo** and the **Palacio de Ovando**, all in 16th-century Renaissance style. Just off the plaza's northeast corner is the **Palacio Carvajal** (☎ 927 25 55 97; Calle de l'Amargura 1; admission free; ☻ 9am-9pm Mon-Fri, 10am-2pm & 5-8pm Sat, 10am-2pm Sun).

Heading back through Arco de la Estrella, you can climb the 12th-century **Torre de Bujaco** (Plaza Mayor; adult/under 12yr €2/free; ☻ 10am-2pm & 5.30-8.30pm Mon-Sat, 10am-2pm Sun Apr-Sep, 10am-2pm & 4.30-7.30pm Mon-Sat, 10am-2pm Sun Oct-Mar; ☻).

SLEEPING

Hotel Don Carlos (☎ 927 22 55 27; www .hoteldoncarloscaceres.net in Spanish; Calle Donoso Cortés 15; s €33-48, d €48-65; ☻ ▣) Rooms are tastefully decorated with bare brick and stone at this welcoming small hotel, sensitively created from a long-abandoned early-19th-century house.

Parador de Cáceres (☎ 927 21 17 59; www .parador.es; Calle Ancha 6; s/d €128/154; ℗ ☻ ☻) A grand 14th-century Gothic stone build-

ing houses this elegant accommodation located deep in the walled town across from the tourist office.

EATING

Mesón El Asador (☎ 927 22 38 37; Calle de Moret 34; raciones €6-8, meals €18-25; ☻ closed Sun) Enter the dining room and you get the picture right away: one wall is covered with hung hams. You won't taste better roast pork (or lamb) in town.

El Racó de Sanguino (☎ 927 22 76 82; www.racodesanguino.es; Plaza de las Veletas 4; meals €30-40; ☻ lunch & dinner Tue-Sat & lunch Sun) Carlos Sanguino has created a traditional *extremeño* menu with an innovative twist, with dishes such as codfish scented with fresh rosemary served with a potato mousse (a nice change from fries).

JAM WORLD IMAGES/ALAMY
Arco de la Estrella, Cáceres

GETTING THERE & AWAY

Up to five trains per day run to/from Madrid (€17.80 to €24.50, four hours), Plasencia (€4.35, 1½ hours) and Mérida (€5.25, one hour).

TRUJILLO

pop 9700

Wander into Plaza Major here and you could be forgiven for thinking that you had stumbled onto the filmset of a medieval blockbuster. The square is surrounded by baroque and Renaissance stone buildings topped with a skyline of towers, turrets, cupolas, crenulations and nesting storks. Stretching beyond the square the illusion continues with a labyrinth of mansions, leafy courtyards, fruit gardens, churches and convents; Trujillo truly is one of the most captivating small towns in Spain.

INFORMATION

Tourist office (☎ 927 32 26 77; www.ay to-trujillo.com in Spanish; Plaza Mayor s/n; 🕑 10am-2pm & 4-7pm Oct-May, 10am-2pm & 5-8pm Jun-Sep)

SIGHTS

Through a twisting alley above the Palacio de la Conquista is the **Palacio Juan Pizarro de Orellana** (admission free; 🕑 10am-1.30pm & 4.30-6.30pm), converted from miniature fortress to Renaissance mansion by one of the Pizarro cousin conquistadors.

Overlooking the Plaza Mayor from the northeast corner is the 16th-century **Iglesia de San Martín** with delicate Gothic ceiling tracing, stunning stained-glass windows and a grand organ (climb up to the choir loft for the best view).

The 900m of walls circling the upper town date from Muslim times. Here, newly settled noble families built their mansions and churches after the Reconquista.

The 13th-century **Iglesia de Santa María la Mayor** (Plaza de Santa María) has a mainly Gothic nave and a Romanesque tower that you can ascend (all 106 steps) for fabulous views.

At the top of the hill, Trujillo's **castle** (☎ 927 32 26 77; Calle del Convento de las Jerónimas 12; 🕹), of 10th-century Muslim origin (evident by the horseshoe-arch gateway

Plaza Mayor, Trujillo

DAVID TOMLINSON

just inside the main entrance) and later strengthened by the Christians, is impressive, although bare but for a lone fig tree. Patrol the battlements for magnificent 360-degree sweeping views.

SLEEPING

Mesón La Cadena (☎ 927 32 14 63; fax 927 32 31 16; Plaza Mayor 8; s/d €36/46; 🚲) Occupying part of a 16th-century mansion on the plaza, the rooms have cool grey-and-white floor tiles and beams. Go for rooms 206 or 207 with their views of the square.

our pick **Posada Dos Orillas** (☎ 927 65 90 79; www.dosorillas.com; Calle de Cambrones 6; d €70-107; 🚲 🖥) This tastefully renovated 16th-century mansion in the walled town once served as a silk-weaving centre. The rooms replicate Spanish colonial taste; those in the older wing bear the names of the 'seven Trujillos' of Extremadura and the Americas.

EATING

Restaurante La Troya (☎ 927 32 13 64; Plaza Mayor 10; menú €15) The restaurant and its founder, the late Concha Álvarez, are *extremeño* institutions. You will be directed to one of several dining areas and there, without warning, be presented with a plate of tortilla, chorizo and salad, followed by a three-course menu (with truly gargantuan portions), including wine and water.

Posada Restaurante Dos Orillas (☎ 927 65 90 79; www.dosorillas.com; Calle de Cambrones 6; meals €25-30; 🕙 lunch & dinner Tue-Sat, lunch Sun; Ⓥ) Just as the hotel is a gem, so the restaurant is a place of quiet, refined eating, whether al fresco on the patio or in the dining room with its soft-hued fabrics.

GETTING THERE & AWAY

The **bus station** (☎ 927 32 12 02; Avenida de Miajadas) is 500m south of Plaza Mayor. There are services to/from Madrid (€15.20

to €19, three to 4¼ hours, up to 10 daily), Guadalupe (€5.75, 1½ hours, two daily), Cáceres (€3.55, 45 minutes, eight daily) and Mérida (€7.35, 1½ hours, three daily).

GUADALUPE

pop 2250

This sparkling white village is like a bright jewel set in the green crown of the surrounding ranges of the Sierra de Villuercas. There are thick woods of chestnut, oak and cork meshed with olive groves and vineyards. Guadalupe (from the Arabic meaning 'hidden river') appears as though from nowhere, huddled around the massive stone hulk of the Real Monasterio de Santa María de Guadalupe.

INFORMATION

Tourist office (☎ 927 15 41 28; www.puebla deguadalupe.net; Plaza Mayor s/n; 🕙 10am-2pm & 4-6pm Mon-Fri Sep-Jun, 10am-2pm & 5-7pm Mon-Fri Jul-Aug, 10am-2pm Sat & Sun)

SIGHTS

The **Real Monasterio de Santa María de Guadalupe** (☎ 927 36 70 00; Plaza Santa María de Guadalupe; 🕙 9am-8pm), a Unesco World Heritage site, was founded in 1340 by Alfonso XI on the spot where, according to legend, a shepherd found an effigy of the Virgin, hidden years earlier by Christians fleeing the Muslims. It remains one of Spain's most important pilgrimage sites.

SLEEPING

Hospedería del Real Monasterio (☎ 927 36 70 00; www.monasterioguadalupe.com; Plaza Juan Carlos I; s/d/tr €43/62/83; Ⓟ 🚲) Centred on the monastery's beautiful 16th-century Gothic cloister with high-ceilinged luxurious rooms (all different), this is *the* sleeping option in Guadalupe.

CENTRAL SPAIN

EXTREMADURA

WITOLD SKRYPCZAK

Belmonte Castle

⬎ IF YOU LIKE...

If you like Trujillo's **castle** (p150), we think you'll also be drawn to the following castles:

- **Almonacid de Toledo** Abandoned and dramatic ruined castle where El Cid may once have lived, southeast of Toledo.
- **Castillo de Montálban** Twelfth-century castle built by the Knights Templar overlooking the Río Torcón Valley, southwest of Toledo.
- **Oropesa** Fourteenth-century hilltop castle with fine mountain views, west of Talavera de la Reina.
- **Belmonte** Textbook turreted castle with sweeping views in Castilla-La Mancha; Don Quijote once paid a visit.
- **Peñafiel** One of Spain's longest and narrowest castles with a wine museum in the heart of Ribera del Duero wine country.

EATING

Hospedería del Real Monasterio (☎ 927 36 70 00; www.monasterioguadalupe.com; Plaza Juan Carlos I; meals €25) Dine grandly under the arches of the magnificent Gothic cloister or in the dining halls, rich with 17th-century timber furnishings and antique ceramics,

GETTING THERE & AWAY

Mirat (☎ 927 23 48 63) runs two daily services to/from Cáceres (€9.35, 2½ hours) via Trujillo (€5.75).

MÉRIDA

pop 74,900

Mérida, seat of the Junta de Extremadura, is remarkable for its archaeological remains. Founded as Augusta Emerita in 25 BC for veterans of Rome's campaigns in Cantabria, it has Spain's most complete Roman ruins and a magnificent classical museum.

INFORMATION

Municipal tourist office (☎ 924 33 07 22; Calle Santa Eulalia 64; ☼ 9.30am-2pm & 4-7pm or 5-8pm)

SIGHTS

The **Teatro Romano** (Calle Alvarez S de Buruaga; adult/under 12yr €7/free, incl Los Columbarios, Casa de Mitreo, Alcazaba, Zona Arqueológica de Morería, Basílica de Santa Eulalia & Circo Romano €10/free; ☼ 9.30am-1.45pm & 5-7.15pm Jun-Sep, 9.30am-1.45pm & 4-6.15pm Oct-May;), built around 15 BC to seat 6000 spectators, has a dramatic and well-preserved two-tier backdrop of stone columns. The adjoining **Anfiteatro**, opened in 8 BC for gladiatorial contests, had a capacity of 14,000.

Don't miss the extraordinarily powerful spectacle of the **Puente Romano** over the Río Guadiana, which at 792m in length with 60 granite arches, is one of the longest bridges built by the Romans.

The excellent **Museo Nacional de Arte Romano** (☎ 924 31 16 90; www.mnar.es; Calle de José Ramón Mélida; adult/senior & 18-25yr/under 18yr €2.40/1.20/1.20; ☼ 10am-2pm & 5-7pm Tue-Sat, 10am-2pm Sun Mar-Nov, 10am-2pm Tue-Sat, 10am-2pm Sun Dec-Feb) has a superb collection of statues, mosaics, frescoes, coins and other Roman artefacts.

SLEEPING

Hotel Cervantes (☎ 924 31 49 61; www.hotel cervantes.com; Calle Camilo José Cela 8; s €40-50, d €60-70; P ✕) The best deal in this price bracket with attractive half-panelled rooms with marble floors, full baths and dark-wood furniture. The bar-restaurant serves a bacon-and-egg breakfast.

Parador Vía de la Plata (☎ 924 31 38 00; www.parador.es; Plaza de la Constitución 3; s/d €118/142; P ✕ ✕ ✕) You're sleeping on the site of a Roman temple in a building that started life as a convent; the lounge was a former chapel, then served as both hospital and prison. Rear-room balconies look onto a quiet garden with fountains.

EATING

Casa Nano (☎ 924 31 82 57; Calle San Salvador Castelar 3; meals €15-20; ✕ Mon-Sat) Tucked behind Plaza de España, the *simpatico* staff here serve dishes like *cordero a la ciruela* (lamb with plums), various *bacalao* (cod) dishes and *patatas al rebujón* (wedges of thick potato omelette).

Restaurante Nicolás (☎ 924 31 96 10; Calle Felix Valverde Lillo 15; meals €20-25; ✕ lunch & dinner Mon-Sat, lunch Sun) Long admired as a local favourite, this is one of the classier city dining options.

GETTING THERE & AROUND

Up to six trains run to/from Cáceres (€5.25, one hour).

ZAFRA

pop 16,400

Gleaming white Zafra resembles an Andalucían *pueblo blanco,* except that the sea is 160km away. The narrow streets are lined with baroque churches, old-fashioned shops and traditional houses decorated by the brilliant red splashes of geraniums.

The **tourist office** (☎ 924 55 10 36; www .ayto-zafra.com in Spanish; ✕ 9.30am-2pm & 4-7pm or 5-8pm Mon-Fri, 10am-1.30pm & 5-7pm or 6-8pm Sat & Sun) is on Plaza de España, the main square.

DAVID TOMLINSON

Real Monasterio de Santa María de Guadalupe (p151)

CENTRAL SPAIN

EXTREMADURA

Teatro Romano (p152), Mérida

OLIVER STREWE

children playing football and decorating the ground with *pipas* (sunflower) shells.

SLEEPING & EATING

Hotel Plaza Grande (☎ 924 56 31 63; Calle Pasteleros 2; s/d €30/60; ﹡) The new owner has created a gem of a hotel here. Go for room 108 with its corner windows overlooking the plaza. Decor is terracotta accentuated by cream paintwork and muted earth colours. The downstairs restaurant and bar are reliably good.

Parador Hernán Cortés (☎ 924 55 45 40; www.parador.es; Plaza Corazón de María 7; s/d €115/144; ﹡ ﹡ ﹡) The large rooms are richly decorated with burgundy-coloured fabrics and antiques. The marble-pillared courtyard is truly magnificent while the secluded pool is surrounded by ivy and turrets.

La Rebotica (☎ 924 55 42 89; Calle Boticas 12; meals €35; ﹡ lunch & dinner Tue-Sat, lunch Sun) This restaurant offers a traditional meaty menu including *rabo de toro* (ox tail) and five different pork fillet dishes subtly prepared by Dutch chef Rudy Koster.

GETTING THERE & AWAY

Zafra is on the main bus and train routes linking Seville to the south with Mérida (€4.55, 65 minutes) and Badajoz (€5.75, 1¼ hours).

Zafra's 15th-century **castle**, now the town's *parador,* was built over the former Muslim Alcázar and dominates the town. **Plaza Grande** and the adjoining **Plaza Chica**, arcaded and bordered by bars, are the place to see Zafra life, from old men in flat caps playing dominoes to

CATALONIA & ARAGÓN

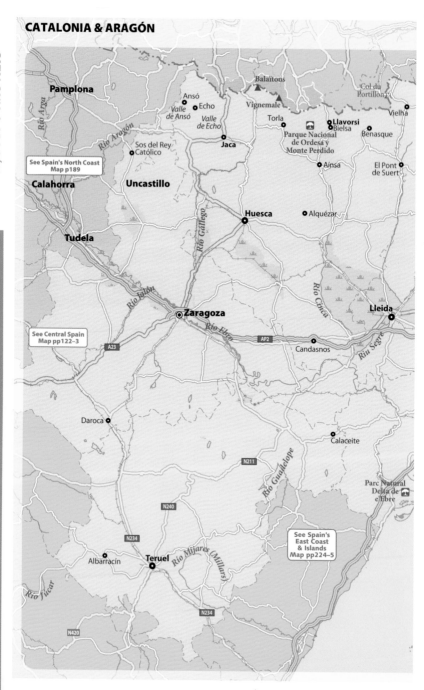

See Spain's North Coast
Map p189

See Central Spain
Map pp122–3

See Spain's
East Coast
& Islands
Map pp224–5

Pamplona

Ansó
Valle
de Ansó
Echo
Valle
de Echo

Balaïtous
Vignemale
Torla
Llavorsi
Bielsa
Benasque
Col du
Portillon
Vielha

Parque Nacional
de Ordesa y
Monte Perdido
Aínsa
El Pont
de Suert

Sos del Rey
Católico
Jaca

Calahorra
Uncastillo

Huesca
Alquézar

Tudela

Río Arga
Río Aragón
Río Gállego
Río Cinca
Río Segre

Zaragoza
Lleida

Río Jalón
Río Ebro
AP2
Candasnos
Riu Segre

A23

Daroca

Calaceite

N211
Río Guadalope

Parc Natural
Delta de
el'Ebre

N240

N234

Albarracín
Teruel
Río Mijares (Millars)

Río Júcar

N234

N420

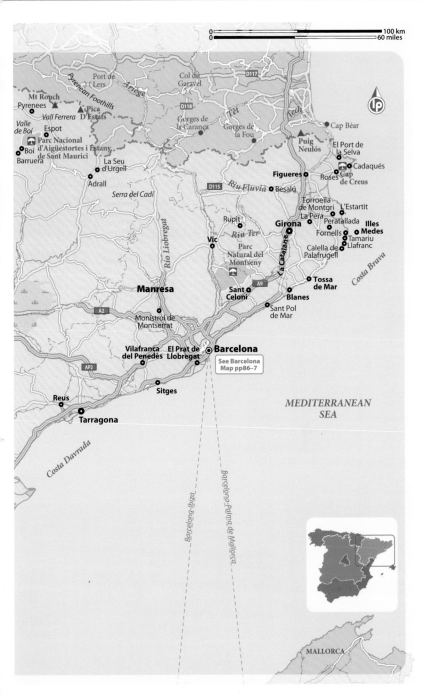

0   100 km
0   60 miles

Port de
Lers

Col du
Garavel

D117

Ariège

Pyrenean Foothills

Mt Rouch
Pyrenees

Vall Ferrera   Pica
D'Estats

D118

Tèt

Gorges de
la Caranca

Gorges de
la Fou

Tech

Cap Béar

Valle
de Boí

Espot

Parc Nacional
d'Aigüestortes i Estany
de Sant Maurici

Boí
Barruera

La Seu
d'Urgell

Puig
Neulós

El Port de
la Selva

Cadaqués

Adrall

Serra del Cadí

D115

Riu Fluvià

Besalú

Figueres

Roses

Cap
de Creus

Rupit

Riu Ter

Girona

Torroella
de Montgrí

La Pera

Peratallada

L'Estartit

Illes
Medes

Rio Llobregat

Vic

Parc
Natural del
Montseny

La Catalane

Fornells

Calella de
Palafrugell

Tamariu
Llafranc

A9

Costa Brava

Manresa

A2

Sant
Celoni

Tossa
de Mar

Blanes

Sant Pol
de Mar

Monistrol de
Montserrat

Vilafranca
del Penedès

El Prat de
Llobregat

Barcelona

See Barcelona
Map pp86–7

AP2

Sitges

Reus

Tarragona

MEDITERRANEAN
SEA

Costa Davrada

Barcelona–Ibiza

Barcelona–Palma de Mallorca

MALLORCA

CATALONIA & ARAGÓN

CATALONIA & ARAGÓN HIGHLIGHTS

CATALONIA & ARAGÓN HIGHLIGHTS

1 TEATRE-MUSEU DALÍ, FIGUERES

BY ANTONI PITXOT, PAINTER & DALÍ-APPOINTED DIRECTOR OF THE TEATRE-MUSEU DALÍ

Dalí said: 'I want my museum to be like a single block, a labyrinth, a great surrealist object. The people who come to see it will leave with the sensation of having had a theatrical dream'. He also described his museum as a self-portrait, showing us in one place his desires, enigmas, obsessions and passions.

ANTONI PITXOT'S DON'T MISS LIST

❶ TREASURE ROOM

In this room upholstered in red velvet to give the impression of a jewellery box, Dalí hung the paintings himself to impress visitors with their analogies or contrasts. It's filled with references to the Renaissance, avant-garde and his obsessions with a scientific approach to form, Gala (his wife and muse) and sex. The star is Atomic Leda with Gala as the centrepiece, Dalí disguised as a swan, and numerous mythological echoes.

❷ THE WIND PALACE

The ceiling in this old foyer of the theatre on the 1st floor is full of Dalí's imagery and iconography represented as a golden rain of money. We see Gala and Dalí flying up to the centre of this Wind Palace, their burial ceremony, and Dalí and Gala watching their own idyllic (and almost cinematic) boat trip to a more spiritual dimension.

❸ MONSTERS

Dalí's grotesque monsters are phantas-magoric beings that contemplate the

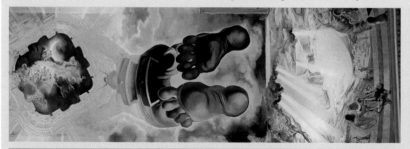

Clockwise from top: Section of Dalí painting in the Teatre-Museu Dalí; Dalí's bedroom display in the museum; Ceiling mural in the Wind Palace

theatre-museum from the courtyard. Made up of everything from rocks and a whale skeleton from Cape Creus to Figueres plane trees and gargoyles, the monsters embody Dalí's dream to decorate by accumulating instead of selecting. When it's hot and dry, they release a pleasant rain of thin water drops.

❹ POETRY OF AMERICA ROOM

Apart from Dalí's 1943 masterpiece *Poetry of America* (also known as *The Cosmic Athletes*) in this room, the delicate green-pen drawing *The Argonauts* is worth a closer look to admire the almost imperceptible details of the foot of one of the Argonauts: there are wings in his shoe with gold, rubies and emeralds.

❺ MONUMENT TO FRANCESC PUJOLS

At the museum's entrance, this monument to the Catalan philosopher is based on a millenary olive tree and repository of the old feelings of the Catalan people. Everything contained in the installation links past and tradition to modern times.

↘ THINGS YOU NEED TO KNOW

Antoni Pitxot Dalí personally appointed Pitxot as director; together they created the monsters in the courtyard and Dalí mandated that the 2nd floor contain a permanent collection of Pitxot's work **Admission** €11 **Website** www.salvador-dali.org **See our author's review, p172**

CATALONIA & ARAGÓN HIGHLIGHTS

2

⤷ THE CATALAN PYRENEES

The Pyrenees are Spain's most extensive and soul-stirring mountains. Although they unfold with similar drama in Aragón, if you had to choose just one mountain corner it would have to be the Catalan Pyrenees (p173). Zooming in a little closer, the Parc Nacional D'Aigüestortes i Estany de Sant Maurici (p173) is the pick, with deep, forested, stream-filled valleys cutting like gashes through the mountains.

3

⤷ DALÍ'S CATALONIAN LEGACY

Catalonia's Costa Brava has numerous sights associated with Dalí, including the Castell de Púbol (p166) and the Casa Museu Dalí (p171), but the highlight is the Teatre-Museu Dalí (p172) in Figueres. Most of the museum's exhibits defy description, but if we tell you that a portrait of his muse, Gala, emerges as if by magic from an Abraham Lincoln visage, you'll get the idea.

CATALONIA & ARAGÓN

CATALONIA & ARAGÓN HIGHLIGHTS

4

↘ ENJOY COASTAL PERFECTION IN CADAQUÉS

Much of the Spanish coast has lost the battle with tourist developments, but Cadaqués (p169) seems to have somehow slipped beneath the radar. This is a Mediterranean village at its most beguiling, combining hundreds of years of human history with more than a hint of sophistication.

5

↘ DIVE INTO ZARAGOZA

Every taste is catered for in Zaragoza (p179). For architecture enthusiasts there's a sacred cathedral beloved by pilgrims, as well as the gilded La Seo and the Aljafería, Spain's finest Islamic building beyond Andalucía. History buffs will love the signposts to Roman Caesaraugusta, while Zaragoza nights are the stuff of legend.

6

↘ TAKE REFUGE IN AÍNSA

Crowning a hilltop in the foothills of the Aragonese Pyrenees, old-world Aínsa (p184) has cobbled streets, a sprinkling of medieval monuments and sweeping views. But it's Aínsa's timeless air that you'll most appreciate, especially if you stay for a few nights during the week when there's scarcely another tourist in sight.

2 DAMIEN SIMONIS; 3 MARTIN LLADO; 4 DAVID TOMLINSON; 5 CESAR LUCAS ABREU/PHOTOLIBRARY; 6 ANTHONY HAM

2 Parc Nacional D'Aigüestortes i Estany de Sant Maurici (173); 3 Summer house patio, Casa Museu Dalí (p171); 4 Cadaqués (p169); 5 Interior of Aljafería (p182), Zaragoza; 6 Aínsa (p184)

CATALONIA & ARAGÓN'S BEST...

⤵ PLACES FOR ROMAN AND ROMANESQUE

- **Tarragona** (p175) Catalonia's premier Roman city.
- **Zaragoza** (p179) Roman remains of Caesaraugusta.
- **Monestir de Sant Pere de Rodes** (p170) Sublime Romanesque monastery, close to Cadaqués.
- **Vall de Boí** (p174) Pyrenean valley strewn with Romanesque churches.

⤵ PLACES TO RECHARGE THE BATTERIES

- **Cadaqués** (p169) Dalí's ghost and whitewashed Costa Brava charm.
- **Aínsa** (p184) Dreamy Aragonese hill-town.
- **Parque Nacional de Ordesa y Monte Perdido** (p174) Just 1800 people are allowed in this Pyrenean park at any one time.
- **Valles de Echo & Ansó** (p174) The Aragonese Pyrenees' least-trammelled valleys.

- **Sos del Rey Católico** (p186) Hill-town perfection in northwestern Aragón.

⤵ PLACES TO GET ACTIVE

- **Illes Medes** (p168) Some of the Mediterranean's best diving.
- **Serra del Cadí** (p174) A rock-climber's paradise in the Pyrenees.
- **Vall de la Noguera Pallaresa** (p174) White-water rafting in the Pyrenees.
- **Alquézar** (p186) World-class canyoning in Aragón.

⤵ PLACES FOR A GREAT MEAL

- **El Celler de Can Roca, Girona** (p168) Two Michelin stars and innovative Catalan cooking.
- **El Tubo, Zaragoza** (p183) Tangled, inner-city *barrio* lined with bars.
- **Serrallo, Tarragona** (p178) Fresh seafood straight from the boat.

MARTIN LLADO

Clear waters of Cadaqués

THINGS YOU NEED TO KNOW

VITAL STATISTICS

- **Population** 8.65 million
- **Area** 79,833 sq km
- **Best time to visit** Year-round; Pyrenees mid-June to September.

LOCALITIES IN A NUTSHELL

- **Costa Brava** (p166) The beautiful Catalan coast from the French border to Barcelona.
- **Pyrenees** (p173 and p184) Separates Spain from the rest of mainland Europe, running from the Mediterranean (Catalonia) to Aragón and beyond.
- **Central & Southern Aragón** (p179) The Aragonese flatlands stretch from the foothills of the Pyrenees, past Zaragoza to Teruel in the south.
- **Costa Daurada** (p175) The southern Catalan coast, from Barcelona to the Valencian border; home to Tarragona.

ADVANCE PLANNING

- **One year before** Reserve your table at El Bulli (p177).
- **One month before** Book your accommodation, earlier along the Costa Brava in summer.

RESOURCES

- **Catalonia** (www.gencat.net/probert) Regional tourist office site for Catalonia.
- **Aragón** (www.turismodearagon.com) Aragón's tourism portal.
- **Romanico Catalan** (www.romanico catalan.com) Terrific resource on Catalonia's Romanesque sites.
- **Fundació Gala-Salvador Dalí** (www.salvador-dali.org) Everything you need to plan your visit to Catalonia's Dalí sights.

EMERGENCY NUMBERS

- **Emergency** (☎112)
- **Policía Nacional** (☎091)

GETTING AROUND

- **Air** International airports in Barcelona, Girona (Ryanair's Spanish hub) and Zaragoza.
- **Bus** Intermittent services in the Pyrenees.
- **Road** Coastal motorways and towards Madrid; small mountain roads in the Pyrenees.
- **Train** Excellent network along the coast with good connections to the rest of Spain (often via Barcelona).
- **Train & Boat** In summer, a combination of *rodalies* (local trains) and boat connects the southern Costa Brava with Barcelona.

CATALONIA & ARAGÓN ITINERARIES

IN DALÍ'S FOOTSTEPS Three Days

Few artists have left such an enduring impression upon the territory they inhabited quite like Salvador Dalí. Your journey through Dalí's Catalonia begins, just as the great man's life did, in **(1) Figueres** (p171), an unexciting town that may have inspired Salvador to seek refuge in a surreal world of his own making. It nonetheless hosts the mind-blowing Teatre-Museu Dalí, the single-most significant legacy to survive Dalí after his death in 1989. South of Figueres, **(2) Girona** (p166) is a charming city that's the ideal overnight base for the **(3) Castell de Púbol** (p166) in La Pera. This mansion's foundations may belong to the Gothic and Renaissance eras, but Dalí transformed it into a zany epitaph to his muse, Gala. Perhaps the least otherworldly exhibit is the blue Cadillac in which Dalí took Gala on her last drive after her death. Away to the northwest, close to mainland Spain's easternmost point, **(4) Cadaqués** (p169) is where Dalí spent much of his adult life. It is such a beautiful coastal village that you may feel tempted to do the same.

THE ESSENCE OF ARAGÓN Five Days

Landlocked Aragón may climb steeply up into the Pyrenees, but its central and southern heartland is the soul of inland Spain. **(1) Zaragoza** (p179) is one of Spain's most engaging cities. By day it's a living museum with weighty landmarks to Roman, Islamic and Christian Spain. But once dark falls, Zaragoza has perfected the art of tapas as a precursor to frenetic nights that are famous throughout the country. The quiet evenings of enchanted **(2) Aínsa** (p184), the quintessential Aragonese hill village within sight of the Pyrenees, offer a radical change of pace away to the northeast. Return to Zaragoza, then continue south. Pause en route in **(3) Daroca** (p186), which is worth exploring for an hour or two, before you make for **(4) Teruel** (p185), known for its extraordinary concentration of Mudéjar architecture. Not far away, **(5) Albarracín** (p186) has fine castle ramparts and the village's every stone seems cast in some earthy shade of red or pink, making for wonderful plays of colour.

COAST & MOUNTAINS One Week

A week is scarcely enough to scratch the surface of Catalonia, and that's to say nothing of Barcelona halfway along its coast. But the itinerary that follows touches on the region's signature experiences. **(1) Tarragona** (p175) is very Catalan, combining a rich Roman history with meals dominated by this morning's catch from the Mediterranean.

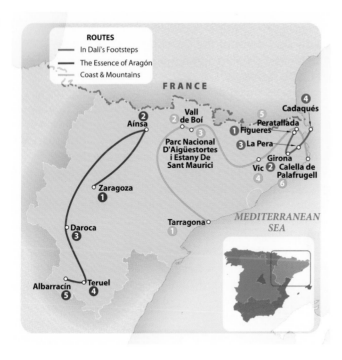

Head north through the Catalonian heartland to the (2) Vall de Boí (p174), dotted with pretty little Romanesque churches, and Pyrenean gateway for the (3) Parc Nacional D'Aigüestortes i Estany De Sant Maurici (p173). This is prime hiking country, with a range of walks the perfect encore to a long day spent travelling to get here. Roads snake eastwards in the Pyrenees' shadows, before you drop down to (4) Vic (p175) where the food is good and the monuments worth spending an evening over. As you wind your way back to the coast, stop off in (5) Peratallada (p170), a soulful *pueblo* just in from the coast, then rest from the exertions of the road in delightful (6) Calella de Palafrugell (p170).

DISCOVER CATALONIA & ARAGÓN

From the Mediterranean coves of the Costa Brava to the high summits of the Pyrenees, Catalonia and Aragón encompass some of Spain's most dramatic scenery.

The Costa Brava boasts much of the wild beauty that first drew visitors here, in spite of the occasional unsightly pocket of tourism-driven construction. Just inland are the medieval cities of Girona and Figueres, the latter home to the 'theatre-museum' of that city's zany son, Salvador Dalí, whose influence ripples across the region. Running across the north of both provinces, the Pyrenees rise to mighty 3000m peaks from a series of green and often remote valleys, dotted with villages that retain a palpable rural and even medieval air. These mountains provide excellent opportunities for a host of activities, especially hiking.

Historic, bustling cities such as Tarragona, Zaragoza and Teruel add urban sophistication to the spectacular open spaces, while the postcard-perfect *pueblos* (villages) of rural Aragón are among Spain's most beautiful.

CATALONIA

COSTA BRAVA

The Costa Brava (stretching from Blanes to the French border) ranks with the Costa Blanca and Costa del Sol as one of Spain's three great holiday coasts. Alongside some occasionally awful concrete development, the 'Rugged Coast' has some spectacular stretches.

A little further inland are the bigger towns of Girona (Castilian: Gerona), with a sizeable and strikingly well-preserved medieval centre, and Figueres (Castilian: Figueras), famous for its bizarre Teatre-Museu Dalí, the foremost of a series of sites associated with the eccentric surrealist artist Salvador Dalí.

CASTELL DE PÚBOL

The **Castell de Púbol** (☎ 972 48 86 55; www.salvador-dali.org; La Pera; adult/student & senior €7/5; ☼ 10.30am-7.15pm mid-Jun–mid-Sep, 10.30am-5.15pm Tue-Sun mid-Mar–mid-Jun & mid-Sep–Oct, 10.30am-4.15pm Tue-Sat Nov-Dec) is at La Pera, just south of the C66 and 22km northwest of Palafrugell.

In 1968 Dalí bought this Gothic and Renaissance mansion, which includes a 14th-century church, and gave it to his wife, Gala, who lived here until her death.

The castle was renovated by Dalí in his inimitable style, with lions' heads staring from the tops of cupboards, statues of elephants with giraffes' legs in the garden, and a stuffed giraffe staring at Gala's tomb in the crypt.

Sarfa buses between Palafrugell and Girona run along the C66.

GIRONA
pop 92,200

A tight huddle of ancient arcaded houses, grand churches, climbing cobbled streets and medieval baths, all enclosed by defensive walls and a lazy river, constitute a powerful reason for visiting north Catalonia's largest city, Girona.

INFORMATION

Tourist office (☎ 972 22 65 75; www.ajun tament.gi/turisme; Rambla de la Llibertat 1; ☉ 8am-8pm Mon-Fri, 8am-2pm & 4-8pm Sat, 9am-2pm Sun)

SIGHTS

CATEDRAL

The billowing baroque facade of the cathedral stands at the head of a majestic flight of steps rising from Plaça de la Catedral. Repeatedly rebuilt and altered down the centuries, it has Europe's widest Gothic nave (23m).

The fee for the museum also admits you to the beautiful 12th-century Romanesque cloister, whose 112 stone columns display some fine, if weathered, carving. From the cloister you can see the 13th-century Torre de Carlemany bell tower.

ESGLÉSIA DE SANT FELIU

Girona's second great church (Plaça de Sant Feliu; ☉ 9.30am-2pm & 4-7pm Mon-Sat, 10am-noon & 4-7pm Sun) is downhill from the cathedral. The nave has 13th-century Romanesque arches but 14th- to 16th-century Gothic upper levels. The northernmost of the chapels, at the far western end of the church, is graced by a masterly Catalan Gothic sculpture, Aloi de Montbrai's alabaster *Crist Jacent* (Recumbent Christ).

BANYS ÀRABS

Although modelled on earlier Muslim and Roman bathhouses, the Banys Àrabs (Arab baths; ☎ 972 21 32 62; Carrer de Ferran Catòlic; admission €1.80; ☉ 10am-7pm Tue-Sat Apr-Sep, 10am-2pm Tue-Sat Oct-Mar, 10am-2pm Sun & holidays) are a 12th-century Christian affair in Romanesque style.

THE CALL

Until 1492 Girona was home to Catalonia's second-most important medieval Jewish community (after Barcelona), and its Jewish quarter, the Call, was centred on Carrer de la Força. For an idea of medieval Jewish life and culture, visit the Museu d'Història dels Jueus de Girona (Jewish History Museum, aka the Centre Bonastruc Ça Porta; ☎ 972 21 67 61; Carrer de la Força 8; adult/under

River Onyar, Girona

GUY MOBERLY

16yr/senior & student €2/free/1.50; 🕐 10am-8pm Mon-Sat Jun-Oct, 10am-6pm Mon-Sat Nov-May, 10am-3pm Sun & holidays).

SLEEPING

Bed & Breakfast Bells Oficis (☎ 972 22 81 70; www.bellsoficis.com; Carrer dels Germans Busquets 2; r €35-85; ✂ 🅿 💻) With just five rooms, this family-run option is perfectly placed just off Rambla de la Llibertat. The two best ones have balconies overlooking the Rambla.

Residència Bellmirall (☎ 972 20 40 09; www.grn.es/bellmirall; Carrer de Bellmirall 3; s/d €40/75; 🕐 closed Jan-Feb; 🅿) Carved out of a 14th-century building in the heart of the old city, this 'residence' of heavy stone blocks and timber beams oozes character.

Hotel Històric (☎ 972 22 35 83; www.hotel historic.com; Carrer de Bellmirall 4A; s/d €102/114; 🅿 🅿 💻) A bijou hotel in a historic building in old Girona, it has eight spacious rooms that are individually decorated.

EATING

König (☎ 972 22 57 82; Carrer dels Calderers 16; meals €8-15) For a quick sandwich, *entrepà* (filled roll) or simple hot dishes, 'King' boasts a broad outdoor terrace shaded by thick foliage. Or just stop by for a drink.

Mimolet (☎ 972 20 21 24; Carrer del Pou Rodó 12; meals €35-40; 🕐 Tue-Sat; ✂ Ⓥ) For refined local cooking in a modern setting just within the old city walls, this is it. A stylish, designer spot, Mimolet offers an excellent wine menu to accompany the seasonally varied menu.

El Celler de Can Roca (☎ 972 22 21 57; www.cellercanroca.com; Carrer Can Sunyer 46; meals €80-100; 🕐 Tue-Sat) About 2km west of the city centre (and not the easiest place to find), this two-star Michelin choice is one of Catalonia's top-ranking restaurants. Housed in a modernised *masia* (country

house), it offers thoroughly inventive and ever-changing takes on Mediterranean cooking.

GETTING THERE & AWAY

Located 11km south of the centre is **Girona-Costa Brava airport**, and just off the AP7 and A2 is Ryanair's Spanish hub. **Sagalés** (☎ 902 13 00 14; www.sagales.com) operates hourly services from Girona-Costa Brava airport to Girona's main bus/train station (€2.05, 25 minutes) in connection with flights. A **taxi** (☎ 972 20 33 73, 972 22 23 33) to/from the airport to central Girona costs around €15.

Girona is on the train line between Barcelona, Figueres and Portbou on the French border.

L'ESTARTIT & THE ILLES MEDES
pop 3050

L'Estartit, 6km east of Torroella de Montgrí, has a long, wide beach of fine sand but nothing over any other Costa Brava package resort – with the rather big exception of the Illes Medes (Islas Medes)! The group of rocky islets barely 1km offshore is home to some of the most abundant marine life on Spain's Mediterranean coast.

The main road in from Torroella de Montgrí is called Avinguda de Grècia as it approaches the beach; the beachfront road is Passeig Marítim, at the northern end of which is the **tourist office** (☎ 972 75 19 10; www.visitestartit.com; Passeig Marítim; 🕐 9.30am-2pm & 4-8pm daily Jul-Sep, 9.30am-2pm & 4-7pm Mon-Sat, 10am-2pm Sun May-Jun & Oct, 9am-1pm & 3-6pm Mon-Fri, 10am-2pm Sat Oct-Apr).

The shores and waters around these seven islets, an offshore continuation of the limestone Montgrí hills, have been protected since 1985 as a *reserva natural submarina* (underwater nature reserve), which has brought a proliferation in their

Illes Medes

CATALONIA & ARAGÓN

CATALONIA

marine life and made them Spain's most popular destination for snorkellers and divers.

Kiosks by the harbour, at the northern end of L'Estartit beach, offer snorkelling and glass-bottomed boat trips to the islands.

SLEEPING & EATING

Hotel Les Illes (☎ 972 75 12 39; www.hotel lesilles.com; Carrer de Les Illes 55; r per person incl breakfast €43) A decent, functional place with comfortable, if unspectacular, rooms, all with sparkling bathroom and balcony. It is basically a divers' hang-out in a good spot back from the port. It has its own dive shop.

If you're looking for a bite, the northern end of Passeig Marítim, by the roundabout, is swarming with eateries.

GETTING THERE & AROUND

Sarfa buses run to and from Barcelona once or twice daily (€17.65, two hours), rising to four times in peak season (July to August).

CADAQUÉS & AROUND

pop 2800

If you have time for only one stop on the Costa Brava, you can hardly do better than Cadaqués. A whitewashed village around a rocky bay, it and the surrounding area have a special magic – a fusion of wind, sea, light and rock – that isn't dissipated even by the throngs of mildly fashionable summer visitors.

A portion of that magic owes itself to Salvador Dalí, who spent family holidays in Cadaqués during his youth, and lived much of his later life at nearby Port Lligat. The empty moonscapes, odd-shaped rocks and barren shorelines that litter Dalí's paintings weren't just a product of his fertile imagination. They're strewn all around the Cadaqués area in what Dalí termed a 'grandiose geological delirium'.

INFORMATION

Tourist office (☎ 972 25 83 15; www.cad aques.org; Carrer del Cotxe 2; ☺ 9am-9pm Mon-Sat, 10am-1pm Sun Easter-Sep, 9.30am-1pm & 3-6pm Mon-Sat, 10am-1pm Sun Oct-Easter)

Tamariu beach

STEPHEN SAKS

⟩ IF YOU LIKE...

If you like **Cadaqués** (p169), we think you'll also enjoy exploring these other villages of the Costa Brava:

- **Calella de Palafrugell** Low-slung buildings strung Aegean-style around a bay of rocky points and small, pretty beaches.
- **Llafranc** A smallish bay but a longer stretch of sand, cupped on either side by pine-dotted craggy coast.
- **Tamariu** A small crescent cove surrounded by pine stands, offering some of the most translucent waters on Spain's Mediterranean coast.
- **Tossa de Mar** A picturesque village of crooked, narrow streets with defensive medieval walls and towers, and marvellous sunsets.
- **Fornells** On one of the Costa Brava's most picturesque bays with a marina, beach and transparent azure water.
- **Peratallada** Warm stone houses and beautifully preserved narrow streets inland from the coast.
- **Besalú** Delightfully well-preserved medieval town with a Tolkeinesque fortified bridge.
- **El Port de la Selva** Home to the Monestir de Sant Pere de Rodes, one of Catalonia's finest Romanesque monasteries.

SIGHTS

Cadaqués is perfect for wandering, either around the town or along the coast (in either direction). The 16th- and 17th-century **Església de Santa Maria**, with a gilded baroque *retablo* (altarpiece), is the focus of the oldest part of town, with its narrow hilly streets. But wandering the

little pedestrian-only lanes anywhere back from the waterfront is a delight.

The **Museu de Cadaqués** (☎ 972 25 88 77; Carrer de Narcís Monturiol 15; ◷ 10am-1.30pm & 4-7pm Mon-Sat) includes Dalí among other local artists.

Cadaqués' main beach, and several others along the nearby coast, are small, with more pebbles than sand, but their picturesqueness and beautiful blue waters make up for that.

Port Lligat, an easy 1.25km walk from Cadaqués, is a tiny settlement around another lovely cove, with fishing boats pulled up on its beach. **Casa Museu Dalí** (☎ 972 25 10 15; www.salvador-dali.org; Port Lligat; adult/student & senior €10/8; 🕙 10.30am-9pm mid-Jun–mid-Sep, 10.30am-6pm Tue-Sun mid-Sep–mid-Jan & mid-Mar–mid-Jun) began as a fisherman's hut and was steadily altered and enlarged by Dalí, who lived here from 1930 to 1982, apart from a dozen or so years abroad during and around the Spanish Civil War. You must book ahead.

Cap de Creus is the most easterly point of the Spanish mainland and is a place of sublime, rugged beauty. With a steep, rocky coastline indented by dozens of turquoise-watered coves, it's an especially wonderful place to be at dawn or sunset.

SLEEPING

Fonda Vehí (☎ 972 25 84 70; Carrer de l'Església 5; s/d without bathroom €30/55, d with bathroom €65; 🔀) Near the church in the heart of the old town, this simple but engaging *pensión* tends to be booked up for July and August.

Hotel La Residència (☎ 972 25 83 12; www.laresidencia.net; Avinguda de la Caritat Serinyana 1; s/d €70/95; 🅿 🔀) In the heart of town, with just a dozen good-sized rooms, this hotel oozes history. It opened in 1904 and Picasso stayed here six years later. Nowadays the place has a studied, classy air.

EATING

Cala d'Or (☎ 972 25 81 49; Carrer de Sa Fitora 1; meals €20-25) Tucked away back from the waterfront, this knockabout place attracts swarms of local workers seeking a good

solid lunch at tables dressed in classic gingham. Tuck into some *llobarro a la planxa* (grilled sea perch).

Es Baluard (☎ 972 25 81 83; Carrer de Nemesi Llorens 2; meals €30; 🕙 daily Jun-Oct, Fri & Sat Mar-May) Tucked into part of what were the town's seaward protective walls, Es Baluard is a family-run spot where local fresh products of the sea dominate. A lucky few get sea views from their tables.

ENTERTAINMENT

L'Hostal (Passeig; 🕙 10pm-5am Sun-Thu, 10pm 6am Fri & Sat Apr-Oct) Facing the beachfront boulevard, this classic has live music on many nights (from midnight). One evening in the 1970s, an effusive Dalí called L'Hostal the *lugar más bonito del mundo* (the most beautiful place on earth).

GETTING THERE & AWAY

Sarfa buses to/from Barcelona (€19.90, 2¼ hours) leave twice daily (up to five daily in July and August). Buses also run to/from Figueres (€4.50, one hour) up to seven times daily (three in winter) via Castelló d'Empúries.

FIGUERES

pop 41,120

Twelve kilometres inland from the Golf de Roses, Figueres (Castilian: Figueras) is a humdrum town (some might say a dive) with a single, unique and unmissable attraction: Salvador Dalí. In the 1960s and '70s Dalí created here, in the town of his birth, the extraordinary Teatre-Museu Dalí.

INFORMATION

Tourist office (☎ 972 50 31 55; www.figueres ciutat.com; Plaça del Sol; 🕙 9am-8pm Mon-Sat, 10am-2pm Sun Jul-Sep, 8am-3pm & 4.30-8pm Mon-Fri, 9.30am-1.30pm & 3.30-6.30pm Sat Easter-Jun & Oct, 8am-3pm Mon-Fri Nov-Easter)

SIGHTS

Salvador Dalí was born in Figueres in 1904. Although his career took him to Madrid, Barcelona, Paris and the USA, he remained true to his roots and lived well over half his adult life at Port Lligat (p171), east of Figueres on the coast. Between 1961 and 1974 Dalí converted Figueres' former municipal theatre, ruined by a fire at the end of the Civil War in 1939, into the Teatre-Museu Dalí (☎ 972 67 75 00; www.salvador-dali .org; Plaça de Gala i Salvador Dalí 5; admission incl Dalí Joies & Museu de l'Empordà adult/student €11/8; ⏰ 9am-8pm Jul-Sep, 10.30am-6pm Tue-Sun Oct-Jun). It's full of surprises, tricks and illusions, and contains a substantial portion of his life's work. Note that you can enter no later than 45 minutes before closing time.

SLEEPING

Hotel Rambla (☎ 972 67 60 20; www.hotelram bla.net; La Rambla 33; s €56, d €70-85; P 🕸 🖵) Hiding behind an 1860 facade on the town's central boulevard, this hotel has pleasant rooms with crisp decor in blues and beiges.

Mas Pau (☎ 972 54 61 54; www.maspau.com; Avinyonet de Puigventós; s/d €88/105; P 🕸 🖵) Four kilometres west of Figueres along the road to Besalú, Mas Pau is an enchanting country hotel-restaurant, created inside the rough-hewn stone of a 16th-century *masia,* and set amid soothing gardens.

EATING

Hotel Durán (☎ 972 50 12 50; Carrer de Lasauca 5; meals €30-40) More than a century of tradition has not tired the Durán clan of serving up fine traditional food. Frequently the stage of gastronomic events, this place offers much clever cooking.

Mesón Castell (☎ 972 51 01 04; Pujada del Castell 4; meals €35-40; ⏰ Mon-Sat) A bustling, rustic eatery where you can sample tapas at the bar or head to the sit-down restaurant for robust local cooking (including lamb and suckling pig – grilled meats are the house speciality).

GETTING THERE & AWAY

Figueres is on the train line between Barcelona, Girona and Portbou on the

Parc Nacional d'Aigüestortes i Estany de Sant Maurici

JOSEP FERRER/ALAMY

French border, and there are regular connections to Girona (€2.60 to €2.90, 30 to 40 minutes) and Barcelona (€8.55 to €9.80, 2¼ hours) and to Portbou and the French border (€2 to €2.30, 25 minutes).

THE PYRENEES

The Pyrenees in Catalonia encompass some awesomely beautiful mountains and valleys. Above all, the Parc Nacional d'Aigüestortes i Estany de Sant Maurici, in the northwest, is a jewel-like area of lakes and dramatic peaks. The area's highest mountain, the Pica d'Estats (3143m), is reached by a spectacular hike past glittering glacial lakes. On arrival at the top, you enjoy a privileged point with 360-degree views over France and Spain.

NORTHWEST VALLEYS

North of the highway that leads northwest from Llavorsí towards the Port de Bonaigua pass, stretches a series of valleys leading up to some of the most beautiful sights in the Catalan Pyrenees.

The Vall de Cardòs and Vall Ferrera, heading back into the hills northeast of Llavorsí, lead to some remote and, in parts, tough mountain-walking country along and across the Andorran and French borders, including Pica d'Estats (3143m), the highest peak in Catalonia. Editorial Alpina's *Pica d'Estats* and *Montgarri* maps will help.

PARC NACIONAL D'AIGÜESTORTES I ESTANY DE SANT MAURICI & AROUND

Catalonia's only national park extends 20km east to west, and only 9km from north to south, but packs in more beauty than most areas 100 times its size. The product of glacial action over two million years, it's essentially two east–west valleys at 1600m to 2000m altitude lined by jagged 2600m to 2900m peaks of granite and slate. Against this backdrop, pine and fir forests, and open bush and grassland, bedecked with wildflowers in spring, combine with some 200 small *estanys* (pools or lakes) and countless streams and waterfalls to create a wilderness of rare splendour.

You can find information (in Spanish) at http://reddeparquesnacionales.mma .es/parques.

ORIENTATION

The main approaches are via the village of Espot (1320m), 4km east of the park's eastern boundary, and Boí, 5.5km from the western side.

The two main valleys are those of the Riu Escrita in the east and the Riu de Sant Nicolau in the west. The Escrita flows out of the park's largest lake, the 1km-long **Estany de Sant Maurici**. The Sant Nicolau's main source is **Estany Llong**, 4km west of Estany de Sant Maurici across the 2423m Portarró d'Espot pass. Three kilometres downstream from Estany Llong, the Sant Nicolau runs through a particularly beautiful stretch known as **Aigüestortes** (Twisted Waters).

MAPS & GUIDES

Editorial Alpina's map guides are adequate, although they don't show every single trail. A better map of the whole area is the Institut Cartogràfic de Catalunya's *Parc Nacional d'Aigüestortes i Estany de Sant Maurici,* scaled at 1:25,000 – but even it is not perfect.

INFORMATION

There are national park information offices in **Espot** (☎ 973 62 40 36; ☷ 9am-1pm & 3.30-6.45pm daily Jun-Sep, 9am-2pm & 3.30-5.45pm Mon-Sat, 9am-2pm Sun Oct-May) and **Boí** (☎ 973 69 61 89; ☷ same as Espot office). The **tourist**

CATALONIA & ARAGÓN

CATALONIA

Serra Del Cadí

JOHN WARBURTON-LEE PHOTOGRAPHY/ALAMY

↘ IF YOU LIKE...

If you like Catalonia's **Parc Nacional D'Aigüestortes i Estany de Sant Maurici** (p173), we think you'll also like these stirring mountain areas:

- **Parque Nacional de Ordesa y Monte Perdido** One of the highest and most spectacular mountain regions in the Spanish Pyrenees, in Aragón.
- **Val D'Aran** Catalonia's northernmost outpost, surrounded by spectacular 2000m-plus mountains and studded with ski resorts, including Baquiera.
- **Valles de Echo & Ansó** Lush, little-visited valleys with old stone villages climbing deep into the Aragonese Pyrenees.
- **Vall Ferrera** Amid the Parc Natural de l'Alt Pirineu (Catalonia's biggest nature reserve), with pretty villages and good walks.
- **Serra del Cadí** Picturesque pre-Pyrenees range with ravines and peaks famous for rock climbing.
- **Vall de la Noguera Pallaresa** Dramatic valley west of La Seu d'Urgell best known for its white-water rafting.

office (☎ 973 69 40 00; ⌚ 9am-2pm & 5-7pm Mon-Sat, 10am-2pm Sun) in Barruera, on the L500, 10km north from the N230, is a

good source of information on the area around the west side of the park.

Private vehicles cannot enter the park.

SIGHTS

The **Vall de Boí** (www.vallboi.com), southwest of the park, is dotted with some of Catalonia's loveliest little Romanesque churches, which together were declared a Unesco World Heritage site in 2000.

Other worthwhile Romanesque churches in the area are at Boí (Sant Joan), Barruera (Sant Feliu), Durro (Nativitat) and Erill la Vall (Santa Eulàlia).

ACTIVITIES

You can walk right across the park in one day. The full Espot–Boí (or vice versa) walk is about 25km and takes nine hours, but you can shorten this by using Jeep-taxis to/from Estany de Sant Maurici or Aigüestortes (3km downstream from Estany Llong) or both.

Numerous good walks of three to five hours return will take you up into spectacular side valleys from Estany de Sant Maurici or Aigüestortes.

SLEEPING

Six *refugis* in the park and nine more inside the *zona perifèrica* provide accommodation for walkers. Most charge €13.50 per person to stay overnight.

The villages of Espot, Boí and Taüll have a range of accommodation options (including several midrange hotels in Espot). There are *hostales* and *cases de pagès* in Barruera, El Pont de Suert, Capdella and La Torre de Capdella.

EATING

Most of the towns have one or two fairly basic restaurants.

Restaurant Juquim (☎ 973 62 40 09; meals €20-25; ⌚ daily Jun–mid-Oct, Wed-Mon mid-Oct–

May) This classic on Espot's main square has a varied menu concentrating largely on hearty country fare, with generous winter servings of *olla pallaresa* (steaming hot-pot) or *civet de senglar* (wild boar stew).

GETTING THERE & AWAY

Daily buses from Barcelona, Lleida and La Pobla de Segur to Esterri d'Àneu (and in summer to the Val d'Aran) will stop at the Espot turning on the C13.

GETTING AROUND

Once you're close to the park, the easiest way of getting inside it is by Jeep-taxi from Espot or Boí.

CENTRAL CATALONIA
VIC

pop 38,320

Vic, with its attractive historic centre and some fine restaurants, dominates the flatlands of La Plana de Vic to the south of the Pyrenees. With some Roman remnants, medieval leftovers, a grand Gothic cloister, excellent art museum and reputation for fine food, it makes a rewarding day trip from Barcelona or first stop en route to the Pyrenees.

For information, visit the **tourist office** (☎ 93 886 20 91; www.victurisme.cat; Carrer de la Ciutat 4; ☺ 10am-2pm & 4-8pm Mon-Fri, 10am-2pm & 4-7pm Sat, 10am-1.30pm Sun).

Plaça Major, the largest of Catalonia's central squares, is lined with medieval, baroque and Modernista mansions. Around it swirl the serpentine streets of medieval Vic, lined by mansions, churches and chapels.

In a town that bristles with eateries, **La Taula** (☎ 93 886 32 29, Plaça de Don Miguel de Clariana 4; meals €30; ☺ daily Jul-Sep, Tue-Sat & lunch only Sun Oct-Jun, closed Feb) is a bright star of traditional cooking, with fair prices and no pretensions (and considered by locals as one of the best in town).

Regular *rodalies* (line C3) run from Barcelona (€4.10, up to 1½ hours).

RUPIT

pop 330

An enchanting excursion northeast of Vic takes you 31km along the C153 to Rupit, a splendid old village set amid rugged grazing country. You cross a suspension footbridge to reach the village, which is full of quaint 17th-century houses, a baroque church and tucked-away squares.

COSTA DAURADA
TARRAGONA

pop 134,160

A seemingly eternally sunny port city, Tarragona is easily Catalonia's most important Roman site, starting with its amphitheatre. The medieval city, dominated by a beautiful cathedral that is surrounded by a compact warren of winding lanes, is worth a trip on its own. You could spend a day getting lost within its defensive walls.

INFORMATION

Tourist office (☎ 977 25 07 95; www.tarragonaturisme.cat; Carrer Major 39; ☺ 9am-9pm Mon-Sat, 10am-3pm Sun Jul-Sep, 10am-2pm & 4-7pm Mon-Sat, 10am-2pm Sun & holidays Oct-Jun)

SIGHTS & ACTIVITIES

Pick up the handy *Ruta Arqueològica Urbana* brochure from the tourist office.

CATEDRAL

Sitting grandly at the top of the old town, Tarragona's **cathedral** (☎ 977 23 86 85; Pla de la Seu; admission €3.50; ☺ 10am-1pm & 4-7pm Mon-Sat mid-Mar–May, 10am-7pm Mon-Sat Jun–mid-Oct, 10am-5pm Mon-Sat mid-Oct–mid-Nov, 10am-2pm Mon-Sat mid-Nov–mid-Mar) is a treasure house deserving 1½ hours or more of

TARRAGONA

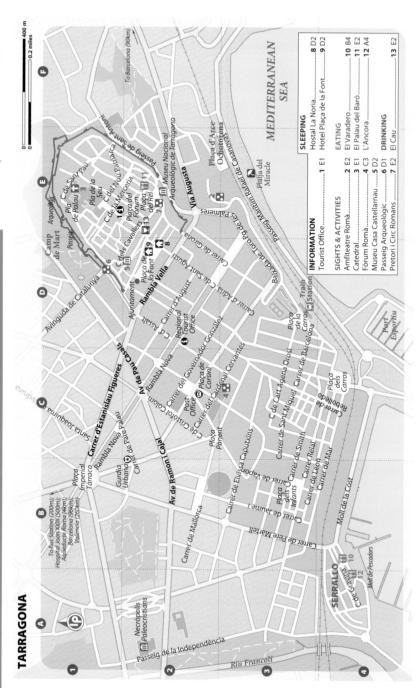

MEDITERRANEAN
SEA

INFORMATION	
Tourist Office....................	1 E1
SIGHTS & ACTIVITIES	
Amfiteatre Romà................	2 E2
Catedral.............................	3 E1
Fòrum Romà.......................	4 C3
Museu Casa Castellarnau.....	5 D2
Passeig Arqueològic...........	6 D1
Pretori i Circ Romans.........	7 E2

SLEEPING	
Hostal La Noria..................	8 D2
Hotel Plaça de la Font........	9 D2
EATING	
El Varadero........................	10 B4
El Palau del Baró................	11 E2
L'Àncora............................	12 A4
DRINKING	
El Cau................................	13 E2

SEEING MICHELIN STARS

Once a simple bar and grill clutching on to a rocky perch high above the bare Mediterranean beach of Cala Montjoi and accessible only by dirt track from Roses, 6km to the west, El Bulli (☎ 972 15 04 57; www.elbulli.com; Cala Montjoi; meals €200; Apr-Sep; ⊠) is now one of the world's most sought-after dining experiences (usually fully booked a year in advance), thanks to star chef Ferran Adrià.

While easily Catalonia's internationally best-known dining experience, it has two stablemates as three-star Michelin eateries (in all Spain there are only six; the other three are in the Basque Country).

Can Fabes (☎ 93 867 28 51; www.canfabes.com; Carrer de Sant Joan 6, Sant Celoni; meals €120-150; Tue-Sat) has long attracted a steady stream of gastronauts from Barcelona (53km to the south). Chef Santi Santamaria (the first Catalan chef ever awarded three Michelin stars) is a local boy who started up here in 1981. Dishes based on local products (seafood landed at Blanes, for example) are at the core of his cooking.

Barely 25km east, on the coast at Sant Pol de Mar, is another foodies' fave. Sant Pau (☎ 93 760 06 62; Carrer Nou 10; meals €120-150; lunch & dinner Tue-Wed, Fri & Sat, dinner Thu, closed most of May & Nov) is a beautifully presented mansion whose garden overlooks the Mediterranean. Carme Ruscalleda is the driving force. Some 20 other restaurants scattered around Catalonia have a Michelin star (and just one has two), in addition to 14 in Barcelona!

your time, if you're to do it justice. Built between 1171 and 1331 on the site of a Roman temple, it combines Romanesque and Gothic features, as typified by the main facade on Pla de la Seu.

PONT DEL DIABLE

The so-called Devil's Bridge is actually the Aqüeducte Romà (admission free; 9am-dusk), yet another marvel left by the Romans. It is a fine stretch of two-tiered aqueduct (217m long and 27m high), along which you can totter to the other side.

SLEEPING

Hostal La Noria (☎ 977 23 87 17; Plaça de la Font 53; s/d €30/48) For a real bargain-basement position right on the old town's main square, you can't do much better than these corner digs. Rooms are

simple enough but have their own attached clean bathroom, and those with a balcony assure you a window on old Tarragona's street life.

Hotel Plaça de la Font (☎ 977 24 61 34; www.hotelpdelafont.com; Plaça de la Font 26; s/d €55/70;) A notch up and also on the town square is this crisp *pensión*. Rooms, although a trifle cramped, have a pleasing modern look, with soft colours, sturdy beds and, in the case of half of the rooms, little balconies overlooking the square.

EATING

El Palau del Baró (☎ 977 24 14 64; www.palaudelbaro.com; Carrer de Santa Anna 3; meals €35-45; lunch & dinner Tue-Sat, lunch Sun) The Baron's palace, a centuries-old mansion, provides a romantic, sumptuous 19th-century setting. Dishes are served with

JORDI CAMI/PHOTOLIBRARY

Architectural remains in the Fòrum Romà

↘ MUSEU D'HISTÒRIA DE TARRAGONA

This museum comprises four separate Roman sites (which, since 2000, together have constituted a Unesco World Heritage site) and a 14th-century noble mansion, which now serves as the Museu Casa Castellarnau.

Start with the Pretori i Circ Romans, which includes part of the vaults of the Roman circus, where chariot races were held. Near the beach is the well-preserved Amfiteatre Romà, where gladiators battled each other, or wild animals, to the death.

Southeast of Carrer de Lleida are remains of the Fòrum Romà, dominated by several imposing columns. This forum was the hub of public and religious life for the Roman town.

The Passeig Arqueològic is a peaceful walk around part of the old town between two lines of city walls; the inner ones are mainly Roman, while the outer ones were put up by the British during the War of the Spanish Succession.

Things you need to know: Museu d'Història de Tarragona (www.museutgn.com; adult/concession per site €2.45/1.25, incl all MHT elements €9.25/4.60; ☾ 9am-9pm Mon-Sat, 9am-3pm Sun Easter-Sep, 9am-7pm Mon-Sat, 10am-3pm Sun & holidays Oct-Easter); Museu Casa Castellarnau (☎ 977 24 22 20; Carrer dels Cavallers 14); Pretori i Circ Romans (☎ 977 23 01 71; Plaça del Rei); Amfiteatre Romà (☎ 977 24 25 79; Plaça d'Arce Ochotorena); Fòrum Romà (☎ 977 24 25 01; Carrer del Cardenal Cervantes)

aplomb, and range from paella to various fish options.

L'Ancora (Carrer de Trafalgar 25; meals €25-30; ☾ 1pm-1am) and its sister establishment El Varadero (Carrer de Trafalgar 13) brim with mouth-watering seafood and open late.

The quintessential Tarragona seafood experience can be had in Serrallo, the town's fishing port. About a dozen bars and restaurants here sell the day's catch, and on summer weekends in particular the place is packed.

CATALONIA & ARAGÓN

DRINKING & ENTERTAINMENT

El Cau (☎ 977 23 12 12; www.elcau.net; Carrer de Trinquet Vell 2; ⏰ daily) Set in one of the vaults of the Roman circus, this is the best place for dancing in central Tarragona.

GETTING THERE & AWAY

At least 38 regional and long-distance trains per day run to/from Barcelona's Passeig de Gràcia via Sants. Many of these trains continue on to Valencia, Alicante and a couple into Andalucía.

ARAGÓN

ZARAGOZA

pop 624,600 / elev 200m

Zaragoza (Saragossa) rocks and rolls. The feisty citizens of this great city on the banks of the mighty Río Ebro make up over half of Aragón's population and they live a fairly hectic lifestyle with great tapas bars and raucous nightlife. But Zaragoza is so much more than a city that loves to live the good life and there's a host of historical sights spanning the great civilisations (Roman, Islamic and Christian) that have left their indelible mark on the Spanish soul.

INFORMATION

Oficina de Turismo de Aragón (☎ 976 28 21 81; www.turismodeAragon.com; Avenida de César Augusto 25; ⏰ 9am-2pm & 5-8pm Mon-Fri, from 10am Sat & Sun)

Plaza del Pilar (☎ 976 39 35 37; www.zaragozaturismo.com; ⏰ 9am-9pm Easter-Oct, 10am-8pm Nov-Easter) The city information office, opposite the basilica.

SIGHTS

BASÍLICA DE NUESTRA SEÑORA DEL PILAR

Brace yourself for the saintly and the solemn in this great baroque cavern of Catholicism. It was here on 2 January AD 40, that Santiago (St James the Apostle) is believed by the faithful to have seen the Virgin Mary descend atop a marble *pilar* (pillar). A chapel was built around the remaining pillar, followed by a series of ever-more-grandiose churches, culminating in the enormous **basilica** (☎ 976 39 74 97; admission free; ⏰ 6.45am-9.30pm) that you see today. The exterior is another story altogether, its splendid main dome lording it over a flurry of 10 mini-domes, each encased in chunky blue, green, yellow and white tiles, creating a kind of rugged Byzantine effect.

The legendary **pilar** is hidden in the Capilla Santa, inside the east end of the basilica.

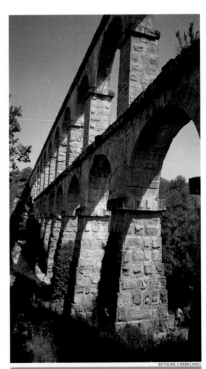

BETHUNE CARMICHAEL

Tarragona's Aqüeducte Romà (p177)

ARAGÓN

CATALONIA & ARAGÓN

ZARAGOZA

ZARAGOZA

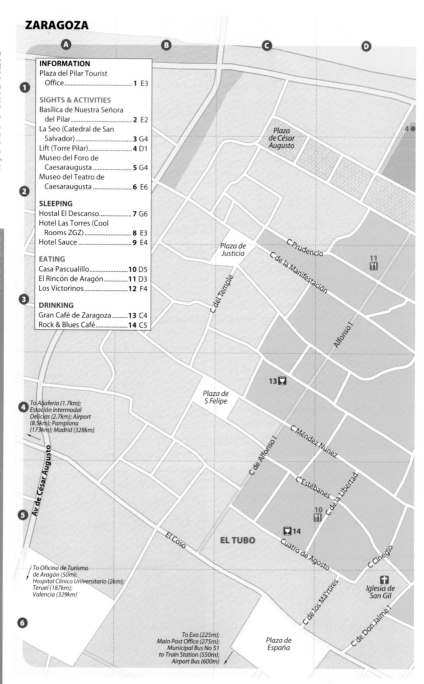

INFORMATION
Plaza del Pilar Tourist
Office................................. **1** E3

SIGHTS & ACTIVITIES
Basílica de Nuestra Señora
del Pilar............................. **2** E2
La Seo (Catedral de San
Salvador)........................... **3** G4
Lift (Torre Pilar)...................... **4** D1
Museo del Foro de
Caesaraugusta.................. **5** G4
Museo del Teatro de
Caesaraugusta.................. **6** E6

SLEEPING
Hostal El Descanso.................. **7** G6
Hotel Las Torres (Cool
Rooms ZGZ)...................... **8** E3
Hotel Sauce **9** E4

EATING
Casa Pascualillo....................... **10** D5
El Rincón de Aragón............... **11** D3
Los Victorinos.......................... **12** F4

DRINKING
Gran Café de Zaragoza.......... **13** C4
Rock & Blues Café.................. **14** C5

Plaza
de César
Augusto

Plaza de
Justicia

C Prudencio

C de la Manifestación

C del Temple

Alfonso I

13

Plaza de
S Felipe

To Aljafería (1.7km);
Estación Intermodal
Delicias (2.7km); Airport
(8.5km); Pamplona
(173km); Madrid (328km)

Av de César Augusto

C Méndez Núñez

C de Alfonso I

C Estébanes

C de la Libertad

10

El Coso

EL TUBO

14

Cuatro de Agosto

C Cinegio

To Oficina de Turismo
de Aragón (50m);
Hospital Clínico Universitario (2km);
Teruel (187km);
Valencia (329km)

C de los Mártires

Iglesia de
San Gil

To Exo (225m);
Main Post Office (275m);
Municipal Bus No 51
to Train Station (550m);
Airport Bus (600m)

Plaza de
España

C de Don Jaime I

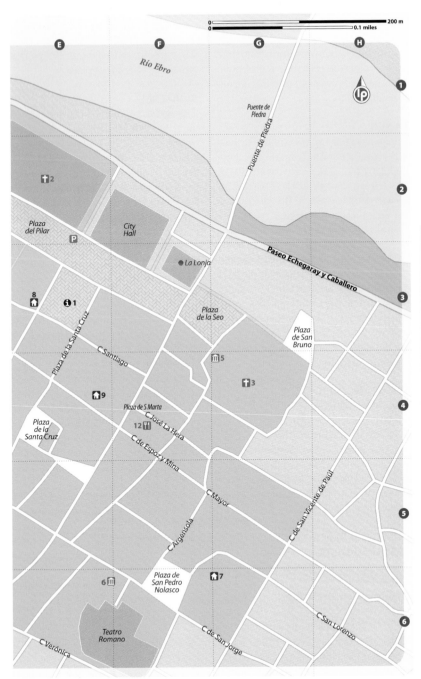

Río Ebro

Puente de Piedra

Puente de Piedra

Paseo Echegaray y Caballero

Plaza del Pilar

City Hall

La Lonja

Plaza de la Seo

Plaza de San Bruno

Plaza de la Santa Cruz

C Santiago

Plaza de la Santa Cruz

Plaza de S Marta

C José La Hera

C de Espoz y Mina

C Mayor

C Argensola

C de San Vicente de Paul

Plaza de San Pedro Nolasco

Teatro Romano

C Verónica

C de San Jorge

C San Lorenzo

200 m
0.1 miles

A lift (admission €2; ☉ 9.30am-1.30pm & 4-6.30pm Sat-Thu) whisks you most of the way up the north tower (Torre Pilar) from where you climb to a superb viewpoint over the domes and out across this ever-expanding city.

LA SEO
Dominating the eastern end of Plaza del Pilar is the Catedral de San Salvador, more popularly known as La Seo (☎ 976 29 12 38; Plaza de la Seo; admission €2.50; ☉ 10am-6pm Tue-Fri, 10am-2pm & 3-6pm Sat, 10-11.30am & 2.30-6pm Sun Jun-Sep, shorter hr rest of year).

La Seo may lack the fame of the Basílica de Nuestra Señora del Pilar, but it's easily its architectural superior. Built between the 12th and 17th centuries, it displays a fabulous spread of architectural styles from Romanesque to baroque. The north-west facade is a Mudéjar masterpiece, deploying classic dark brickwork and colourful ceramic decoration in eye-pleasing geometric patterns.

MUSEO DEL FORO DE CAESARAUGUSTA
The trapezoid building on Plaza de la Seo is the entrance to an excellent reconstruction of part of Roman Caesaraugusta's forum (☎ 976 39 97 52; Plaza de la Seo 2; admission €2; ☉ 10am-2pm & 5-8pm Tue-Sat, 10am-2pm Sun, last entry 1hr before closing), now well below ground level.

MUSEO DEL TEATRO DE CAESARAUGUSTA
Discovered during the excavation of a building site in 1972, the ruins of Zaragoza's Roman theatre are the focus of this interesting museum (☎ 976 20 50 88; Calle de San Jorge 12; admission €3; ☉ 10am-9pm Tue-Sat, 10am-2pm Sun). Great efforts have been made to help visitors reconstruct the edifice's former splendour, including

evening projections of a virtual performance (admission €1; ☉ 10pm Fri & Sat) on the stage; get there 15 minutes before performances to ensure a place.

ALJAFERÍA
If we had to choose one place that on its own is worth the trip to Zaragoza, it would be the Aljafería (☎ 976 28 96 84; Calle de los Diputados; adult/under 12yr/concession €3/free/1, free Sun; ☉ 10am-2pm Sat-Wed, 4-6.30pm Mon-Wed & Fri-Sat Nov-Mar, 10am-2pm Sat-Wed, 4.30-8pm Fri-Wed Apr-Jun & Sep-Oct, daily Jul & Aug). This is Spain's finest Islamic-era edifice outside Andalucía – it's not in the league of Granada's Alhambra or Córdoba's Mezquita, but it's nonetheless a glorious monument.

SLEEPING
Hostal El Descanso (☎ 976 29 17 41; Calle de San Lorenzo 2; s/d without bathroom €20/30) Simple, bright rooms, a family-run atmosphere and a central location overlooking a pretty plaza near the Roman theatre add up to a good budget deal.

Hotel Sauce (☎ 976 20 50 50; www.hotelsauce.com; Calle de Espoz y Mina 33; s/d €58.85/74.90; P ⊠ ▣) This small hotel has good rooms with a mix of styles from traditional and cosy to pastel tones and a modern, classy look.

Hotel Las Torres (Cool Rooms ZGZ; ☎ 976 39 42 50; www.coolroomshotels.com; Plaza del Pilar 11; s €69-110, d €79-120; ⊠ ▣) This place was a work-in-progress when we visited but it promises to be Zaragoza's best place to stay. Many of the rooms overlook Plaza del Pilar and all are being renovated with a designer, contemporary flourish.

EATING
Zaragoza has some terrific tapas bars, with dozens of places on or close to Plaza de Santa Marta and towards the southern

Museo del Foro de Caesaraugusta, Zaragoza

end of Calle Heroísmo. Otherwise the narrow streets of El Tubo, north of Plaza de España, are tapas central.

ourpick Casa Pascualillo (☎ 976 39 72 03; Calle de la Libertad 5; lunch & dinner Tue-Sat, lunch Sun) When *Metropoli,* the respected weekend magazine of *El Mundo* newspaper, set out to find the best 50 tapas bars in Spain, it's no surprise that Casa Pascualillo made the final cut. The bar groans under the weight of every tapas variety imaginable, with seafood and meat in abundance, but the house speciality is El Pascualillo, a 'small' *bocadillo* of *jamón,* mushrooms and onion.

Los Victorinos (☎ 976 39 42 13; Calle José La Hera 6; Mon-Sat) This place, tucked away in a pedestrian lane just west of Calle de Don Jaime I, also made *Metropoli*'s Top-50 list. Although there aren't as many options on the bar, there are plenty more on the menu, and choices for vegetarians.

ourpick El Rincón de Aragón (☎ 976 20 11 63; Calle de Santiago 3-5; menú del día €12.95) The sort of place that Spaniards love, El Rincón de Aragón offers hearty Aragonese

specialities. There's no time for unnecessary elaborations here – the decor is basic and the food stripped down to its essence – but the eating is top-notch and ideal for finding out why people get excited about Aragonese cooking.

DRINKING

Gran Café de Zaragoza (☎ 976 39 41 25; Calle de Alfonso I 25; breakfasts from €2.50; 8.30am-10pm Sun-Thu, 9am-2.30am Fri & Sat) This Zaragoza institution evokes the grand old cafes of Spain's past with a gold-plated facade and an old-style civility in the service.

Calle del Temple, southwest of Plaza del Pilar, is the spiritual home of Zaragoza's roaring nightlife.

Exo (Plaza del Carmen 11; 7am-1am Mon-Thu, 7am-3.30am Fri, 5pm-3.30am Sat, 5-11pm Sun) You don't need to be as sleek and cool as the bar staff or as shiny as the modernist decor at this smart but easygoing bar.

Rock & Blues Café (Cuatro de Agosto 5-9; 3pm-2.30am, later on weekends) Rock 'n' roll paraphernalia and homage to the likes of Jimi Hendrix set the tone for the music and style of this long-standing favourite.

GETTING THERE & AWAY

The **Zaragoza-Sanjurjo airport** (☎ 976 71 23 00) has direct **Ryanair** (www.ryanair.com) flights to/from London-Stansted, Brussels (Charleroi), Rome, Milan and Alicante.

Zaragoza is connected by almost hourly high-speed AVE services to Madrid (€50.90, 1½ hours, approximately 10 daily) and Barcelona (€58.90, one hour).

Agreda Automóvil (☎ 976 55 45 88) runs airport buses (€2.15) to/from Paseo Pamplona via Plaza San Francisco and Gran Via 4 (the stop for municipal bus 30) that link with flights.

THE NORTH (THE PYRENEES)

The Aragonese Pyrenees boast several peaks well over the 3000m mark and they're the most dramatic and rewarding on the Spanish side of the range. Viewed from the south their crenellated ridges fill the northern horizon wherever you turn and their valleys offer magnificent scenery, several decent ski resorts and great walking.

Aragón's mountains are more popular in summer than in winter. Some 6000km of long-distance trails (Grandes Recorridos; GR) and short-distance trails (Pequeños Recorridos; PR) are marked all across Aragón.

The optimum time for walking is mid-June to early September, though the more popular parks and paths can become crowded in midsummer.

Dotted throughout the mountains are several mountain *refugios* (refuges). The **Federación Aragonesa de Montañismo** (FAM; ☎ 976 22 79 71; www.fam.es in Spanish; 4th fl, Calle Albareda 7) in Zaragoza can provide

information and a FAM card will get you substantial discounts on *refugio* stays.

The Aragonese publisher Prames produces some of the best maps for walkers.

AÍNSA
pop 1400 / elev 589m

The hilltop village of medieval Aínsa (L'Aínsa in the local dialect), which stands above the modern town of the same name, is one of Aragón's gems, a stunning village of uneven stone. From its perch, you'll have commanding panoramic views of the mountains, particularly of the great rock bastion of La Peña Montañesa.

There's an excellent **regional tourist office** (☎ 974 50 05 12; www.turismosobrarbe.com in Spanish; Plaza del Castillo 1, Torre Nordeste; ☼ 10am-2pm & 4-7pm) within the castle walls.

The restored Romanesque **Iglesia de Santa María**, rising above the Plaza Mayor, lights up when you pop a €1 coin into a box, with five minutes of Gregorian chants thrown in. The crypt and Gothic cloister are charming, while you can also climb the **belfry** (admission €1; ☼ approx 11am-1.30pm & 4-7pm) for stunning views of the mountains to the north and down over the terracotta rooftops of the old town; climb as close to sunset as the opening hours allow. Otherwise, simply wander down through the village along either Calle de Santa Cruz or Calle Mayor, pausing in the handful of artsy shops en route.

SLEEPING

Casa El Hospital (☎ /fax 974 50 07 50; Calle del Arco del Hospital; s €25-29, d €39-55) The cheapest place to stay in the old town, Casa El Hospital sits just off Plaza Mayor in a lovely stone building.

our pick **Hotel Los Siete Reyes** (☎ 974 50 06 81; www.lossietereyes.com in Spanish; Plaza Mayor s/n; d €90-120; ✂ ▢) Set in a charming stone building overlooking Plaza Mayor,

Aínsa

ANTHONY HAM

this temple of style has stunning bathrooms, polished floorboards, flat-screen TVs and some lovely period detail wedded to a contemporary look (eg contemporary art adorning exposed stone walls).

EATING & DRINKING

our pick **L'Alfil** (☎ 974 50 02 99; Calle Traversa; raciones €6.50-11; Thu-Tue) A pretty little place with floral accompaniment to its outside tables, in a side street along from the church, this cafe-bar does a whole heap of *raciones* that are more creative than you'll find elsewhere, from ostrich chorizo, snails and deer sausage to wild boar paté and cured duck.

Bodegón de Mallacán (☎ 974 50 09 77; Plaza Mayor 6; menú €22, meals from €20) One of the most popular places on Plaza Mayor, this place has an extensive wine cellar, high-quality traditional local cooking and a number of pretty dining rooms.

GETTING THERE & AWAY

ALOSA (☎ 902 21 07 00; www.alosa.es in Spanish) sends a daily bus to Aínsa from

Barbastro (€4.88, one hour), while the same company also has one bus a day to Torla (€3.10, one hour).

THE SOUTH
TERUEL

pop 32,400 / elev 917m

Teruel is one of Aragón's most engaging cities, an open-air museum of ornate Mudéjar monuments almost without peer in Spain.

INFORMATION

Regional tourist office (☎ 978 64 14 61; Calle de San Francisco 1; 9am-2pm & 4.30-7pm Mon-Sat, 10am-2pm & 4.30-7pm Sun mid-Sep–Jun, 10am-2pm & 4.45-7.45pm Mon-Sat, 10am-2pm & 4.45-7.45pm Sun Jul–mid-Sep)

SIGHTS

Teruel's **cathedral** (☎ 978 61 80 16; Plaza de la Catedral; adult/child €3/2; 11am-2pm & 4-8pm Easter-Oct, 11am-2pm & 4-7pm Nov-Easter) is a rich example of the Mudéjar imagination at work with its kaleidoscopic brickwork and colourful ceramic tiles.

Village and fortress walls of Albarracín
GEOFFREY GRACE/ALAMY

⚲ IF YOU LIKE...

If you like Aínsa (p184), Aragón has many similarly charming villages:

- **Sos del Rey Católico** If this gorgeous medieval hilltop village in northwestern Aragón were in Tuscany, it would be world famous.
- **Albarracín** Epic fortress walls and ancient, maze-like streets with centuries-old buildings leaning over them, west of Teruel.
- **Alquézar** A beautiful stone village, draped along a ridgeline and famous as a destination for canyoning.
- **Daroca** Sleepy medieval town with castle walls snaking along the surrounding ridges.

The most impressive of Teruel's other Mudéjar monuments is the Torre de El Salvador (☎ 978 60 20 61; www.teruelmudejar.com in Spanish; Calle El Salvador; adult/child €2.50/1.80; ☽ 10am-2pm & 4-8pm mid-Jul–mid-Sep, 11am-2pm & 4.30-7.30pm Tue-Sat, 11am-2pm Sun rest of year), an early-14th-century extravaganza of brick and ceramics built around an older Islamic minaret. The views from the top are Teruel's best.

FESTIVALS & EVENTS

On the weekend closest to 14 February, thousands of Teruel's inhabitants (and even more visitors from elsewhere) don medieval dress for the Fiesta Medieval, which includes markets and food stalls.

SLEEPING

Hostal Aragón (☎ 978 61 18 77; Calle Santa María 4; s with/without bathroom €25/22, d with/without bathroom €44/37) An unassuming place on a narrow side street with well-kept wood-panelled rooms, Hostal Aragón drops its prices by a few euros midweek.

our pick **Hotel El Mudayyan** (☎ 978 62 30 42; www.elmudayyan.com in Spanish; Calle Nueva 18; s/d €60/90; ✗ ▣) Certainly the most character-filled of Teruel's hotels, El Mudayyan has lovely rooms with polished wood floors, wooden beams and charming interior design that's different in every room.

EATING

Landlocked Teruel is utterly devoted to meat eating and promotes its local *jamón* and other *embutidos* (cured meats) with enthusiasm.

La Torre de Salvador (☎ 978 61 73 76; Calle El Salvador; dishes €10-19; ☽ Tue-Sun) Right opposite the Torre de El Salvador, this smart restaurant raises the stakes on style with its *nouveau cuisine Aragonese,* with subtle dishes such as quail in a fruity sauce and cod with mushrooms.

Mesón Óvalo (☎ 978 61 82 35; Paseo del Óvalo 8; menú €12, mains €12-18; ☽ lunch & dinner Tue-Sat, lunch Sun) There's a strong emphasis on regional Aragonese cuisine at this pleasant place, with meat and game dishes to the fore. One fine local speciality is *jarretes* (Mozarabic hock of lamb stewed with wild mushrooms).

GETTING THERE & AWAY

Teruel is on the railway between Zaragoza (€12.25, two hours) and Valencia (€11, 2½ hours), with three trains each way daily.

BRUCE ESBIN

Galicia coastline and lighthouse

SPAIN'S NORTH COAST

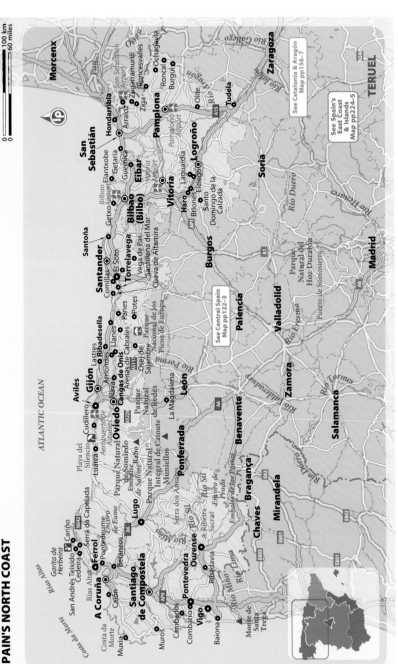

See Catalonia & Aragón Map pp156–7

See Spain's East Coast & Islands Map pp224–5

See Central Spain Map pp122–3

TERUEL

Zaragoza

Madrid

Salamanca

Zamora

Valladolid

Palencia

Burgos

Soria

Logroño

Vitoria

Pamplona

San Sebastián

Bilbao (Bilbo)

Santander

Torrelavega

Gijón

Oviedo

Avilés

Ponferrada

León

Benavente

Bragança

Chaves

Mirandela

Ourense

Pontevedra

Vigo

Santiago de Compostela

A Coruña

Ferrol

Lugo

Tudela

Eibar

Haro

ATLANTIC OCEAN

100 km
60 miles

0
0

Morcenx

Río Gállego

Osse

Roncal
Ochagavía
Roncesvalles
Burguí
Zugarramurdi
Arraiz
Ziga
Olite
Río Aragón

San Sebastián Airport
Hondarribia
Elantxobe
Getaria
Guernica
Getxo
Bilbao Airport
Laguardia
Briones
Santo Domingo de la Calzada
Vitoria Airport
Pamplona Airport

Río Duero
Río Henares

Parque Natural del Hoz Duratón
Puerto de Somosierra

Río Eresma
Río Pisuerga
Río Tormes

Río Porma

Río Órbigo

Santoña
Comillas
El Soto
Vega de Pas
Santillana del Mar
Cueva de Altamira
Potes
Panes
Ribadesella
Lastres
Llanes
Naves
Arriondas
Arenas de Cabrales
Cangas de Onís
Oseja de Sajambre
Parque Nacional de los Picos de Europa

Playa del Silencio
Cudillero
Luarca
Aeropuerto de Asturias
Parque Natural de Somiedo
Embalse de Salime
Parque Natural Integral de Catoute de Muniellos

La Magdalena

Río Sil
Río Sil
Embalse de las Portas
Río Cúa
Serra dos Ancares
Embalse de Prada
Río Navia
Sacraf

Garita de Herbeira
San Andrés de Teixido
Cedeira
Cariño
Serra da Capelada
Pontedeume
Betanzos
Sada
Rías Altas
Costa da Morte
Muxía

Cambados
Combarro
O Grove
Muros
Baiona
Ribadavia
Monte de Santa Tregá
Río Miño
Río Limia

E82
E801
E805
E802

A1
A8
A15
A68
N-621
N632
N634
N-VI
A6
A3

SPAIN'S NORTH COAST HIGHLIGHTS

1   CATEDRAL DE SANTIAGO DE COMPOSTELA

BY IÑAKI GAZTELUMENDI, SANTIAGO TOURISM GURU

Ernest Hemingway described Santiago's cathedral as the building that meant the most to him in all the world. It's an intense and eclectic monument and loaded with spiritual symbolism, but thanks to its position on Unesco's World Heritage list, it has become the focal point for the regeneration of Santiago de Compostela's old town.

⤢ IÑAKI GAZTELUMENDI'S DON'T MISS LIST

❶ OBRADOIRO FACADE

I've lived in Santiago all my life, but it's still a privilege to see the overwhelmingly baroque Fachada del Obradoiro every day. Study it closely, but step back into the middle of the plaza where the 360-degree views are a journey through the evolution of art, from the Middle Ages to the 18th century.

❷ MAIN ENTRANCE

I'm always surprised how many people rush inside. Pause instead to contemplate the splendour of El Pórtico de la Gloria where I have a special weakness for the 24 elders of the apocalypse with musical instruments (an echo of Santiago de Compostela's strong musical tradition). Inside, near the Altar Mayor, the figure of Maestro Mateo moves me with its simplicity amid the extravagant beauty elsewhere.

❸ PLAZA DE LA QUINTANA

Of the four plazas that connect the cathedral to the rest of the old town, Plaza de la Quintana is the most enigmatic, divided as it is between Quintana of

Clockwise from top: Obradoiro square; Baroque cathedral facade; Interior chapel; Catedral de Santiago de Compostela and Plaza de la Quintana; Strolling past Santiago de Compostela's masterpiece

the Dead and Quintana of the Living. Seek out the subtly beautiful granite panel on the monastery facade of the Mosteiro de San Paio de Anteáltares.

❹ **THE CATHEDRAL'S ROOF**
As you climb through the labyrinth of staircases, you'll see the great eras of the cathedral's architectural history. But the cathedral was built not just through the genius of its architects, but through the labour of local people, and from the summit the panoramic views are a reminder that the cathedral is the centrepiece of a living, breathing city.

❺ **EL PALACIO GELMÍREZ**
Don't miss the interior of this palace, an annex to the cathedral, with its numerous Romanesque gems. I particu-

larly like the kitchen and dining room with their scenes of Galician banquets, including traditional local foods. It's rare to find two main pillars of Santiago life (gastronomy and the social life that grew up around the cathedral) in one place.

↘ **THINGS YOU NEED TO KNOW**

Top festival Feast of Saint James (25 July) **Peak pilgrim season** June to August **Best photo op** Take the cathedral rooftop tour (p217) **See our author's review, p217**

SPAIN'S NORTH COAST HIGHLIGHTS

2 PINTXOS IN SAN SEBASTIÁN

BY GABRIELLA RANELLI, COOKING SCHOOL TEACHER AND GASTRONOMIC TOUR LEADER

San Sebastián is a culinary Mecca: if you love food you must come here. The city holds 18 Michelin stars (and counting), more per capita than any other city in the world. It all owes a debt to the New Basque Cuisine Movement, which has lightened up traditional dishes and emphasised the remarkable local products.

⬆ GABRIELLA RANELLI'S DON'T MISS LIST

❶ THE PINTXO CRAWL

The *pintxos* tradition is to go from bar to bar trying one *pintxo* and a drink in each spot, then moving on. The idea is to try the house speciality in each one. Don't count on sitting down. It's more like a movable cocktail party.

❷ CALLE DE FERMÍN CALBETÓN & CALLE DE 31 DE AGOSTO

If you only have one day, you can't miss Calle de Fermín Calbetón or Calle de 31 de Agosto in the Parte Vieja (Old Town). Any place with a lot of people is probably a good bet, but remember that if you come at any time other than before lunch and before dinner, an empty bar might just mean that you are off schedule.

❸ GROS

The other great area for *pintxos* in San Sebastián is in Gros, east of the Parte Vieja across the Río Urumea. Gros is where you will find more wine bars and sophisticated contemporary *pintxos*. The pace is slower here and people

Clockwise from top: Basque-style tapas; Pouring a glass of *txacoli;* Shrimp brochette; *Pintxos,* Gros; Food and drink served San Sebastián—style

might linger longer in some of the bars on this side because the wine lists are especially tempting. Don't forget to try the cider.

❹ GILDA

The most emblematic *pintxo* in San Sebastian is the Gilda. Its base always consists of pickled guindilla peppers (a mild green chilli), anchovies and olives and is traditionally served piled on a plate and doused in extra-virgin olive oil. But this being San Sebastián, some bars do creative variations on the theme.

❺ TXAKOLI DE GETARIA

The perfect (and most traditional) accompaniment to many *pintxos* in San Sebastián is a glass of *txacoli*, the tart

local white wine, which is often poured into your glass from a great height. And not just any *txacoli*: it really should be Txakoli de Getaria, which is produced west of San Sebastián. It goes especially well with a shrimp brochette.

⬊ THINGS YOU NEED TO KNOW

Top survival tip The local cider, with its low alcohol content, is ideal if you're visiting lots of bars **Don't be put off** Not all San Sebastián bars have *pintxos* lined up along the bar – if it's made to order it's worth the wait **See the author's coverage of eating in San Sebastián, p208**

SPAIN'S NORTH COAST HIGHLIGHTS

SPAIN'S NORTH COAST

SPAIN'S NORTH COAST HIGHLIGHTS

3

⬊ SCENERY & TAPAS IN SAN SEBASTIÁN

At one level, the elegant seaside city of San Sebastián (p204) is one of Spain's most beautiful cities, with a perfect arc of beach watched over by two soaring headlands. For most cities this would be enough. But San Sebastián is best known for its culture of *pintxos* (Basque tapas), and the bars of its Parte Vieja (old town) have made this one of the culinary capitals of the world.

4

⬊ SANTIAGO DE COMPOSTELA

The cathedral city of Santiago de Compostela (p216) is one of the most sacred in the Catholic world. A much-coveted destination for pilgrims along the Camino de Santiago, the city is laden with spiritual significance, and its staggering cathedral cannot fail to leave you moved. Santiago's monumental splendour co-exists alongside the wonderful food culture for which Galicia is famed.

↘ PICOS DE EUROPA

The Pyrenees may be Spain's best-known mountain range, but the Picos de Europa (p215) in Asturias are their equal for sheer mountain beauty. Rising from the hinterland of the Asturian and Cantabrian coasts, the Picos are extraordinarily picturesque. By car or on foot, this is the place to immerse yourself in hidden villages and quiet trails.

↘ NAVARRA'S HIDDEN VALLEYS

The quiet back roads of Navarra's Pyrenees are among Spain's most rewarding. The mountains run like a spine along the Spain–France border and shelter gorgeous valleys filled with old-world villages. The Valle del Roncal (p209) is our favourite, but it's closely followed by dozens of others seemingly cut off from the modern world.

↘ ASTURIAN & GALICIAN COASTS

Fronting onto the Bay of Biscay and the Atlantic, Spain's northwestern coast will linger in the memory. In Asturias, villages like Cudillero (p214) combine a strong fishing culture with stunning natural beauty. Further west in Galicia, the Rías Altas (p220) and Costa da Morte (p221) are worlds of windswept drama.

3 San Sebastián's Playa de la Concha (p205); 4 Pilgrims on the Camino de Santiago, Santiago de Compostela (p216); 5 Hiking in the Picos de Europa (p215); 6 Roncal (p209); 7 Costa da Morte (p221)

SPAIN'S NORTH COAST

SPAIN'S NORTH COAST'S BEST...

⬊ DRIVES

- **Valle del Roncal** (p209) Storybook villages and panoramic mountain views in Navarra.
- **Rías Altas** (p220) Towering cliffs and untamed beaches in Galicia.
- **Costa da Morte** (p221) Follow the haunting coastline of Galicia's 'Coast of Death'.

⬊ PLACES FOR A LOCAL DROP

- **Briones** (p210) Home to one of Spain's most interactive wine museums.
- **Laguardia** (p210) Charming hilltown in the heart of La Rioja wine country with plenty of wineries to visit nearby.
- **Cambados** (p211) Heartland of Galicia's Albariño wine country with a wine festival.
- **Asturian bars** (p216) Cider is a local obsession, poured from the barrel in almost all Asturian bars.

⬊ VILLAGE ESCAPES

- **Santillana del Mar** (p212) Achingly perfect medieval Cantabrian village.
- **Cudillero** (p214) The pick of many Asturian fishing villages.
- **Elantxobe** (p204) Stunning Basque village hard up against the cliffs.
- **Muxía** (p213) One of countless perfect villages along Galicia's coast.
- **Zugarramurdi** (p209) Perfect Pyrenean village in Navarra.

⬊ PLACES FOR CITY LIFE

- **San Sebastián** (p204) Gorgeous city and extraordinary food.
- **Santiago de Compostela** (p216) Cathedral city beloved by pilgrims and aesthetes alike.
- **Lugo** (p221) Encircled by 3rd-century Roman walls.

DAMIEN SIMONIS

Fishing fleet on the Costa da Morte (p221)

THINGS YOU NEED TO KNOW

⬎ VITAL STATISTICS

- **Population** 7.47 million
- **Area** 68,169 sq km
- **Best time to visit** May to September

⬎ LOCALITIES IN A NUTSHELL

- **Basque Country** (p200) Home to Bilbao and San Sebastián.
- **Navarra** (p209) Mountain area with the Pyrenees in the north.
- **La Rioja** (p210) Spain's premier wine country, south of the Basque Country.
- **Cantabria** (p211) Coastal region west of the Basque Country.
- **Asturias** (p214) Coastal region with the Picos de Europa inland.
- **Galicia** (p216) Home to Santiago de Compostela and isolated coastal stretches.

⬎ ADVANCE PLANNING

- **Two months before** Book your table at Arzak (p208).
- **One month before** Make sure you have your accommodation reserved.

⬎ RESOURCES

- **Basque Country** (www.basquecountry -tourism.com) Informative site for the Basque Country.
- **Navarra** (www.turismo.navarra.es) Everything you need to know about Navarra.
- **La Rioja** (www.lariojaturismo.com) Official tourist office site for La Rioja.

- **Asturias** (www.infoasturias.com) Tourist office website for Asturias.
- **Cantabria** (www.turismocantabria .net) One of the better Cantabrian portals.
- **Galicia** (www.turgalicia.es) Excellent window on Galicia.

⬎ EMERGENCY NUMBERS

- **Emergency** (☎ 112)
- **Policía Nacional** (☎ 091)

⬎ GETTING AROUND

- **Air** International airports in Bilbao, Santander, Oviedo, Santiago de Compostela, A Coruña and Vigo.
- **Train** Renfe (www.renfe.es) trains connect to the rest of Spain, FEVE (www.feve.es) runs along the coast.
- **Bus** Intermittent services where trains don't reach.
- **Road** Good network of roads.

⬎ BE FOREWARNED

- **Accommodation** Can be hard to find in San Sebastián (May to September) and Santiago de Compostela (July).
- **Arzak** The Basque Country's most celebrated restaurant closes the last two weeks in June and most of November.
- **Summer** Book your coastal accommodation months in advance.

SPAIN'S NORTH COAST

THINGS YOU NEED TO KNOW

SPAIN'S NORTH COAST ITINERARIES

BASQUE CITIES Three Days

Basque culture is one of the oldest in Europe, but (1) Bilbao (p200) offers confirmation that a willingness to embrace the outrageously modern is central to the Basque psyche. This is a town of fiercely guarded Basque traditions, not least in the seven streets of the Parte Vieja (old town) where Bilbao was born. Not far away, the futuristic Museo Guggenheim is one of Europe's most extraordinary architectural innovations. Put together, it's a fascinating cultural mix that deserves at least a day. For the remaining two days, lose yourself in (2) San Sebastián (p204), a gorgeous seaside city arrayed around a near-perfect beach. High-altitude vantage points also allow you to take in the town's panoramic beauty. In the impossibly narrow lanes of the old town, bar tops groan under the weight of *pintxos* (Basque tapas), from the basic Basque staples to the experimental high cuisine in miniature for which the region has become famous. Elsewhere in town, Michelin-starred restaurants provide a more formal but equally delicious dining experience.

WINE & THE PYRENEES Five Days

La Rioja, Spain's most prestigious wine-producing region, is studded with wine museums, wineries and towns where all they think about is wine. Away to the northeast, Navarra's Pyrenees are home to some of northern Spain's prettiest scenery.

For La Rioja, base yourself in (1) Laguardia (p210), a medieval hilltop town surrounded by vineyards. One of the best bodegas nearby is the Guggenheim-esque (2) Bodegas Marqués de Riscal (p211) in Elciego. Also along the Río Ebro, Briones has the astonishing (3) Dinastía Vivanco (p210), arguably La Rioja's best wine museum. Close by, (4) Haro (p211) also has a wine museum, wine festival and winery visits. A couple of hours' drive to the east, small-but-monumental (5) Olite (p211) is stunning in its own right, but it also hosts a terrific wine museum specialising in little-known Navarran wines. North of here, you could easily spend two to three days exploring the Navarran Pyrenees, in particular the (6) Valle del Roncal (p209), where you can pick up fine cheese to accompany your wine, and the area around (7) Ochagavía (p209).

ALONG THE COAST One Week

This itinerary takes you along the length of Spain's northern coast, connecting two of the region's most beguiling cities, with beautiful coastal villages all along the way.

After savouring the visual and culinary delights of (1) San Sebastián (p204), wind your way around the coves and cliffs of the Basque Coast. Pause in (2) Elantxobe (p204), which clings to vertiginous cliffs, then continue on to (3) Santillana del Mar (p212), which has, not unreasonably, been mentioned as a candidate for Spain's most beautiful village. As you cross the provincial border into Asturias, the coast becomes more rugged by degrees, throwing up charming settlements like (4) Comillas (p213), (5) Lastres (p213) and (6) Cudillero (p214). By the time you reach Galicia's (7) Rías Altas (p220) and the (8) Costa da Morte (p221), you'll have used up all your superlatives – this is coastal Spain at its most stirring. Although more beautiful villages line the waterfront all the way south to the Portuguese border, it's time to cut inland to (9) Santiago de Compostela (p216), a sacred city whose magnificent cathedral is the dream of many a pilgrim.

DISCOVER SPAIN'S NORTH COAST

Home to some of the most dramatic scenery in the country – from the Pyrenees of Navarra to wild coastline with picture-perfect villages – Spain's north coast and its hinterland is the Spain that most foreign visitors have yet to discover.

The diversity and culinary innovation of the Basque Country finds expression in two cities: magnificent San Sebastián, one of the world's most beautiful seaside cities, and Bilbao, whose stirring Guggenheim Museum has become the symbol for the region. The wine country of La Rioja is also not far away. The Basque Coast trails westwards and even more spectacularly into Cantabria and Asturias. Not far inland, the Picos de Europa rank among southern Europe's most eye-catching mountain areas.

By the time you reach Galicia in the northwest, you've left behind tourist Spain and the cliff-strewn coast has to be seen to be believed. It all culminates in Santiago de Compostela, whose cathedral is as splendid as it is spiritually significant.

BASQUE COUNTRY

No matter where you've just come from, be it the hot, southern plains of Spain or gentle and pristine France, the Basque Country is different. Known to Basques as Euskadi or Euskal Herria (the 'land of Basque Speakers'), and called El Pais Vasco in Spanish, this is where mountain peaks reach for the skies and sublime rocky coves are battered by mighty Atlantic swells. It's a place that demands exploration beyond the delightful main cities of Bilbao and San Sebastián.

BILBAO

pop 354,200

Bilbao (Basque: Bilbo) had a tough upbringing. But, like the kid from the estates who made it big, Bilbao's graft paid off when a few wise investments left it with a shimmering titanium fish called the Museo Guggenheim and a horde of arty groupies around the world.

INFORMATION

Tourist office (☎ 944 79 57 60; www.bilbao .net/bilbaoturismo) Main Office (Plaza del Ensanche 11; ☺ 9am-2pm & 4-7.30pm Mon-Fri); Guggenheim (Avenida Abandoibarra 2; ☺ 10am-7pm Mon-Sat, 10am-6pm Sun Jun-Sep, 11am-6pm Tue-Fri, 11am-7pm Sat, 11am-3pm Sun Oct-May)

SIGHTS

MUSEO DE BELLAS ARTES

A mere five minutes from Museo Guggenheim is Bilbao's **Museo de Bellas Artes** (Fine Arts Museum; ☎ 944 39 60 60; www .museobilbao.com; Plaza del Museo 2; adult/ student €5.50/4, admission free Wed; ☺ 10am-8pm Tue-Sun). More than just a complement to the Guggenheim, it often seems to actually exceed its more famous cousin for content.

There are three main subcollections: Classical Art, with works by Murillo, Zurbarán, El Greco, Goya and van Dyck; Contemporary Art, featuring works by Gauguin, Francis Bacon and Anthony

BILBAO

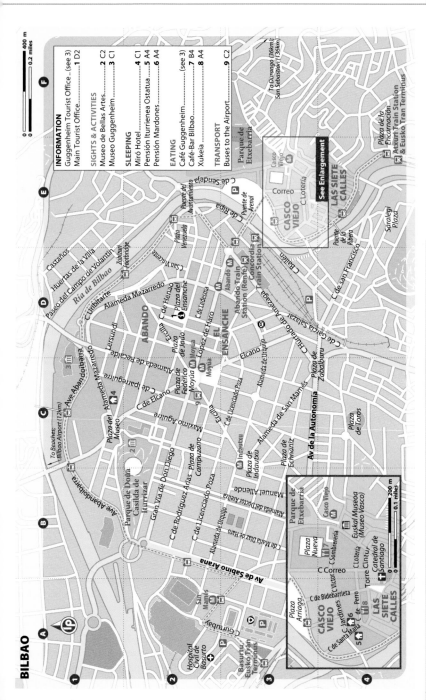

INFORMATION
Guggenheim Tourist Office...(see 3)
Main Tourist Office...................1 D2

SIGHTS & ACTIVITIES
Museo de Bellas Artes...............2 C2
Museo Guggenheim...................3 C1

SLEEPING
Miró Hotel...............................4 C1
Pensión Iturrienea Ostatua........5 A4
Pensión Mardones....................6 A4

EATING
Café Guggenheim..................(see 3)
Café-Bar Bilbao.......................7 B4
Xukela...................................8 A4

TRANSPORT
Buses to the Airport..................9 C2

Caro; and Basque Art, with the works of the great sculptors Jorge de Oteiza and Eduardo Chillida, and also strong paintings by the likes of Ignacio Zuloago and Juan de Echevarria.

CASCO VIEJO

The compact Casco Viejo, Bilbao's atmospheric old quarter, is full of charming streets, boisterous bars, and plenty of quirky and independent shops. At the heart of the Casco are Bilbao's original 'seven streets', Las Siete Calles, which date from the 1400s.

SLEEPING

Bilbao, like the Basque Country in general, is increasingly popular, and it can be very hard to find decent accommodation (especially at weekends). The Bilbao tourism authority has a very useful **reservations department** (☎ 902 87 72 98; www .bilbaoreservas.com).

Pensión Mardones (☎ 944 15 31 05; www.pensionmardones.com; Calle Jardines 4; s/d €34/48; 🖳) This well-kept number has nice carved wooden wardrobes in the rooms and lots of exposed wooden roof beams. The cheerful owner is very helpful and all up it offers great value.

ourpick Pensión Iturrienea Ostatua (☎ 944 16 15 00; www.iturrieneaostatua.com; Calle de Santa María 14; d/tr €70/96) Easily the most eccentric hotel in Bilbao, it's part farmyard, part old-fashioned toyshop, and a work of art in its own right. Try to get a room on the 1st floor; they are so full of character there'll be barely enough room for your own!

Miró Hotel (☎ 946 61 18 80; www.miro hotelbilbao.com; Alameda Mazarredo 77; s/d from €87/112; 🅿 ✂ 🖳 🎏) Dreamt up by fashion designer Antonio Miró, everything about this hotel is subtle, classy and absolutely in tune with the new Bilbao.

EATING

Though it lacks San Sebastián's stellar reputation for *pintxos,* prices are generally slightly lower here and the quality is about equal.

Xukeia (☎ 944 15 97 72; Calle de Perro) One of the more character-infused places in the old town, it has something of the look of a small-town French bistro overlaid with raucous Spanish soul. The drool-inducing *pintxos* have won awards and at only €1 to €1.50 a go are cheaper than elsewhere.

Café-Bar Bilbao (☎ 944 15 16 71; Plaza Nueva 6) This place, with its cool blue southern tile work and warm northern atmosphere, prides itself on very creative *pintxos,* so plunge straight in, if you dare, for a taste of *mousse de pata sobre crema de melocotón y almendras* (duck, cream, peach and almond mousse). Don't ask; just eat…

ourpick Café Guggenheim (☎ 944 23 93 33; www.restauranteguggenheim.com; lunch menú €19, restaurant mains €30-35) El Goog's modernist, chic restaurant and cafe are under the direction of multi-Michelin-starred chef Martin Berasategui. Needless to say, the *nueva cocina vasca* (Basque nouvelle cuisine) is breathtaking, including such mouth-waterers as roast vine tomato stuffed with baby squid with black risotto and fresh cream. Reservations are essential in the evening.

GETTING THERE & AWAY
AIR

Bilbao's **airport** (☎ 944 86 96 64; www.aena .es) is near Sondika, 12km northeast of the city.

TRAIN

The **Renfe** (☎ 902 24 02 02; www.renfe.es) Abando train station is just across the river from Plaza Arriaga and the Casco Viejo. There are two trains daily to Madrid (from

SPAIN'S NORTH COAST

ALDO PAVAN

Museo Guggenheim, Bilbao

BASQUE COUNTRY

⬊ MUSEO GUGGENHEIM

Opened in September 1997, Bilbao's Museo Guggenheim lifted modern architecture and Bilbao into the 21st century – with sensation.

Some might say, probably quite rightly, that structure overwhelms function here and that the Guggenheim is probably more famous for its architecture than its content. But Canadian architect Frank Gehry's inspired use of flowing canopies, cliffs, promontories, ship shapes, towers and flying fins is irresistible.

The interior of the Guggenheim is purposefully vast. The cathedral-like atrium is more than 45m high. Light pours in through the glass cliffs. Leading off from the atrium is Gallery 104, the Arcelor Gallery (formerly the Fish Gallery), a vast arena (128m by 30m) that houses Richard Serra's *Snake* and *The Matter of Time*.

Galleries 103 and 105 house selections from the Guggenheim permanent collection, and can include works by Picasso, Braque, Mondrian, Miró, Rothko, Klee and Kandinsky. But for most people it is the temporary exhibitions that are the main attraction (check the Guggenheim's website for a full program of upcoming exhibitions).

Excellent self-guided audio tours in various languages are free with admission.

Things you need to know: ☎ 944 35 90 80; www.guggenheim-bilbao.es; Avenida Abandoibarra 2; adult/under 12yr/student €12.50/free/7.50; ⏲ 10am-8pm daily Jul & Aug, 10am-8pm Tue-Sun Sep-Jun

€39.80, six hours) and Barcelona (€39.80, nine hours).

Next door is the Concordia train station with its handsome art-nouveau facade of wrought iron and tiles. It is used by the FEVE (☎ 944 23 22 66; www.feve.es) private rail company for running trains west into Cantabria and Asturias.

The Atxuri train station is about 1km upriver from Casco Viejo. From here, **Eusko Tren/Ferrocarril Vasco** (**ET/FV**; ☎ 902 54 32 10; www.euskotren.es in Spanish & Basque) operates services every half-hour to Bermeo (€2.40, 1½ hours) via Guernica (€2.40, one hour) and Mundaka (€2.40, 1½ hours), and hourly to San Sebastián (€6.50, 2¾ hours) via Durango, Zumaia and Zarautz.

GETTING AROUND

The airport bus (Bizkaibus A3247; €1.25, 30 minutes) departs from a stand on the extreme right as you leave Arrivals. It runs through the northwestern section of the city, passing the Museo Guggenheim, stopping at Plaza Moyúa and terminating at the Termibus (bus station). It runs every 20 minutes from 5.20am to 10.20pm.

Taxis from the airport to the Casco Viejo cost about €25.

There are metro stations at all the main focal points of the Ensanche and at Casco Viejo. Tickets start at €1.30.

Bilbao's Eusko Tran tramline is a boon to locals and visitors alike. It runs to and fro between Basurtu, in the southwest of the city, and the Atxuri train station. Stops include the Termibus station, the Guggenheim and Teatro Arriaga by the Casco Viejo. Tickets cost €1 and need to be verified in the machine next to the ticket dispenser before boarding.

CENTRAL BASQUE COAST

The coast road from Bilbao to San Sebastián is a glorious journey past spectacular seascapes, with cove after cove stretching east and verdant fields suddenly ending where cliffs plunge into the sea. *Casas rurales* (village or farmstead accommodation) and camping grounds are plentiful and well signposted.

ELANTXOBE

pop 460

The tiny hamlet of Elantxobe, with its colourful houses clasping like geckos to an almost sheer cliff face, is undeniably one of the most attractive spots along the entire coast. The difficulty of building here, and the lack of a beach, has meant that it has been saved from the worst of tourist-related development. Public-transport fans will be so excited by Elantxobe that the earth really will move for them – the streets are so narrow that buses don't have space to turn around, so the road spins around for them!

SAN SEBASTIÁN

pop 183,300

It's impossible to lay eyes on San Sebastián (Basque: Donostia) and not fall madly in love. This stunning city is everything that grimy Bilbao is not: cool, svelte and flirtatious by night, charming and well mannered by day. For it's setting, form and attitude, Playa de la Concha is the equal of any city beach in Europe. As the sun falls on another sweltering summer's day, you'll sit back with a drink and an artistic *pintxo* and realise that yes, you too are in love with sexy San Sebastián.

INFORMATION

Centro de Atracción y Turismo (**CAT**; ☎ 943 48 11 66; www.sansebastianturismo.com; Blvd Reina Regente 3; ☻ 8.30am-8pm Mon-Sat, 10am-7pm Sun Jun-Sep, 9am-2pm & 3.30-7pm Mon-Sat, 10am-2pm Sun Oct-May)

SIGHTS & ACTIVITIES

You can walk to the top of **Monte Urgull**, topped by low castle walls and a grand statue of Christ, by taking a path from Plaza de Zuloaga or from behind the aquarium. The views are breathtaking.

San Sebastián and the peak of Monte Igueldo

DAVID TOMLINSON

The views from the summit of **Monte Igueldo**, just west of town, will make you feel like a circling hawk staring over the vast panorama of the Bahía de la Concha and the surrounding coastline and mountains. The best way to get there is via the old-world **funicular railway** (return adult/child €2.30/1.70; ☼ 10am-10pm Jul & Aug, 10 or 11am-6 or 9pm depending on the month rest of the year) to the **Parque de Atracciones** (amusement park; ☎ 943 21 02 11; ☼ 11am-6pm Mon-Tue & Thu-Fri, 11am-8pm Sat & Sun).

Fulfilling almost every idea of how a perfect city beach should be formed, **Playa de la Concha** and its westerly extension, **Playa de Ondarreta**, are easily among the best city beaches in Europe. Throughout the long summer months a fiesta atmosphere prevails, with thousands of tanned and toned bodies spread across the sands.

FESTIVALS & EVENTS

Among San Sebastián's top draws is the **International Jazz Festival**, held in July. The world-renowned, two-week **Film Festival** (www.sansebastianfestival.com) has been an annual fixture in the second half of September since 1957.

SLEEPING

Accommodation standards in San Sebastián are generally good, but prices are high and availability in high season very tight. If you turn up without a booking, the tourist office keeps a list of available rooms.

ourpick **Pensión Amaiur Ostatua** (☎ 943 42 96 54; www.pensionamaiur.com; Calle de 31 de Agosto 44; s/d without bathroom €55/60; ☐) With only nine rooms, getting a space here is tough, but well worth the battle. The rooms are small but have had a great deal of thought put into them – there's chintzy wallpaper in the hallways, brazen primary colours in the bedrooms and everywhere a bizarre mix of African savannah and French street-scene paintings.

Pensión Aida (☎ 943 32 78 00; www .pensionesconencanto.com; Calle de Iztueta 9; s/d €59/78; ☐) The owners of this excellent *pensión* read the rule book on what makes a good hotel and have complied exactly.

SAN SEBASTIÁN

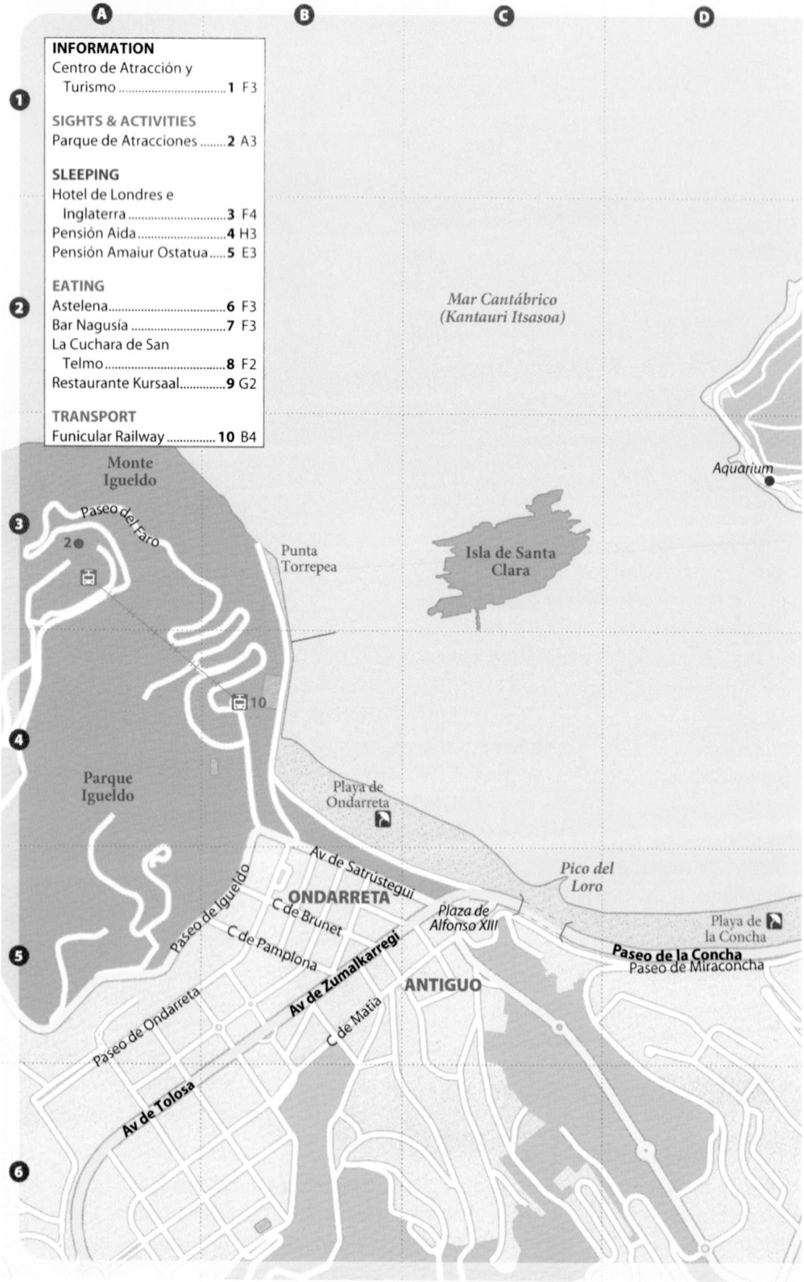

INFORMATION
Centro de Atracción y
  Turismo **1** F3

SIGHTS & ACTIVITIES
Parque de Atracciones **2** A3

SLEEPING
Hotel de Londres e
  Inglaterra **3** F4
Pensión Aida **4** H3
Pensión Amaiur Ostatua.....**5** E3

EATING
Astelena...................................**6** F3
Bar Nagusía **7** F3
La Cuchara de San
  Telmo **8** F2
Restaurante Kursaal.............**9** G2

TRANSPORT
Funicular Railway **10** B4

*Mar Cantábrico
(Kantauri Itsasoa)*

Aquarium

Monte
Igueldo

Paseo del Faro

2

10

Punta
Torrepea

*Isla de Santa
Clara*

Parque
Igueldo

Playa de
Ondarreta

*Pico del
Loro*

*Playa de
la Concha*

Av de Satrústegui

ONDARRETA

C de Brunet

*Plaza de
Alfonso XIII*

Paseo de la Concha
Paseo de Miraconcha

Paseo de Igueldo

C de Pamplona

Av de Zumalkarregi

ANTIGUO

Paseo de Ondarreta

C de Matia

Av de Tolosa

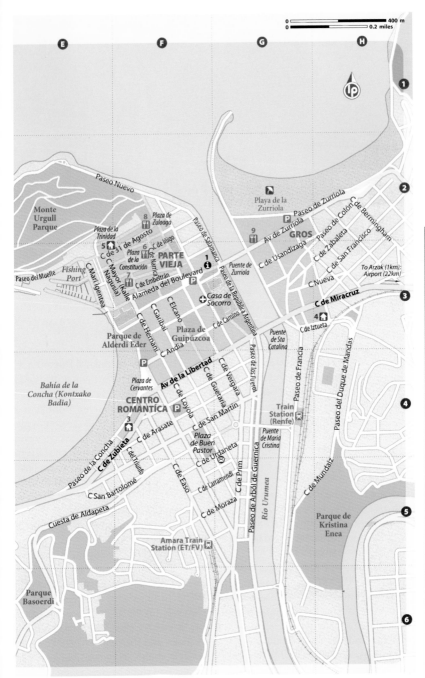

Beech forest in the Pyrenees

ROBERTO GEROMETTA

The rooms are bright and bold, full of exposed stone, and everything smells fresh and clean.

Hotel de Londres e Inglaterra (☎ 943 44 07 70; www.hlondres.com; Calle de Zubieta 2; s/d from €175/225; P X 🖳) Queen Isabel II set the tone for this hotel well over a century ago and things have stayed pretty regal ever since. It oozes class and some rooms have stunning views over Playa de la Concha.

EATING

There are *pintxos* and then there are San Sebastián *pintxos*. To prove it's not just a one-trick pony, San Sebastián has some superb restaurants and is home to more Michelin stars than even Paris.

our pick **Astelena** (Calle de Iñigo 1) The *pintxos* draped across the counter in this bar, tucked into the corner of Plaza de la Constitución, stand out as some of the best in the city. Many of them are a fusion of Basque and Asian inspirations.

Bar Nagusía (Kalle Nagusia 4) This old-San-Sebastián-style bar has a counter that

moans under the weight of its *pintxos*. You'll be moaning after a few as well – in sheer pleasure.

our pick **La Cuchara de San Telmo** (☎ 943 42 08 40; Calle de 31 de Agosto 28) This unfussy, hidden-away bar offers miniature *nueva cocina vasca* from a supremely creative kitchen, where chefs Alex Montiel and Iñaki Gulin conjure up such delights as *carrílera de ternera al vino tinto* (calf cheeks in red wine), with meat so tender it starts to dissolve almost before it's past your lips.

Restaurante Kursaal (☎ 943 00 31 62; Avenida de Zurriola 1; tasting menus from €48; 🕒 closed mid-Dec–mid-Jan) The Michelin-starred Restaurante Kursaal is another of top chef Martin Berasategui's outstations. Downstairs is what is being touted as a 'gastro pub' (open Sunday to Wednesday; *menú* from €24). A gastro pub with a Michelin-starred chef – we like that!

Arzak (☎ 943 27 84 65; Avenida Alcalde Jose Elosegui 273; meals €100-160) With more Michelin stars than we've had hot dinners (well OK, three), acclaimed Chef Juan Mari Arzak takes some beating when it comes to *nueva cocina vasca*. Reservations, well in advance, are obligatory. The restaurant is closed for the last two weeks in June and for most of November. Prices are high, but then this man has cooked for the Queen of England.

GETTING THERE & AWAY
The city's **airport** (☎ 902 40 47 04) is 22km out of town, near Hondarribia. There are regular flights to Madrid and occasional charters to major European cities.

The main **Renfe train station** (Paseo de Francia) is just across Río Urumea, on a line linking Paris to Madrid.

NAVARRA

The Navarran capital, Pamplona, tends to grab the headlines with its world-famous running of the bulls, but the region's real charm is in its peppering of small towns and villages, each one with a unique history and an iconography that covers every kind of architecture.

THE PYRENEES
Awash in greens and often concealed in mists, the rolling hills, ribboned cliffs, clammy forests and snow-plastered mountains that make up the Navarran Pyrenees are a playground for outdoor enthusiasts and pilgrims on the Camino de Santiago.

Trekkers and skiers should be thoroughly equipped at any time of the year and note emergency numbers in case of difficulties: ☎ 112 in Navarra or ☎ 17 in Aquitaine (France).

Further information on these wonderful mountains can be obtained from the **Federación Navarra de Deportes de Montaña y Escalada** (☎ in Pamplona 948 22 46 83, in San Sebastián 943 47 42 79; www.fed me.es).

VALLE DEL RONCAL
Navarra's most spectacular mountain area is around **Roncal**, and this easternmost valley is an alternative route for leaving or entering the Navarran Pyrenees. For details of *casas rurales* in the valley, visit the **Roncal-Salazar** (www.roncal-salazar.com) website.

The gateway to this part of the Pyrenees is **Burgui** – an enchanting huddle of stone houses built beside a clear, gushing stream (the Río Esca) bursting with frogs and fish and crossed via a humpbacked Roman bridge. You can swim from a small beach on the banks of the stream.

MELBA PHOTO AGENCY/ALAMY

Ziga

➘ IF YOU LIKE...

If you like the Pyrenees' **Valle del Roncal** (above), we think you'll also like these other mountain areas of Navarra:

- **Valle del Baztán** Charming villages such as Arraioz, Ziga and Zugarramurdi in Navarra's northern foothills.
- **Valle del Salazar** Valley leading down from the Pyrenees with medieval villages.
- **Roncesvalles** World-famous pilgrimage site just across the border from France.
- **Ochagavía** Grey slate, stone and cobblestone village in the heart of the Pyrenees.

The largest centre along this road, though still firmly a village, Roncal is a place of cobblestone alleyways that twist and turn between dark stone houses and meander down to a river full of trout. Roncal is renowned for its Queso de Roncal, a sheep's-milk cheese that's sold in the village.

The **tourist office** (☎ 948 47 52 56; www .valledaroncal.es; ☉ 10am-2pm & 4.30-8.30pm Mon-Sat, 10am-2pm Sun mid-Jun–mid-Sep, 10am-2pm Mon-Thu & Sun, 10am-2pm & 4.30-7.30pm Fri & Sat mid-Sep–mid-Jun), on the main road towards the Isaba exit from town, has an excellent interpretation centre (€1.20).

LA RIOJA

Get out the *copas* (glasses) for La Rioja and for some of the best red wines produced in the country. Wine goes well with the region's ochre earth and vast blue skies, which seem far more Mediterranean than the Basque greens further north. The bulk of the vineyards line Río Ebro around the town of Haro, but extend also into neighbouring Navarra and the Basque province of Álava.

La Rioja wine rolls on and off the tongue with ease, by name as well as taste. All wine fanciers know the famous wines of La Rioja, where the vine has been cultivated since Roman times. The region is classic vine country and vineyards cover the hinterland of Río Ebro. On the river's north bank, the region is part of the Basque Country and is known as La Rioja Alavesa.

BRIONES

pop 900 / elev 501m

The sunset-gold village crawls gently up a hillside and offers commanding views over the surrounding vine-carpeted plains, where you will find the fantastic

Dinastía Vivanco (Museo de la Cultura del Vino; ☎ 902 32 00 01; adult/child/student €7.50/ free/6.50; ☉ 10am-8pm Tue-Sun Jun-Sep, 10am-6pm Tue-Thu & Sun, 10am-8pm Fri & Sat Oct-May). This space-age museum is the creation of Pedro Vivanco Paracuello. Over several floors and numerous rooms you will learn all about the history and culture of wine and the various processes that go into its production. At the end of the tour you can enjoy some wine tasting and, by booking in advance, you can join a tour of the winery (€6.50; in Spanish only).

Currently the only place to rest wine-heavy heads is **Los Calaos de Briones** (☎ 941 32 21 31; www.loscalaosdebriones.com; Calle San Juan 13; r €58), which has pleasant rooms in shades of peach and sky-blue. Some have suitably romantic four-posters. The attached restaurant is stuffed with excellent locally inspired cuisine (mains €12 to €13).

LAGUARDIA

pop 1490 / elev 557m

It's easy to spin back the wheels of time in the medieval fortress town of Laguardia, or the 'Guard of Navarra' as it was once appropriately known, sitting proudly on its rocky hilltop.

The **tourist office** (☎ 945 60 08 45; Plaza de San Juan; ☉ 10am-2pm & 4-7pm Mon-Fri, 10am-2pm & 5-7pm Sat, 10.45am-5pm Sun) has a list of bodegas that can be visited in the local area.

Maybe the most impressive feature of the town is the castlelike **Puerta de San Juan**, one of the most stunning city gates in Spain. Also impressive is the **Iglesia de Santa María de los Reyes** (☎ 945 50 08 45; guided tours €2), which has a breathtaking late-14th-century Gothic doorway, covered with beautiful sculptures of the disciples and other motifs.

SLEEPING & EATING

ourpick **Casa Rural Legado de Ugarte**
(☎ 945 60 01 14; legadodeugarte@hotmail.com;
Calle Mayor 17; r incl breakfast €75) This is one
that you're going to either love or hate –
we love it. Recently renovated, the entrance and reception have more of the
same old-world flavour you'll be starting
to get bored of, but the bright and very
comfortable rooms are an arresting mix
of purple, silver and gold pomp.

Posada Mayor de Migueloa (☎ 945
62 11 75; www.mayordemigueloa.com; Mayor de
Migueloa 20; s/d €90/115; Ⓟ Ⓧ) For the ultimate in gracious La Rioja living, this old
mansion-hotel is simply irresistible. The
in-house restaurant offers fine local cuisine with meals starting at about €20.

GETTING THERE & AWAY

Six slow daily buses connecting Vitoria
and Logroño pass through Laguardia.

AROUND LAGUARDIA

Your own transport is essential for exploring here. There are several wine cellars that
can be visited, often with advance notice –
contact the tourist office in Laguardia for
details. **Bodegas Palacio** (☎ 945 60 00 57;
Carretera de Elciego), only 1km from Laguardia
on the Elciego road, is one of the most re-
ceptive to visitors. The star attraction of
the area, though, is the **Bodegas Marqués
de Riscal** (☎ 945 60 60 00; www.marquesderiscal
.com), on the edge of the village of Elciego,
designed by Frank Gehry and known as
Spain's second Guggenheim.

CANTABRIA

Sliced up by deep mountain valleys
dotted with the occasional settlement,
Cantabria remained until recently virtually untouched by the modern legions of
visitors that flock to Spain each year.

OLIVER STREWE

Harvest time in Galicia

⬎ IF YOU LIKE...

If you like the Dinastía **wine museum** (p210), we think you'll also
like these other wine attractions:

- **Haro** The unattractive capital of
  La Rioja wine country, Haro has
  an informative Museo del Vino
  and winery visits.
- **Museo del Vino, Olite** Outstanding wine museum in one of
  Navarra's most charming small
  towns.
- **Museo de la Sidra, Nava** Fine
  museum in the capital of Asturian cider production.
- **Cambados** Pretty seaside capital
  of Galicia's Albariño wine country with a fine wine festival at
  the end of July.
- **Ribadavia** The headquarters of
  the Ribeiro wine region, which
  produces Galicia's best whites.

It offers a little of everything for the traveller looking for an escape. Some pretty
beaches make summer seaside days quite
possible (unreliable weather permitting),
while the inland valleys, sprinkled with
quiet towns and villages, offer a feast of
natural beauty for the eyes, whether you
choose to drive the country roads or walk
the trails. The rugged ranges culminate in
the west in the abrupt mountainous walls
of the Picos de Europa.

Dotted around the region are more than 400 often beautifully restored country homes to stay in (which go by various names, such as *casas rurales* and *posadas*). Check out www.turismocantabria.net, www.turismoruralcantabria.com or www.cantabriarural.com for listings.

EASTERN CANTABRIA

Short on specific sights but rich in unspoiled rural splendour, the little-visited valleys of eastern Cantabria are ripe for exploration. Plenty of routes suggest themselves: what follows is but a sample.

From El Soto, on the N623 just south of Puente Viesgo, take the CA270 southeast towards Vega de Pas. The town is of minimal interest, but the drive is something. The views from the **Puerto de la Braguía**

Santillana del Mar

PHILIP GAME

pass, in particular, are stunning. From Vega de Pas continue southeast, briefly crossing into Castilla y León, before turning north again at Río de Trueba, then following Río Miera down through San Roque de Riomiera towards Santander.

WESTERN CANTABRIA

SANTILLANA DEL MAR

pop 4000

This medieval jewel is in such a perfect state of preservation, with its bright cobbled streets and tanned stone and brick buildings huddling in a muddle of centuries of history, that it seems too good to be true. Surely it's a film set! Well, no. People still live here, passing their precious houses down from generation to generation.

You'll find an informative **tourist office** (☎ 942 81 88 12; Calle del Escultor Jesús Otero 20; ⏱ 9am-9pm Jul-Sep, 9.30am-1.30pm & 4-7pm Oct-Jun) at the main car park. You can also get information on the town at www.santillanadelmar.com.

SIGHTS

A stroll along the cobbled main street, past solemn nobles' houses from the 15th to 18th centuries, leads you to the lovely 12th-century Romanesque **Colegiata de Santa Juliana** (admission €3; ⏱ 10am-1.30pm & 4-7.30pm daily Jun-Sep, 10am-1.30pm & 4-6.30pm Tue-Sun Oct-May).

Santillana also hosts an eclectic bunch of museums, cultural foundations and exhibitions.

SLEEPING

Posada Santa Juliana (☎ 942 84 01 06; Calle Carrera 19; d €57) A short walk in from the main road, this charming *casona* (medieval house) has six smallish but tastefully restored doubles with creaking timber floors and wooden furniture.

ourpick La Casa del Organista (☎ 942 84 03 52; www.casadelorganista.com; Camino de Los Hornos 4; s/d €79/96; Ⓟ) Rooms at this elegant 18th-century house, once home to the *colegiata*'s organist, are particularly attractive, with wood-rail balconies, plush rugs, antique furniture and plenty of exposed heavy beams and stonework.

EATING

La Villa (☎ 942 81 83 64; Plaza de la Gándara s/n; meals €25-30; ◔ Thu-Tue) Wander through the great timber doors into the courtyard. To your left is a bar with benches; to the right and upstairs is the dining area. They're brought together as though under a big top of heavy, dark timber beams. The meat dishes, such as the *solomillo con salsa de queso* (sirloin in cheese sauce; €15), are its strong suit.

Restaurante Gran Duque (☎ 942 84 03 86; www.granduque.com; Calle del Escultor Jesús Otero 5; meals €35; ◔ lunch & dinner daily Jul-Aug, lunch & dinner Tue-Sat, lunch Sun, dinner Mon Sep-Jun) The food is high-quality local fare and what sets it apart is the setting, a grand stone house with noble trappings and nice decorative touches such as the exposed brick and beams.

GETTING THERE & AWAY

Autobuses La Cantábrica (☎ 942 72 08 22) has buses four times a day Monday to Friday, with three on Saturday and Sunday, from Santander to Santillana (€2.15, 35 minutes), and on to Comillas and San Vicente de la Barquera.

MUSEO & CUEVA DE ALTAMIRA

The country's finest prehistoric art, in the Cueva de Altamira (Altamira Cave), 2km southwest of Santillana del Mar, is now off limits to all but the scientific community.

Lastres

ROGER DAY/ALAMY

⟩ IF YOU LIKE...

If you like close-to-seaside villages like Santillana del Mar (p212), we think you'll also like:

- Lastres Precarious cliff-side fishing village with some 16th-century churches thrown in, east of Gijón.
- Comillas Cobbled streets, a golden beach and a Gaudí-designed building, west of Santillana del Mar.
- Pontedeume Medieval Galician hillside town overlooking the Eume estuary northeast of A Coruña.
- Combarro Postcard-perfect village set around a bay close to Pontevedra.
- Baiona Medium-sized town with a village feel and spectacular seaside fortress in Galicia's far southwest.
- Muxía Quaint village in Galicia's extreme west.
- Getaria Highly attractive medieval fishing settlement west of San Sebastián.

Since 2001, however, Museo Altamira (☎ 942 81 80 05; http://museodealtamira.mcu.es; adult/senior & under 18yr/student €2.40/free/1.20, Sun & from 2.30pm Sat free; ◔ 9.30am-8pm Tue-Sat, 9.30am-3pm Sun & holidays May-Oct, 9.30am-

SPAIN'S NORTH COAST

CANTABRIA

6pm Tue-Sat, 9.30am-3pm Sun & holidays Nov-Apr; Ⓟ) has allowed all comers to view the inspired, 14,500-year-old depictions of bison, horses and other beasts (or rather, their replicas) in this full-size, dazzling re-creation of the cave's most interesting chamber, the Sala de Polícromos (Polychrome Hall).

During the Easter period and from July to September it's worth purchasing tickets in advance at branches of **Banco de Santander** (☎ 902 24 24 24; www.banco santander.es in Spanish), or by phoning or visiting the website (click on 'Get your tickets'). Those without vehicles must walk or take a taxi from Santillana del Mar.

ASTURIAS

Asturias' beauty lies in its stunning countryside. Much of the Picos de Europa are on Asturian territory, and fishing villages such as Llanes and Cudillero make great bases for exploring the lovely coast, dotted with picture-postcard coves (it is said there are more than 600 beaches on the Asturian coast) and inlets.

WEST COAST
CUDILLERO
pop 1710

Cudillero is the most picturesque fishing village on the Asturian coast, and it knows it. The houses, painted in varying pastel shades, cascade down to a tiny port on a narrow inlet. Despite its touristy feel, Cudillero is cute and remains reasonably relaxed, even in mid-August when almost every room in town is occupied.

For a good map of area beaches, stop by the **tourist office** (☎ 985 59 13 77; www .ayuntamientodecudillero.org; ☑ 10am-9pm daily Jul-Sep, 10am-2pm & 5-8pm Mon-Sat, 11am-2pm Sun Oct-Jun) by the port, which is also the only place to park.

The main activity is watching the fishing boats come in (between 5pm and 8pm) and unload their catch, then sampling fish, molluscs and urchins at the *sidrerías* (cider houses). The former *lonja* (fish market) is now a minor fishing museum.

BEACHES
The coast around here is a particularly appealing sequence of cliffs and beaches.

Playa del Silencio (also called El Gavieiru), 15km west of Cudillero, could certainly qualify as one of Spain's most beautiful beaches: a long sandy cove backed by a natural rock amphitheatre. Take the exit for Novellana and follow signs to Castañeras.

SLEEPING
Hotel Casa Prendes (☎ 985 59 15 00; Calle San José 4; d €82) This blue-fronted stop is a nicely maintained port hotel. Single rates (€48 to €58) are available outside August. The owners also rent apartments.

La Casona de Pío (☎ 985 59 15 12; www .arrakis.es/~casonadepio in Spanish; Calle del Ríofrío; s/d €66/84) Just back from the port area is this charming stone house, featuring 11 very comfortable rooms with a rustic touch, and a good restaurant.

EATING
Sidrería El Patrón (Calle de Suárez Inclán 2; meals €20) Back up the road a bit from the port, this is where many locals hang out for *raciones* of seafood or cheese, and sausage or ham platters (€6 to €16).

El Faro (☎ 985 59 15 32; Calle del Ríofrío; meals €30; ☑ Thu-Tue) This is an attractive eatery hidden one street back from the port. A combination of stone, timber and blue decor creates a welcoming atmosphere in which to dig into an *arroz caldoso* (a seafood and rice stew).

GETTING THERE & AWAY

The bus station is at the top of the hill, 800m from the port, and the FEVE train station is 1km further inland.

PICOS DE EUROPA

These jagged, deeply fissured mountains straddling Asturias, Cantabria and the northeast of Castilla y León province amount to some of the finest walking country in Spain, offering plentiful short and long outings for striders of all levels, plus lots of scope for climbers and cavers, too.

Beginning only 15km from the coast, and stretching little more than 40km from east to west and 25km north to south, the Picos still encompass enough spectacular mountain and gorge scenery to ensure a continual flow of Spanish and international visitors. They comprise three limestone massifs, whose geological structure is unique in Spain and similar to that of the Alps: the eastern Macizo Andara, with a summit of 2444m; the western Macizo El Cornión, rising to 2596m; and the particularly rocky Macizo Central or Macizo Los Urrieles, reaching 2648m. The 647-sq-km Parque Nacional de los Picos de Europa covers all three massifs and is Spain's second-biggest national park. Virtually deserted in winter, the area is full to bursting in August and you should always try to book ahead.

The main access towns for the Picos are Cangas de Onís in the northwest, Arenas de Cabrales in the central north and Potes in the southeast. Paved roads lead from Cangas southeast up to Covadonga, Lago de Enol and Lago de la Ercina; from Arenas south up to Poncebos then east up to Sotres and Tresviso; and from Potes west to Fuente Dé.

MAPS

The best maps of the Picos, sold in shops in Cangas de Onís, Potes and elsewhere for €4 to €5 each, are Adrados Ediciones' *Picos de Europa* (1:80,000), *Picos de Europa Macizos Central y Oriental* (1:25,000) and *Picos de Europa Macizo Occidental* (1:25,000).

SPAIN'S NORTH COAST

ASTURIAS

ROBIN CHAPMAN

Cudillero

SAMPLING CIDER

Ancient documents show Asturians were sipping apple cider as far back as the 8th century! The region, which produces 80% of Spanish cider (the rest is made in Galicia, the Basque Country and Navarra), churns out anything up to 30 million litres a year, depending on the apple harvest. Apples are reaped in autumn and crushed to a pulp (about three-quarters of the apple winds up as apple juice). A mix of bitter, sour and sweet apples is used. The cider is fermented in *pipes* (barrels) kept in *llagares* (the place where the cider is made) over winter. It takes about 800kg of apples to fill a 450L *pipa*, which makes 600 bottles.

Traditionally, the *pipes* were transported to *chigres* (cider taverns) all over Asturias, and punters would be served direct from the *pipa*. The *chigre* is dying out, though, and most cider is now served in bottles in *sidrerías* (cider houses), usually with tapas or full meals. The cider is *estanciado* – that is, served by pouring it from the bottle, which the barman holds overhead, into a glass held low. This gives it some fizz. Such a glass of cider is known as a *culete* or *culín* and should be knocked back in one hit.

INFORMATION

The national park's main information office, in Cangas de Onís, is **Casa Dago** (☎ 985 84 86 14; Avenida de Covadonga 43; ☻ 9am-2.30pm). Sometimes it opens in the afternoon too. Other park information offices are in **Posada de Valdeón** (☎ 987 74 05 49; Travesía de los Llanos; ☻ 9am-5pm daily Jul & Aug, 9am-2pm Sat & Sun Sep-Jun) in the southwest, where hours can vary considerably, and in **Tama** (☎ 942 73 81 09; Avenida Luis Cuevas 2A; ☻ 9am-8pm Jun-Sep, 9am-6pm Oct-May) in east Cantabria. Basic information on walks and accommodation is available at these offices. Local tourist offices can usually provide information too.

GETTING THERE & AROUND

Trying to taste the main delights of the Picos by public transport can be frustrating, if you're not hanging around long enough to criss-cross them on foot. Just a few bus and train services – mostly in summer only – will get you into the hills.

GALICIA
SANTIAGO DE COMPOSTELA

pop 88,000 / elev 260m

Whether you're wandering its medieval streets, nibbling on tapas in the taverns along Rúa do Franco, gazing down at the rooftops from atop the cathedral, or immersed in the gold-tinged splendour of its ecclesiastical monuments, Santiago seduces.

The faithful believe that Santiago Apóstol (St James) preached in Galicia and, after his death in Palestine, was brought back by stone boat and was buried here. The tomb was supposedly rediscovered in 813 by a religious hermit who followed a guiding star (hence 'Compostela', from the Latin *campus stellae, campo de estrella*, or field of the star). The grave became a rallying symbol for Christian Spain, the Asturian king Alfonso II turned up to have a church erected above the holy remains, pilgrims began flocking to it and the rest is history.

SPAIN'S NORTH COAST

GALICIA

INFORMATION

City tourist office (☎ 981 55 51 29; www
.santiagoturismo.com; Rúa do Vilar 63; ⏲ 9am-
9pm Jun-Sep, 9am-2pm & 4-7pm Oct-May)

SIGHTS

CATEDRAL DE SANTIAGO DE COMPOSTELA

The grand heart of Santiago, the **cathedral** (Praza do Obradoiro; www.catedraldesan
tiago.es; ⏲ 7am-9pm) soars above the city
centre in a splendid jumble of moss-
covered spires and statues. Though
Galicia's grandest monument was built
piecemeal through the centuries, its
beauty is only enhanced by the enticing
mix of Romanesque, baroque and Gothic
flourishes.

Most people enter via the lavish
staircase and facade on the Praza do
Obradoiro. Just behind the grand doorway is the artistically unparalleled **Pórtico
de la Gloria** (Galician: Porta da Gloria), the
original entryway. Its impact is undoubtedly muted by the exterior baroque facade, which protects the 200 sculptures of
Maestro Mateo, the architect and sculptor
placed in charge of the program of cathedral building in the late 12th century by
Fernando II of León.

Approaching the Churrigueresque
Altar Mayor (Main Altar), a small staircase
on the right side leads to a 13th-century
statue of Santiago. You emerge on the
left side, then proceed down some steps
to contemplate what you are assured is
his **tomb**.

A special pilgrims' Mass is celebrated
at noon daily. Other High-Altar masses
take place Monday through Saturday at
9.30am and 7.30pm and on Sundays at
10am. You may catch one of the special
Masses where the world's greatest dispenser of incense, the **botafumeiro**, is
swung across the church.

OTHER ATTRACTIONS

Santiago's greatest pleasures are simply
wandering its arcaded streets and drift-
ing in and out of the tapas bars along the
Rúas Franco and Raíña.

The **Museo das Peregrinacións** (☎ 981 58
15 58; Rúa de San Miguel 4; admission €2.40; ⏲ 10am-
8pm Tue-Fri, 10.30am-1.30pm & 5-8pm Sat, 10.30am-
1.30pm Sun) explores the Camino de Santiago
phenomenon over the centuries.

TOURS

For an unforgettable bird's-eye view of
the city, take the **cathedral rooftop tour**
(☎ 981 55 29 85; www.archicompostela.com; per
person €10; ⏲ 10am-2pm & 4-8pm) organised
by the Museo da Catedral. This tour is
the only way to visit the Gothic **Pazo de**

CHRISTOPHER HERWIG

Camino pilgrim route, Santiago de Compostela

SANTIAGO DE COMPOSTELA

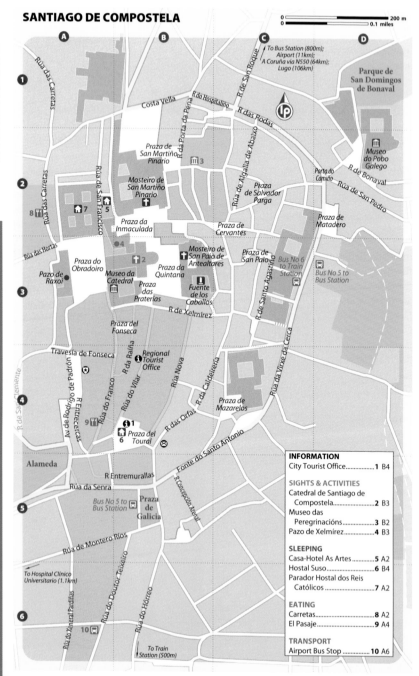

0 — 200 m
0 — 0.1 miles

To Bus Station (800m);
Airport (11km);
A Coruña via N550 (64km);
Lugo (106km)

Parque de
San Domingos
de Bonaval

Rúa das Carretas

Costa Vella

R do Hospitaliño

R de San Roque

R das Rodas

Praza de
San Martiño
Pinario

Museo
do Pobo
Galego

R de Bonaval

Rúa de San Pedro

Rúa de San Francisco

Rúa das Carretas

Mosteiro de
San Martiño
Pinario

Porta do
Camiño

Praza de
Salvador
Parga

Praza da
Inmaculada

Praza de
Cervantes

Rúa de Algalia de Abaixo

Praza de
Matadero

Rúa das Hortas

Pazo de
Raxoi

Praza do
Obradoiro

Museo da
Catedral

Praza
das
Praterías

Praza da
Quintana

Mosteiro de
San Paio de
Antealtares

Fuente
de los
Caballos

Praza de
San Paio

R de Xelmírez

Bus No 6
to Train
Station

Bus No 5 to
Bus Station

R de Santo Agostiño

Praza del
Fonseca

Travesía de Fonseca

Regional
Tourist
Office

R de San Clemente

R de Rodrigo de Padrón

R Entrecercas

Rúa do Franco

Rúa do Vilar

Rúa da Raíña

Rúa Nova

R da Caldeirería

Praza de
Mazarelos

Rúa da Virxe da Cerca

Praza del
Toural

R das Orfas

Fonte do Santo Antonio

Alameda

R Entremurallas

Rúa da Senra

Bus No 5 to
Bus Station

Praza
de
Galicia

R Concepción Arenal

Rúa de Montero Ríos

To Hospital Clínico
Universitario (1.1km)

Rúa do Xeneral Pardiñas

Rúa do Doutor Teixeiro

Rúa do Hórreo

To Train
Station (500m)

INFORMATION
City Tourist Office.................**1** B4

SIGHTS & ACTIVITIES
Catedral de Santiago de
  Compostela.........................**2** B3
Museo das
  Peregrinacións...................**3** B2
Pazo de Xelmírez.................**4** B3

SLEEPING
Casa-Hotel As Artes............**5** A2
Hostal Suso...........................**6** B4
Parador Hostal dos Reis
  Católicos **7** A2

EATING
Carretas.................................**8** A2
El Pasaje................................**9** A4

TRANSPORT
Airport Bus Stop **10** A6

Xelmírez (1120), where the main banquet hall is adorned with exquisite little wall busts depicting feasters, musicians, kings and jugglers.

FESTIVALS & EVENTS

July is Santiago's busiest month. The **Feast of Saint James** (Día de Santiago) is on 25 July and is simultaneously Galicia's 'national' day. Two weeks of festivities surround the festival, which culminates in a spectacular fireworks display on 24 July.

SLEEPING

Hostal Suso (☎ 981 58 66 11; Rúa do Vilar 65; s/d €20/40) Stacked above a bar, this family-run *hostal* represents the best deal in town. Immaculate rooms with spic-and-span bathrooms have firm beds and modern wood furniture. Light sleepers should request an interior room.

our pick **Casa-Hotel As Artes** (☎ 981 55 52 54; www.asartes.com; Travesía de Dos Puertas 2; r €88-98; ⌨) Located on a quiet street close to the cathedral, the Casa-Hotel As Artes' lovely stone-walled rooms exude a romantic rustic air. Breakfast (€9) is served in a homey dining room overlooking the street.

Parador Hostal dos Reis Católicos (☎ 981 58 22 00; www.parador.es; Praza do Obradoiro 1; r €225; Ⓟ ⌗ ⌨) Built in 1499 and rubbing shoulders with the cathedral, the palatial *parador* is Santiago's top hotel. Even if you don't book one of its regal rooms, stop in for tea at the elegant cafe.

EATING

Central Santiago is packed with eateries, especially along Rúa do Franco (named for the French, not the dictator) and parallel Rúa da Raíña. Don't leave without trying a *tarta de Santiago,* an iconic almond cake.

Carretas (☎ 981 56 31 11; Rúa das Carretas 21; mains €10-18, menú €18) Located at the edge of the old town, this classic *marisquería* (seafood eatery) is known for its shellfish platters (€48 per person) and excellent *ría*-fresh fish.

El Pasaje (☎ 981 55 70 81; Rúa do Franco 54; mains €14-25) For a special meal, this classic spot offers melt-in-your-mouth Galician seafood, shellfish and steaks.

DRINKING

The centre is packed with bars and cafes. If you're after tapas and wine, graze along the Rúas do Franco and da Raíña. For people-watching, hit the cafes along Praza da Quinatana and Rúa do Vilar. The liveliest area lies east of Praza da Quintana, especially along Rúa de San Paio de Antealtares, a hot spot for live music. Things get lively after dinner, especially Thursday to Sunday nights, when Santiago's large student population comes out in full force.

GETTING THERE & AWAY

The **Lavacolla airport** (☎ 981 54 75 00; www.aena.es) is 11km east of the city and connects Santiago with Spanish and European destinations.

Renfe (www.renfe.es) travels to/from Madrid (Chamartín station; €45) on a daytime Talgo (seven hours) or an overnight Trenhotel (nine hours).

Regional trains run roughly every hour up and down the coast, linking Santiago with Vigo (€5.90 to €8, 90 minutes), Pontevedra (€3.90 to €5.25, 50 minutes) and A Coruña (€3.90 to €5.25, 45 to 70 minutes).

GETTING AROUND

Santiago de Compostela is walkable, although it's a bit of a hike from the train and bus stations to the centre.

Up to 21 **Empresa Freire** (☎ 981 58 81 11) buses run daily between Lavacolla airport and the bus station (€1.70). Taxis charge around €20.

RÍAS ALTAS

If you're seeking dramatic scenery, look no further. Here, towering forests open to views of sheer sea cliffs, sweeping beaches and vivid green fields studded with farmhouses. Add in medieval villages like Betanzos and Pontedeume and the constant roar of the Atlantic, and it's easy to see why the Rías Altas may be Galicia's most beautiful area. The water may be colder up here, but beaches are far less crowded, making this an ideal destination for travellers yearning to get off the beaten path.

BETANZOS

pop 13,300

The medieval city of Betanzos straddles the Ríos Mendo and Mandeo, which meet here to flow north into the Ría de Betanzos. Once a thriving port rivalling A Coruña (until that city eclipsed it), Betanzos today offers a well-preserved old town, although its best face is seen by strolling along the riverbank, sipping local wines in its taverns, or enjoying the sunlight on your face in one of the cafes in the centre.

Get a map at the **tourist office** (☎ 981 77 66 66; Praza da Galicia 1; ⏰ 10am-2pm & 4-7pm Oct-May, 10am-2pm & 5-8pm Jun-Sep).

SLEEPING & EATING

A 10-minute walk from the old town, the **San Roque** (☎ 981 77 55 55; www.complejosan roque.com; s/d €81/91; ℗ ✗ ▯), a modernist-mansion-turned-hotel, has sleek, sunny rooms with a vaguely maritime air. The peachy facade is unmissable from the main road. It's wheelchair friendly.

In town, **Hotel Garelos** (☎ 981 77 59 30; www.hotelgarelos.com; Calle Alfonso IX 8; s/d incl breakfast €79/90; ℗ ✗) has spic-and-span rooms endowed with parquet floors, marble bathrooms and countryside views. It's wheelchair accessible.

A string of terrace cafes flanks the expansive Praza Irmáns Garcia Naviera. Be sure to try the local *tortilla de patata*, a runny potato omelette that's Betanzo's culinary claim to fame.

GETTING THERE & AWAY

Betanzos Cidade train station is northwest of the old town, across Río Mendo. Five trains go daily to Ferrol and A Coruña (both €2.60, 45 minutes).

SERRA DA CAPELADA

The wild, rugged coastline that the Rías Altas are famous for begin above Cedeira. If you have your own car (or even better, time for long-distance hikes), Galicia's northwestern corner is truly a captivating place to explore, with lush forests, vertigo-inducing cliffs and stunning oceanscapes.

SAN ANDRÉS DE TEIXIDO & GARITA HERBEIRA

In summer, great busloads of tourists descend on the hamlet of Texeido (12km past Cediera), a jumble of stone houses renowned as a sanctuary of relics of St Andrew.

More exciting is its natural setting. Hit the winding CP-2205 highway, a lovely road that runs northwest towards Cariño and the Cabo Ortegal, for incredible views. Six kilometres beyond San Andrés is the must-see **Garita Herbeira Mirador**, 600m above sea level. This is the best place to wow over southern Europe's highest sea cliffs. Further on, make a 9km detour to the **Mirador da**

Miranda, a sublime vantage point over the Estaca de Bares that's only slightly marred by the presence of two communications towers.

CABO ORTEGAL

The magnificent cape where the Atlantic Ocean meets the Bay of Biscay, **Cabo Ortegal** overlooks the craggy coastline from its perch above tall cliffs. Just offshore, **Os Tres Aguillóns**, three islets, provide a home to hundreds of **marine birds** like yellow-leg seagulls and storm petrels. If you come with binoculars, you may also spot dolphins or whales near the cape.

Sitting 4km beyond the workaday town of **Cariño**, the cape is worth visiting just for the views, but there are also some lovely walks out here. On the road out, stop at the first *mirador* (viewpoint) to take the 3.2km/30-minute cliff-top trail to the **San Xiáo de Trebo** chapel. This well-marked path traverses a forest, crosses the Soutullo River and affords grand views. The vastly more ambitious **GR-50** long-distance trail also begins nearby.

Rural hotels are the way to go in the area. **Río da Cruz** (☎ 981 42 80 57; www .riodacruz.com; Landoi; r €60-80; P) offers six rooms in a rustic country house 15 minutes outside Cariño. They feature solid, if slightly careworn, wooden furnishings.

COSTA DA MORTE

Long, remote beaches broken up by ragged, rocky points and peaks make up the eerily beautiful 'Coast of Death', the relatively isolated and unspoilt shore that runs from Caión down to Muros. The idyllic landscape can undergo a rapid transformation when ocean mists blow in.

If you're looking for a quiet base from which to explore the region, consider stay-

Galicia coastline near Cabo Ortegal
GLOBE EXPOSURE/ALAMY

ing in a rural hotel. Many are listed online at www.turismocostadamorte.com.

THE EAST
LUGO
pop 93,900 / elev 475m

The grand Roman walls encircling old Lugo are considered the world's best-preserved and are the number one reason visitors land here. Yet within the fortress is a beautifully preserved labyrinth of streets and squares, most of them traffic-free and ideal for strolling.

INFORMATION

Regional tourist office (☎ 982 23 13 61; www.lugoturismo.com; Rúa de Conde Pallarés 2; ☾ 10am-2pm & 4-7pm Mon-Sat Sep-Jun, 10am-2pm & 4-8pm daily Jul & Aug)

CRACKIN' GOOD SHELLFISH

Galician shellfish and seafood is plentiful, fresh and may well be the best you have ever tasted. The region's signature dish is *pulpo a la gallega,* tender pieces of octopus sprinkled with olive oil and paprika (*pulpo á feira* has chunks of potato added). Mollusc mavens will enjoy the variety of *ameixas* (clams) and *mexillons* (mussels). Special shellfish of the region include *vieiras* and *zamburiñas* (types of scallop), *berberechos* (cockles), *navajas* (razor clams) and the tiny, much-prized goose barnacles known as *percebes,* which bear a curious resemblance to fingernails. Other delicacies include various crabs, from little *necoras* to the great big *buey del mar* – the 'ox of the sea'. Also keep an eye open for the *bogavante* or *lubrigante,* a large, lobster-like creature with two enormous claws.

SIGHTS

The path running along the top of the **Roman walls** is to Lugo what a maritime promenade is to a seaside resort: a place to jog, take an evening stroll, see and be seen.

The walls, which make a 2.25km loop around the old city, rise 15m high, are studded with 82 stout towers and represent 18 centuries of history. Until well into the 19th century the city gates were closed at night and tolls were charged to bring in goods from outside.

Southwest of the centre cluster more Roman remains. Cross the 1st-century **Ponte Romana** (Roman bridge), spanning the Río Miño, to access **As Termas de Lugo** (☎ 982 22 12 28; Barrio da Ponte s/n; admission free; ✆ 9am-1pm & 6.30-8.30pm), where ancient baths taking advantage of the 44°C sulphurous waters are hidden inside the modern spa of the Balneario de Lugo hotel.

SLEEPING

Orban e Sangro (☎ 982 24 02 17; Travesía do Miño; s/d €80/100; P ⊠ ☐) The 12 rooms of this new inner-wall boutique hotel (opened 2008) are regal, with rich linen, antique furnishings and huge 2m beds.

EATING

Rúa de Cruz and Rúa Nova, north of the cathedral, are packed with tempting tapas bars and restaurants.

Casa Rivas (☎ 982 22 10 58; Ronda Muralla 177; menú €8) Stepping through the doorway of this family-run spot is like crossing into 1970s Spain. A neighbourhood crowd files in to the mustard-coloured dining room for noodle soup, grilled veal, fried hake, squid or chickpea stew.

A Nosa Terra (☎ 982 22 92 35; Rúa Nova 8; mains €7-18) A dark but inviting bar with a long by-the-glass wine list, this popular spot doles out good tapas (free with a drink). The downstairs bodega is a good place to try *pulpo á feira* or *lacón con grelos.*

GETTING THERE & AWAY

Up to five daily Renfe trains head to A Coruña (€6.50 to €16.90, two hours) and Monforte de Lemos (€3.60 to €13.50, one hour). An Atlantico overnight train goes all the way to Madrid (€52, nine hours).

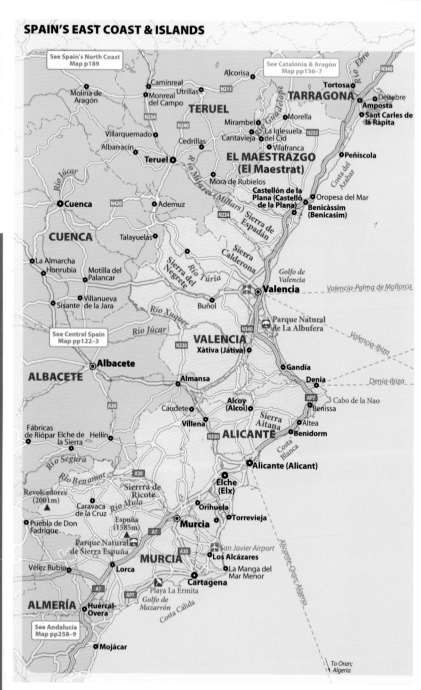

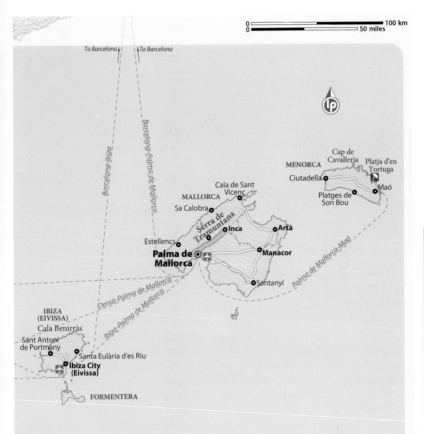

MEDITERRANEAN SEA

SPAIN'S EAST COAST & ISLANDS

EAST COAST & ISLANDS HIGHLIGHTS

EAST COAST & ISLANDS HIGHLIGHTS

1 CITY OF ARTS & SCIENCES

BY MANUEL TOHARIA, SCIENTIFIC DIRECTOR OF THE CIUDAD DE LAS ARTES Y LAS CIENCIAS

The Ciudad de las Artes y las Ciencias is one of the most spectacular cultural complexes on earth. Apart from the astonishing architecture, the interior houses one of Europe's best interactive science museums, a world-class opera theatre (Palau de les Arts Reina Sofía) and an aquarium where you can experience all marine ecosystems on the planet.

➦ MANUEL TOHARIA'S DON'T MISS LIST

❶ WALK BENEATH THE OCEAN

Even if you wouldn't normally visit an aquarium, you can't miss the Oceanogràfic. The most memorable experience is the 30m-long transparent tunnel through a world of giant crabs, sharks, and more sea creatures than you imagined possible. Take it slowly and, at some point, stand still to be swept along by this world in motion.

❷ THE CHROMOSOME FOREST

On the 3rd floor of the Museo de las Ciencias (Science Museum), the Bosque de Cromosomas (Chromosome Forest) is dedicated to 'Life and the Genome' and is filled with more than 150 interactive modules that include giant chromosomes, genes, plants, and animal and human models. Genetics has never been this much fun.

❸ IMAX

In the IMAX theatre in the Hemisfèric (planetarium), make sure you try for a seat in one of the upper rows. From here, vertigo is almost guaranteed, but the projections are so powerful that

Clockwise from top: Palau de les Arts Reina Sofía (left) and the Hemisfèric; Science Museum interior; Oceanogràfic aquarium; L'Umbracle promenade, Ciudad de las Artes y las Ciencias, Valencia City

CLOCKWISE FROM TOP: GREG ELMS; ALFREDO MAIQUEZ; GREG ELMS; ALFREDO MAIQUEZ

you'll soon lose yourself to the extent that you're no longer a spectator but an integral part of the show itself.

❹ THE BEST PHOTO

It's hard to take a bad photo of the Ciudad de las Artes y las Ciencias, but my favourite is from the south side of the Museo de las Ciencias. From here, you have an unrivalled view of the whole complex in perspective, with the rest of the museum, the Hemisfèric and the beautiful Palau de les Arts Reina Sofía in the background.

❺ VISIT THE INTERNATIONAL SPACE STATION

You've gone beneath the ocean, now head into space. The Spanish astronaut Pedro Duque takes you by the hand and guides you through the Estación Espacial Internacional (International Space Station). In the Academia del Espacio (Space Academy), strap yourself into the simulator and you're transformed into a crew member for an unforgettable launch into space.

↘ THINGS YOU NEED TO KNOW

Architect Local-boy-turned-international-star Santiago Calatrava **Area** 350,000 sq metres **Getting there** Take bus 35 from Plaza del Ayuntamiento, bus 95 from Torres de Serrano or walk the lovely Jardines de Turia **Best time to visit** First thing in the morning **See our author's review, p234**

EAST COAST & ISLANDS HIGHLIGHTS

↘ SOAK UP VALENCIA'S SOPHISTICATION

Less well known than Barcelona, Madrid or Seville, **Valencia** (p234) well deserves its place as one of Spain's most exciting cities. A magnificent cathedral, the old quarter of Barrio del Carmen, and fine beaches and restaurants are reason enough to visit. But Valencia is also home to the Ciudad de las Artes y las Ciencias, an exceptional showpiece for the exciting new wave of innovative Spanish architecture.

↘ LAZE ON BALEARIC BEACHES

It's not for nothing that Spain's beaches have been the destination of choice for sun-starved northern Europeans. Yes, there are resorts overwhelmed by high-rises, but the Balearic Islands have plenty of idyllic spots. **Menorca's north coast** (p253), **Mallorca's northwest coast** (p247) and **Formentera** (p253) in particular have lovely beaches, and even party-island **Ibiza** (p248) has plenty to offer.

↘ DIVE INTO IBIZA'S NIGHTLIFE

When it comes to hedonism, **Ibiza** (p248) takes some beating. On the island that brought you the chill-out strains of Café del Mar, this is a place to watch the sunset over the Mediterranean with cocktail in hand, before diving into the city's nightclubs, which rank among the biggest and best in Europe. You won't emerge until after dawn.

↘ EXPLORE PALMA DE MALLORCA

Palma de Mallorca (p243) is proof that these islands have more to them than days in the sun and nights in the *discotecas*. Its old town has a grand cathedral leavened with Gaudí flourishes, its art galleries are among Spain's best, and its signature *patis* (elegant courtyards) provide some of the island's most intimate moments.

↘ MURCIA & CARTAGENA

Away from the tourist trails, the main attraction in **Murcia** (p254) is the city's cathedral – its baroque facade could be Spain's finest. On Murcia's coast, the former Carthaginian and Roman port of **Cartagena** (p255) has numerous signposts to antiquity, as well as one of Spain's richest concentrations of Modernista architecture.

2 GREG ELMS; 3 HOLGER LEUE; 4 GIANNI MURATORE/ALAMY; 5 HOLGER LEUE; 6 ECLECTIC IMAGES/ALAMY

2 Enjoying a night out in Valencia (p234); 3 Postcard-perfect bay in Mallorca (p243); 4 Sunset in Ibiza (p248); 5 Palma de Mallorca township and cathedral (p246); 6 Palacio Aguirre (p255), Cartagena

EAST COAST & ISLANDS' BEST...

↘ ARCHITECTURAL LANDMARKS

- **Ciudad de las Artes y las Ciencias, Valencia** (p234) They'll talk about this building for centuries to come.
- **D'Alt Vila, Ibiza** (p248) Ibiza's World Heritage–listed old town, this is the island's other face.
- **Palma de Mallorca's cathedral** (p246) A heady mix of Gothic, Gaudí and the other-worldly work of artist Miquel Barceló.
- **Palma de Mallorca's courtyards** (p244) A delightful counterpoint to the region's grand-scale architecture.

↘ PLACES FOR REGIONAL COOKING

- **Valencia** (p238) Paella as it should taste but rarely does elsewhere in Spain.
- **Morella** (p242) Heart-warming mountain-cooking best enjoyed in winter.

- **Palma de Mallorca** (p244) Lobster paella is pricey but oh-so-worth-it.
- **Ibiza** (p250) The freshest seafood and typical Balearic cuisine.

↘ PLACES TO KILL THE NIGHT

- **Ibiza** (p250) The Mediterranean's wildest nights. Without question.
- **Barrio del Carmen, Valencia** (p239) The epicentre for Valencia's famous nightlife.
- **Palma de Mallorca** (p246) Slightly more low-key evenings than Ibiza, but only just.

↘ PLACES TO ESCAPE THE CROWDS

- **Morella** (p241) The antithesis of coastal clamour.
- **Altea** (p242) Benidorm's alter-ego and Valencia's prettiest village.
- **Menorca's North Coast** (p253) One of the Balearics' quietest corners.

DAVID TOMLINSON

Ibiza's marina and D'Alt Vila (p248)

THINGS YOU NEED TO KNOW

◥ VITAL STATISTICS

- **Population** 6.83 million
- **Area** 39,561 sq km
- **Best time to visit** Year-round

◥ LOCALITIES IN A NUTSHELL

- **Valencia** (p234) Dominated by Valencia city, but long coastline and hilly coastal hinterland.
- **Balearic Islands** (p243) Mediterranean islands of Mallorca, Ibiza, Menorca and Formentera.
- **Murcia** (p254) Wedge of south-eastern Spain running inland from the Costa Cailda (Hot Coast).

◥ ADVANCE PLANNING

- **One month before** Make sure you have your accommodation reserved, even earlier in summer.
- **Two weeks before** Book your ferry to the Balearic Islands (p243), even earlier in summer.

◥ RESOURCES

- **Region of Valencia** (www.comunitat valenciana.com) Valencia region's excellent official tourism site.
- **Valencia city** (www.turisvalencia.com) Best of several competing tourism sites about the city.
- **Murcia** (www.murciaturistica.es) Regional tourist authority website.
- **Balearic Islands** (www.illesbalears.es) Good site dedicated to the islands.
- **Balearic Islands** (www.baleares.com) Accommodation-focused website for the Balearic Islands.

- **Inland Trips from the Costa Blanca** (Derek Workman) Twenty one-day car excursions into the interior.
- **Small Hotels and Inns of Eastern Spain** (Derek Workman) Ideal if you'd like to spend a night or two away from the crowds.

◥ EMERGENCY NUMBERS

- **Emergency** (☎ 112)
- **Policía Nacional** (☎ 091)

◥ GETTING AROUND

- **Air** International airports (served by charter and some regular airlines) in Valencia, Ibiza, Palma de Mallorca and Murcia.
- **Boat** Ferries connect the Balearics (Mallorca, Ibiza and Menorca) with the mainland (Valencia and Barcelona); there are also services between and around the islands.
- **Bus** Intermittent services around the islands.
- **Road** Good network of roads.
- **Train** Renfe (www.renfe.es) connects Valencia, Murcia and Cartagena with the rest of mainland Spain.

EAST COAST & ISLANDS ITINERARIES

FOOD FOR BODY & SOUL Three Days

Begin in **(1) Valencia** (p234). Its jaw-dropping Ciudad de las Artes y las Ciencias is the perfect complement to the charming Barrio del Carmen and its cathedral, which showcases the major architectural genres from centuries of European history, has sweeping summit views and contains what could be the Holy Grail. At least once (and preferably more than once), order a paella at La Pepica (Valencia and its hinterland are where paella was born and it's still home to the most authentic paellas in Spain) and spend a night prowling the bars of the Barrio del Carmen. Journey north along the coast and, just as you begin to despair of the over-development, stop off in **(2) Peñíscola** (p241) and let yourself be drawn into the quiet embrace of its castle and medieval byways. Venture inland to El Maestrazgo, a secluded mountain region, and especially to **(3) Morella** (p241). Here you'll find an ancient fortified town strewn with monuments and restaurants serving up the hearty mountain cooking for which Valencia province is famous.

FAR FROM THE MADDING CROWD Five Days

Tens of millions of visitors may converge on the region every year, but the vast majority of these head for the coast and scarcely move thereafter. This itinerary shows you what they're missing. After a day spent sampling the delights of **(1) Valencia** (p234), head down the N340 to **(2) Xàtiva** (p241) with its epic castle, cool mountain air and expansive views. Veer south, then southwest to **(3) Villena** (p241), another town with a medieval castle that's at its best when floodlit at night. Continue on to **(4) Orihuela** (p241) and spend at least a day here exploring its Gothic, Renaissance and baroque buildings, as well as a fortress that dates back to Muslim times. Just across the provincial border, **(5) Murcia** (p254) is a window on urban Spain without the tourists; you could spend hours admiring the Gothic cathedral and its Capilla de los Vélez. A short trip down the A30 brings you to **(6) Cartagena** (p255), a study in late-19th-century architecture, and with a slew of Roman ruins set back from the water.

MEDITERRANEAN PLAYGROUND One Week

You couldn't come to this corner of Spain and not take at least a day getting to know **(1) Valencia** (p234). That pleasurable task completed, catch a ferry to **(2) Palma de Mallorca** (p243), the Balearics' sophisticated urban outpost with its enchanted old quarter and distinguished Gothic, baroque and courtyard architecture. The northwestern coast is close but a world away with its stone-built *pueblos* (villages) such

as (3) Estellencs (p247) and a jagged coast with a vertiginous backdrop. Ferries connect Palma de Mallorca to (4) Ibiza (p248) where the nightlife may be clichéd, but will surpass even the most club-weary expectations. The walled old town is well worth exploring, and you could detour to one of Ibiza's beaches such as clothing-optional (5) S'Aigua Blanca (p253). But if you're pushed for time, save your search for the perfect beach for (6) Menorca (p251), the quietest (and for many travellers, their favourite) of the three main Balearic Islands.

DISCOVER SPAIN'S EAST COAST & ISLANDS

If you visit Valencia, Murcia or the Balearic Islands in summer, you'll soon discover that this is Europe's holiday playground. And yet, even as tourism at times threatens to overwhelm the region, the reasons for its popularity – a beautiful sun-drenched coastline with gorgeous beaches, charming villages and vibrant cities – remain intact.

Valencia is one of Spain's most engaging cities, filled as it is with monuments spanning the centuries and an increasingly avant-garde spirit. The birthplace of paella, Valencia province also has some lovely villages along the coast and in its hilly hinterland. Away to the south, Murcia's cathedral and Cartagena's Roman and Modernista architecture are drawcards that see fewer tourists than they deserve.

Out in the Mediterranean, the Balearic Islands have far more to recommend them than fine beaches (although they have these in abundance). Pretty Ibiza could just be Europe's nightlife capital, Palma de Mallorca is a stunning city and Menorca's coastline is the region's most untouched corner.

VALENCIA

VALENCIA CITY

pop 805,300

Valencia, Spain's third-largest city, for ages languished in the long shadows cast by Madrid, Spain's political capital, and Barcelona, the country's cultural and economic powerhouse. No longer. Stunning public buildings have changed the city's skyline – Sir Norman Foster's Palacio de Congresos, David Chipperfield's award-winning Veles i Vents structure beside the inner port, and, on the grandest scale of all, the Ciudad de las Artes y las Ciencas, designed in the main by Santiago Calatrava, local boy made good.

An increasingly popular short-break venue (the number of overseas visitors has almost doubled in the last four years), Valencia is where paella first simmered over a wood fire. It's a vibrant, friendly, mildly chaotic place with two outstanding fine-arts museums, an accessible old quarter, Europe's newest cultural and scientific complex – and one of Spain's most exciting nightlife scenes.

INFORMATION

Regional tourist office (☎ 96 398 64 22; Calle Paz 48; ☼ 9am-2.30pm & 4.30-8pm Mon-Fri) **Turismo Valencia (VLC) tourist office** (☎ 96 315 39 31; www.turisvalencia.es) Plaza de la Reina (**Plaza de la Reina 19;** ☼ 9am-7pm Mon-Sat, 10am-2pm Sun); Train Station (**Calle Xàtiva**) Also has a branch at the airport arrivals area.

SIGHTS & ACTIVITIES

CIUDAD DE LAS ARTES Y LAS CIENCIAS

The aesthetically stunning **Ciudad de las Artes y las Ciencias** (City of Arts & Sciences; ☎ reservations 902 10 00 31; www.cac.es; Autovía a El Saler; combined ticket for all 3 attractions adult/child €30.60/23.30) occupies a massive 350,000-sq-metre swath of the old Turia riverbed.

The **Hemisfèric** (adult/child €7.50/5.80) is planetarium, IMAX cinema and laser show, all in one.

The **Museo de las Ciencias Príncipe Felipe** (adult/child €7.50/5.80; ⏰ 10am-7pm or 9pm) is an interactive science museum where each section has a pamphlet in English summarising its contents.

Highlight of the complex, especially if you have young children, will probably be the **Oceanogràfic** (adult/child €23.30/17.60; ⏰ 10am-6pm or 8pm Sep–mid-Jul, 10am-midnight mid-Jul–Aug). The aquariums of this watery world have sufficient water sloshing around to fill 15 Olympic-size swimming pools. There are also polar zones, a dolphinarium, a Red Sea aquarium, a Mediterranean seascape – and a couple of underwater tunnels, one 70m long, where the fish have the chance to gawp at visitors.

The **Palau de les Arts Reina Sofía** (☎ 902 20 23 83; www.lesarts.com; **Autovía a El Saler**) broods over the riverbed like a giant beetle, its shell shimmering with translucent mosaic tiles. With four au-ditoriums and seating for 4400, it's exceeded in capacity only by the Sydney Opera House.

MUSEO DE BELLAS ARTES

Bright and spacious (and with a great little cafe for a drink or snack lunch), the **Museo de Bellas Artes** (Fine Arts Museum; ☎ 96 378 03 00; Calle San Pío V 9; admission free; ⏰ 10am-8pm Tue-Sun) ranks among Spain's best. Its highlights include the grandiose Roman *Mosaic of the Nine Muses,* a collection of magnificent late medieval altarpieces and works by El Greco, Goya, Velázquez, Murillo and Ribalta, plus artists such as Sorolla and Pinazo of the Valencian Impressionist school.

CATHEDRAL

Valencia's **cathedral** (adult/under 3yr/3-12yr incl audioguide €4/free/2.70; ⏰ 10am-5.30pm or 6.30pm Mon-Sat, 2-5.30pm Sun) is a microcosm of the city's architectural history: the Puerta del Palau on the east side is pure Romanesque; the dome, tower and Puerta de los Apóstoles on Plaza de la Virgen are

KRZYSZTOF DYDYNSKI

Museo de Bellas Artes, Valencia

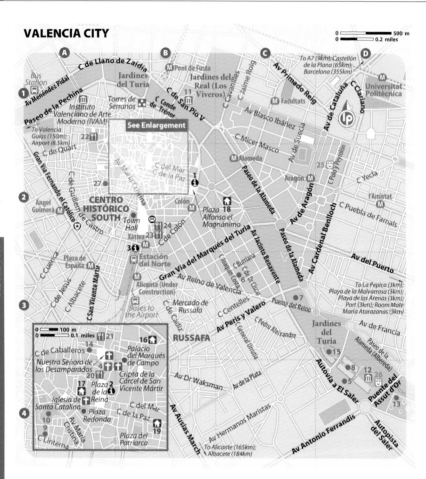

VALENCIA CITY

Gothic; the presbytery and main entrance on Plaza de la Reina are baroque; and there are a couple of Renaissance chapels inside.

Don't miss the recently revealed Italianate frescoes above the main altarpiece. In the flamboyant Gothic Capilla del Santo Cáliz, right of the main entrance, is what's claimed to be the **Holy Grail**, the chalice from which Christ sipped during the Last Supper. The next chapel north has a pair of particularly sensitive Goyas.

Left of the main portal is the entrance to the **Miguelete bell tower** (adult/under 14yr €2/1; ⏰ 10am-7.30pm). Climb the 207 steps of its spiral staircase for great city-and-skyline views.

PLAZA DEL MERCADO

Facing each other across Plaza del Mercado are two emblematic buildings, each a masterpiece of its era. Pop into the 15th-century Gothic **Lonja** (adult/child €2/1, free Sat & Sun; ⏰ 10am-2pm & 4.30-8.30pm Mon-Sat, 10am-3pm Sun), an early Valencian commodity exchange, now a World Heritage site, with its striking colonnaded hall. And set aside time to prowl the **Mercado**

VALENCIA CITY

INFORMATION		
Regional Tourist Office	1	B2
Turismo Valencia (VLC) Tourist Office	2	A4
Turismo Valencia (VLC) Tourist Office	3	B2
SIGHTS & ACTIVITIES		
Cathedral	4	A4
Ciudad de las Artes y las Ciencias	5	D4
Escuela de Cocina Eneldo	6	C3
Gulliver	7	C3
Hemisfèric	8	D4
Lonja	9	A4
Mercado Central	10	A4
Museo de Bellas Artes	11	B1
Museo de las Ciencias Príncipe Felipe	12	D4
Oceanogràfic	13	D4
Palau de la Generalitat	14	A3
Palau de les Arts Reina Sofía	15	D3
SLEEPING		
Ad Hoc	16	B3
Hostal Antigua Morellana	17	A4
Palau del Mar	18	C2
Red Nest Hostel	19	B4
EATING		
La Lola	20	A4
Las Cuevas	21	A3
L'Hamadríada	22	A1
Marisquería Civera	23	B2
Palacio de la Bellota	24	B2
ENTERTAINMENT		
Black Note	25	D2
L'Umbracle Terraza	26	D4
TRANSPORT		
Orange Bikes	27	A2

Central (**Plaza del Mercado; ⌚ 7.30am-2.30pm Mon-Sat**), Valencia's Modernista covered market. Constructed in 1928, it's a swirl of smells, movement and colour.

BEACHES

Spread your towel on broad **Playa de la Malvarrosa** running into **Playa de las Arenas**, each bordered by the **Paseo Marítimo** promenade and a string of restaurants. One block back, lively bars and discos thump out the beat in summer. Take buses 1, 2 or 19, or the high-speed tram from Pont de Fusta or the Benimaclet Metro junction.

COURSES

Escuela de Cocina Eneldo (**☎ 96 395 54 57; www.cocinaeneldo.com in Spanish; Calle Joaquín Costa 45**) Cooking's a very demonstrable discipline, so even if your Spanish isn't up to scratch, pitch in and get your hands floury.

VALENCIA FOR CHILDREN

Beaches (above), of course: nearest is the combined beach of Malvarrosa and Las Arenas (the latter meaning 'sand'), a shortish bus or tram ride from the centre. The other great playground, year-round, is the diverted Río Turia's former 9km riverbed. Of its formal playgrounds, **Gulliver** just asks to be clambered all over.

Of the diversions of the Ciudad de las Artes y las Ciencias, the **Oceanogràfic** (p235), with more than 45,000 aquatic beasts and plants, has something for all ages.

TOURS

Valencia Guías (**☎ 96 385 17 40; www.valenciaguias.com; Paseo de la Pechina 32**) conducts 3½-hour guided bicycle tours (€25 including rental) of Valencia in English, leaving from its premises at 10am. They require a minimum of only two cyclists. They also offer two-hour walking tours in Spanish and English (adult/child €15/7.50), leaving Plaza de la Reina tourist office at 10am each Saturday.

FESTIVALS & EVENTS

The exuberant, anarchic swirl of **Las Fallas de San José** is a must if you are in Spain between 12 and 19 March.

The *fallas* themselves are huge sculptures of papier-mâché on wood built by teams of local artists. Each neighbourhood sponsors its own *falla*, and when the town wakes after the *plantà* (overnight construction of the *fallas*), more than 350 have been erected.

Around-the-clock festivities include street parties, paella-cooking competitions, parades, open-air concerts, bullfights and nightly free firework displays.

La Tomatina, Buñol

SIMON GREENWOOD

➥ IF YOU LIKE...

If you like Valencia's **Las Fallas festival** (p237), we think you'll also love:

- **Semana Santa, Lorca** Among Spain's most flamboyant Easter celebrations, in inland Murcia.
- **La Tomatina, Buñol** The world's biggest tomato fight on the last Wednesday in August, in Valencia province.
- **Misteri d'Elx, Elche** Annual Unesco World Heritage–listed mystery play, held in mid-August, in Valencia province.
- **Moros y Cristianos, Alcoy** Re-enactments of ancient battles between Moors and Christians, held 22 to 24 April, inland from Valencia's Costa Blanca.
- **Carthagineses y Romanos, Cartagena** Battles between Carthaginians and Romans bring to life Cartagena's history in the second half of September.
- **Dia de Sant Joan, Ciutadella** Quintessentially Catalan festival with processions, prancing horses and traditional music in Menorca.

SLEEPING

Red Nest Hostel (☎ 96 342 71 68; www.nesthostelsvalencia.com; Calle Paz 36; dm €14-21, d €41-65, q €68-100) This hugely welcoming hostel has brightly decorated rooms that

range from doubles to dorms that can accommodate 12.

Hostal Antigua Morellana (☎ 96 391 57 73; www.hostalam.com; Calle En Bou 2; s €45-55, d €55-65; ☒) The friendly, family-run 18-room Hostal Antigua Morellana is tucked away near the central market. Occupying a renovated 18th-century *posada* (a place where wealthier merchants bringing their produce to the nearby food market could spend the night), it has cosy, good-sized rooms, most with balconies.

Ad Hoc (☎ 963 91 91 40; www.adhochoteles.com; Calle Boix 4; s €76-101, d €89-125; ☒) Friendly, welcoming Ad Hoc offers comfort and charm deep within the old quarter and also runs a splendid small restaurant. The late-19th-century building has been restored to its former splendour with great sensitivity, revealing original ceilings, mellow brickwork and solid wooden beams.

Room Mate María Atarazanas (☎ 96 320 30 10; www.room-matehotels.com; Plaza Tribunal de las Aguas 5; r €70-130) The cream walls and fabrics of each bedroom contrast with the dark, stained woodwork. From the breezy rooftop terrace there's a magnificent wraparound view of sea and city.

Palau del Mar (☎ 96 316 28 84; www.hospes.es; Calle Navarro Reverter 14; r €160-350; ☒ ☒ ☒) Created by the merging of two elegant 19th-century mansions (with 18 very similar rooms, newly constructed, surrounding a tranquil internal garden), this boutique hotel, all black, white, soft fuscous and beige, is cool, confident and ultramodern.

EATING

There's a cluster of superb upmarket seafood restaurants along pedestrianised Calle Mosén Femades, including **Palacio** de la Bellota (☎ 96 351 53 61; Calle Mosén Femades 7; ◔ Mon-Sat) and **Marisquería Civera** (☎ 96 352 97 64; Calle Mosén Femades 10). For both, count on at least €50 per head, including wine.

Las Cuevas (☎ 96 391 71 96; Calle Samaniego 9; tapas €3-7) 'The Caves', low-ceilinged, semi-basement and aptly named, carries a huge range of fresh tapas.

La Lola (☎ 96 391 80 45; Subida del Toledano 8; mains €17-22; ◔ Tue-Sat) Up an alley beside the cathedral, here's a very suave number where cool jazz warbles. The all-white walls and furnishings offset stark reds, blacks and giant polka dots, and the food (save a space for one of the gooey desserts) is equally innovative.

L'Hamadríada (☎ 96 326 08 91; www .hamadriada.com in Spanish; Plaza Vicente Iborra 3; lunch menú €10, menú degustación €26-40; ◔ lunch daily, dinner Wed-Sat) Down a short, blind alley, this slim white rectangle of a place does an innovative midday *menú,* perfectly simmered rice dishes that change daily, and grills where the meat, like the vegetables, is of prime quality.

La Pepica (☎ 96 371 03 66; Paseo Neptuno 6; meals around €25; ◔ lunch & dinner Mon-Sat, lunch Sun) More expensive than its competitors and run for over a century by three generations of the same family, La Pepica, renowned for its rice dishes and seafood, is where Ernest Hemingway, among many other luminaries, once strutted.

DRINKING

The Barrio del Carmen has both the grungiest and grooviest collection of bars. The other major area is around the university; Avenidas de Aragón and Blasco Ibáñez and surrounding streets have enough bars and *discotecas* (clubs) to keep you busy beyond sunrise.

ENTERTAINMENT

Best of the online 'what's on' guides is www.thisisvalencia.com.

L'Umbracle Terraza (◔ from 8pm Jun-Sep) Within the City of Arts and Sciences, this is a cool, sophisticated spot to spend a hot summer night. Catch the evening breeze under the stars on the terrace, then drop below to **Mya**, a top-of-the-line club with an awesome sound system. Admission (€18) covers both venues.

For more life after 3am, head to the university area along and around Avenidas Blasco Ibáñez and de Aragón. Most clubs have cover charges (€10 to €20), so keep an eye out for discounted passes, carried by many local bars.

Black Note (☎ 96 393 36 63; www.black noteclub.com in Spanish; Calle Polo y Peyrolón 15)

KRZYSZTOF DYDYNSKI

Mercado Central (p236), Valencia City

Valencia city's most active jazz venue, Black Note has live music Monday to Thursday and good canned jazz, blues and soul on Friday and Saturday.

GETTING THERE & AWAY

Valencia's **Aeropuerto de Manises** (☎ 96 159 85 00) is 10km west of the city centre along the A3, direction Madrid.

Acciona Trasmediterránea (☎ 902 45 46 45; www.acciona-trasmediterranea.es) operates car and passenger ferries to Mallorca and Ibiza.

From Valencia's Estación del Norte, up to 10 Alaris express trains travel daily to/from Madrid (€43.50, 3½ hours), at least 12 to Barcelona (€35.30 to €39.60, three to 3¾ hours) and 10 to Alicante (€26.30, 1¾ hours).

GETTING AROUND

Valencia has an integrated bus, tram and metro network. EMT buses ply town routes, while MetroBus serves outlying towns and villages. Tourist offices stock maps for both services.

TO/FROM THE AIRPORT

Metro line 5 connects the airport, downtown and the port. A taxi into the centre costs around €17 (there's a supplement of €2.50 above the metered fee for journeys originating at the airport).

BICYCLE

Orange Bikes (☎ 96 391 75 51; www.orange bikes.net; Calle Editor Manuel Aguilar 1) rents out mountain bikes and town bikes (€9 to €12 per day, €45 to €55 per week) and electric bikes (€15 per day).

CAR & MOTORCYCLE

Street parking can be a real pain. There are large underground car parks beneath Plazas de la Reina and Alfonso el Magnánimo and, biggest of all, near the train station, covering the area between Calle Xàtiva and the Gran Vía.

EL MAESTRAZGO

Straddling northwestern Valencia and southeast Aragón, El Maestrazgo (Valenciano: El Maestrat) is a mountainous

Barrio del Carmen (p239)

GREG ELMS

land, a world away from the coastal flesh-pots, that's fertile territory for cyclists and walkers. Here ancient *pueblos* (villages) huddle on rocky outcrops and ridges.

MORELLA

pop 2700 / elev 1000m

Bitingly cold in winter and refreshingly cool in summer, Morella is the Maestrazgo's principal town. This outstanding example of a medieval fortress town, perched on a hilltop and crowned by a castle, is girdled by an intact rampart wall over 2km long.

ORIENTATION & INFORMATION

The **tourist office** (☎ 964 17 30 32; www .morella.net; Plaza San Miguel 3; ☺ 10am-2pm & 4-6pm or 7pm Mon-Sat, 10am-2pm Sun Apr-Oct, closed Mon Nov-Mar) is just behind Torres de San Miguel, twin 14th-century towers flanking the main entrance gate.

SIGHTS & ACTIVITIES

Morella's **castle** (adult/under 16yr €2/1.50; ☺ 11am-7pm Apr-Oct, 11am-5pm Nov-Mar), though badly knocked about, well merits the strenuous ascent to savour the breathtaking views of the town and surrounding countryside.

The imposing Gothic **Basílica de Santa María la Mayor** (Plaza Arciprestal; ☺ 11am-2pm & 4-6pm or 7pm) has two elaborately sculpted doorways on its south facade. A richly carved stone staircase leads to the elaborately sculpted overhead choir.

Among several imposing civil buildings are the 14th-century **Casa del Consell** (town hall; Calle Segura Barreda 28) and manorial houses such as the **Casa de la Cofradía de Labradores** (House of the Farmers' Guild; Calle de la Confraría).

On the outskirts of town stretch the arches of a very handsome 13th-century **aqueduct**.

Castle of Peñíscola

FAN TRAVELSTOCK/ALAMY

↘ IF YOU LIKE...

If you like Morella and its evocative **castle**, you'll love these hilltop fortresses:

- **Xàtiva** (adult/child €2.10/1.10; ☺ 10am-6pm or 7pm Tue-Sun) A mighty castle strung along the Serra Vernissa with spectacular views, south of Valencia.
- **Castillo de la Atalaya, Villena** (admission free by guided visit) Dramatic 12th-century castle inland from Valencia's Costa Blanca.
- **Orihuela** Muslim-era battlements overlook Orihuela's old quarter in Valencia province.
- **Peñíscola** (adult/under 10yr €3.50/free; ☺ 9.30am-9.30pm Easter–mid-Oct, 10.30am-5.30pm rest of year) Fourteenth-century Knights Templar castle above this white-washed and cobbled Valencian village.
- **Fort Marlborough, Maö** (☎ 971 36 04 62; adult/under 7yr/senior & student €3/free/1.80; ☺ 9.30am-8.30pm Tue-Sat, 9.30am-3pm Sun-Mon Jun-Sep, 10am-2.30pm Tue-Sun Oct-Apr) British-built fort overlooking an emerald-green inlet on Menorca.
- **Artà** Fourteenth-century hilltop fortress with fine panoramas over northeastern Mallorca.

WHAT'S COOKING IN VALENCIA?

Arroz (rice) underwrites much Valencian cuisine – such as paella, first simmered here and exported to the world. For a more original experience, try alternatives such as *arroz a banda* (simmered in a fish stock); *arroz negro* (with squid, including its ink); *arroz al horno* (baked in the oven). For *fideuá*, Valencian cooks simply substitute noodles for rice.

Other regional specialities include *horchata*, an opaque sugary drink made from pressed *chufas* (tiger nuts), into which you dip large finger-shaped buns called *fartons*. Finally, despite its name, *Agua de Valencia* couldn't be further from water. The local take on Buck's Fizz, it mixes *cava* (sparkling Champagne-method wine), orange juice, gin and vodka.

SLEEPING & EATING

Hotel El Cid (☎ 964 16 01 25; www.hotelelcid morella.com; Puerta San Mateu 3; s/d €33/56.60) Beside the ramparts and above its popular bar and restaurant, Hotel El Cid has smart, attractively furnished modern rooms and strictly contemporary bathrooms. Most rooms have balconies and top-floor ones have magnificent views of the surrounding countryside.

Hotel Cardenal Ram (☎ 964 17 30 85; www.cardenalram.com; Cuesta Suñer 1; s/d €45/70; ✷) This venerable hotel, with its ancient stone floors, high ceilings and antique furniture, is a wonderfully transformed 16th-century cardinal's palace.

Mesón del Pastor (☎ 964 16 02 49; Cuesta Jovaní 5-7; mains €8.35-15.50; ✷ lunch Thu-Tue, dinner Sat) It's all about strong mountain cuisine, thick gruels in winter, rabbit, juicy sausages, partridge and, yes, wild boar and goat. In February, you can eat truffle-flavoured dishes from starter to dessert. Ditto for wild mushrooms during peak autumn collecting time.

GETTING THERE & AROUND

On weekdays, **Autos Mediterráneo** (☎ 964 22 00 54) runs two daily buses to/from Castellón (€7.60, 2¼ hours) with a change in Sant Mateu for Vinaròs (€4.55).

COSTA BLANCA

The long stripe of the Costa Blanca (White Coast) is one of Europe's most heavily visited areas. If you're after a secluded midsummer beach, stay away – or head inland to enjoy traditional villages and towns that have scarcely heard the word tourism.

ALTEA

pop 26,600

Altea, separated from Benidorm only by the thick wedge of the Sierra Helada, could be a couple of moons away. Altogether quieter, its beaches are mostly of pebbles. The modern part, extending along the coast, is a bog-standard coastal resort. By contrast, the whitewashed old town, perched on a hilltop overlooking the sea, is just about the prettiest *pueblo* in all the Comunidad Valenciana.

The **tourist office** (☎ 96 584 41 14; Calle San Pedro 9; ✷ 10am-2pm & 5-7.30pm or 8pm Mon-Fri, 10am-1pm Sat) is on the beachfront.

Spain's first organic hotel, **Aparthotel & Restaurante Venus Albir** (☎ 96 686 48 20; www.venusalbir.com; Plaza Venus, Albir-Alfaz del Pi; d €47-90, tr €63-121; P ✷ ✷ ✷) was awarded a national prize for its ecofriendliness. Located in Albir, a continuation of Altea southwards, its 24 comfortable apartments have self-catering facilities and a balcony, and you can indulge in a variety of healthy, de-stressing activities.

Off Plaza de la Iglesia in Altea's old town, and especially down Calle Major, there's a profusion of cute little restaurants, many open for dinner only except in high summer.

BALEARIC ISLANDS

GETTING THERE & AROUND

If already in Spain, scheduled flights from major cities on the mainland are operated by Iberia, Air Europa, Clickair, Spanair and Vueling.

In summer, masses of charter and regular flights converge on Palma de Mallorca and Ibiza from all over Europe.

The main ferry company, **Acciona Trasmedi-terránea** (☎ 902 45 46 45; www .trasmediterranea.es), runs services between Barcelona and Valencia on the mainland, and Ibiza City, Maó and Palma de Mallorca.

You can compare prices and look for deals at **Direct Ferries** (www.directferries.es).

MALLORCA

There's much more to Mallorca than the beach. Palma de Mallorca (or simply Palma) is the main centre and a charming stop. The northwest coast, dominated by the Serra de Tramuntana mountain range, is a beautiful region of olive groves, pine forests and ochre villages, with a spectacularly rugged coastline.

GETTING AROUND

Palma and the major resorts and beaches around the island are connected by boat tours and water-taxi services.

Most of the island is accessible by bus from Palma.

PALMA DE MALLORCA

pop 383,100

Palma de Mallorca is the islands' only true city. Central Palma's old quarter is an enchanting blend of tree-lined boulevards and cobbled laneways, Gothic churches and baroque palaces, designer bars and slick boutiques.

INFORMATION

Consell de Mallorca tourist office (☎ 971 71 22 16; www.infomallorca.net; Plaça de la Reina 2; ☺ 9am-8pm Mon-Fri, 9am-2pm Sat) **Municipal tourist office** (☎ 902 10 23 65; www.palmademallorca.es) Main office (Casal Solleric, Passeig d'es Born 27; ☺ 9am-8pm); Branch office (Parc de les Estacions; ☺ 9am-8pm)

Valencian *fideuá* – paella made with noodles

GREG ELMS

SIGHTS

MUSEUMS

Housed in an 18th-century mansion, the **Museu d'Art Espanyol Contemporani** (☎ 971 71 35 15; www.march.es/arte/palma; Carrer de Sant Miquel 11; admission free; ⏲ 10am-6.30pm Mon-Fri, 10.30am-2pm Sat) offers a good introduction to Spanish modern art. On permanent display are some 70 pieces held by the Fundación Juan March, a veritable who's who of mostly 20th-century artists, including Picasso, Miró, Juan Gris (of cubism fame), the sculptor Julio González and Salvador Dalí.

OLD PALMA HOUSES

Can Marquès (☎ 971 71 62 47; www.casascon historia.net; Carrer de Zanglada 2A; adult/student & senior €6/5; ⏲ 10am-3pm Mon-Fri, 11am-2pm Sat) is one of few such places in Palma open to visitors. Dating to the 14th century, it gives a fascinating insight into how the well-to-do lived around the turn of the 20th century.

Another fine mansion houses the **Casa-Museu Joaquim Torrents Lladó** (☎ 971 72 98 35; www.jtorrentsllado.com; Carrer de la Portella 9; adult/student & senior €3/1.80; ⏲ 11am-7pm Tue-Fri, 10am-2pm Sat mid-Jun–mid-Sep, 10am-6pm Tue-Fri, 10am-2pm Sat mid-Sep–mid-Jun), with a timber gallery overlooking a courtyard.

OTHER ATTRACTIONS

Further south, the circular **Castell de Bellver** (☎ 971 73 06 57; adult/senior & student €2/1; ⏲ 8am-8.30pm Mon-Sat, 10am-7pm Sun & holidays Apr-Sep, 8am-7.15pm Mon-Sat, 10am-5pm Sun & holidays Oct-Mar) is an unusual, circular 14th-century castle (with a unique round tower) set atop a pleasant park.

The **Fundació Pilar i Joan Miró** (☎ 971 70 14 20; http://miro.palmademallorca.es; Carrer de Joan de Saridakis 29; adult/under 17yr/student & senior €6/free/3; ⏲ 10am-7pm Tue-Sat, 10am-3pm Sun & holidays mid-May–mid-Sep, 10am-6pm Tue-Sat, 10am-3pm Sun & holidays mid-Sep–mid-May) in Cala Major (about 4km southwest of the city centre) is housed in a modern complex on the site of Joan Miró's former studios. On show is a permanent collection of the works stored here at the time of his death.

SLEEPING

Hostal Brondo (☎ 971 71 90 43; www.hostal brondo.net; Carrer de Ca'n Brondo 1; s/d without bathroom €40/55, d with bathroom €70) Climb the courtyard stairs to arrive in a homey sitting room overlooking the narrow lane. High-ceilinged rooms (No 3 with a glassed-in gallery) furnished in varying styles (from Mallorcan to vaguely Moroccan) are atmospheric.

Hotel Born (☎ 971 71 29 42; www.hotelborn .com; Carrer de Sant Jaume 3; s €55, d €80-100) A superb place in the heart of the city, this hotel is in an 18th-century palace. The rooms combine elegance and history, with all the mod cons.

ourpick **Misión de San Miguel** (☎ 971 21 48 48; www.hotelmisiondesanmiguel.com; Carrer de Can Maçanet 1; r €125-130; P ⊠ ▣) The hotel is on a side alley off Carrer Oms and its spacious rooms are quiet, with free wi-fi, firm mattresses and rain showers. The restaurant serves a fabulous made-to-order breakfast and the patio area is romantic and relaxing.

Hotel Portixol (☎ 971 27 18 00; www .portixol.com; Carrer de la Sirena 27; s/d from €135/225; ⊠ ▣) Boasting one of the trendiest seafood restaurants around, Portixol is also one of the hippest hotels in town. The best rooms have sea views, and a drink on the terrace bar is a pleasant way to begin the evening.

EATING

A mess of eateries and bars cater to Palma's visitors in the maze of streets between Plaça

HOLGER LEUE

Catedral de Mallorca (La Seu), Palma de Mallorca

◥ CATEDRAL DE MALLORCA

Palma's enormous **cathedral** is often likened to a huge ship moored at the city's edge. This awesome structure is predominantly Gothic, apart from the main facade (replaced after an earthquake in 1851) and parts of the interior (renovated in Modernista style by Antoni Gaudí at the beginning of the 20th century).

It doesn't happen often, but Gaudí is completely upstaged by the island's top contemporary artist, Miquel Barceló, who completely reworked the Capella del Santíssim i Sant Pere, at the rear of the south aisle, in a dream-fantasy ceramic rendition of the miracle of the loaves and fishes.

Things you need to know: ☎ 971 72 31 30; www.catedraldemallorca.org; Carrer del Palau Reial 9; adult/under 10yr/student €4/free/3; ☷ 10am-6.30pm Mon-Fri, 10am-2.30pm Sat Jun-Sep, 10am-5.30pm Mon-Fri, 10am-2.30pm Sat Apr-May & Oct, 10am-2.30pm Mon-Fri, 10am-2.30pm Sat Nov-Mar

de la Reina and the port. Take a look around the *barrio* (district) of Santa Catalina, west of Passeig de Mallorca, especially around the east end of Carrer de la Fàbrica.

Casa Eduardo (☎ 971 72 11 82; Travessia Pesquera (Mollet); meals €35-45; ☷ lunch & dinner Tue-Sat, lunch Sun) What better place to get stuck into fish than behind the fresh fish market? Casa Eduardo has been serving meals since the 1940s and comes up with such things as lobster paella (€25 a head)!

our pick Refectori (☎ 971 22 73 47; Carrer de la Missió 7A; meals €70-80; ☷ lunch & dinner Mon-Fri, dinner Sat; ✗) Lovingly prepared Mediterranean grub with a special touch is the order of the day in the convent refectory.

DRINKING & ENTERTAINMENT

The old quarter is the city's most vibrant nightlife zone. Particularly along the narrow streets that lie between Plaça de la Reina and Plaça de la Drassana, you'll find an enormous selection of bars, pubs and bodegas (wine cellars). Look around the Santa Catalina (especially Carrer de Sant

CENTRAL PALMA DE MALLORCA

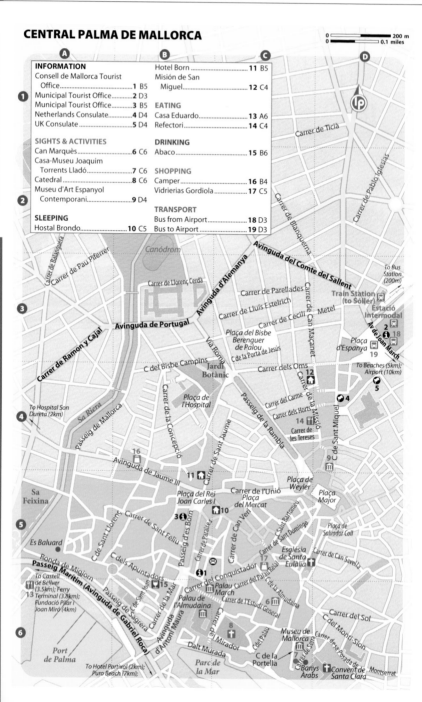

INFORMATION
Consell de Mallorca Tourist
  Office...................................1 B5
Municipal Tourist Office..........2 D3
Municipal Tourist Office..........3 B5
Netherlands Consulate.............4 D4
UK Consulate 5 D4

SIGHTS & ACTIVITIES
Can Marquès.............................6 C6
Casa-Museu Joaquim
  Torrents Lladó.......................7 C6
Catedral...................................8 C6
Museu d'Art Espanyol
  Contemporani.......................9 D4

SLEEPING
Hostal Brondo.........................10 C5

Hotel Born 11 B5
Misión de San
  Miguel................................12 C4

EATING
Casa Eduardo.........................13 A6
Refectori................................14 C4

DRINKING
Abaco....................................15 B6

SHOPPING
Camper..................................16 B4
Vidrierias Gordiola................17 C5

TRANSPORT
Bus from Airport....................18 D3
Bus to Airport........................19 D3

Magí) and Es Molinar districts too. Most bars shut by 1am Sunday to Thursday (3am Friday and Saturday).

Abaco (☎ 971 71 59 47; Carrer de Sant Joan 1; cocktails €15; ⏱ 8pm-1am Tue-Thu, 8pm-3am Fri & Sat) Behind a set of ancient timber doors is the bar of your wildest dreams. Inside, a Mallorcan *pati* and candlelit courtyard are crammed with elaborate floral arrangements and bizarre artworks.

our pick **Puro Beach** (☎ 971 74 47 44; www .purobeach.com; ⏱ 11am-2am) This uber laid-back, sunset chill lounge has an all-white bar with a tapering outdoor promontory area that is perfect for sunset cocktails, DJ sessions and fusion food escapes.

SHOPPING

Camper (☎ 971 71 46 35; Avinguda de Jaume III 16) The best known of Mallorca's famed shoe brands, funky, eco-chic Campers are now trendy worldwide.

Vidrierias Gordiola (☎ 971 71 15 41; Carrer de la Victoria 8; ⏱ closed Sat pm) Mallorca's best-known glassmakers offer everything from traditional goblets and vases to surprisingly modern works of art.

GETTING THERE & AWAY

Sant Joan airport is about 10km east of Palma.

Bus 1 runs every 15 minutes between Sant Joan airport and Plaça d'Espanya in central Palma (€1.85, 15 minutes) and on to the ferry terminal. Alternatively, a taxi will charge you around €15 to €18 for the trip.

NORTHWEST COAST & SERRA DE TRAMUNTANA

Dominated by the rugged Serra de Tramuntana range, Mallorca's northwest coast and its hinterland make up 'the other Mallorca'. No sandy beach resorts here. The coastline is rocky and largely in-

accessible, the villages are mostly built of local stone, and the mountainous interior is much loved by walkers for its beautiful landscapes of pine forests, olive groves and spring wildflowers.

ESTELLENCS

pop 350

Estellencs is a pretty village of stone buildings scattered around rolling hills below the **Puig Galatzó** (1025m) peak. A rugged walk of about 1km leads down to the local 'beach', a cove with crystal-clear water.

The higgledy-piggledy, stone **Petit Hotel Sa Plana** (☎ 971 61 86 66; www.sa plana.com; Carrer de Eusebi Pascual; d up to €98; P ⏱ ⏰) dominates a rise that catches

TRAVEL DIVISION IMAGES/ALAMY

Abaco, Palma de Mallorca

the evening sun. Rooms (there are five) are quite different and tastefully decorated with period furnishings.

IBIZA (EIVISSA)

Birthplace of the rave, Ibiza is home to some of Spain's most (in)famous clubs and plenty of bars. But coastal walking trails, woods and quiet (if not deserted) beaches allow you to elude Ministry of Sound–style madness too.

IBIZA CITY (EIVISSA)

pop 44,100

Set on a protected harbour on the southeast coast, Ibiza's capital is a vivacious, enchanting town with a captivating old quarter. It's also a focal point for some of the island's best nightlife.

INFORMATION

Tourist office (☎ 971 30 19 00; www.ibiza .travel; Passeig de Vara de Rei 1; ☽ 9am-8pm Mon-Fri, 9am-7pm Sat, 9am-3pm Sun) There is another office in Dalt Vila (☎ 971 39 92 32; Carrer Major 2; ☽ 10am-2pm & 6-8pm Mon-Sat).

SIGHTS & ACTIVITIES

From Sa Penya wander up into **D'Alt Vila**, the old walled town (and Unesco World Heritage site).

You can **walk** the entire perimeter of these impressive Renaissance-era walls (with great views along the way), designed to withstand heavy artillery.

A steep and well-worn route leads from Plaça de la Vila along narrow streets to the **cathedral**, which overlooks all.

SLEEPING

Casa de Huéspedes Navarro (☎ 971 31 07 71; Carrer de sa Creu 20; s/d €30/55) Right in the thick of things, this simple place has 10 rooms at the top of a long flight of stairs. The front rooms have harbour views, the interior rooms are quite dark (but cool in summer) and there's a sunny rooftop terrace. Bathrooms are shared but spotless.

Hostal La Marina (☎ 971 31 01 72; www .hostal-lamarina.com; Carrer de Barcelona 7; s €68; d €85-175; ✷) Looking onto the waterfront and bar-lined Carrer de Barcelona, this

Ibiza's D'Alt Vila

FAN TRAVELSTOCK/ALAMY

IBIZA CITY (EIVISSA)

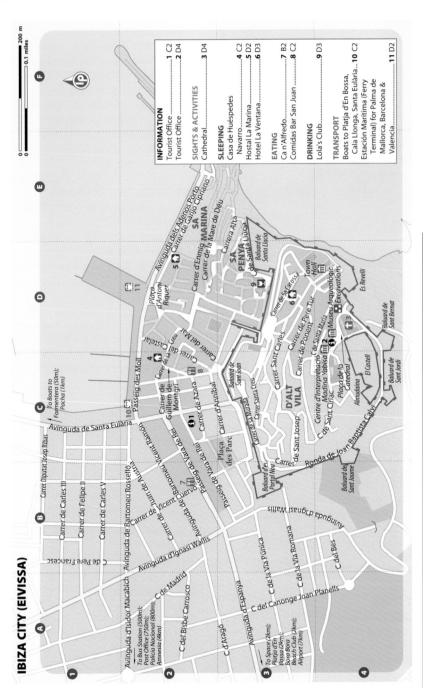

INFORMATION	
Tourist Office	**1** C2
Tourist Office	**2** D4
SIGHTS & ACTIVITIES	
Cathedral	**3** D4
SLEEPING	
Casa de Huéspedes	
Navarro	**4** C2
Hostal La Marina	**5** D2
Hotel La Ventana	**6** D3
EATING	
Ca n'Alfredo	**7** B2
Comidas Bar San Juan	**8** C2
DRINKING	
Lola's Club	**9** D3
TRANSPORT	
Boats to Platja d'En Bossa,	
Cala Llonga, Santa Eulària	**10** C2
Estación Marítima (Ferry	
Terminal) for Palma de	
Mallorca, Barcelona &	
Valencia	**11** D2

LARRY LILAC/ALAMY
Amnesia nightclub, Ibiza

mid-19th-century building has all sorts of brightly coloured rooms. Pricier doubles and attics have panoramic views.

Hotel La Ventana (☎ 971 39 08 57; www .laventanaibiza.com; Carrer de Sa Carossa 13; d from €177; P ✺) Just wander into this charming 15th-century mansion in the old town, set on a little tree-shaded square. Some rooms come with stylish four-poster beds and mosquito nets, and the rooftop terrace, gardens and restaurant are added reasons to choose this spot.

EATING
our pick Comidas Bar San Juan (☎ 971 31 16 03; Carrer de Guillem de Montgri 8; meals €15-20; ☾ lunch & dinner Mon-Sat) A family-run operation with two small dining rooms, this simple eatery offers outstanding value,

with fish dishes for around €10 and many small mains for €6 or less.

Ca n'Alfredo (☎ 971 31 12 74; Passeig de Vara de Rei 16; meals €40-45; ☾ lunch & dinner Tue-Sat, lunch Sun) Locals have been flocking to Alfredo's place since 1934. This is no new-wave Thai-fusion experience, but a great place for the freshest of seafood and other island cuisine that's so good it's essential to book.

DRINKING & ENTERTAINMENT
Sa Penya is the nightlife centre. Dozens of bars keep the port area jumping from sunset until the early hours. Alternatively, various bars at Platja d'En Bossa combine sounds, sand, sea and sangria (among other tipples).

BARS
Lola's Club (Via de Alfonso XII 10) Anyone who remembers Ibiza in the '80s will have fond memories of Lola's Club, one of the first on the island. It's a hip miniclub (with a gay leaning).

Bora Bora Beach Club At Platja d'en Bossa, about 2km from the old town, this is *the* place – a long beachside bar where sun- and fun-worshippers work off hangovers and prepare new ones. The ambience is chilled, with low-key club sounds wafting over the sand.

CLUBS
In summer (late May to the end of September) the west of the island is a continuous party from sunset to sunrise and back again. In 2007, the International Dance Music Awards named three Ibiza clubs (Amnesia, Pacha and Space) among the top five in the world.

The major clubs operate nightly from around 1am to 6am.

Entertainment Ibiza-style doesn't come cheaply. Admission can cost anything from €25 to €60 (and mixed beverages/cocktails then go for around €10 to €15).

Amnesia (☎ 971 19 80 41; www.amnesia.es; ◷ nightly early Jun-Sep) Four kilometres out on the road to Sant Rafel, with a sound system that seems to give your body a sound massage. A huge glasshouse-like internal terrace, filled with palms and bars, surrounds the central dance area, a seething mass of mostly tireless 20-something dancers.

Pacha (www.pacha.com; ◷ nightly Jun-Sep, Fri & Sat Oct-May) In business on the northern side of Ibiza City's port since 1973, Pacha contains 15 bars (!) and various dance spaces that can hold 3000 people.

Space (☎ 971 39 67 93; www.space-ibiza .es; ◷ 4.30pm-6am Jun–mid-Oct) One of the biggest of them all, south of Ibiza City in Platja d'en Bossa, with as many as 40 DJs and up to 12,000 clubbers – the action here starts in the mid-afternoon!

Ibiza's **Discobus** (☎ 971 31 34 47) operates nightly from midnight until 6am (June to September), doing circuits between the major discos, bars and hotels in Ibiza City, Platja d'en Bossa, Sant Rafel, Santa Eulària d'es Riu (and an extension to Es Canar) and Sant Antoni.

GETTING THERE & AWAY

Ibiza's airport (Aeroport d'Eivissa) is 7km southwest of the capital and receives direct flights from various mainland Spanish cities as well as London and a host of European centres.

Buses between the airport and the central port area via Platja d'en Bossa operate hourly between 6.30am and 11.30pm (€1.50, 20 to 25 minutes). A taxi from the airport costs around €12 to €14.

MENORCA

pop 90, 240

Menorca is the least overrun and most tranquil of the Balearics.

The untouched beaches, coves and ravines around its 216km coastline allow the more adventurous the occasional sense of discovery! This must be one of the few places in the Mediterranean where it is possible to have a beautiful beach largely to yourself in summer.

GUY MOBERLY

Port of Ciutadella (p252)

CIUTADELLA

pop 28,000

Known as Vella i Bella (The Old and the Beautiful), Ciutadella is an attractive and distinctly Spanish city with a picturesque port and an engaging old quarter.

INFORMATION

Tourist office (☎ 971 38 26 93; Plaça de la Catedral 5; ☽ 9am-2pm & 4-9pm Mon-Fri, 9am-2pm Sat May-Sep, 9am-1pm & 5-7pm Mon-Fri Oct-Apr); Port (☽ 10.30am-2pm & 6.30-9pm Tue-Sat, 10am-3pm Sun May-Sep)

SIGHTS & ACTIVITIES

The main square, Plaça d'es Born, is surrounded by palm trees and gracious 19th-century buildings, including the

ALBERTO PAREDES/ALAMY

Cala Macarelleta, Menorca

post office, the **ajuntament** (town hall) and the **Palau Torresaura**.

Architectural landmarks worth looking out for include the 14th-century **cathedral** (☎ 971 38 07 39; Plaça de la Catedral; ☽ 8am-1pm & 6-9pm), built in Catalan Gothic style (although with a baroque facade) on the site of Medina Minurqa's central mosque. Impressive noble families' mansions, such as **Palau Martorell** (Carrer del Santíssim 7) and **Palau Saura** (Carrer del Santíssim 2) are sometimes used for temporary exhibitions.

West of the town centre, the southern head of the port entrance is dominated by the stout little **Castell de Sant Nicolau** (☎ 676 807649; Plaça del Almirante Ferragut; admission free; ☽ 10am-1pm & 5-9pm Tue-Sat May-Sep).

SLEEPING

Hostal-Residencia Oasis (☎ 971 38 21 97; Carrer de Sant Isidre 33; s/d €40/55) Set around a spacious garden courtyard, this quiet place close to the heart of the old quarter has pleasant rooms, some of them done up in the past two years and most with bathrooms.

Hotel Gèminis (☎ 971 38 46 44; www.hotel geminismenorca.com; Carrer de Josepa Rossinyol 4; s/d €65/96; 🖫) A friendly, stylish two-star place on a backstreet, this graceful, three-storey, rose-white lodging offers comfortable if somewhat neutral rooms.

EATING

ourpick Café Balear (☎ 971 38 00 05; Placa de Sant Joan 15; meals €25-30; ☽ Mon-Sat) Sometimes the old timers are the best. Set apart from the town's more frenetic restaurant activity, this remains one of Ciutadella's classic seafood stops.

Ca's Ferrer de sa Font (☎ 971 48 07 84; Carrer del Portal de Sa Font 16; meals €35; ☽ lunch & dinner Tue-Sat, dinner Sun) Located in an 18th-century two-storey building with timber shutters, this is a romantic place offering a mix of quality inventive Mediterranean cooking.

GETTING THERE & AWAY
Boats for Mallorca (Port d'Alcúdia and Cala Ratjada) leave from the northern side of the Port de Ciutadella. For ferry details, see p368.

TMSA runs regular buses between Ciutadella and Maó.

NORTH COAST
Menorca's north coast is rugged and rocky, dotted with small and scenic coves. It's less developed than the south and, with your own transport and a bit of footwork, you'll discover some of the Balearics' best off-the-beaten-track beaches.

CAP DE CAVALLERIA & AROUND
Three kilometres shy of Fornells, turn west and follow the signs for 7km to reach a parking area for the stunning double-crescent, golden beach of **Platja Cavalleria** (a five-minute walk from the car park).

SOUTH COAST
Menorca's southern flank tends to have the better beaches – and thus the greater concentration of development. The recurring image is of a jagged coastline, occasionally interrupted by a small inlet with a sandy beach and backed by a cluster of gleaming-white villas.

CIUTADELLA TO PLATGES DE SON BOU
Between Son Xoriguer and Santa Galdana lies some of the least accessible southern coast. A narrow country road leads south of Ciutadella (follow the 'Platjes' sign from the *ronda*, or ring road) and then forks twice to (almost) reach the unspoiled

Sa Calobra bay on Malloca's northwest coast
HOLGER LEUE

⤷ IF YOU LIKE...
If you like the small, sandy beach at **Platja Cavalleria** (left), we're sure you'll enjoy the following Balearic beaches:

- **Menorca's North Coast** Rugged, rocky and largely undeveloped coast with Cala Presili and Platja d'en Tortuga the pick of the beaches.
- **Mallorca's Northwest Coast** Largely inaccessible rocky coastline with terrific beaches at Cala de Sant Vicenç and Sa Calobra.
- **Ibiza's East Coast** Platja Es Figueral and S'Aigua Blanca rank among Ibiza's best beaches.
- **Ibiza's North Coast** The unspoiled bay of Cala Benirràs has a beach backed with high, forested cliffs.
- **Ibiza's West Coast** Lovely beaches at Cala Compte, Cala Codolars and Cala d'Hort.
- **Formentera** The terrific beaches of the Balearics' fourth island include Platja de Llevant, Platja de ses Illetes, Illa s'Espalmador, Es Arenals and Cala Saona.

beaches (from west to east) of **Arenal de Son Saura, Cala en Turqueta, Cala des Es Talaier, Cala Macarelleta** and **Cala Macarella**.

MURCIA

MURCIA CITY

pop 417,000

Officially twinned with Miami, Murcia is the antithesis of the city of vice; it's a laid-back provincial capital that comes alive during the weekend *paseo* (stroll). Bypassed by most tourists and treated as a country cousin by too many Spaniards, the city nevertheless merits a visit.

INFORMATION

Tourist office (☎ 968 35 87 49; www.mur ciaciudad.com; Plaza del Cardenal Belluga; 🕙 10am-2pm & 5-9pm Mon-Sat, 10am-2pm Sun Jun-Sep, 10am-2pm & 4.30-8.30pm Mon-Sat, 10am-2pm Sun Oct-May)

SIGHTS

Murcia's sumptuous **cathedral** (Plaza del Cardenal Belluga; 🕙 7am-1pm & 5-8pm) was built in 1394 on the site of a mosque. The initial Gothic architecture was given a playful facelift in 1748, receiving an exuberant baroque facade complete with tumbling cherubs. The 15th-century Capilla de los Vélez is a highlight; the chapel's flutes and curls resemble piped icing.

SLEEPING

ourpick Hotel Casa Emilio (☎ 968 22 06 31; www.hotelcasaemilio.com; Alameda de Colón 9; s/d €45/55; P ⊠) Across from the leafy Floridablanca gardens, near the river, this is a well-maintained and nicely designed hotel with spacious, brightly lit rooms, large bathrooms and good firm mattresses.

Arco de San Juan (☎ 968 21 04 55; www .arcosanjuan.com; Plaza de Ceballos 10; s/d €75/130; P ⊠) This four-star hotel in a former palace hints of its palatial past with a massive 5m-high original door and some hefty repro columns. The rooms are classic and comfortable with hardwood details and classy fabrics.

EATING

Restaurante Hispano (☎ 968 21 61 52; Calle Arquitecto Cerdán; meals €16-25; 🕙 closed dinner Sun) The warm and inviting bar area here

Murcia Cathedral

IMAGEBROKER/ALAMY

has some wonderfully inventive *raciones* (large tapas serving), such as baby broad beans sautéed with artichokes and onion. The smarter restaurant beyond has an appealing combination of similarly creative and more traditional dishes.

Los Arroces del Romea (☎ 968 21 84 99; Plaza Romea s/n; meals €20-25; V) Watch the speciality paella-style rice dishes being prepared in cartwheel-sized pans over the flames while you munch on circular *murciano* bread drizzled with olive oil. There are five rice dishes to choose from, including vegetarian.

GETTING THERE & AWAY

Murcia's **San Javier airport** (☎ 968 17 20 00) is situated beside the Mar Menor, closer to Cartagena than Murcia city.

Up to five trains travel daily to/from Madrid (€41.30, 4¼ hours).

A taxi between the airport and Murcia city costs around €40.

CARTAGENA

pop 208,600

This is a city where you should walk with your eyes raised to the skyline (when you're not looking down at the map). The Modernista buildings, with their domes, swirly decorations and pastel colours, add a sumptuous quality to the architecture. The city is equally laden with archaeological sites, as well as excellent restaurants and sights.

INFORMATION

Tourist office (☎ 968 50 64 83; www .cartagena.es; Plaza del Almirante Bastarreche; ☺ 10am-2pm & 4-6pm or 5-7pm Mon-Fri, 10am-1pm Sat)

SIGHTS & ACTIVITIES

Cartagena is rich in Modernista buildings, including **Casa Cervantes** (Calle Mayor 11);

the **Casino** (Calle Mayor 13), which has a cafeteria; **Casa Llagostera** (Calle Mayor 25); the zinc-domed **Gran Hotel** (Calle del Aire s/n); the strawberries-and-cream confection of **Casa Clares** (Calle del Aire 4); and the resplendent **Palacio Aguirre** (Plaza de la Merced), now an exhibition space for modern art.

Puerto de Culturas (☺ 968 50 00 93; www.puertoculturas.com) offers four different combined tickets (€11 to €18) covering Murcia's sights and tours.

For a sweeping panoramic view, stride up to **Castillo de la Concepción**, or hop on the lift (€1).

Some other Roman sites include the **Augusteum** (Calle Caballero; adult/under 12yr/12-25yr €2.50/free/2; ☺ 10am-2.30pm Tue-Sun Jul-Sep, 4-6.30pm Tue-Sun Oct-Jun), which has an exhibition on the Roman Forum; the **Decumanus** (adult/under 12yr/12-25yr €2/free/1; ☺ 10am-2.30pm & 4-6pm Tue-Sun Jul-Sep, 10am-2.30pm Tue-Sun Oct-Jun), shop-lined remains of one of the town's main Roman streets, located just off Calle Honda; and the **Casa de la Fortuna** (Plaza Risueño; adult/under 12yr/12-25yr €2.50/free/2; ☺ 10am-2.30pm & 4-8.30pm Tue-Sun Jul-Sep, 10am-2.30pm Tue-Sun Oct-Jun), a Roman villa dating back to the 2nd and 3rd centuries AD, demonstrating the daily life of the aristocracy at the time.

To the northeast are the remains of the 13th-century **cathedral**, devastated by aerial bombardment during the Spanish Civil War and originally built from recycled slabs and pillars from the adjacent **roman theatre** (currently undergoing reconstruction).

SLEEPING

Pensión Oriente (☎ /fax 968 50 24 69; 2nd fl, Calle Jara 27; s/d without bathroom €25/34) The Oriente has 12 simple rooms with high ceilings, pine furniture and fans. The one

Gran Hotel (p255), Cartagena

ED RHODES/ALAMY

spacious double en suite (€38) is worth the extra, although all the rooms could do with a lick of paint.

Hotel Restaurante Los Habaneros (☎ 968 50 52 50; www.hotelhabaneros.com in Spanish; Calle de San Diego 60; s €52-57, d €69-73; P 🔀 ▣) Located across from the Murcia Púnica visitors centre, this shiny modern hotel has good-sized rooms decorated in cream and burgundy.

EATING

ourpick **La Tartana** (☎ 968 50 00 11; Puerta de Murcia 14; tapas €1.50, raciones €4-8) With 60-plus choices lined up along the bar, this is the best place in town to come for tapas and *raciones*.

Plaza de la Isla has two large popular fish restaurants where you can indulge in the catch of the day: **Casa del Pescador** (☎ 968 50 63 75; meals €20-35; ⌚ closed dinner Sun & Mon year-round, lunch & dinner Tue Aug) and its cheaper neighbour **Techos Bajos** (☎ 968 50 50 20; meals €15-20; ⌚ lunch Tue-Sun, dinner Fri & Sat).

GETTING THERE & AWAY

A taxi to or from San Javier airport will cost you approximately €35.

For Renfe train destinations, you need to change in Murcia (€4.20, 50 minutes, four to seven daily).

↘ ANDALUCÍA

ANDALUCÍA

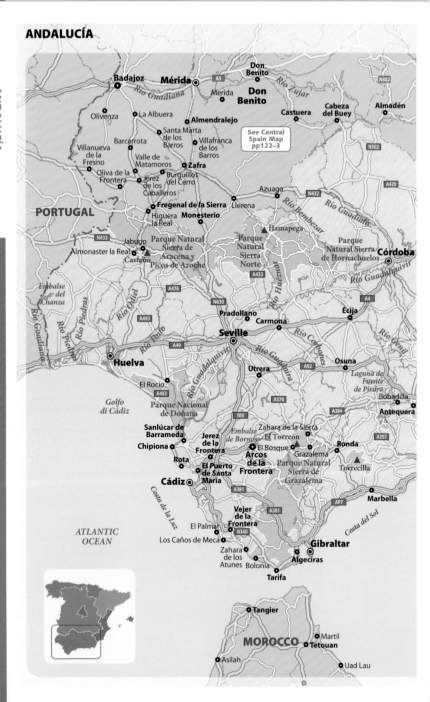

ANDALUCÍA

Badajoz
Rio Guadiana
Mérida
Merida
Don Benito
Don Benito
Rio Zujar
A5
Olivenza
La Albuera
Almendralejo
Santa Marta de los Barros
Villafranca de los Barros
Castuera
Cabeza del Buey
Almadén
N502
N502
Barcarrota
Villanueva de la Fresno
Valle de Matamoros
Zafra
See Central Spain Map pp122–3
A420
Oliva de la Frontera
Jerez de los Caballeros
Burguillos del Cerro
Azuaga
N432
Rio Bembezar
Rio Guadiato
PORTUGAL
Fregenal de la Sierra
Higuera la Real
Monesterio
Llerena
Parque Natural Sierra Norte
Hamapega
Parque Natural Sierra de Hornachuelos
Córdoba
N433
Jabugo
Parque Natural Sierra de Aracena y Picos de Aroche
Rio Huezna
Rio Guadalquivir
Almonaster la Real
Castaño
A432
A4
Embalse del Chanza
A476
Rio Odiel
N630
Pradollano
Carmona
Écija
Rio Corbones
Rio Genil
Rio Piedras
A493
Rio Tinto
Seville
A49
Huelva
Rio Guadaíra
A92
Osuna
Laguna de Fuente de Piedra
Rio Guadiana
El Rocio
A483
Rio Guadalquivir
Utrera
A376
Golfo di Cádiz
Parque Nacional de Doñana
NIV
Bobadilla
Antequera
A384
A357
Sanlúcar de Barrameda
Jerez de la Frontera
Embalse de Bornos
Zahara de la Sierra
El Torreón
Ronda
Chipiona
El Bosque
Grazalema
Rota
Arcos de la Frontera
Parque Natural Sierra de Grazalema
Torrecilla
El Puerto de Santa María
AP7
Cádiz
A381
Marbella
Costa del Sol
Vejer de la Frontera
A381
ATLANTIC OCEAN
Costa de la Luz
El Palmar
N340
Los Caños de Meca
Zahara de los Atunes
Bolonia
Gibraltar
Algeciras
Tarifa

Tangier

MOROCCO
Martil
Tetouan
Asilah
Uad Lau

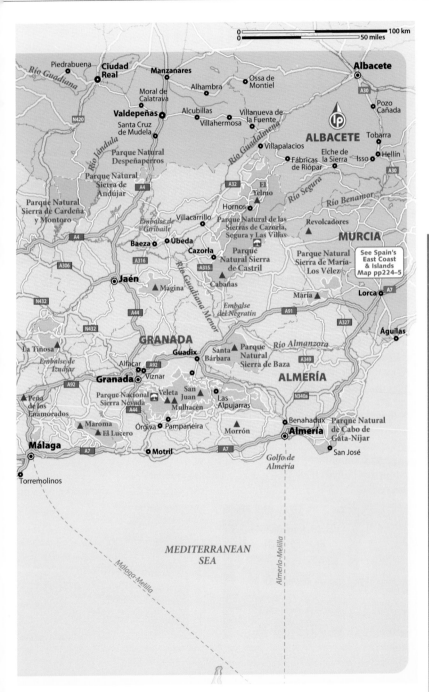

0   100 km
0   50 miles

Piedrabuena

Ciudad Real

Manzanares

Río Guadiana

Alhambra

Ossa de Montiel

Albacete

A30

Moral de Calatrava

Valdepeñas

Alcubillas

Villanueva de la Fuente

Pozo Cañada

Santa Cruz de Mudela

N420

Villahermosa

Río Guadalmena

ALBACETE

Tobarra

Parque Natural Despeñaperros

Villapalacios

Elche de la Sierra

Hellín

Parque Natural Sierra de Andújar

A4

A32

El Yelmo

Fábricas de Riópar

Isso

A30

Parque Natural Sierra de Cardeña y Montoro

Hornos

Río Segura

Río Benamor

A4

Embalse de Giribaile

Villacarrillo

Parque Natural de las Sierras de Cazorla, Segura y Las Villas

Revolcadores

MURCIA

Baeza

Úbeda

A316

Cazorla

Parque Natural Sierra de María-Los Vélez

See Spain's East Coast & Islands Map pp224–5

A306

A315

Parque Natural Sierra de Castril

Jaén

Mágina

Cabañas

María

Lorca

A7

N432

A44

Embalse del Negratín

A91

A327

Águilas

N432

GRANADA

Guadix

Santa Bárbara

Parque Natural Sierra de Baza

Río Almanzora

A349

La Tiñosa

Alfacar

A92

Embalse de Iznájar

Viznar

Granada

A92

Veleta

San Juan

Las Alpujarras

ALMERÍA

N340a

Peña de los Enamorados

Parque Nacional Sierra Nevada

A44

Mulhacén

Maroma

Órgiva

Pampaneira

Morrón

Benahadux

Almería

Parque Natural de Cabo de Gata-Níjar

El Lucero

San José

Málaga

A7

Motril

A7

Golfo de Almería

Torremolinos

Málaga-Melilla

MEDITERRANEAN SEA

Almería-Melilla

ANDALUCÍA HIGHLIGHTS

ANDALUCIA HIGHLIGHTS

1 LA ALHAMBRA

BY MARÍA DEL MAR VILLAFRANCA, DIRECTOR OF PATRONATO DE LA ALHAMBRA Y GENERALIFE

The Alhambra is exceptional, the only medieval palace of its type and cultural significance to have survived anywhere in the world. It also represents a shining example of the conservation and restoration of heritage buildings. But what I love most about the Alhambra is its harmonious relationship between architecture and landscape.

⬎ MARÍA DEL MAR VILLAFRANCA'S DON'T MISS LIST

❶ FACADE OF THE PALACIO DE COMARES

Unlike many visitors, take the time to contemplate this iconic and perfectly proportioned facade. So many of the Alhambra's signature decorative forms are on display here, including *epigrafía* (inscriptions and calligraphy), *lacerías* (interlocking wooden lengths to form geometric patterns), *atauriques* (stylised plant motifs) in plaster and ceramics, and a magnificent wooden *dosel* (canopy) to round it all off.

❷ PATIO DE LOS ARRAYANES

Visit here for the overall majesty, but what's special is the use of water, which is at once decorative and functional. It has the effect of making the porticos seem longer, adding a symbolic dimension and amplifying the sense of light, even as it gives the visitor the feeling that this is not just a garden but an oasis.

❸ PATIO DE LOS LEONES

My favourite place from which to view this famous patio is from the Sala de

Clockwise from top: Palacio Nazaríes; Palacio de Comares internal patio; Carved archway; Tilework in Patio de los Arrayanes; Courtyard garden in the Alhambra

Dos Hermanas (Hall of the Two Sisters) on the patio's northern side. This perspective reveals the glorious pinnacle of Nasrid architecture, blending the careful designs of Al-Andalus' most skilled artisans with the wider heritage of oriental art.

❹ PEINADOR DE LA REINA

The 'Queen's Dressing Room' is like a bridge between the Islamic and Christian periods of the Alhambra. As such, it's an outstanding example of cultural synthesis, where the beautiful decorative art of the Renaissance occupies the heart of an earlier Nasrid tower. It also serves as one of the Alhambra's open windows with sweeping views out onto the world beyond the palace.

❺ THE SPIRIT OF THE AGE

Two corners of the Alhambra in particular give a powerful sense of what it was like to live here. The base of the Torre de la Vela conserves that spirit perfectly, while the baths are unique in enabling you to understand the social, cultural and religious practices that gave meaning to life in Al-Andalus.

↘ THINGS YOU NEED TO KNOW

Admission €12 **Top tip** Of the 6600 daily tickets issued, just 2000 are available at the gate so book ahead **Night visits** Possible for Palacio Nazaríes 10pm to 11.30pm Tuesday to Saturday March to October, 8pm to 9.30pm Friday & Saturday November to February **See the author's review, p303**

ANDALUCÍA

ANDALUCÍA HIGHLIGHTS

ANDALUCÍA HIGHLIGHTS

2 CÓRDOBA

BY SEBASTIÁN DE LA OBRA, EMINENT LOCAL HISTORIAN

Córdoba's diverse and surprising fingerprints of the past are not always what they seem. Yes, there are reminders of a tolerant past where three religions co-existed. But the reality of Córdoba as a symbol of historical coexistence is far more complicated. Discovering whether this Córdoba was myth or reality is a fascinating journey.

SEBASTIÁN DE LA OBRA'S DON'T MISS LIST

❶ LA MEZQUITA DE CÓRDOBA

Córdoba's Mezquita is one of the most prestigious buildings in Arab-Islamic culture. The interior is indescribably beautiful – a labyrinth of bicoloured columns with horseshoe arches, a forest of palm trees rendered in stone and brickwork that is most beautiful in the *mihrab* (which was finished with golden mosaics from Byzantium).

❷ LA SINAGOGA DE CÓRDOBA

Built in 1315 (5075 in the Jewish calendar), Córdoba's synagogue is richly decorated with Mudéjar art and fragments of the Psalms in Hebrew. After Jews were expelled from Spain, the synagogue served as a school, hermitage, hospital and even a brotherhood of shoemakers, but is now one of the few remaining signposts to Spain's Jewish heritage.

❸ TEMPLO ROMANO DE CÓRDOBA

Away from the heart of tourist Córdoba, the city's spectacular Roman temple is a reminder that Córdoba's fame predates

Clockwise from top: Templo Romano de Córdoba (off Map p298); Iglesia de Santa Marina (off Map p298); La Mezquita (p297); Hebrew inscription in La Sinagoga de Córdoba (p297); La Mezquita (p297) interior

CLOCKWISE FROM TOP: JEAN DOMINIQUE DALLET/ALAMY; PHOTAS LTD/ALAMY; KARL BLACKWELL; DBIMAGES/ALAMY; MICHAEL TAYLOR

Al-Andalus. Córdoba was the capital of Hispania Ulterior (and later Córdoba Bética), and in the 3rd century was considered the cultural and economic powerhouse of Roman Iberia. The ruins wonderfully evoke this period.

❹ CHURCHES OF THE FERNANDO PERIOD

In the 14th century, churches were built in all the city's neighbourhoods and today provide the focal point for a beautiful route through the city. Thirteen of the original 14 churches survive and all share common architectural features – three naves with an apse, rose windows, stone walls and Mozarabic windows. My favourites are the Capilla de San Bartolomé and the Iglesia de Santa Marina.

❺ CASA DE SEFARAD

This privately run museum and cultural space occupies a beautiful 14th-century house and serves as a centre for recovering the heritage and historical memory of Spain's Jewish community. It's home to one of the most prestigious libraries in Andalucía (with numerous ancient manuscripts), but also hosts concerts of Sephardic and other Andalucian music.

↘ THINGS YOU NEED TO KNOW

Best time to visit Mid-April to mid-June **Avoid** July and August when Córdoba is fiercely hot **Córdoba's Roman Temple** Can be found on the corner of Calle de Claudio Marcelo and Calle de los Capitulares **See our author's coverage of the city, p296**

ANDALUCÍA HIGHLIGHTS

3

↘ GRANADA'S ARCHITECTURAL MASTERPIECE

If you visit one place in Andalucía, make it the **Alhambra** (p303), the peak of seven centuries of Islamic architectural achievement in Europe. Epic in scale, exquisite in the intricacy of its close-up detail, this is a place modelled on an Islamic vision of paradise. The iconic Palacio Nazaríes is the extraordinary centrepiece, while the Generalife gardens bring to fruition the Qur'anic claim that paradise is a garden.

4

↘ SAVOUR CÓRDOBA'S MEZQUITA

If Granada's Alhambra impresses on a grand scale, Cordoba's **Mezquita** (p297) is an altogether more intimate experience. The striped horseshoe arches of the mosque's interior are, if you can ignore the monstrosity of the 16th-century cathedral in its midst, as close to perfection as you'll come. As such, it's a fitting tribute to Córdoba's glory days when it was the most enlightened city on earth.

5

↘ CÁDIZ

Ask any Spaniard for their favourite Spanish city, and chances are that many will say Cádiz (p280), usually accompanied with a broad smile. Renowned for its sense of fun – especially during Carnaval – and famous for its fantastic food and many stunning high-above-the-rooftops vantage points, Cádiz is one of our favourite Andalucian cities, too.

6

↘ SEVILLE'S TAPAS AND FLAMENCO

If you want to experience the essence of Spain, Seville (p270) is the place to do it. Its architecture – a mix of Islamic splendour and Catholic extravagance – and its festivals are quintessentially Spanish. But Seville is known above all for its obsession with tapas (p278) and as the possible birthplace of flamenco (p279).

7

↘ ARCOS DE LA FRONTERA

One of Andalucía's signature images, Arcos de la Frontera (p285) ranks among Andalucía's most beautiful *pueblos blancos* (white villages). Stretched out along a ridge like a string of pearls, surveying the plains from its clifftop perch, Arcos combines small-town Andalucian charm with architecture that will live long in the memory.

3 WITOLD SKRYPCZAK; 4 KARL BLACKWELL; 5 PAUL BERNHARDT; 6 KARL BLACKWELL; 7 DIANA MAYFIELD

3 View of the Alhambra (p303) from Granada's Albayzín; 4 Mezquita (p297), Cordoba; 5 Cádiz (p280); 6 Flamenco guitarist, Seville (p270); 7 Arcos de la Frontera (p285)

ANDALUCÍA

ANDALUCÍA'S BEST...

ANDALUCÍA'S BEST...

⬎ SIGNATURE SIGHTS BEYOND GRANADA & CÓRDOBA

- **Alcázar, Seville** (p271) One of Andalucía's architectural gems.
- **Museo Picasso Málaga** (p289) Stunning collection of Picasso's works in the city of his birth.
- **Baeza** (p309) A treasure-trove of Renaissance architecture.

⬎ BEACHES

- **Tarifa** (p287) Windsurfing, whales and horse-riding.
- **Cabo de Gata** (p311) Hidden coves without the crowds.
- **Zahara de los Atunes** (p288) Expanse of sand as the Spanish coast used to be.
- **Los Caños de Meca** (p288) Long laid-back beaches around the Cabo de Trafalgar.

⬎ JOURNEYS BACK IN TIME

- **Hammam Baños Árabes, Córdoba** (p299) The indulgent echo of medieval Córdoba's sophistication.
- **Santiponce** (p280) Second-century Roman town with a massive amphitheatre.
- **Bolonia** (p288) Spain's most extensive Roman town with a great beach.
- **Mini Hollywood** (p311) Western film set with the ghost of Clint Eastwood before he became respectable.

⬎ WALKING COUNTRY

- **Sierra Nevada** (p308) Andalucía's most spectacular natural area.
- **Las Alpujarras** (p309) Berber-style villages and snaking valleys.
- **Sierra de Grazalema** (p286) Verdant mountains and pretty white villages.

DIANA MAYFIELD

Puente Nuevo (p295), Ronda, Málaga province

THINGS YOU NEED TO KNOW

VITAL STATISTICS

- **Population** 7.9 million
- **Area** 87,000 sq km
- **Best time to visit** Year-round; avoid the interior in July and August.

LOCALITIES IN A NUTSHELL

- **Seville** (p270) Home to all things Andalucian.
- **Cádiz province** (p280) From the coastal city of Cádiz to the hill-towns of the north in eastern Andalucía.
- **Málaga province** (p289) Includes Málaga, Marbella and Ronda.
- **Córdoba province** (p296) Córdoba boasts the Mezquita and a fine Jewish quarter.
- **Granada province** (p300) Contains Granada city, the Sierra Nevada and Las Alpujarras.
- **Jaén & Almería provinces** (p309 & p311) Away from well-worn tourist trails with Baeza and Cabo de Gata respectively.

ADVANCE PLANNING

- **One month before** Reserve your entry ticket for the Alhambra (p303) and your accommodation, earlier in summer.
- **Two weeks before** Reserve your high-speed AVE ticket (www .renfe.es) from Madrid to Seville or Málaga.

RESOURCES

- **Andalucía Te Quiere** (www.anda lucia.org) Terrific tourist office site for the entire region.
- **Andalucia.com** (www.andalucia .com) Excellent privately run site on Andalucía.
- **La Guía de Flamenco** (www.guia flama.com in Spanish) The best source of upcoming flamenco concerts.
- **Centro Andaluz de Flamenco** (www.centroandaluzdeflamenco.es) Another good resource for flamenco performances.
- **The Ornament of the World** (Maria Rosa Menocal) A fascinating insight into Andalucía's Islamic centuries.

EMERGENCY NUMBERS

- **Emergency** (☎ 112)
- **Policía Nacional** (☎ 091)

GETTING AROUND

- **Air** International airports with intra-Spain connections in Málaga, Seville, Granada, Jerez de la Frontera and Almería.
- **Train** Renfe has good north–south connections, fewer from east to west.
- **Bus** Wherever trains don't reach.
- **Road** Excellent network of roads.

BE FOREWARNED

- The Alhambra has 6600 daily tickets, but just 2000 are available at the gate, so book ahead.

ANDALUCÍA ITINERARIES

AL-ANDALUS HEARTLAND Three Days

Any attempt to catch a glimpse of Islamic Al-Andalus just has to begin in **(1) Granada** (p300), which served as the capital of Islamic Spain long after the rest of the country had fallen to the Christian Reconquista. Having had centuries to perfect their distinctive architectural style, Granada's Islamic rulers created the Alhambra, quite possibly one of the most exquisite collections of buildings on earth. You could spend a day in the Alhambra alone, but the Albayzín, Granada's historical and present-day heartbeat, the Capilla Real and the city's wonderful tapas culture deserve another day at least. Away to the northwest by road or by rail (change in Bobadilla), **(2) Córdoba** (p296) is every bit as impressive. Córdoba's Mezquita, which dates from the early Islamic period, is the perfect complement to Granada's Alhambra: together they stand as bookends to the historical story of Al-Andalus. Córdoba's Judería, which surrounds the Mezquita, deserves as much time as you can give it, its tangled, whitewashed lanes once a symbol of Córdoba's enlightened religious tolerance in the Middle Ages; here you'll also find one of just three medieval synagogues left in Spain.

FLAMENCO & SHERRY Five Days

Flamenco was born in eastern Andalucía, and it's in the intimate tiled courtyards of **(1) Seville** (p270), the genre's reputed birthplace, where you can still hear flamenco in its purest form. With hundreds of tapas bars nearby and monuments to visit, Seville deserves at least two days. An hour south of Seville by regular train, or just off the AP4, **(2) Jerez de la Frontera** (p283) shares many of the same passions – it's a hotbed of authentic flamenco (ask at the Centro Andaluz de Flamenco for the latest performances), a fantastic place to eat, and famous for its Andalucian horses. Jerez also has world-renowned sherry bodegas, most of which run tours. A short train journey away, **(3) El Puerto de Santa María** (p285) is another capital of the sherry world, not to mention a lovely whitewashed town with some excellent beaches. Just across the bay, **(4) Cádiz** (p280), reached by ferry or train, is Europe's oldest continuously inhabited city, and one of Spain's most engaging seaside towns.

PUEBLOS BLANCOS & THE SIERRA NEVADA One Week

You know you're in Andalucía when a dazzling village looms into view, perched atop a rocky crag. **(1) Arcos de la Frontera** (p285) is spectacular from a distance, and equally pretty within its narrow lanes, which close off any view of the horizon. After a night in Arcos, detour into the Sierra de Grazalema where **(2) Grazalema** (p286) and

ANDALUCÍA

ANDALUCÍA ITINERARIES

(3) Zahara de la Sierra (p286) are perfectly sited and heartbreakingly picturesque, before continuing down to (4) Vejer de la Frontera (p286) for the night. The most artsy of the hill towns in Cádiz province, Vejer is enchanting. Northwest of Vejer, (5) Ronda (p295) is a special place, clinging precariously to the summit of vertiginous cliffs. After a night here, a longish drive east brings you to (6) Las Alpujarras (p309), a peerless succession of white villages. Trekking from village to village in Las Alpujarras, or walking to the summit of the Mulhacén (at 3479m, it's mainland Spain's highest peak) in the neighbouring (7) Sierra Nevada (p308), is Andalucía at its best.

DISCOVER ANDALUCÍA

What aspect of Spain does Andalucía represent? To millions of visitors, this southern powerhouse *is* Spain. Since the country began to reinvent itself as a major destination in the 1950s, Andalucía has been the generator of national stereotypes.

There's Cádiz, Europe's oldest living city, contrasting with the shiny new metropolises of the Costa del Sol still waiting to be inhabited. The narrow streets of Andalucía's provincial capitals, rich in historic treasures left by Phoenician, Roman, Moorish, Jewish and Catholic conquerors, offset a vast outdoor adventure playground with Spain's widest swathes of protected land, the mainland's highest mountain, and Europe's stiffest breezes powering kitesurfing in Tarifa.

Andalucía is a clash of sensory impressions as fierce as its searing light and impenetrable shade. Andalucía is both superstitious and irreligious. Yet it is not sentimental, and its young people are impatient for change. Andalucía is taking its place in 21st-century Spain – the past can come along if it likes.

HISTORY

Andalucía was the obvious base for the Muslim invaders who surged onto the Iberian Peninsula from Africa in 711 under Arab general Tariq ibn Ziyad. Until the 11th century Córdoba was the leading city of Islamic Spain, followed by Seville until the 13th and finally Granada until the 15th century. At its peak in the 10th century, Córdoba was the most dazzling city in Western Europe, famed for its 'three cultures' coexistence of Muslims, Jews and Christians.

The Emirate of Granada, the last bastion of Al-Andalus, finally fell to the Catholic Monarchs, Fernando and Isabel, in 1492. Columbus' landing in the Americas the same year brought great wealth to Seville and later Cádiz, the Andalucian ports through which Spain's trade with the Americas was conducted. But the Castilian conquerors killed off Andalucía's deeper prosperity by handing out great swathes of territory to their nobles, who set sheep to run on former food-growing lands.

SEVILLE

pop 700,000

Conjure your most vivid image of Andalucía – proud men in black *sombreros,* flamenco dancers, hooded penitents following a candlelit statue of the Virgin, a matador unfurling his scarlet cape – and it comes alive in Seville. All this and more is played out with intense passion in Andalucía's capital city, especially during the city's Semana Santa (Holy Week) and its annual *feria* (fair) in spring. Yet Seville doesn't rest on its historic laurels; increasingly, its historic buildings coexist with stark and stylish hotels and bars playing the latest beats.

INFORMATION

Municipal tourist office (☎ 954 22 17 14; barranco.turismo@sevilla.org; Calle de Arjona 28; ☽ 9am-7.30pm Mon-Fri, 9am-2pm Sat & Sun, reduced hrs during Semana Santa & Feria de Abril) **Regional tourist offices** Avenida de la Constitución 21 (☎ 954 22 14 04; otsevilla@ andalucia.org; ☽ 9am-7pm Mon-Fri, 10am-2pm

& 3-7pm Sat, 10am-2pm Sun, closed holidays); Estación Santa Justa (☎ 954 53 76 26; ⏰ 9am-8pm Mon-Fri, 10am-2pm Sat & Sun, closed holidays).

Turismo Sevilla (☎ 954 21 00 05; www.turis mosevilla.org; Plaza del Triunfo 1; ⏰ 10.30am-7pm Mon-Fri)

SIGHTS
ALCÁZAR

Residence of many generations of kings and caliphs, the **Alcázar** (☎ 954 50 23 23; adult/under 16yr, senior, student, disabled €7/free; ⏰ 9.30am-8pm Tue-Sat, to 6pm Sun & holidays Apr-Sep, to 6pm Tue-Sat, to 2.30pm Sun & holidays Oct-Mar) is Seville's answer to Granada's Alhambra.

Originally founded as a fort for the Cordoban governors of Seville in 913, the Alcázar has been expanded and rebuilt many times in its 11 centuries of existence. The Catholic Monarchs, Fernando and Isabel, set up court here in the 1480s as they prepared for the conquest of Granada. Later rulers created the Alcázar's lovely gardens.

PATIO DEL LEÓN

The Lion Patio was the garrison yard of the Al-Muwarak palace. Off here, the **Sala de la Justicia** (Hall of Justice), with beautiful Mudéjar plasterwork, was built in the 1340s by Alfonso XI, who disported here with his mistress Leonor de Guzmán. The room gives on to the pretty **Patio del Yeso**, a 19th-century reconstruction of part of the 12th-century Almohad palace.

PATIO DE LA MONTERÍA

The **Sala de Audiencias** contains the earliest known painting on the discovery of the Americas (by Alejo Fernández, 1530s), in which Columbus, Fernando El Católico, Carlos I, Amerigo Vespucci and Native Americans can be seen sheltered beneath the Virgin in her role as protector of sailors.

PALACIO DE DON PEDRO (MUDEJAR PALACE)

He might have been 'the Cruel', but between 1360 and 1364 Pedro I humbly built his exquisite palace in 'perishable'

Seville's cathedral and Giralda tower (p274)

DIANA MAYFIELD

ANDALUCÍA

SEVILLE

ANDALUCÍA

SEVILLE

SEVILLE

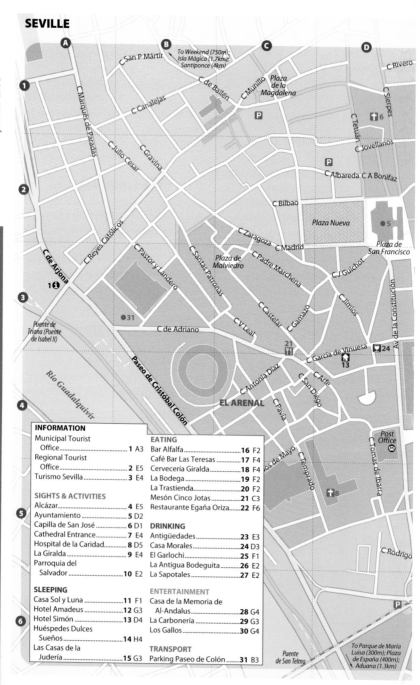

To Weekend (750m);
Isla Mágica (1.7km);
Santiponce (4km)

C San P. Mártir

C Rivero

C de Bailén

C Munillo
Plaza
de la
Magdalena

C Canalejas

C Sierpes

6

C Marqués de Paradas

C Julio César

C Gravina

P

C Tetuán

C Jovellanos

C Albareda C A Bonifaz

P

C Bilbao

Plaza Nueva

5

C Reyes Católicos

C de Arjona

C Zaragoza

C Madrid

Plaza de
San Francisco

1

C Pastor y Landero

C Santas Patronas

Plaza de
Malviedro

C Padre Marchena

C J Guichot

Av de la Constitución

Puente de
Triana (Puente
de Isabel II)

31

C de Adriano

C Castelar

C Gamazo

C Jimios

CV Leal

21
13

C García de Vinuesa

24

Río Guadalquivir

Paseo de Cristóbal Colón

C Antonia Díaz

C San Diego

C Arfe

Post
Office

C Tomás de Ibarra

EL ARENAL

C Pavia

C Temprado

Puente
de San Telmo

C Rodrigo

P

To Parque de María
Luisa (300m); Plaza
de España (400m);
Aduana (1.3km)

8

INFORMATION

Municipal Tourist
  Office.......................... **1** A3
Regional Tourist
  Office.......................... **2** E5
Turismo Sevilla..................... **3** E4

SIGHTS & ACTIVITIES

Alcázar................................ **4** E5
Ayuntamiento **5** D2
Capilla de San José.............. **6** D1
Cathedral Entrance.............. **7** E4
Hospital de la Caridad.......... **8** D5
La Giralda **9** E4
Parroquia del
  Salvador **10** E2

SLEEPING

Casa Sol y Luna **11** F1
Hotel Amadeus **12** G3
Hotel Simón **13** D4
Huéspedes Dulces
  Sueños.............................**14** H4
Las Casas de la
  Judería **15** G3

EATING

Bar Alfalfa..........................**16** F2
Café Bar Las Teresas **17** F4
Cervecería Giralda..............**18** F4
La Bodega **19** F2
La Trastienda......................**20** F2
Mesón Cinco Jotas..............**21** C3
Restaurante Egaña Oriza......**22** F6

DRINKING

Antigüedades......................**23** E3
Casa Morales......................**24** D3
El Garlochi..........................**25** F1
La Antigua Bodeguita.........**26** E2
La Sapotales.......................**27** E2

ENTERTAINMENT

Casa de la Memoria de
  Al-Andalus......................**28** G4
La Carbonería.....................**29** G3
Los Gallos..........................**30** G4

TRANSPORT

Parking Paseo de Colón **31** B3

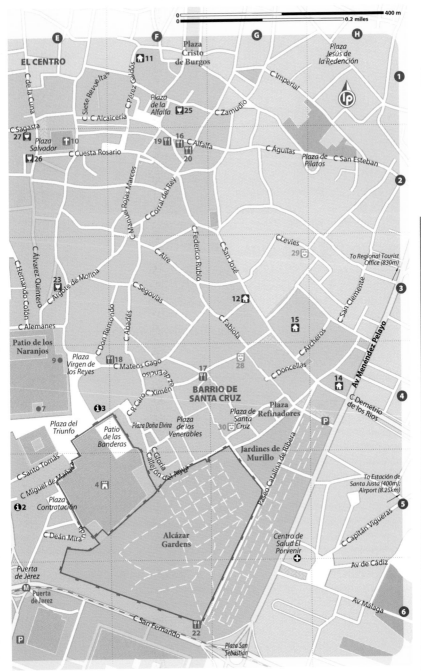

0 400 m
0 0.2 miles

E · F · G · H

EL CENTRO

Plaza Cristo de Burgos

Plaza Jesús de la Redención

11

C Imperial

C de la Cuna

C Siete Revueltas

C Pérez Galdós

Plaza de la Alfalfa

25

C Zamudio

C Águilas

C San Esteban

Plaza de Pilatos

C Sagasta

27

Plaza Salvador

10

C Alcaicería

C Cuesta Rosario

19 16

C Alfalfa

20

26

C Manuel Rojas Marcos

C Corral del Rey

C Federico Rubio

C Levíes

29

C San José

C Álvarez Quintero

23

C Argote de Molina

C Aire

C Segovias

C Don Remondo

C Abadés

C San Clemente

12

C Fabiola

15

C Archeros

C Hernando Colón

C Alemanes

Patio de los Naranjos

9

Plaza Virgen de los Reyes

18

C Mateos Gago

C de Enciso

C Ximénez de Enciso

28

17

C Doncellas

7

3

C R Caro

BARRIO DE SANTA CRUZ

Plaza Doña Elvira

Plaza de los Venerables

Plaza de Santa Cruz

30

Plaza de Refinadores

14

Av Menéndez Pelayo

C Demetrio de los Ríos

Plaza del Triunfo

Patio de las Banderas

Gloria

Callejón del Agua

Jardines de Murillo

Paseo Catalina de Ribera

C Santo Tomás

C Miguel de Mañara

4

Plaza Contratación

2

Alcázar Gardens

Centro de Salud El Porvenir

C Capitán Vigueras

C Deán Mira S

5

Puerta de Jerez

Puerta de Jerez

Av de Cádiz

Av Málaga

6

C San Fernando

22

Plaza San Sebastián

To Regional Tourist Office (830m)

To Estación de Santa Justa (400m); Airport (8.25km)

ANDALUCÍA

SEVILLE

WAYNE WALTON

Cathedral and Giralda, Seville

⬈ CATHEDRAL & GIRALDA

Seville's cathedral is one of the largest in the world: the main building is 126m long and 83m wide. It was completed by 1507 and was originally Gothic, though work done after its central dome collapsed in 1511 was mostly in the Renaissance style.

Inside the cathedral's southern door stands the elaborate tomb of Christopher Columbus, dating from 1902.

Towards the east end of the main nave is the Capilla Mayor, whose Gothic altarpiece is the jewel of the cathedral and reckoned to be the biggest altarpiece in the world.

In the northeastern corner of the cathedral interior you'll find the passage for the climb up the Giralda. The climb affords great views.

Over 90m high, La Giralda was the minaret of the mosque that stood on the site before the cathedral, constructed in brick by Almohad caliph Yusuf Yacub al-Mansur between 1184 and 1198. Its proportions, decoration and colour make it perhaps Spain's most perfect Islamic building.

Things you need to know: ☎ 954 21 49 71; adult/under 12yr/concession €7.50/free/1.50, admission Sun free; ☒ 11am-6pm Mon-Sat, 2.30-7pm Sun Sep-Jun, 9.30am-4.30pm Mon-Sat, 2.30-7pm Sun Jul & Aug

ceramics, plaster and wood, obedient to the Quran's prohibition against 'eternal' structures, reserved for the Creator.

At the heart of the palace is the wonderful **Patio de las Doncellas** (Patio of the Maidens), surrounded by beautiful arches and exquisite plasterwork and tiling.

The **Cámara Regia** (King's Quarters) on the northern side of the patio has two rooms with stunning ceilings. Just west is the small **Patio de las Muñecas** (Patio of the Dolls), the heart of the palace's private quarters, with delicate Granada-style decoration; indeed, plasterwork was actually brought here from the Alhambra in the 19th century. The **Cuarto del Príncipe** (Prince's Quarters), to its north, has a excellent wooden cupola ceiling recreating a starlit night sky and was probably the queen's bedroom.

The spectacular **Salón de Embajadores** (Hall of Ambassadors), off the western end of the Patio de las Doncellas, was Pedro I's throne room and incorporates caliphal-style door arches from the earlier Al-Muwarak palace. Its fabulous wooden dome of multiple star patterns was added in 1427. On its western side, the **Arco de Pavones**, with peacock motifs, leads into the **Salón del Techo de Felipe II**.

BARRIO DE SANTA CRUZ

Seville's medieval *judería* (Jewish quarter), east of the cathedral and Alcázar, is today a tangle of quaint, winding streets and lovely plant-decked plazas perfumed with orange blossom. Its most characteristic plaza today is **Plaza de Santa Cruz**, which gives the *barrio* its name.

EL CENTRO

The real centre of Seville is the densely packed zone of narrow streets north of the cathedral.

PLAZA DE SAN FRANCISCO & CALLE SIERPES

Plaza de San Francisco has been Seville's main public square since the 16th century. The southern end of the **ayuntamiento** (town hall) here is encrusted with lovely Renaissance carving from the 1520s and '30s.

Pedestrianised Calle Sierpes, heading north from the plaza, and the parallel Calle Tetuán/Velázquez are the hub of Seville's fanciest shopping zone. Between the two streets is the 18th-century **Capilla de San José** (Calle Jovellanos; 🕙 8am-12.30pm

& 6.30-8.30pm), with breathtakingly intense baroque ornamentation.

PLAZA SALVADOR

This plaza, which has a few popular bars, was once the forum of Roman Hispalis. It's dominated by the **Parroquia del Salvador**, a big baroque church built between 1674 and 1712 on the site of Muslim Ishbiliya's main mosque. The interior reveals a fantastic richness of carving and gilding.

EL ARENAL

A short walk west from Avenida de la Constitución brings you to the bank of Río Guadalquivir, lined by a pleasant footpath. The nearby district of El Arenal is home to some of Seville's most interesting sights.

HOSPITAL DE LA CARIDAD

A marvellous sample of Sevillean golden-age art adorns the church in this **charity hospice** (☎ 954 22 32 32; Calle Temprado 3; admission €5 with audioguide, free Sun & holidays for EU citizens; 🕙 9am-1.30pm & 3.30-7.30pm Mon-Sat, to 1pm Sun & holidays) a block from the river.

SOUTH OF THE CENTRE
PARQUE DE MARÍA LUISA & PLAZA DE ESPAÑA

A large area south of the tobacco factory was transformed for Seville's 1929 international fair, the Exposición Iberoamericana, when architects adorned it with fantastical buildings, many of them harking back to Seville's past glory or imitating the native styles of Spain's former colonies. In its midst is the large **Parque de María Luisa** (🕙 8am-10pm, to midnight Jul & Aug), a living expression of Seville's Moorish and Christian past.

Plaza de España, one of the city's favourite relaxation spots, faces the park

ANDALUCÍA

SEVILLE

SEMANA SANTA IN SEVILLE

Nowhere in Spain is Holy Week marked with quite such intense spectacle, solemnity and joy as in Seville.

Every day from Palm Sunday to Easter Sunday, large, richly bedecked images and life-size tableaux from the Easter story are carried from Seville's churches through the streets to the cathedral, accompanied by processions that may take more than an hour to pass. These rites have been going on in their present form since the 17th century, when many of the images were created.

The processions are organised by over 50 different *hermandades* or *cofradías* (brotherhoods, some of which include women), each normally with two *pasos* (sculptural representations of events from Christ's Passion).

The first *paso* focuses on Christ; the second is an image of the Virgin. They are carried by teams of about 40 bearers called *costaleros*, who work in relays as each supports a weight of about 50kg. The *pasos* move with a hypnotic swaying motion to the rhythm of their accompanying bands and the commands of their bell-striking *capataz* (leader).

From Palm Sunday to Good Friday, about eight brotherhoods leave their churches in the afternoon or early evening, arriving between 5pm and 11pm at Calle Campana, at the northern end of Calle Sierpes. This is the start of the *carrera oficial* (official route), which all then follow along Calle Sierpes, Plaza San Francisco and Avenida de la Constitución to the cathedral. They enter the cathedral at its western end and leave at the east, emerging on Plaza Virgen de los Reyes.

The climax of the week is the *madrugada* (early hours) of Good Friday, when some of the most respected brotherhoods file through the city.

On the Saturday evening, just four brotherhoods make their way to the cathedral, and finally, on Easter Sunday morning, only one, the Hermandad de la Resurrección.

Procession schedules are widely available during Semana Santa, and the website www.semana-santa.org (in Spanish) is devoted to Holy Week in Seville. Arrive near the cathedral in the early evening for a better view.

across Avenida de Isabel la Católica. Around it is the most grandiose of the 1929 buildings, a semicircular brick-and-tile confection featuring Seville tilework at its gaudiest.

SEVILLE FOR CHILDREN

Open spaces such as the banks of the Guadalquivir, Parque de María Luisa (p275) and the Alcázar gardens are great places for young children to let off some steam. They'll enjoy feeding the doves at Plaza de América in Parque de María Luisa. **Isla Mágica** (☎ 902 16 17 16; www.islamagica .es; adult/under 16yr & senior €23.50/19; ⊙ 11am-7pm Tue-Fri, to 10pm Sat & Sun Apr-late Jun, to 11pm Mon-Fri & Sun, to midnight Sat late Jun-early Sep, to 9pm Fri & Sat early Sep-Oct, closed Nov-Mar) is a huge day of fun: those aged over 10 will get the most out of the rides. Another sure hit is a **city tour** (p277) in a horse-drawn carriage.

TOURS

Horse-drawn carriages wait near the cathedral, Plaza de España and Puerta de Jerez, charging €40 for up to four people for a one-hour trot around the Barrio de Santa Cruz and Parque de María Luisa areas.

Discover Sevilla (☎ 954 22 66 42; Calle Joaquín Guichot 6; ☺ 8pm-late Wed & Fri) For €59, your guide will take you on a flamenco walking tour through the labyrinth of Barrio Santa Cruz, often claimed as the birthplace of flamenco.

Sevilla Walking Tours (☎ 902 15 82 26; www.sevillawalkingtours.com) Tours of the main monumental area in English, at 10.30am Monday to Saturday lasting about two hours for €12.

FESTIVALS & EVENTS

In the second half of the month, the **Feria de Abril** (April Fair) is the joyful celebration after the solemnity of Semana Santa. The biggest and most colourful of all Andalucía's *ferias*, it takes place on a special site, El Real de la Feria, in the Los Remedios area southwest of the city centre.

SLEEPING

BARRIO DE SANTA CRUZ

Huéspedes Dulces Sueños (☎ 954 41 93 93; Calle Santa María La Blanca 21; s/d €40/50, without bathroom €20/45; ☒) 'Sweet Dreams' is a friendly little *hostal* (budget hotel) with spotless rooms. Only the doubles have air-conditioning.

Hotel Amadeus (☎ 954 50 14 43; www.hotelamadeussevilla.com; Calle Farnesio 6; s/d €80/90; P ☒ ◻) This musician family converted their 18th-century mansion into a stylish hotel with 14 elegant rooms. Five new rooms have been added, one or two soundproofed for piano or violin practice.

Las Casas de la Judería (☎ 954 41 51 50; www.casasypalacios.com; Callejón Dos Hermanas 7;

s/d from €140/175; P ☒) This charming five-star hotel is in fact a series of luxuriously restored houses and mansions based around several patios and fountains.

EL ARENAL

Hotel Simón (☎ 954 22 66 60; www.hotelsimonsevilla.com; Calle García de Vinuesa 19; s €60-70, d €95-110; ☒) A charming small hotel in a grand old 18th-century house, with spotless and comfortable rooms. Even the light filtering into the antique patio seems dipped in tea.

EL CENTRO

Casa Sol y Luna (☎ 954 21 06 82; www.casasolyluna1.com; Calle Pérez Galdós 1A; d €45, s/d/tr without bathroom €22/38/60) This is a first-rate

Feria de Abril, Seville

BRUCE B...

hostal in a beautifully decorated house dating from 1911, with embroidered white linen that makes you feel as if you're staying at your grandma's.

EATING
Seville is one of Spain's tapas capitals, so plunge straight in and follow the winding tapas trail.

BARRIO DE SANTA CRUZ & AROUND
Café Bar Las Teresas (☎ 954 21 30 69; Calle Santa Teresa 2; tapas €2.20-4) Head barman Pepe has served thousands of punters here since 1962, including Edward Kennedy in 1964. He will be happy to share the experience with you in this convivial corner of old Seville.

Cervecería Giralda (☎ 954 22 82 50; Calle Mateos Gago 1; tapas €3.50-5) Exotic tapas variations are merged with traditional dishes in this one-time Muslim bathhouse.

Restaurante Egaña Oriza (☎ 954 22 72 11; Calle San Fernando 41; mains €22-32; ☽ closed Sat lunch & Sun) Regarded as one of the city's best restaurants, Egaña Oriza cooks up superb Andalucian-Basque cuisine, including lasagne with seafood, lobster and truffles.

EL ARENAL
Mesón Cinco Jotas (☎ 954 21 05 21; Calle Castelar 1; tapas/media raciones €3.80/9.45) Try some of the best j*amón* in town here and move on to the *solomillo ibérico* (Iberian pork sirloin) in sweet Pedro Ximénez wine for the peak of porcine flavour.

EL CENTRO
Plaza de la Alfalfa is the hub of the tapas scene, with a flush of first-rate bars serving tapas from around €1.80 to €3. On Calle Alfalfa just off the plaza, hop from sea-themed La Trastienda to the intimate Bar Alfalfa and on to La Bodega where you can mix head-spinning quantities of ham and sherry.

DRINKING
Bars usually open 6pm to 2am weekdays and 8pm to 3am at the weekend. In summer, dozens of open-air late-night bars *(terrazas de verano)* spring up along both banks of the river.

Antigüedades (Calle Argote de Molina 40) Blending mellow beats with offbeat decor, this place boasts tiled window seats with a view of the busy street – they're the best place to nurse your drink.

ourpick **Casa Morales** (☎ 954 22 12 42; Garcia de Vinuesa 11) Founded in 1850, not much has changed in this defiantly old-world bar, with charming anachronisms wherever you look. Towering clay *tinajas* (wine storage jars) carry the chalked-up tapas choices of the day.

Plaza del Salvador is brimful of drinkers from mid-evening to 1am. Grab a drink from **La Antigua Bodeguita** (☎ 954 56 18 33) or **La Sapotales** next door and sit on the steps of the Parroquia del Salvador.

El Garlochi (Calle Boteros 4) Named after the *gitano* word for 'heart', this deeply camp bar hits you with clouds of incense, Jesus and Virgin images displayed on scarlet walls, and potent cocktails with names like Sangre de Cristo (Blood of Christ).

In terms of hipness and trendy places to go out, the slightly shabby Alameda is where it's at, and it's also the heartbeat of gay Seville.

ENTERTAINMENT
Seville comes to life at night with live music, experimental theatre and steamy flamenco. See www.discoversevilla.com or www.exploreseville.com for the latest action.

ANDALUCÍA

SEVILLE

KARL BLACKWELL

Guitarists of Los Gallos flamenco show, Seville

CLUBS

Weekend (☎ 954 37 88 73; Calle del Torneo 43; admission €7; ⏲ 11pm-8am Thu-Sat) This is one of Seville's top live-music and DJ spots.

Aduana (☎ 954 23 85 82; www.aduana .net; Avenida de la Raza s/n; admission varies; ⏲ midnight-late Thu-Sat) Aduana is where Seville's best-dressed party-goers show off their moves.

FLAMENCO

La Carbonería (☎ 954 21 44 60; Calle Levíes 18; admission free; ⏲ about 8pm-4am) A converted coal yard in the Barrio de Santa Cruz with two large bars, thronged nearly every night, which offer live flamenco from about 8pm to 4am.

Casa de la Memoria de Al-Andalus (☎ 954 56 06 70; Calle Ximénez de Enciso 28; adult/child €14/8; ⏲ 9pm & 10.30pm) Authentic nightly shows with a focus on medieval and Sephardic Al-Andalus styles, in a room of shifting shadows. Space is limited, so reserve tickets in advance.

Hotels and tourist offices tend to steer you towards *tablaos* (expensive, tourist-oriented flamenco venues), which can lack atmosphere, though **Los Gallos** (☎ 954 21 69 81; www.tablaolosgallos.com; Plaza de Santa Cruz 11; admission incl 1 drink €30; ⏲ 2hr shows 8-10pm & 10.30pm-12.30am) is a cut above the average.

GETTING THERE & AWAY

Seville's **Aeropuerto San Pablo** (☎ 902 40 47 04; ⏲ 24hr) has a fair range of international and domestic flights.

The **Estación de Santa Justa** (☎ 902 24 02 02; Avenida Kansas City) is 1.5km northeast of the city centre.

GETTING AROUND

The airport is 7km east of the city centre on the A4 Córdoba road. **Amarillos Tour** (☎ 902 21 03 17) runs buses between the airport and the Puerta de Jerez (€2.20 to €2.50, 30 to 40 minutes, at least 15 daily). A taxi costs about €18.

Parking Paseo de Colón (cnr Paseo de Cristóbal Colón & Calle Adriano; per hr up to 10hr €1.20, 10-24hr €13.50) is a relatively inexpensive underground car park.

SeVici (☎ 902 01 10 32; www.sevici.es; ⏰ 7am-9pm) is a bright, green idea from Seville's urban authority: a cycle hire network comprising almost 200 fully automated pick-up/drop-off points dotted all over the city (clearly shown on a nifty folding pocket map).

AROUND SEVILLE

The small town of **Santiponce**, 8km northwest of Seville, is the location of **Itálica** (☎ 955 99 73 76; adult/EU citizen €1.50/free; ⏰ 8.30am-8.30pm Tue-Sat, 9am-3pm Sun Apr-Sep, 9am-5.30pm Tue-Sat, 10am-4pm Sun Oct-Mar). Situated on the northern edge of town and founded in 206 BC, Itálica was the first Roman town in Spain and also the home town of the 2nd-century-AD Roman emperors Trajan and Hadrian. The partly reconstructed ruins include one of the biggest of all the Roman amphitheatres, broad paved streets, ruins of several houses with beautiful mosaics and a theatre.

Buses run to Santiponce (€1.20, 40 minutes) from Seville's Plaza de Armas bus station, at least twice an hour from 6.35am to 11pm Monday to Friday, and a little less often at weekends.

CÁDIZ PROVINCE

CÁDIZ

pop 128,600

Once past the coastal marshes and industrial sprawl around Cádiz, you emerge into an elegant, historic port city of largely 18th- and 19th-century construction. The old part of Cádiz is crammed onto the head of a promontory like some huge, crowded, ocean-going ship, and the tang of salty air and ocean vistas are never far away. Cádiz has a long and fascinating history, absorbing monuments and museums, and plenty of enjoyable places to eat and drink.

INFORMATION

Municipal tourist office (☎ 956 24 10 01; Paseo de Canalejas s/n; ⏰ 8.30am-6pm Mon-Fri, 9am-5pm Sat & Sun)

Regional tourist office (☎ 956 20 31 91; Avenida Ramón de Carranza s/n; ⏰ 9am-7.30pm Mon-Fri, 10am-2pm Sat, Sun & holidays)

SIGHTS & ACTIVITIES

Broad Plaza San Juan de Dios is lined with cafes and is dominated by the imposing neoclassical **ayuntamiento** built around 1800. At the nearby **Roman Theatre** (☎ 956 25 17 88; Campo del Sur; admission free; ⏰ 10am-2.30pm Wed-Mon) you can walk along a gallery beneath the tiers of seating.

Cádiz's yellow-domed **cathedral** (☎ 956 28 61 54; Plaza de la Catedral; adult/student €5/3, free during services; ⏰ 10am-6.30pm Mon-Fri, 10am-4.30pm Sat, 1-6.30pm Sun, services 7-8pm Tue-Fri, 11am-1pm Sun) is an impressively proportioned baroque-cum-neoclassical construction but by Spanish standards very sober in its decoration. From a separate entrance on Plaza de la Catedral, climb to the top of the **Torre de Poniente** (Western Tower; ☎ 956 25 17 88; adult/child/senior €4/3/3; ⏰ 10am-6pm, to 8pm 15 Jun-15 Sep) for marvellous vistas.

A short walk northwest from the cathedral, Plaza de Topete is one of Cádiz's liveliest squares, bright with flower stalls and adjoining the large, lively **Mercado Central** (Central Market). Nearby, the **Torre Tavira** (☎ 956 21 29 10; Calle Marqués del Real Tesoro 10; adult/student €4/3.30; ⏰ 10am-6pm, to 8pm 15 Jun-15 Sep) is the highest of Cádiz's old watchtowers (in the 18th century the city had no less than 160 of these, built so that citizens could observe the comings and goings of ships without leaving home). It provides great panoramas and has a **camera obscura** projecting live images of the city onto a screen.

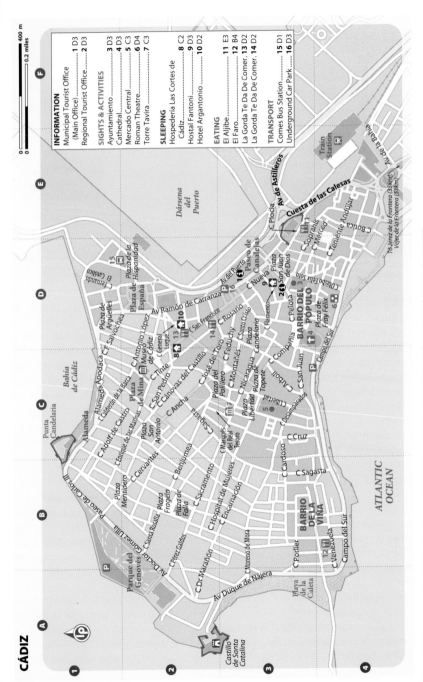

ANDALUCÍA

CÁDIZ PROVINCE

Cádiz Cathedral (p280)
PAUL BERNHARDT

FESTIVALS & EVENTS

No other Spanish city celebrates **Carnaval** with the enthusiasm and originality of Cádiz, where it turns into a 10-day party spanning two weekends. Groups called *murgas,* in fantastic costumes, tour the city on foot or on floats, singing witty satirical ditties, dancing or performing sketches.

Some of the liveliest scenes are in the working-class Barrio de la Viña and on Calle Ancha and Calle Columela, where *ilegales* tend to congregate.

SLEEPING

Hostal Fantoni (☎ 956 28 27 04; www.hostal fantoni.net; Calle Flamenco 5; s/d €45/70; ⌘) The Fantoni offers a dozen attractive and spotless rooms, all with air-con, in an attractively modernised 18th-century house. The panoramic roof terrace catches a breeze in summer.

Hotel Argantonio (☎ 956 21 16 40; www .hotelargantonio.com in Spanish; Calle Argantonio 3; s/d incl breakfast €74/101; ⌘ ⌨) A very attractive small new hotel in the old city

with an appealing Mudéjar accent to its decor.

Hospedería Las Cortes de Cádiz (☎ 956 21 26 68; www.hotellascortes.com; Calle San Francisco 9; s/d incl breakfast €109/148; P ⌘ ⌨) This excellent hotel occupies a remodelled 1850s mansion. The 36 rooms, each themed around a figure, place or event associated with the Cortes de Cádiz, sport classical furnishings and modern comforts.

EATING

El Aljibe (☎ 956 26 66 56; www.pablogrosso .com; Calle Plocia 25; tapas €2-3.50, mains €10-15) *Gaditano* (Cádiz native) chef Pablo Grosso concocts delicious combinations of the traditional and the adventurous. You can enjoy his creations as tapas in the stone-walled downstairs bar.

El Faro (☎ 956 22 99 16; Calle San Félix 15; mains €15-25) Over in Barrio de la Viña, El Faro has a famous and excellent seafood restaurant, decorated with pretty ceramics, and an adjoining, less-pricey, tapas bar.

Also recommended, **La Gorda Te Da De Comer** (tapas €2-2.40, media raciones €6; Luque Calle General Luque 1; 🕑 9-11.30pm Mon, 1.30-4pm & 9-11.30pm Tue-Sat; Rosario cnr Calles Rosario & Marqués de Valdeiñigo; 🕑 1-4pm & 9-11.30pm Tue-Sat) has incredibly tasty food at low prices amid trendy pop design at both its locations.

DRINKING

In the old city, the Plaza de Mina-Plaza San Francisco-Plaza de España area is the main hub of the nocturnal bar scene; things start to get going around midnight at most places, but can be quiet in the first half of the week.

GETTING THERE & AROUND

Most buses are run by **Comes** (☎ 956 80 70 59; Plaza de la Hispanidad).

There's a handily placed **underground car park** (Paseo de Canalejas; per 24hr €9) near the port area.

From the **train station** (☎ 902 24 02 02) up to 36 trains run daily to El Puerto de Santa María (€2.35 to €2.90, 40 minutes) and Jerez de la Frontera (€2.90 to €3.65, 50 minutes), up to 15 to Seville (€9.80, two hours), three to Córdoba (€34 to €43, three hours) and two to Madrid (€63, five hours).

JEREZ DE LA FRONTERA

pop 202,700

Jerez (heh-*reth*), 36km northeast of Cádiz, is a beguiling town with a uniquely eclectic and intense character. Visitors come to see its famous sherry bodegas, but Jerez is also Andalucía's horse capital and has a creative artistic and nightlife scene and a large *gitano* community that is one of the hotbeds of flamenco. It stages fantastic, showy, hedonistic fiestas with sleek horses, beautiful people, fine food and drink, and passionate music.

INFORMATION

Municipal tourist office (☎ 956 33 88 74; www.turismojerez.com; Alameda Cristina; 🕑 9am-3pm & 5-6.30pm Mon-Fri, 9.30am-2.30pm Sat & Sun)

SIGHTS
OLD QUARTER

The obvious place to start a tour of old Jerez is the 11th- or 12th-century Almohad fortress, the **Alcázar** (☎ 956 35 01 33; Alameda Vieja; admission €5.40; 🕑 10am-6pm Mon-Sat, 10am-3pm Sun 16 Sep-30 Apr, 10am-8pm Mon-Sat, 10am-3pm Sun 1 May-15 Sep).

The orange tree–lined promenade around the Alcázar overlooks the mainly 18th-century **cathedral** (🕑 11.30am-1pm & 6.30-8pm Mon-Sat, Mass 11.30am, 1.30pm, 7.30pm & 9pm Sun), built on the site of Scheris' main mosque.

A couple of blocks northeast of the cathedral is Plaza de la Asunción, with the handsome 16th-century **Antiguo Cabildo** (Old Town Hall) and lovely 15th-century Mudéjar **Iglesia de San Dionisio**.

Northwest of here is the **Barrio de Santiago**, with a sizeable *gitano* population. Also in this area is the **Centro Andaluz de Flamenco** (Andalucian Flamenco Centre; ☎ 956 34 92 65; http://caf.cica.es in Spanish; Plaza San Juan 1; admission free; 🕑 9am-2pm Mon-Fri). This centre is a kind of flamenco museum, library and school, with a different flamenco video screened each day.

Try not to miss what is arguably Jerez's loveliest church, the 15th/16th-century Gothic **Iglesia de San Miguel** (Plaza San Miguel; 🕑 Mass 8pm Mon-Sat, 9am, noon & 8pm Sun), just southeast of Plaza del Arenal.

SHERRY BODEGAS

Bodegas González Byass (☎ 902 44 00 77; www.bodegastiopepe.com; Calle Manuel María González 12; tour €10; 🕑 11am-6pm) is home of the Tio Pepe brand and one of the biggest sherry houses, handily located just west of the Alcázar.

Another interesting bodega is **Bodegas Tradición** (☎ 956 16 86 28; www.bodegastradicion.com; Plaza Cordobeses 3; ☻ 9am-2pm & 4.30-6.30pm Mon-Fri) – not only for its extra-aged sherries (20 or more years old) but also because it houses the Colección Joaquín Rivera, a private Spanish art collection that includes important works by Goya, Velázquez and Zurbarán.

REAL ESCUELA ANDALUZA DEL ARTE ECUESTRE

The famed **Royal Andalucian School of Equestrian Art** (☎ 956 31 80 08; www.realescuela.org; Avenida Duque de Abrantes; ☻) trains horses and riders in equestrian skills, and you can watch them going through their paces in **training sessions** (admission adult/child €10/6; ☻ 11am-1pm Mon, Wed & Fri Sep-Jul, Mon & Wed Aug). There's an official **exhibición** (show; admission adult/child €24/15; ☻ noon Tue & Thu Sep-Jul, noon Tue, Thu & Fri Aug), where the handsome white horses show off their tricks to classical music.

FESTIVALS & EVENTS

Festival de Jerez (www.festivaldejerez.es in Spanish) Late February/early March – Jerez's biggest celebration of flamenco.

Feria del Caballo Late April or first half of May – Jerez's week-long Horse Fair is one of Andalucía's biggest festivals, with music, dance and bullfights as well as all kinds of equestrian competitions and parades.

SLEEPING

Hostal Las Palomas (☎ 956 34 37 73; www.hostal-las-palomas.com; Calle Higueras 17; s with/without bathroom €25/20 d with/without bathroom €35/30) A faint Moroccan theme, touches of art, earthy colours and a good roof terrace are among the pluses of this recently revamped hostal.

Hotel Chancillería (☎ 956 30 10 38; www.hotelchancilleria.com; Calle Chancillería 21; s/d incl breakfast €65/90; ☒ ▣) This 14-room hotel in the atmospheric Barrio de Santiago is a great addition to Jerez's accommodation. The hotel's restaurant, **Sabores** (☎ 956 32 98 35), has a prize-winning young chef; mains cost €14 to €18 and include a good vegie selection.

EATING

Mesón El Patio (☎ 956 34 07 36; Calle San Francisco de Paula 7; mains €8-17; ☻ closed Sun evening & Mon) Convivial yet a touch refined, El Patio serves terrific fish and meat dishes.

Central Jerez is littered with great tapas bars. The pedestrian streets just north of

MARK DYBALL
Feria del Caballo, Jerez de la Frontera

ANDALUCÍA

Plaza del Arenal are a fine place to start. Head for the cavelike **El Almacén** (☎ 956 18 71 43; Calle Latorre 8; tapas €3; ☽ 1-4pm Thu & Fri, 8.30pm-1.30am daily; Ⓥ) or **Reino de León** (☎ 956 32 29 15; Calle Latorre 8; tapas €3) next door. Close by, **Cruz Blanca** (☎ 956 32 45 35; Plaza de la Yerva; tapas €3) whips up good fish, egg, meat and salad offerings and has tables on a quiet little plaza.

About 500m north, further brilliant tapas bars surround little Plaza Rafael Rivero.

ENTERTAINMENT
The tourist office is very helpful with what's-on information; also visit www.turismojerez.com and look out for posters. Several *peñas flamencas* (flamenco clubs) welcome genuinely interested visitors.

El Lagá Tio Parrilla (☎ 956 33 83 34; Plaza del Mercado; show & 2 drinks €18; ☽ 10.30pm Mon-Sat) The best of the places staging regular flamenco shows. The emphasis is on the more upbeat styles such as *bulería*, but this is still the genuine article with gutsy performers.

GETTING THERE & AROUND
Jerez airport (☎ 956 15 00 00), 7km northeast of town on the NIV, is increasingly busy with flights from European cities and has at least six car rental offices.

Jerez train station (☎ 956 34 23 19; Plaza de la Estación) is beside the bus station, with up to 36 daily trains to El Puerto de Santa María (€1.40, 15 minutes) and Cádiz (€2.90 to €3.65, 50 minutes), and 10 or more to Seville (€6.50 to €16.80, 1¼ hours).

ARCOS DE LA FRONTERA
pop 29,900 / elev 185m

Bathed in burning white light, the walled, hilltop town of Arcos, 30km east of Jerez, could not be more thrillingly sited: it perches on a high, unassailable ridge

WITOLD SKRYPCZAK

Sherry cellars, Sanlúcar de Barrameda

↘ **IF YOU LIKE...**
If you like the bodegas in **Jerez de la Frontera** (p283), we think you'll also like these towns famous for their wine and sherry culture:

- **El Puerto de Santa María** Seven sherry bodegas offer tours, including Osborne and Terry; El Puerto is across the bay from Cádiz.
- **Sanlúcar de Barrameda** Visitable bodegas devoted to a distinctive sherry-like wine, manzanilla, as well as fine seafood in its restaurants; northwest of El Puerto.

with sheer precipices plummeting away on both sides.

Arcos' charm today lies in exploring the mazelike upper town with its whitewashed houses and spectacular setting.

ORIENTATION & INFORMATION
The **tourist office** (☎ 956 70 22 64; Plaza del Cabildo; ☽ 10am-2.30pm & 5.30-8pm Mon-Fri, 10.30am-1.30pm & 5-7pm Sat, 10.30am-1.30pm Sun) is on the old town's main square.

SIGHTS
The old town is a delight to get lost in with every turn revealing something new. The centre of this quarter is the Plaza del

CÁDIZ PROVINCE

Grazalema

BRUCE ESBIN

↘ IF YOU LIKE...

If you like **Arcos de le Frontera** (p285) and are eager for more hill villages all dressed in white nearby, we think you'll also like:

- **Vejer de la Frontera** Enchanted hill village with a castle, labyrinthine streets and an artsy vibe just inland from the Costa de la Luz.
- **Grazalema** Whitewashed, red-roofed village hunched under an enormous shaft of rock in the heart of the Sierra de Grazalema.
- **Zahara de la Sierra** Topped by a crag with a ruined castle and near-perfect when viewed from across the lake; just north of the Sierra de Grazalema.

Cabildo. The square itself has been somewhat spoilt by being turned into a car park, but the surrounding fine old buildings and a vertiginous **mirador** (lookout) with views over Río Guadalete make up for a lot. The 11th-century **Castillo de los Duques** is firmly closed to the public. On the plaza's northern side is the Gothic-cum-baroque **Basíllica-Parroquia de Santa María**, which was closed for renovations at the time of research. On the eastern side, the **Parador Casa del Corregidor** hotel is a reconstruction of a 16th-century magistrate's house.

SLEEPING & EATING

our pick **Hotel Real de Veas** (☎ 956 71 73 70; www.hotelrealdeveas.com; Calle Corredera 12; s/d €48/55; 🅿 🖳) A superb option inside a lovingly restored building. The dozen or so rooms are arranged around a glass-covered patio and are cool and comfortable.

Hotel El Convento (☎ 956 70 23 33; www .hotelconvento.es; Calle Maldonado 2; s/d with breakfast from €55/70; 🅿 🖳) The nuns who used to live in this beautiful, former 17th-century convent obviously appreciated a good view. Now it's been turned into a slightly chintzy hotel.

Mesón Don Fernando (☎ 956 71 73 26; Calle Boticas 5; mains €9-11, ⏱ closed Mon) Up in the old-town maze, Mesón Don Fernando has a lively Spanish atmosphere. You can enjoy treats like rabbit stew and deer steaks while sitting on an outside table relishing the evening breeze.

GETTING THERE & AWAY

Services from the **bus station** (☎ 956 70 49 77; Calle Corregidores) run to Jerez (€2.55, 45 minutes, 12-15 daily), Cádiz (€5.59, 1¼ hours, five daily), El Bosque (€2.55, one hour, seven daily), Ronda (€8.14, two hours, three daily) and Seville (€7.45, two hours, two daily).

SOUTHERN COSTA DE LA LUZ

The 90km coast between Cádiz and Tarifa is Andalucía's finest, and miraculously mass tourism development has no more than a toehold here. The coast can be windy, and its Atlantic waters are cooler than the Mediterranean, but these are small prices to pay for a wild stretch of coastline where you can enjoy a host of water- and land-based activities. Andalucian holidaymakers swarm in with a fiesta atmosphere in July and August.

TARIFA

pop 17,200

Set at mainland Spain's southernmost tip, Tarifa has grown in two decades from a down-at-heel coastal town into Europe's hip kitesurfing and windsurfing capital.

Add the setting of a quaint, white-washed old town, stunning white-sand beaches, views of Morocco, and rolling green countryside, and you'll understand why for a growing number of people Tarifa has a magic unique in Spain. To boot, it's one of the best places in Europe for watching not just birds but also dolphins and whales.

INFORMATION

Tourist office (☎ 956 68 09 93; www.ayto tarifa.com in Spanish; Paseo de la Alameda; ⏰ 10am-2pm daily, 4-6pm Mon-Fri Oct-May, 6-8pm Mon-Fri Jun-Sep)

SIGHTS

A wander round the old town's narrow streets, of mainly Islamic origin, is a must. The Mudéjar **Puerta de Jerez** was built after the Reconquista. Look in at the bustling **market** (Calle Colón) before wending your way to the mainly 15th-century **Iglesia de San Mateo** (Calle Sancho IV El Bravo; ⏰ 9am-1pm & 5.30-8.30pm). South of the church, the **Mirador El Estrecho**, atop part of the castle walls, has spectacular views across to Africa, only 14km away.

The **Castillo de Guzmán** (Calle Guzmán El Bueno) is named after the Reconquista hero Guzmán El Bueno. The imposing fortress was closed for refurbishment at research time.

ACTIVITIES
BEACHES

On the isthmus leading out to Isla de las Palomas, **Playa Chica** is sheltered but very small indeed. From here the spectacular **Playa de los Lances** stretches northwest to the huge sand dune at **Ensenada de Valdevaqueros**.

KITESURFING & WINDSURFING

Most of the action occurs along the coast between Tarifa and Punta Paloma, 11km

ANDALUCÍA

CÁDIZ PROVINCE

Costa de la Luz

ROBIN CHAPMAN

ANDALUCÍA

CÁDIZ PROVINCE

WITOLD SKRYPCZAK

Zahara de los Atunes

↘ IF YOU LIKE...

If you like the beaches around Tarifa (p287), you'll also appreciate the long stretches of white sand northwest along the Costa de La Luz:

- **Zahara de los Atunes** Twelve kilometres of uninterrupted sand and very little development next to the beach.
- **Bolonia** A beautiful bay, a long beach, views of Africa, and Baelo Claudia, the most complete Roman town yet uncovered in Spain.
- **Los Caños de Meca** Bohemian village with fine beaches around the Cabo de Trafalgar, which marks the site of the famous eponymous battle in 1805.
- **El Palmar** Almost 5km of sand with few buildings; beloved by surfers from October to May and less-active beach-lovers the rest of the year.

northwest. Both wind- and kitesurfing are practised year round, but the biggest season is from about April to October.

Tarifa now has around 30 kitesurf and windsurf schools, many of them with offices or shops along Calle Batalla del Salado or on Calle Mar Adriático. Others are based along the coast. Some experienced, recommended schools:

Club Mistral (www.club-mistral.com) Hurricane (☎ 956 68 90 98; Hurricane Hotel, N340 Km78); Valdevaqueros (☎ 619 340913; Cortijo Valdevaqueros, Ensenada de Valdevaqueros, N340 Km75) Windsurf and kitesurf.

Hot Stick Town (☎ 956 68 04 19; www.hot sticktarifa.com; Calle Batalla del Salado 41) Offers six-hour kitesurf courses with lower rates; windsurf classes too.

HORSE RIDING

On Playa de los Lances, **Aventura Ecuestre** (☎ 956 23 66 32; www.aventura ecuestre.com; Hotel Dos Mares, N340 Km79.5) and **Hurricane Hípica** (☎ 646 964279; Hurricane Hotel, N340 Km78) both offer well-kept horses with excellent guides.

WHALE-WATCHING

The Strait of Gibraltar is a top site for viewing whales and dolphins. Killer whales visit in July and August, huge sperm and fin whales lurk here from spring to autumn, and pilot whales and three types of dolphin stay all year. Most trips cost €27/18 for passengers over/under 14 years; special 3½-hour killer-whale trips in July and August are around €40/30.

firmm (☎ 956 62 70 08; www.firmm.org; Calle Pedro Cortés 4; ☉ Mar-Oct) uses every trip to record data.

SLEEPING

Hostal Africa (☎ 956 68 02 20; hostal_africa@ hotmail.com; Calle María Antonia Toledo 12; s with/without bathroom €50/35, d with/without bathroom €65/50; ☉ closed 24 Dec-31 Jan) The well-travelled owners of this revamped house know just what travellers need. Rooms are attractive and there's an expansive terrace with wonderful views. Short-term storage for boards, bicycles and baggage is available.

La Estrella de Tarifa (☎ 956 68 19 85; www.laestrelladetarifa.com in Spanish; Calle San Rosendo 2; r €75-110, ste €120-145, incl breakfast) Full of intriguing nooks and crannies, this comfortable small hotel in an old town-house rambles up and down over four floors with Moroccan decor in soothing blue and white.

Posada La Sacristía (☎ 956 68 17 59; www.lasacristia.net; Calle San Donato 8; r incl breakfast €115-135) Tarifa's most elegant accommodation is in a beautifully renovated 17th-century townhouse. The 10 white rooms have some lovely details. There's a new in-house massage and therapy centre too.

EATING

Chilimoso (☎ 956 68 50 92; Calle Peso 6; dishes €4-6; Ⓥ) This tiny place serves tasty vegan and vegetarian food with oriental leanings. Try the falafel with hummus, tzatziki and salad.

Bodega La Casa Amarilla (☎ 956 68 19 93; Calle Sancho IV El Bravo 9; mains €14-18) With an attractive, flowery patio, this is a top place in town for local grilled meats and fish, good *revueltos* (scrambled egg dishes) and tapas.

GETTING THERE & AROUND

Comes (☎ 902 19 92 08, 956 68 40 38; Calle Batalla del Salado 13) runs six or more daily buses to Cádiz (€7.91, 1¾ hours), Algeciras (€1.90, 30 minutes) and La Línea de la Concepción (€3.59, 45 minutes), four to Seville (€15.30, three hours), two each to Jerez de la Frontera (€8.34, 2½ hours) and Málaga (€12.45, two hours), and one to Zahara de los Atunes (€3.24, 40 minutes).

In July and August local buses run about every 1½ hours northwest along the coast as far as Camping Jardín de las Dunas on Ensenada de Valdevaqueros.

MÁLAGA PROVINCE
MÁLAGA
pop 720,000

This exuberant and very Spanish port city, set against the sparkling Mediterranean, is both historic and pulsing with modern life; more than any other major Andalucian city, Málaga seems to be focusing on the future, though with plenty to boast about from the past. The centre presents the visitor with narrow old streets and wide, leafy boulevards, beautiful gardens and impressive monuments, fashionable shops and a burgeoning cultural life. The historic centre is being restored and much of it pedestrianised, and the port is being developed as a leisure zone. The city's terrific bars and nightlife, the last word in Málaga *joie de vivre,* stay open very late.

INFORMATION

Municipal tourist office (www.malaga turismo.com in Spanish; Ⓧ 9am-7pm Mon-Fri, 10am-7pm Sat & Sun Apr-Oct, to 6pm Mon-Fri, 10am-6pm Sat & Sun, Nov-Mar; Casita del Jardinero ☎ 952 13 47 31; Avenida de Cervantes 1; Plaza de la Marina ☎ 952 12 20 20)
Regional tourist office (☎ 951 30 89 11; Pasaje de Chinitas 4; www.andalucia.org; Ⓧ 9am-7.30pm Mon-Fri, 10am-7pm Sat, to 2pm Sun)

SIGHTS
MUSEO PICASSO MÁLAGA

The **Museo Picasso Málaga** (☎ 902 44 33 77; www.museopicassomalaga.org; Palacio de Buenavista, Calle San Agustín 8; permanent collection €6, temporary exhibition €4.50, combined ticket €8, seniors & under-26yr students half price; Ⓧ 10am-8pm Tue-Thu & Sun, to 9pm Fri & Sat) has 204 Picasso works, donated and lent by his daughter-in-law Christine Ruiz-Picasso and grandson

MÁLAGA

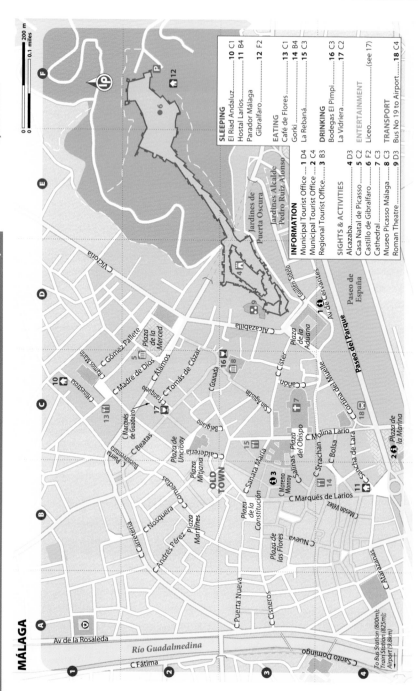

Av de la Rosaleda

Río Guadalmedina

C Fátima

To Bus Station (800m);
Train Station (825m);
Airport (9.8km)

Av de Cervantes

Paseo del Parque

Paseo de
España

C Molina Lario

C Strachan

C Bolsa

C Sancha de Lara

C Marqués de Larios

C Mesón Vélez

C Nueva

C Puerta Nueva

C Cisneros

C Santo Domingo

C Atarazanas

OLD
TOWN

Plaza
de la
Constitución

Plaza
de las Flores

Plaza
Marfines

Plaza
Mitjana

Plaza de
Uncibay

C Comedias

C Nosquera

C Carretería

C Andrés Pérez

C Beatas

C Marqués
de Guadiaro

C Madre de Dios

C Gómez Pallete

Ramos María

C Tinteros

C Alamos

C Tomás de Cózar

C Granada

C Císter

C Cañón

C San Agustín

C Calderería

C Santa María

C Salinas

C Moreno Monroy

Plaza
del Obispo

Plaza
de la
Aduana

C Alcazabilla

Camino Gibralfaro

C Victoria

Jardines de
Puerta Oscura

Jardines Alcalde
Pedro Ruiz Alonso

Plaza
de la
Merced

Continuación Muralla

Plaza de
la Marina

INFORMATION
Municipal Tourist Office....... 1 D4
Municipal Tourist Office....... 2 C4
Regional Tourist Office......... 3 B3

SIGHTS & ACTIVITIES
Alcazaba............................... 4 D3
Casa Natal de Picasso.......... 5 C2
Castillo de Gibralfaro........... 6 F2
Cathedral............................. 7 C3
Museo Picasso Málaga......... 8 C3
Roman Theatre..................... 9 D3

SLEEPING
El Riad Andaluz.................. 10 C1
Hostal Larios...................... 11 B4
Parador Málaga
Gibralfaro.......................... 12 F2

EATING
Café de Flores.................... 13 C1
Gorki................................. 14 B4
La Rebaná.......................... 15 C3

DRINKING
Bodegas El Pimpi................ 16 C3
La Vidriera......................... 17 C2

ENTERTAINMENT
Liceo.............................. (see 17)

TRANSPORT
Bus No 19 to Airport........... 18 C4

0   200 m
0   0.1 miles

ANDALUCÍA

MÁLAGA PROVINCE

Museo Picasso Málaga (p289)

KARL BLACKWELL

Bernard Ruiz-Picasso, and also stages high-quality temporary exhibitions on Picasso themes. The Picasso paintings, drawings, engravings, sculptures and ceramics on show (many never previously on public display) span almost every phase and influence of the artist's colourful career – blue period, cubism, surrealism and more, with a fascinating emphasis on early, formative works. The museum is housed in the 16th-century Palacio de Buenavista, sensationally restored at a cost of €66 million. Picasso was born in Málaga in 1881 but moved to northern Spain with his family when he was nine.

CATHEDRAL

Málaga's cathedral (☎ 952 21 59 17; www.3planalfa.es/catedralmalaga; Calle Molina Lario, entrance Calle Císter; admission €3.50; 🕑 10am-5.30pm Mon-Fri, to 5pm Sat, closed Sun & holidays) was begun in the 16th century on the former site of the main mosque. The chapels vie with each other in splendour.

ALCAZABA

At the lower, western end of the Gibralfaro hill, the wheelchair-accessible Alcazaba (☎ 952 22 51 06; Calle Alcazabilla; admission €2, incl Castillo de Gibralfaro €3.20; 🕑 9.30am-8pm Tue-Sun Apr-Oct, 8.30am-7pm Tue-Sun Nov-Mar, closed Mon & major holidays) was the palace-fortress of Málaga's Muslim governors, dating from 1057. Roman artefacts and fleeting views of the harbour and city enliven the walk, while honeysuckle, roses and jasmine perfume the air. Go before noon during the hot months. Below the Alcazaba is a Roman theatre.

CASTILLO DE GIBRALFARO

Above the Alcazaba rises the older Castillo de Gibralfaro (☎ 952 22 72 30; admission €2; 🕑 9am-9pm Apr-Sep, to 6pm Oct-Mar), built by Abd ar-Rahman I, the 8th-century Cordoban emir, and rebuilt in the 14th and 15th centuries. Nothing much remains of the interior of the castle, but the walkway around the ramparts affords exhilarating views and there's a tiny museum with a military focus.

KEN WELSH/ALAMY

View from Parador Málaga Gibralfaro, Málaga

OTHER MUSEUMS

Casa Natal de Picasso (☎ 952 06 02 15; Plaza de la Merced 15; admission free; ☽ 9.30am-7.45pm, closed major holidays), Picasso's birthplace, is a centre for exhibitions and academic research on contemporary art, with a few compelling items of personal memorabilia and a well-stocked shop.

FESTIVALS & EVENTS

Lasting nine days, the **Feria de Málaga** (mid- to late August) is the biggest and most ebullient of Andalucía's summer fairs. During daytime, especially on the two Saturdays, celebrations take over the city centre, with music, dancing and horses. At night the fun switches to large *feria* grounds at Cortijo de Torres, 4km southwest of the city centre, with fairground rides, music and dancing.

SLEEPING

Hostal Larios (☎ 952 22 54 90; www.hostal larios.com; Calle Marqués de Larios 9; s/d/tr €48/58/78, s/d without bathroom €39/49; P 🅿️ 🖥️). This central *hostal* outclasses all others in the budget range. The 12 rooms are painted in shades of apricot and blue.

El Riad Andaluz (☎ 952 21 36 40; www .elriadandaluz.com; Calle Hinestrosa 24; s/d €70/90; 🅿️ 🖥️) Colourful and exotic, this gorgeous restored monastery offers eight rooms with Moroccan decor set around an atmospheric patio, with tea and coffee on tap all day. Situated in the rapidly gentrifying Centro Historico, it's an easy stroll to all the funkiest bars and restaurants in surrounding plazas. The French owner infuses the Riad with a special magic.

Parador Málaga Gibralfaro (☎ 952 22 19 02; www.parador.es; Castillo de Gibralfaro, s/n; s/n €134/170; P 🅿️ 📱) With an unbeatable location up on the pine-forested Gibralfaro hill, Málaga's modern but rustic *parador* provides spectacular views of city and harbour from its upper floors, an excellent terrace restaurant and a rooftop pool.

EATING

La Rebaná (Calle Molina Lario 5; tapas €4.20-8.50, raciones €7-11.50) A great, noisy tapas bar near the Picasso Museum and the cathedral. Dark wood, tall windows and exposed brick walls create a modern, minimal but laid-back space. Try the foie gras with salted nougat for a unique tapa.

Gorki (☎ 952 22 14 66; Calle Strachan 6; platos combinados €7.50-16) A popular upmarket tapas bar with pavement tables and a modern interior full of wine-barrel tables and stools.

Café de Flores (☎ 952 60 85 24; Calle Madre de Dios 29; menú €9.50, mains €14-23; ☺ 1.30pm-late, closed Mon) Formerly La Casa del Ángel, the once eccentric interior has been replaced with sleek plexiglass furniture, abstract art and a highly rated DJ to become a haunt of smart young *malagueños* in up-and-coming Plaza Madre de Dios, right opposite the blue-and-gold Teatro Cervantes. By day it's a coffee bar and lunch place; by night good food is complemented by great sounds.

DRINKING
On weekend nights, the web of narrow old streets north of Plaza de la Constitución comes alive. Look for bars around Plaza de la Merced, Plaza Mitjana and Plaza de Uncibay.

Bodegas El Pimpi (☎ 952 22 89 90; Calle Granada 62; ☺ 7pm-2am) A Málaga institution with a warren of charming rooms and mini-patios, El Pimpi attracts a fun-loving crowd of all nationalities and generations with its sweet wine and traditional music.

La Vidriera (☎ 952 228 943; Marqués de Guadiaro 2; ☺ midnight-late) Next to the popular Liceo music bar in this lively part of the city, each table in the long upper room of this bar is fitted with its own tap for pulling long cold glasses of Alhambra beer. A range of *raciones* is available (€4 to €12).

ENTERTAINMENT
Liceo (Calle Beatas 21; ☺ 9pm-1am Thu-Sat) A grand old mansion turned young music bar, which buzzes with a student crowd after midnight. Go up the winding staircase and discover more rooms.

GETTING THERE & AWAY
Málaga's busy **airport** (☎ 952 04 88 38), the main international gateway to Andalucía, receives flights by dozens of airlines (budget and otherwise) from around Europe.

The main station, **Málaga-Renfe** (☎ 952 36 02 02; Explanada de la Estación), renamed the María Zambrano in 2007, is round the corner from the bus station. The superfast AVE service runs to Madrid (€71.20 to €79.20, 2½ hours, six daily).

GETTING AROUND
Bus 19 to the city centre (€1.10, 20 minutes) leaves from the 'City Bus' stop outside the arrivals hall, every 20 or 30 minutes, 6.35am to 11.45pm, stopping at Málaga-Renfe train station and the bus station en route.

A taxi from the airport to the city centre costs €20 to €24 depending on traffic and pick-up location.

Málaga is responding to green issues and citizen pressure by building its own Metro system. **Metro Málaga** (☎ 902 93 49 44; www.metrodemalaga.info), with the first section of track, from the port towards the city centre and including the train station, is set to launch in 2010.

COSTA DEL SOL
Strewn along the seaboard from Málaga almost to Gibraltar, the Costa del Sol stretches like a wall of wedding cakes several kilometres thick. Its recipe for success is sunshine, convenient beaches (of grey-brown sand), cheap package deals and bountiful nightlife and entertainment. The *costa* (coast) is also a haven for sport lovers, with around 40 golf clubs, several busy marinas, tennis courts, riding schools, swimming pools, gyms and beaches offering every imaginable water sport.

The resorts were once fishing villages, but there's little evidence of that now. In July and August it's best to ring ahead.

MARBELLA

pop 132,000

Overlooked by the dramatic Sierra Blanca 28km west of Fuengirola, Marbella has been the Costa del Sol's glossiest resort since the 1950s. Yet Marbella proper and its Casco Antiguo or old town has little to do with the conspicuous consumption of the notorious Golden Mile, heading west towards Puerto Banús.

INFORMATION

Municipal tourist office (www.marbella.es in Spanish; 9am-9pm Mon-Fri, 9.30am-2.30pm Sat, closed Sun); Fontanilla (952 77 14 42; Glorieta de la Fontanilla); Naranjos (952 82 35 50; Plaza de los Naranjos 1)

SIGHTS & ACTIVITIES

Pretty Plaza de los Naranjos, with its 16th-century town hall, is at the heart of the largely pedestrianised, postcard-perfect old town. Nearby are the Iglesia de la Encarnación (Plaza de la Iglesia), begun in the 16th century, and the Museo del Grabado Español Contemporáneo (Museum of Contemporary Spanish Prints; 952 76 57 41; Calle Hospital Bazán s/n; admission €3, free Sat; 9am-2pm & 6-9pm Tue-Fri, 9am-2pm Mon & Sat). In beautifully uncluttered vaulted rooms, you can see work by Picasso, Joan Miró and Salvador Dalí, among others.

Avenida del Mar, leading down to the central Playa de Venus, a standard Costa del Sol beach, is peppered with crazed sculptures by Salvador Dalí.

Puerto Banús, the Costa del Sol's flashiest marina, is 6km west of Marbella. Marbella's 'spend, be seen, have fun' ethos is at its purest in Puerto Banús, with a constant parade of the glamorous, the would-be glamorous and the normal in front of the boutiques and busy restaurants strung along the waterfront.

SLEEPING

Hostal Berlin (952 82 13 10; www.hostal berlin.com; Calle San Ramón 21; s/d/tr €45/65/80; P ⊠ 🖳) A very friendly *hostal* simply but brightly furnished and with spotless shower rooms, on a quiet street parallel to Calle La Luna. Breakfast is €3.

our pick Town House (952 90 17 91; www .townhouse.nu; Calle Alderete 7; s/d incl breakfast €115/130; ⊠ 🖳) Occupying a traditional town house, with nine chic rooms, the Swedish-owned Town House reminds you what a luxury hotel is for: to pamper you with feather bedding and leather sofas, cashmere throws and great coffee; to serve you a healthy fruit and Greek yoghurt breakfast, and to send you out again at peace with yourself and the whole world.

EATING

La Taberna del Pintxo (Avenida Miguel Cano 7; tapas €1-2) Grab a table and a plate and choose from a huge range of hot and cold tapas, such as the goats' cheese tart with cranberry jelly. At the end of the night, the toothpicks from each tapa are counted and you are charged accordingly. This big, busy bar is just a block or two from the beach and all the evening *paseo* action.

El Balcón de la Virgen (952 77 60 52; Calle Virgen de los Dolores; mains €9-18; closed Sun) One of the best restaurants near Plaza de los Naranjos, this has a lovely summer *terraza* overlooked by a 300-year-old grieving Virgin and a large bougainvillea, vibrant pink against the bright blue paintwork. The fare is typical Andalucian.

GETTING THERE & AROUND

Half-hourly buses to Fuengirola (€2.65, 1¼ hours), Puerto Banús (€1.10, 20 minutes) and Estepona (€2.51, 1¼ hours) have stops on Avenida Ricardo Soriano.

RONDA

pop 37,000 / elev 744m

Perched on an inland plateau riven by the 100m fissure of El Tajo gorge and surrounded by the beautiful Serranía de Ronda, Ronda is the most dramatically sited of all the *pueblos blancos*. Just an hour north of the Costa del Sol, it is nevertheless a world away from the coastal scene.

INFORMATION

Municipal tourist office (☎ 952 18 71 19; www.turismoderonda.es; Paseo de Blas Infante; ⏰ 10am-7.30pm Mon-Fri May-Sep, to 6pm Oct-Apr, 10.15am-2pm & 3.30-6.30pm Sat, Sun & holidays)

SIGHTS

The majestic **Puente Nuevo** (New Bridge), spanning El Tajo from Plaza de España, the main square on the north side of the gorge, was completed in 1793. Folklore claims that its architect, Martín de Aldehuela, fell to his death while trying to engrave the date on the bridge's side.

The first street to the left, after you cross the Puente Nuevo, leads down to the **Casa del Rey Moro** (☎ 952 18 72 00; Calle Santo Domingo 17). This romantically crumbling 18th-century house, supposedly built over the remains of an Islamic palace, is itself closed, but you can visit its cliff-top **gardens** and descend the 200 dimly lit steps of **La Mina** (gardens & La Mina adult/child €4/2; ⏰ 10am-7pm), an Islamic-era stairway cut inside the rock right down to the bottom of the gorge (take care!).

A minute's walk southeast is Plaza Duquesa de Parcent, where the **Iglesia de Santa María La Mayor** (☎ 952 87 22 46; admission adult/student/senior €3/1.50/2; ⏰ 10am-8pm Apr-Oct, to 6pm Nov-Mar), as grand as a cathedral, stands on the site of Islamic Ronda's main mosque.

Nearby, the amusing **Museo del Bandolero** (☎ 952 87 77 85; Calle de Armiñán

Plaza de Toros, Ronda

JOHN ELK III

65; admission €3; ⏰ 10.30am-8pm Apr-Sep, to 6pm Oct-Mar) is dedicated to the banditry for which central Andalucía was renowned in the 19th century.

Beside the museum, a long flight of cobbled steps leads down to an impressive stretch of La Ciudad's old **walls**. Follow the path down to the beautiful horseshoe arches of the 13th- and 14th-century **Baños Árabes** (Arab Baths; ☎ 656 950937; Hoyo San Miguel; admission €3; ⏰ 10am-7pm Mon-Fri, to 3pm Sat & Sun), the best preserved baths on the whole Iberian Peninsula.

Ronda's elegant bullring, the **Plaza de Toros** (☎ 952 87 41 32; Calle Virgen de la Paz; admission €6; ⏰ 10am-8pm Apr-Sep, to 6pm Oct-Mar), is one of the oldest in Spain – it opened in 1785 – and has seen some of the most important events in bullfighting history.

SLEEPING

Hotel Alavera de los Baños (☎ 952 87 91 43; www.andalucia.com/alavera; Hoyo San Miguel s/n; s/d incl breakfast €65/85; ⊠ ⚏) A magical hotel with style echoes of the Arab baths next door, this one-time tannery is sumptuously decorated, with a flower-filled patio and pool.

Parador de Ronda (☎ 952 87 75 00; www .parador.es; Plaza de España s/n; s/d €127/159; P ⊠ ⚏ ⚏) Acres of shining marble and deep-cushioned furniture give this modern *parador* a certain appeal. The terrace is a wonderful place to drink in views of the gorge with your coffee or wine.

EATING

our pick **Bar Restaurant Almocábar** (☎ 952 87 59 77; Calle Ruedo Alameda 5; tapas €2, mains €12-20; ⏰ 1.30-5pm & 8pm-1am Wed-Mon, closed Aug; V) In the Barrio San Francisco, a little off the tourist path, tiny Almocábar features inspired and exceptional cooking, with a surprising range of vegetarian salads, as well as meaty classics and fish.

Restaurante Tragabuches (☎ 952 19 02 91; Calle José Aparicio 1; mains €27-32; ⏰ closed Mon) Sleek, modern Tragabuches is famous for its creativity. Try venison and sweet potatoes or pork trotters with squid and sunflower seeds.

GETTING THERE & AWAY

From the **bus station** (Plaza Concepción García Redondo 2), **Los Amarillos** (☎ 952 18 70 61) goes to Málaga (€9.11, two hours, at least four daily), Grazalema (€2.46, 35 minutes, two daily) and Seville (€10.85, 2½ hours, three to six daily); **Comes** (☎ 952 87 19 92) has three or four buses daily to Arcos de la Frontera (€8.14, two hours), Jerez (€10.67, 2½ hours) and Cádiz (€13.74, 2½ hours); and **Portillo** (☎ 952 87 22 62) runs to Málaga (€10.21, 1½ hours, at least three daily) via Marbella.

CÓRDOBA PROVINCE
CÓRDOBA

pop 302,000 / elev 110m

Standing on a sweep of Río Guadalquivir, Córdoba is a handsome, conservative city. Apart from its great historical attractions, it also features some of the region's best restaurants and taverns, and there is a small but growing nightlife scene. The best time to visit is between temperate mid-April and mid-June, when the city's patios and lanes, like the Calleja de las Flores, are at their fragrant best.

HISTORY

Córdoba's heyday came under Abd ar-Rahman III (912–61). The biggest city in Western Europe had dazzling mosques, libraries, observatories and aqueducts, a university and highly skilled artisans in leather, metal, textiles and glazed tiles. And the multicultural court was frequented by Jewish, Arab and Christian scholars.

In 1236, Córdoba was captured by Fernando III of Castilla and became a provincial town of shrinking importance.

INFORMATION

Municipal tourist office (☎ 957 20 05 22; Plaza de Judá Levi; ⏰ 8.30am-2.30pm Mon-Fri) **Regional tourist office** (☎ 957 35 51 79; Calle de Torrijos 10; ⏰ 9am-7.30pm Mon-Fri, 9.30am-3pm Sat, Sun & holidays) Faces the western side of the Mezquita.

SIGHTS & ACTIVITIES
JUDERÍA

The medieval *judería,* extending northwest from the Mezquita almost to Avenida del Gran Capitán, is today a maze of narrow streets and whitewashed buildings with flowery window boxes.

WITOLD SKRYPCZAK

La Mezquita, Córdoba

↘ MEZQUITA

It's hard to exaggerate the beauty of the Córdoba mosque, one of the great creations of Islamic architecture, with its shimmering golden mosaics and rows of red-and-white-striped arches disappearing into infinity.

Emir Abd ar-Rahman I founded the Mezquita in 785 on the site of a Visigothic church that had been partitioned between Muslims and Christians. In the 9th and 10th centuries, the Mezquita was enlarged and embellished until it extended over nearly 23,000 sq metres in total, making it one of the biggest mosques in the world. Its 14,000-sq-metre prayer hall incorporated 1293 columns, some of which had stood in the Visigothic church, in Roman buildings in Córdoba and even in ancient Carthage. Today 856 of the columns remain.

What we see today is the Mezquita's original architectural form with two big changes: a 16th-century cathedral plonked right in the middle (which explains the often-used description 'Mezquita-Catedral'); and the closing of the 19 doors, which would once have filled the Mezquita with light.

Things you need to know: ☎ 957 47 05 12; adult/child €8/4; ☻ 10am-7pm Mon-Sat Apr-Oct, to 6pm Mon-Sat Nov-Mar, 9-10.45am & 1.30-6.30pm Sun year-round

The beautiful little 14th-century **Sinagoga** (Calle de los Judíos 20; admission adult/EU citizen €0.30/free; ☻ 9.30am-2pm & 3.30-5.30pm Tue-Sat, 9.30am-1.30pm Sun & holidays) is one of only three surviving medieval synagogues in Spain and the only one in Andalucía.

In the heart of the *judería*, and once connected by an underground tunnel to the Sinagoga, is the 14th-century **Casa de Sefarad** (☎ 957 42 14 04; www.casadesefarad .es; admission €4; ☻ 10am-6pm Mon-Sat, 11am-2pm Sun). Opened in 2008 on the corner of Calle Judios and Calle Averroes, this small, beautiful museum is devoted to reviving interest in the Sephardic-Judaic-Spanish tradition.

ANDALUCÍA

CÓRDOBA

CÓRDOBA

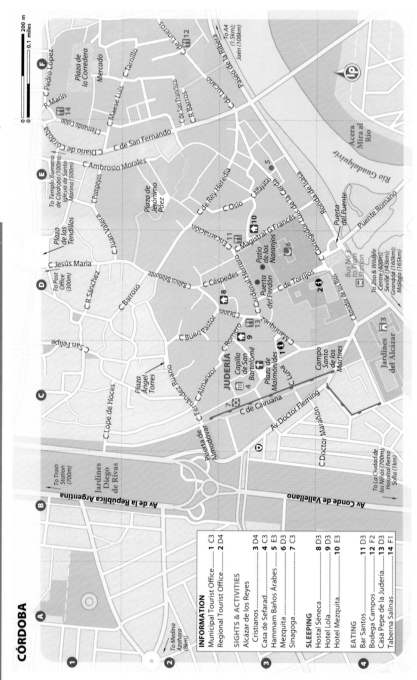

ALCÁZAR DE LOS REYES CRISTIANOS

Just southwest of the Mezquita, the Alcázar, or Castle of the Christian Monarchs (☎ 957 42 01 51; Campo Santo de Los Mártires s/n; adult/student €4/2, Fri free; ✦ 10am-2pm & 4.30-6.30pm Tue-Sat mid-Oct–Apr, 10am-2pm & 5.30-7.30pm Tue-Sat May-Jun & Sep–mid-Oct, 8.30am-2.30pm Tue-Sat Jul-Aug, 9.30am-2.30pm Sun & holidays year-round), began as a palace and fort for Alfonso X in the 13th century. From 1490 to 1821 the Inquisition operated from here. Today its gardens are among the most beautiful in Andalucía.

HAMMAM BAÑOS ÁRABES

Follow the lead of the medieval Cordobans and indulge your senses at the beautifully renovated Arab baths (☎ 957 48 47 46; www.hammamspain.com/cordoba; Calle Corregidor Luis de la Cerda 51; bath/bath & massage €12/16; ✦ 2hr sessions at 10am, noon, 2pm, 4pm, 6pm, 8pm & 10pm) where you can enjoy an aromatherapy massage, with tea, hookah and Arabic sweets in the cafe later.

CÓRDOBA FOR CHILDREN

Just southwest of the city centre and adjoining the city Zoo and Wildlife Centre (Avenida de Linneo; adult/child €4/2; ✦ 10am-7pm Tue-Sun Apr & May, to 8pm Jun-Aug, to 7pm Sep, to 5-6pm Oct-Mar), historic buildings morph into brightly coloured climbing equipment. Welcome to La Ciudad de los Niños (☎ 663 035709; laciudaddelosninos.com; Avenida Menéndez Pidal; admission free; ✦ 10am-2pm & 7-11pm Jun–mid-Sep, 10am-6pm Nov-Mar), Córdoba's City for Kids. A calendar of special events aimed at four to 12 year olds runs throughout the summer – check its website for details, or ask at the regional tourist office. Buses 2 and 5 from the city centre stop here.

JOHN ELK III

Alcázar courtyard, Córdoba

FESTIVALS & EVENTS

Concurso & Festival de Patios Cordobeses (Early May) Look for 'Patio' signs in Córdoba's streets, inviting you to view blooming gardens. Entrance is free, though donations are welcome.

Festival Internacional de Guitarra (Late June/early July) Two-week celebration of the guitar, with live classical, flamenco, rock, blues and more; top names play in the Alcázar gardens at night.

SLEEPING

Hostal Séneca (☎ /fax 957 47 32 34; Calle Conde y Luque 7; s/d incl breakfast €36/48; ✦ closed 1 week Aug & Christmas week) The charming, friendly Séneca occupies a rambling house with a marvellous pebbled patio that's filled with greenery. Some rooms have air-conditioning.

Hotel Mezquita (☎ 957 47 55 85; hotel mezquita@wanadoo.es; Plaza Santa Catalina 1; s €37-39, d €53-74; ⚡) One of the best-value places in town, this hotel is right opposite the Mezquita itself. The 16th-century mansion has sparkling bathrooms and elegant rooms, some with views of the great mosque.

Hotel Lola (☎ 957 20 03 05; www.hotel conencantolola.com; Calle Romero 3; d incl breakfast €114; ⓟ ⚡) A quirky hotel with large antique beds and full of smaller items that you just wish you could take home. You can eat your breakfast on the roof terrace overlooking the Mezquita bell tower.

EATING

Dishes common to most Cordoban restaurants include *salmorejo,* a very thick tomato-based gazpacho (cold vegetable soup), and *rabo de toro.*

There are lots of places to eat right by the Mezquita, but beware inflated prices and uninspired food.

Bar Santos (Calle Magistral González Francés 3; tortillas €2.50) The legendary Bar Santos serves the biggest *tortilla de patata* in town – eaten with plastic forks on paper plates, while gazing at the Mezquita. Don't miss it.

Taberna Salinas (☎ 957 48 01 35; Calle Tundidores 3; tapas/raciones €2.50/8; ⌚ closed Sun & Aug) Dating back to 1879, this large patio restaurant fills up fast. Try the delicious aubergines with honey or potatoes with garlic. The tavern side is quieter in the early evening.

Casa Pepe de la Judería (☎ 957 20 07 44; Calle Romero 1; tapas/media raciones €2.50-9.50, mains €11-18, menú €27.82) A great roof terrace with views of the Mezquita and a labyrinth of busy dining rooms. Down a complimentary glass of Montilla before

launching into the house specials, including Cordoban oxtails or venison fillets.

Bodega Campos (☎ 957 49 75 00; Calle de Lineros 32; tapas/raciones €6.50-16, mains €17.50-29; ⌚ closed Sun evening) This many-roomed, atmospheric winery-cum-restaurant offers the peak dining experience in Cordoba.

GETTING THERE & AWAY

Córdoba's **train station** (☎ 957 40 02 02; Avenida de América) is on the high-speed AVE line between Madrid and Seville.

AROUND CÓRDOBA

Even in the cicada-shrill heat and stillness of a summer afternoon, the Madinat al-Zahra whispers of the power and vision of its founder, Abd ar-Rahman III. The self-proclaimed caliph began the construction of a magnificent new capital 8km west of Córdoba around 936, and took up full residence around 945. **Medina Azahara** (Madinat al-Zahra; ☎ 957 32 91 30; adult/EU citizen €1.50/free; ⌚ 10am-6.30pm Tue-Sat, to 8.30pm May–mid-Sep, to 2pm Sun) was a resounding declaration of his status, a magnificent trapping of power.

Today, though less than a tenth of it has been excavated, and only about a quarter of that is open to visitors, Medina Azahara is still a fascinating place to visit.

GRANADA PROVINCE
GRANADA

pop 300,000 / elev 685m

Spain's most visited monument, the Alhambra palace, presides over a city full of architectural and historic treasures. Alongside them flourish smart new tapas bars, tiny flamenco dives and chrome-and-neon clubs that support a dynamic student and gay scene.

ANDALUCÍA

GRANADA PROVINCE

Alhambra (p303), Granada

JOHN BANAGAN

HISTORY

Granada's history reads like a thriller. After the fall of Córdoba (1236) and Seville (1248), Muslims sought refuge in Granada, where Mohammed ibn Yusuf ibn Nasr had set up an independent emirate. Stretching from the Strait of Gibraltar to east of Almería, this 'Nasrid' emirate became the final remnant of Al-Andalus, ruled from the increasingly lavish Alhambra palace for 250 years. Granada became one of the richest cities in medieval Europe.

However, in the 15th century the economy stagnated and violent rivalry developed over the succession. One faction supported the emir, Abu al-Hasan, and his harem favourite Zoraya. The other faction backed Boabdil, Abu al-Hasan's son by his wife Aixa. In 1482 Boabdil rebelled, setting off a confused civil war. The Christian armies invading the emirate took advantage, besieging towns and devastating the countryside, and in 1491 they finally laid siege to Granada. After eight months, Boabdil agreed to surrender the city in return for the Alpujarras valleys and 30,000 gold coins, plus political and religious freedom for his subjects. On 2 January 1492 the conquering Catholic Monarchs, Isabel and Fernando, entered Granada ceremonially in Muslim dress. They set up court in the Alhambra for several years.

INFORMATION
INTERNET RESOURCES

Where2 (www.where2.es) is an excellent, comprehensive English-language website with information on 'Where To' eat, sleep, find entertainment or even buy property in Granada.

TOURIST INFORMATION

Municipal tourist office (off Map pp302-3; ☎ 958 22 52 17; www.granadatur.com; Calle Almona del Campillo, 2; ☺ 9am-7pm Mon-Fri, to 6pm Sat, 10am-2pm Sun & holidays)
Provincial tourist office (Map pp302-3; ☎ 958 24 71 28; www.turismodegranada.org; Plaza de Mariana Pineda 10; ☺ 9am-8pm Mon-Fri, 10am-2pm & 4-7pm Sat, 10am-3pm Sun May-Sep, 9am-8pm Mon-Fri, 10am-1pm Sat, to 3pm Sun Nov-Apr)

GRANADA

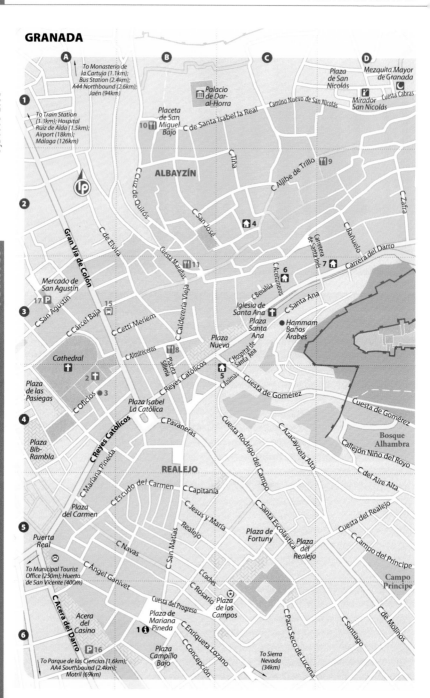

A
To Monasterio de
la Cartuja (1.1km);
Bus Station (2.4km);
A44 Northbound (2.6km);
Jaén (94km)

To Train Station
(1.3km); Hospital
Ruiz de Alda (1.5km);
Airport (18km);
Málaga (126km)

B
Palacio
de Dar-
al-Horra

Placeta
de San
Miguel
Bajo

10

C de Santa Isabel la Real

C de Quiñós

C Cruz de Quirós

ALBAYZÍN

C San José

Cuesta Marañas

C Calderería Vieja

C
Plaza
de San
Nicolás

Camino Nuevo de San Nicolás

C Tiña

C Aljibe de Trillo   9

4

C Benalúa

6
C Arcedianos

Iglesia de
Santa Ana

Plaza
Santa
Ana

Hammam
Baños
Árabes

C Santa Ana

D
Mezquita Mayor
de Granada

Mirador
San Nicolás

Cuesta Cabras

Carretera de Santa Inés

7

Carrera del Darro

C Zafra

C Bañuelo

11

Gran Vía de Colón

C de Elvira

Mercado de
San Agustín

17   P

C San Agustín

C Cárcel Baja

15

C Cetti Meriem

C Almireceros   8

Cathedral

2

3

Plaza
de las
Pasiegas

C Oficios

Plaza
Bib-
Rambla

C Reyes Católicos

Puerta
Silería

C Reyes Católicos

Plaza Isabel
La Católica

C Pavaneras

Plaza
Nueva

C Hospital de
Santa Ana

C Ánimas

5

Cuesta de Gomérez

Cuesta de Gomérez

Bosque
Alhambra

Callejón Niño del Royo

C del Aire Alta

REALEJO

C Mariana Pineda

C Escudo del Carmen

C Capitanía

C Jesús y María

Realejo

Plaza de
Fortuny

Cuesta Rodrigo del Campo

C Azacayuela Alta

C Santa Escolástica

Plaza
del
Realejo

Cuesta del Realejo

C Campo del Príncipe

Campo
Príncipe

Plaza
del Carmen

Puerta
Real

C Navas

C San Matías

C Ángel Ganivet

C Cochés

C Rosario

Plaza
de los
Campos

C Paco Seco de Lucena

C Santiago

C de Molinos

To Municipal Tourist
Office (250m); Huerta
de San Vicente (400m)

Acera
del
Casino

C Acera del Darro

1

Cuesta del Progreso

Plaza de
Mariana
Pineda

C Enriqueta Lozano

C Concepción

Plaza
Campillo
Bajo

To Sierra
Nevada
(34km)

16   P

To Parque de las Ciencias (1.6km);
AA4 Southbound (2.4km);
Motril (69km)

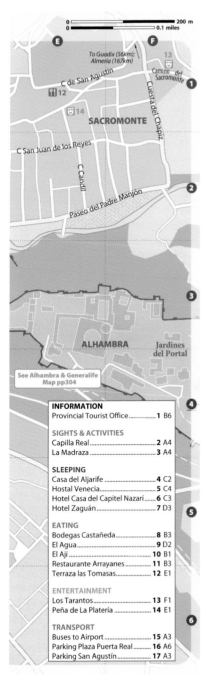

SIGHTS & ACTIVITIES
ALHAMBRA

Stretched along the top of the hill known as La Sabika, the **Alhambra** (Map p304; ☎ 902 44 12 21; adult/EU senior/EU student €12/9/9, disabled & under 8yr free, Generalife only €6; ⏰ 8.30am-8pm Mar-Oct, to 6pm Nov-Feb, closed 25 Dec & 1 Jan) is the stuff of fairy tales. It's highly advisable to book in advance (€1 extra per ticket). You can book up to a year ahead in two ways:

Alhambra Advance Booking (☎ 902 88 80 01 for national calls, 0034 934 92 37 50 for international calls; ⏰ 8am-9pm every day)

Servicaixa (www.servicaixa.com) Online booking in Spanish and English.

Palacio Nazaríes

This is the Alhambra's true gem, the most brilliant Islamic building in Europe, with its perfectly proportioned rooms and court-yards, intricately moulded stucco walls, beautiful tiling, fine carved wooden ceil-ings and elaborate stalactite-like *muqarnas* vaulting, all worked in mesmerising, sym-bolic, geometrical patterns. Arabic inscrip-tions proliferate in the stuccowork.

Built for Emir Yusuf I, the **Palacio de Comares** served as a private residence for the ruler. It's built around the lovely **Patio de los Arrayanes** (Patio of the Myrtles) with its rectangular pool.

The Patio de los Arrayanes leads into the **Palacio de los Leones** (Palace of the Lions), built under Mohammed V – by some accounts as the royal harem. The palace rooms surround the famous **Patio de los Leones** (Lion Courtyard), with its marble fountain channelling water through the mouths of 12 marble lions. On the northern side of the patio is the richly decorated **Sala de Dos Hermanas** (Hall of Two Sisters), probably named after the slabs of white marble at either side of its fountain.

ANDALUCÍA

GRANADA PROVINCE

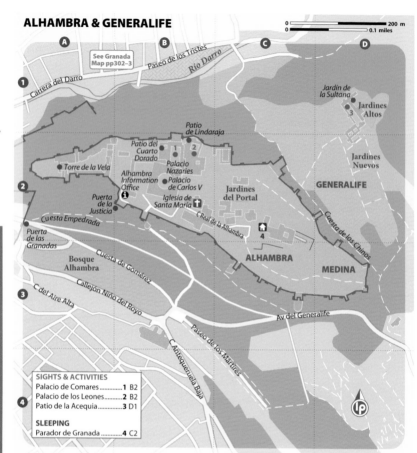

ALHAMBRA & GENERALIFE

SIGHTS & ACTIVITIES
Palacio de Comares **1** B2
Palacio de los Leones...........**2** B2
Patio de la Acequia.............**3** D1

SLEEPING
Parador de Granada **4** C2

Generalife

The name Generalife means 'Architect's Garden'. The Muslim rulers' summer palace is in the corner furthest from the entrance. Within the palace, the **Patio de la Acequia** (Court of the Water Channel) has a long pool framed by flowerbeds and 19th-century fountains, whose shapes echo the arched porticos at each end.

CAPILLA REAL

The **Royal Chapel** (Map pp302-3; ☎ 958 22 92 39; www.capillareal.granada.com; Calle Oficios; admission €3.50; ⏱ 10.30am-12.45pm & 4-7pm

Mon-Sat, 11am-12.45pm & 4-7pm Sun Apr-Oct, 10.30am-12.45pm & 3.30-6.15pm Mon-Sat, 11am-12.45pm & 3.30-6.15pm Sun Nov-Mar), adjoining the cathedral, is Granada's outstanding Christian building.

The monarchs Isabel and Fernando, who commissioned this elaborate mausoleum, lie in simple lead coffins in the crypt beneath their marble monuments in the chancel, which is enclosed by a stunning gilded wrought-iron screen created in 1520 by Bartolomé de Jaén.

Just opposite is **La Madraza** (Map pp302-3; admission free; ⏱ 8am-10pm), founded in

1349 by Sultan Yusuf I as a school and university. Gaze into the splendid prayer hall with its elaborate *mihrab*. The light here has a special mellow quality.

ALBAYZÍN

On the hill facing the Alhambra across the Darro valley, Granada's old Muslim quarter, the Albayzín, is an open-air museum in which you can lose yourself for a whole morning. The cobblestone streets are lined with gorgeous *cármenes* (large mansions with walled gardens, from the Arabic *karm* for garden). It survived as the Muslim quarter for several decades after the Christian conquest in 1492.

MONASTERIO DE LA CARTUJA

Another architectural gem stands 2km northwest of the city centre, reached by bus 8 from Gran Vía de Colón. **La Cartuja Monastery** (off Map pp302-3; ☎ 958 16 19 32; Paseo de la Cartuja; admission €3.50; ☷ 10am-1pm & 4-8pm every day Apr-Oct, to 1pm & 3-6pm Nov-Mar) was built between the 16th and 18th centuries and features a church bursting with gold, marble and sculptures and an exuberantly baroque sacristy.

HUERTA DE SAN VICENTE

This **house** (off Map pp302-3; ☎ 958 25 84 66; Calle Virgen Blanca s/n; admission €3, free Wed) where Federico García Lorca spent summers and wrote some of his best-known works, is a 15-minute walk south of the city centre, though it still retains the evocative aura of an early 20th-century country villa.

TOURS

Granavisión (☎ 902 33 00 02) Offers guided tours of the Alhambra and Generalife (€49) and Historic Granada tours (€48). Phone direct or book through a travel agent.

Granada Tapas Tours (☎ 619 444984; www.granadatapastours.com)

GRANADA FOR CHILDREN

With four buildings and eight interactive exhibition areas, Granada's popular **Parque de las Ciencias** (off Map pp302-3;

Patio de la Acequia, Generalife, Granada

JOHN ELK III

Parque de las Ciencias (p305), Granada

KEN WELSH/ALAMY

☎ 958 13 19 00; www.parqueciencias.com; Avenida del Mediterráneo s/n; adult/under 18yr €4.50/3.50; ⏰ 10am-7pm Tue-Sat, 10am-3pm Sun & holidays), south of the centre, should keep the kids happily absorbed for hours.

SLEEPING

Hostal Venecia (Map pp302-3; ☎ 958 22 39 87; Cuesta de Gomérez 2; r €32, s/d/tr/q without bathroom €19/30/53/60) A lovely *hostal* with friendly hosts and flower-and-picture-filled turquoise corridors, just off Plaza Nueva.

There are several hotels in beautiful renovated Albayzín mansions, including **Hotel Casa del Capitel Nazarí** (Map pp302-3; ☎ 958 21 52 60; www.hotelcasacapitel .com; Cuesta Aceituneros 6; s/d €73/91;), **Casa del Aljarife** (Map pp302-3; ☎/fax 958 22 24 25; www.granadainfo.com/most; Placeta de la Cruz Verde 2; r €96.30;) and **Hotel Zaguán** (Map pp302-3; ☎ 958 21 57 30; www .hotelzaguan.com; Carrera del Darro; s €55, r €95;).

Parador de Granada (Map p304; ☎ 958 22 14 40; www.parador.es; Calle Real de la Alhambra s/n; s/d €220/310;) The most expensive *parador* in Spain can't be beaten for its location within the Alhambra and its historical connections. Book ahead.

EATING

Granada is one of the last bastions of that fantastic practice of free tapas with every drink, and some have an international flavour.

The labyrinthine Albayzín holds a wealth of eateries all tucked away in the narrow streets.

Bodegas Castañeda (Map pp302-3; Calle Almireceros; raciones from €6) An institution, and reputedly the oldest bar in Granada, this restaurant located near Plaza Nueva whips up traditional food in a typical bodega setting. Its tasty free tapa of paella is almost enough for a light lunch. Get a table before 2pm as it gets very busy around then.

Restaurante Arrayanes (Map pp302-3; ☎ 958 22 84 01; Cuesta Marañas 4; mains €8.50-19; ⏰ from 8pm) Pop in to fill up on delicious Moroccan tagine casseroles. Note that

Restaurante Arrayanes does not serve alcohol.

El Ají (Map pp302-3; ☎ 958 29 29 30; San Miguel Bajo 9; menú €10.50, mains €10-20; **V**) We like the cool, modern interior, soft jazz, and its menu of nontraditional meat and lively vegetarian choices.

El Agua (Map pp302-3; ☎ 958 22 33 58; Plaza Aljibe de Trillo 7; fondues per person €14-19, minimum 2 people; ☾ lunch Wed-Mon, dinner daily) and **Terraza las Tomasas** (Map pp302-3; ☎ 958 22 41 08; Carril de San Agustín 4; mains €18-22; ☾ dinner Wed-Sat) offer fabulous views of the Alhambra.

ENTERTAINMENT

Peña de la Platería (Map pp302-3; ☎ 958 21 06 50; Placeta de Toqueros 7) Buried deep in the Albayzín warren, this is a genuine aficionados' club with a large outdoor patio. Catch a 9.30pm performance on Thursday or Saturday.

Situated above and to the northwest of the city centre, and offering panoramic views over the Alhambra, the Sacromonte is Granada's centuries-old *gitano* quarter. The Sacromonte caves harbour touristy flamenco haunts for which you can pre-book through hotels and travel agencies, some of whom offer free transport. Try the Friday or Saturday midnight shows at **Los Tarantos** (Map pp302-3; ☎ day 958 22 45 25, night 958 22 24 92; Camino del Sacromonte 9; admission €24) for a lively experience.

GETTING THERE & AWAY

Iberia (☎ 902 40 05 00; www.iberia.com) flies daily to and from Madrid and Barcelona. From the UK, **Ryanair** (www.rynanair.com) flies daily to Granada.

The **train station** (off Map pp302-3; ☎ 958 24 02 02; Avenida de Andaluces) is 1.5km west of the centre, off Avenida de la Constitución.

GETTING AROUND

The **airport** (off Map pp302-3; ☎ 958 24 52 23) is 17km west of the city on the A92. **Autocares J González** (☎ 958 49 01 64) runs buses between the airport and a stop near the Palacio de Congresos (€3, five daily), with a stop in the city centre on Gran Vía de Colón, where a schedule is posted opposite the cathedral, and at the entrance to the bus station. A taxi costs €18 to €22 depending on traffic conditions and pick-up point.

Central underground public car parks include **Parking San Agustín** (Map pp302-3; Calle San Agustín; per hr/day €1/16), **Parking Neptuno** (Calle Neptuno, A44-E902, exit 129) and **Parking Plaza Puerta Real** (Map pp302-3; Acera del Darro; per hr/day €1/12). Free parking is available at the Alhambra car parks.

AROUND GRANADA

The **Parque Federico García Lorca**, between the villages of Víznar and Alfacar (about 2.5km from each), marks the site where Federico García Lorca and hundreds, possibly thousands, of others are believed to have been shot and buried by the Nationalists, at the start of the Civil War.

The touchingly modest house where Lorca was born in 1898, in the otherwise unremarkable suburb of Fuente Vaqueros, 17km west of Granada, is now the **Casa Museo Federico García Lorca** (☎ 958 51 64 53; www.museogarcialorca.org in Spanish; Calle Poeta Federico García Lorca 4; admission €1.80; ☾ guided visits hourly 10am-1pm & 5-7pm Tue-Sat Apr-Jun, to 2pm & 6-8pm Tue-Sat Jul-Sep, 10am-1pm & 4-6pm Tue-Sat Oct-Mar). The place brings his spirit to life, with numerous charming photos, posters and costumes from his plays, and paintings illustrating his poems. A short video captures him in action with the touring Teatro Barraca.

SIERRA NEVADA

The Sierra Nevada, which includes mainland Spain's highest peak, Mulhacén (3479m), forms an almost year-round snowy southeastern backdrop to Granada. The upper reaches of the range form the 862-sq-km **Parque Nacional Sierra Nevada**, Spain's biggest national park, with a rare high-altitude environment that is home to about 2100 of Spain's 7000 plant species. Andalucía's largest ibex population (about 5000)

MICHAEL SPARROW/ALAMY

Parque Natural Sierra de Grazalema

↘ IF YOU LIKE...

If you like **Sierra Nevada** (above) and its combination of wilderness areas and possibilities for getting active, we also recommend the following:

- **Parque Natural Sierra de Grazalema** One of Andalucía's greenest areas and best walking country with pastoral river valleys and precipitous gorges; in Cádiz province.
- **Parque Natural de las Sierras de Cazorla, Segura y Las Villas** A stunning region of rugged mountain ranges divided by high plains and deep, forested valleys and one of the best places in Spain for spotting wildlife; in eastern Jaén province.
- **Parque Natural Sierra de Aracena y Picos de Aroche** Lovely, rolling hill country of northern Huelva province, with fortress-like villages and fine walking.
- **La Axarquía** Wild landscapes, orchards and deep valleys with quiet walking trails; in Málaga province.
- **Laguna de Fuente de Piedra** Hosts up to 20,000 pairs of the spectacular greater flamingo from January or February until August; close to Antequera in Málaga province.
- **Parque Nacional de Doñana** Important refuge for the endangered Spanish imperial eagle and Iberian lynx with a hauntingly beautiful landscape; in southern Huelva province.

is here too. Surrounding the national park at lower altitudes is the 848-sq-km **Parque Natural Sierra Nevada**. The mountains and the Alpujarras valleys (see below) comprise one of the most spectacular areas in Spain, and the area offers wonderful opportunities for walking, horse riding, climbing, mountain biking and, in winter, good skiing and snowboarding.

The **Centro de Visitantes El Dornajo** (☎ 958 34 06 25; ⏰ 10am-2pm & 6-8pm Apr-Sep, 10am-2pm & 4-6pm Oct-Mar), about 23km from Granada, on the A395 towards the ski station, has plenty of information on the Sierra Nevada. Knowledgeable, English-speaking staff are happy to help.

The **Sierra Nevada Ski Station** (☎ 958 24 91 36; www.sierranevadaski.com; ⏰ 10am-2pm & 4-6pm), at Pradollano, 33km southeast of Granada, is one of Spain's biggest and liveliest ski resorts. The ski season normally lasts from December to April.

GETTING THERE & AWAY

In the ski season **Autocares Bonal** (☎ 958 46 50 22) operates three daily buses (four at weekends) from Granada bus station to the ski station (one way/return €4.20/7.50, one hour). A taxi from Granada to the ski station costs around €45.

LAS ALPUJARRAS

Below the southern flank of the Sierra Nevada lies the 70km-long jumble of valleys known as Las Alpujarras. Arid hillsides split by deep ravines alternate with oasis-like white villages set beside rapid streams and surrounded by gardens, orchards and woodlands. Countless good walking routes link valley villages and head up into the Sierra Nevada: the best times to visit are between April and mid-June, and mid-September and early November.

ANDALUCÍA

JAÉN PROVINCE

SIERRA NEVADA & ALPUJARRAS MAPS

The best overall maps of the area are Editorial Alpina's *Sierra Nevada, La Alpujarra* (1:40,000) and Editorial Penibética's *Sierra Nevada* (1:50,000). Both come with booklets, in English or Spanish, describing walking, biking and skiing routes. An invaluable resource is *34 Alpujarras Walks* by Charles Davis, published by Discovery Walking Guides, which has an accompanying Tours & Trails map.

INFORMATION

Punto de Información Parque Nacional de Sierra Nevada (☎ 958 76 31 27; www .nevadensis.com; Plaza de la Libertad, Pampaneira; ⏰ 10am-2pm & 4-6pm Tue-Sat, to 3pm Sun & Mon Oct-Mar) Plenty of information about Las Alpujarras and Sierra Nevada.

Servicio de Interpretación de Altos Cumbres (☎ 958 76 34 86, 686 41 45 76; ⏰ approx 9am-2pm & 4.30-7.30pm) By the main road in Capileira.

JAÉN PROVINCE

BAEZA

pop 17,000 / elev 790m

This country town, 48km northeast of Jaén, is replete with gorgeous Gothic and Renaissance buildings from the 16th century, when local nobility ploughed much of their wealth from grain-growing and textiles into magnificent architecture.

INFORMATION

The **tourist office** (☎ 953 77 99 82/83; Plaza del Pópulo; ⏰ 9am-7.30pm Mon-Fri, 9.30am-3pm Sat, Sun & fiestas Apr-Sep) is just southwest of Paseo de la Constitución.

ANDALUCÍA

JAÉN PROVINCE

SIGHTS

In the centre of beautiful **Plaza del Pópulo** is the **Fuente de los Leones** (Fountain of the Lions), topped by an ancient statue believed to represent Imilce, a local Iberian princess who was married to Hannibal. On the southern side of the plaza is the Plateresque Casa del Pópulo

DAVID TOMLINSON

Cathedral of Jaén

⬎ IF YOU LIKE...

If you like the Renaissance splendour of **Baeza** (p309), we think you'll also enjoy the following gems dating from the same period:

- **Úbeda** Baeza's neighbour and rival for extensive Renaissance architecture, especially surrounding the Plaza Vázquez de Molina.
- **Cathedral, Jaén** Worth the trip to this otherwise uninspiring city, Renaissance mingled with the baroque.
- **Monasterio de la Encarnación, Osuna** Lovely country town with baroque mansions and this amazing Renaissance monastery; 91km southeast of Seville.
- **Colegiata de Santa María la Mayor, Antequera** The Renaissance facade of this church is one of many reasons to visit this spire-studded town; in Málaga province.

from about 1540 (housing Baeza's helpful tourist office).

Now a high school, Baeza's **Antigua Universidad** (Old University; Calle Beato Juan de Ávila; admission free; ⏰ 10am-1pm & 4-6pm Thu-Tue) was founded in 1538. The main patio has two levels of elegant Renaissance arches. Round the corner is the early-16th-century **Palacio de Jabalquinto** (Plaza Santa Cruz; admission free; ⏰ 9am-2pm Mon-Fri), a mansion with a flamboyant Isabelline-Gothic facade and lovely Renaissance patio with a fantastically carved baroque stairway.

Across the square, the 13th-century **Iglesia de la Santa Cruz** (⏰ 11am-1pm & 4.30-6pm Mon-Sat, 11am-1pm Sun), one of the first churches to be built in Andalucía after the Reconquista, may be the only Romanesque church in Andalucía.

A block north of Paseo de la Constitución, the **ayuntamiento** (Town Hall; Paseo del Cardenal Benavides 9) has a marvellous plateresque facade.

SLEEPING & EATING

Hotel Palacete Santa Ana (☎ 953 74 16 57; www.palacetesantana.com; Calle Santa Ana Vieja 9; s/d €42/66; ☒) Stylishly restored, this hotel has its own museum in what was a 16th-century nunnery.

Hospedería Fuentenueva (☎ 953 74 31 00; www.fuentenueva.com; Calle del Carmen 15; s/d incl breakfast €52/78; ☒ ☐ ☒) This former women's prison now has big, beautiful rooms with black-slate shower rooms.

Restaurante Vandelvira (☎ 953 74 81 72; Calle de San Francisco 14; mains €8-22; ⏰ closed Sun night & Mon) Treat yourself to dishes such as partridge pâté salad or *solomillo al carbón* (char-grilled steak) in this restored convent.

GETTING THERE & AWAY

From the **bus station** (☎ 953 74 04 68; Paseo Arco del Agua), 700m east of Plaza de

España, buses go to Jaén (€3.85, 45 minutes, 11 daily), Úbeda (€1.10, 30 minutes, 15 daily), Cazorla (€4.41, 2¼ hours, two daily) and Granada (€11.34, 2¼ hours, five daily)

ALMERÍA PROVINCE
AROUND ALMERÍA

Beyond Benahadux, north of Almería, the landscape becomes a series of canyons and rocky wastelands that look straight out of the Arizona badlands, and in the 1960s and '70s movie-makers shot around 150 Westerns here.

The movie industry has left behind three Wild West town sets that are open as tourist attractions. **Mini Hollywood** (☎ 950 36 52 36; poblado@playasenator.com; adult/child €19/9; ☉ 10am-9pm Apr-Oct, to 7pm Tue-Sun Nov-Mar), the best known and the best preserved of these, is 25km from Almería on the N340 Tabernas road. Parts of more than 100 movies, including *A Fistful of Dollars* and *The Good, the Bad and the Ugly*, were filmed here.

CABO DE GATA

Some of Spain's most beautiful and least crowded beaches are strung between grand cliffs and capes east of Almería city, where dark volcanic hills tumble into a sparkling turquoise sea. Though Cabo de Gata is not undiscovered, it still has a wild, elemental feel and, with a couple of exceptions in July and August, its scattered villages remain low-key. You can walk along, or not far from, the coast right round from Retamar in the northwest to Agua Amarga in the northeast (61km), but in summer there's little shade.

The **Parque Natural de Cabo de Gata-Níjar** covers Cabo de Gata's 60km coast

Antigua Universidad, Baeza

DAVID TOMLINSON

plus a slice of hinterland. The park's main information centre is the **Centro de Interpretación Las Amoladeras** (☎ 950 16 04 35; ☉ 10am-2pm & 5.30-9pm mid-Jul–mid-Sep, to 3pm Tue-Sun mid-Sep–mid-Jul), about 2.5km west of Ruescas.

Some of the best beaches on Cabo de Gata lie along a dirt road southwest from San José. **Playa de los Genoveses**, a broad strip of sand about 1km long with shallow waters, is 4.5km away. **Playa de Mónsul**, 2.5km further from town, is a shorter length of grey sand, backed by huge lumps of volcanic rock. Away from the road, the coast between these two beaches is strung with a series of isolated, sandy, cove beaches, the **Calas del Barronal**, which can be reached only on foot.

↘ SPAIN IN FOCUS

SPAIN IN FOCUS

FAMILY TRAVEL

FAMILY TRAVEL

Feria de Abril (p47)

Spain is a great place to bring your kids, not least because children are made to feel welcome just about everywhere. Children are such an integral part of Spanish life that you'll see families together in the most unlikely places, such as bars. The main difficulties arise from the late hours that Spaniards keep. At fiestas it's common to see even tiny ones toddling the streets at 2am or 3am. Visiting kids like this idea, too – but can't always cope with it quite so readily.

Accompanied children are welcome at all kinds of accommodation, as well as in many cafes, bars and restaurants. Before you baulk at taking your kids into a bar, remember that Spanish bars are as much hubs of social life as they are places to drink. There is, however, the problem of smoke, which you can get around in warmer weather by taking to the outside tables, which usually allow kids a bit of space and freedom while the grown-ups sit and eat or drink.

Food and children are two of the great loves for Spaniards and they make for a happy combination in most restaurants. If highchairs aren't available, staff will improvise and you shouldn't be made to feel uncomfortable as your children run amok. As for the food, children's menus may be scarce, but Spanish fare is rarely spicy and kids tend to like it. Toddlers are usually fed straight from their parents' plate. When kids get hungry between meals it's easy to zip into the nearest *tasca* and get them a snack and there are also sweet shops every few blocks.

For more general information on travelling with children, pick up a copy of Lonely Planet's *Travel with Children* or visit the websites www.travelwithyourkids.com and www.familytravelnetwork.com.

SIGHTS & ACTIVITIES

Many child-focused attractions (such as zoos and amusement parks) are often inconveniently located on the outskirts of cities, but most larger places have swimming pools and plentiful playgrounds. There are also some fabulous parks, including **Park Güell** (p107) in Barcelona and **Parque del Buen Retiro** (p71) in Madrid. Football-addicted youngsters will probably want to visit either FC Barcelona's **Camp Nou** (p107) or Real Madrid's **Santiago Bernabéu** (p81).

> ### ↘ THE NITTY GRITTY
> - **Change facilities** Extremely rare in bars and restaurants
> - **Cots** Available in midrange and top-end hotels, but reserve in advance
> - **Health** High health-care standards
> - **Highchairs** Many restaurants have at least one
> - **Nappies (diapers)** Widely available
> - **Strollers** Bring your own
> - **Transport** Trains are fine; car-hire companies (but not taxis) have car seats

Interactive museums are another sure-fire winner, especially the bells-and-whistles science attractions of Barcelona's **CosmoCaixa** (p106) or Granada's **Parque de las Ciencias** (p305). Castles, of which Spain is full, are often another easy sight to sell to the young ones – especially Segovia's fairy-tale fortress, **Alcázar** (p138). Alternatively, there's always the obvious appeal of beaches and other seaside activities, including **whale watching** (p288) or the fishy lure of aquariums – seek out **Oceanogràfic** (p235) in Valencia or **L'Aquàrium** (p109) in Barcelona. For something a little different, head to **Mini Hollywood** (p311), a Wild West movie set situated in the Almería desert.

The larger the city, the greater the range of choices for children; this is particularly the case in Madrid (p70), Barcelona (p109), Valencia (p237), Seville (p276), Córdoba (p299) and Granada (p305). Wherever you find yourself, your first stop should be the local tourist office where staff can point you in the direction of family-friendly activities.

FLAMENCO

RICHARD NEBESKY

Flamenco dancer, Madrid

Flamenco, Spain's soul-stirring gift to the world of music, provides the ever-present soundtrack to Spanish life. The passion of the genre is clear to anyone who has heard its melancholy strains in the background in a crowded Spanish bar or during an uplifting live performance. At the same time, flamenco can seem like an impenetrable world of knowledgeable yet taciturn initiates. Where these two worlds converge is in that rare yet famous, almost mystical flamenco moment known as *duende*, when a flamenco performer sends shivers down your spine, and you are oblivious to all else.

No one is quite sure where flamenco came from, although it probably owes its origins to a mosaic of ancient sources. Songs brought to Spain by the *gitanos* (Roma people) were almost certainly part of the mix, wedded to the music and verses of medieval Muslim Andalucía. Some historians argue that the Byzantine chant used in Visigothic churches prior to the Muslim arrival also played their part.

Wherever it came from, flamenco first took recognisable form in the late-18th and early 19th centuries among *gitanos* in the lower Guadalquivir Valley in western Andalucía. Suitably, for a place considered the cradle of the genre, the Seville–Jerez de la Frontera–Cádiz axis is still considered flamenco's heartland and it's here, purists believe, that you must go for the most authentic flamenco experience. Early flamenco was *cante jondo* (deep song), an anguished form of expression for a people on the margins of society. *Jondura* (depth) is still the essence of flamenco.

MODERN FLAMENCO LEGENDS

All flamenco performers aspire to the fame enjoyed by Manuel Torre (1878–1933); Torre's singing, legend has it, could drive people to rip their shirts open and upturn tables. One man who undoubtedly achieved this aim was El Camarón de la Isla (whose real name was José Monge Cruz) from San Fernando near Cádiz. El Camarón's incredible vocal and emotional range and his wayward lifestyle made him a legend well before his tragically early death in 1992 at the age of 42. As his great guitar accompanist Paco de Lucía observed, 'Camarón's cracked voice could evoke, on its own, the desperation of a people'.

Paco de Lucía, born in Algeciras in 1947, is the doyen of flamenco guitarists with a virtuosity few can match. He is also almost single-handedly responsible for transforming the guitar, formerly the junior partner of the flamenco trinity, into an instrument of solo expression far beyond traditional limits. Such is his skill that de Lucía can sound like two or three people playing together and, for many in the flamenco world, he is the personification of *duende*.

NEW FLAMENCO

Flamenco is enjoying something of a golden age, but part of its appeal lies in a new generation of artists broadening flamenco's horizons. In the 1970s, musicians began mixing flamenco with jazz, rock, blues, rap and other genres. At the forefront of the transformation was Enrique Morente (b 1942), referred to by one Madrid paper as 'the last bohemian', and a cult figure who enjoys rare popularity among both purists and the new generation of flamenco aficionados. While careful not to alienate flamenco purists,

FLAMENCO RESOURCES

- **Flama** (www.guiaflama.com) Good for upcoming live concerts.
- **Duende** (Jason Webster) The author's gripping search for the true flamenco spirit.
- **Camarón** (Director Jaime Chávarri; 2005) A terrific biopic of El Camarón de la Isla.
- **Bodas de Sangre** (1981) and **Flamenco** (1995) These two Carlos Saura films are flamenco classics; the former is a film version of Federico García Lorca's dramatic play of the same name.

MICHAEL TAYLOR

Bailaor (male dancer), Córdoba

SPAIN IN FOCUS

FLAMENCO

⬎ THE BEST

Dancer at flamenco festival

NEIL SETCHFIELD

FLAMENCO FESTIVALS

- **Bienal de Flamenco, Seville** (September; p49)
- **Festival de Jerez, Jerez de la Frontera** (February–March; p46)
- **Festival Internacional de la Guitarra, Córdoba** (June–July; p48)
- **Festival Flamenco, Madrid** (February; p70)
- **Suma Flamenca, Madrid** (May; p70)

Morente, through his numerous collaborations across genres, helped lay the foundations for Nuevo Flamenco (New Flamenco) and Fusion.

Other genres to have made their way into the repertoire of Nuevo Flamenco include rock (Kiko Veneno and Raimundo Amador), jazz and blues (Pata Negra), Latin and African rhythms (Ketama and Diego El Cigala), reggae, Asian and dance rhythms (Ojos de Brujo), and electronica (Chambao). When it comes to dance, Joaquín Cortés fuses flamenco with contemporary dance, ballet and jazz, to music at rock-concert amplification.

SEEING FLAMENCO

If you're eager to catch some live flamenco while in Spain, Seville (p279) has the widest number of regular, high-quality shows, followed by Jerez de la Frontera (p285), Granada (p307) and Madrid (p80).

Aside from widely advertised concerts held in large arenas, the best places for live performances are usually *peñas,* clubs where flamenco fans band together. The atmosphere in such places is authentic and at times very intimate and proof that the best flamenco feeds off an audience that knows their flamenco. Most Andalucian towns in particular have dozens of *peñas* and most tourist offices have a list.

The other option is to attend a performance at a *tablao,* which hosts regular shows put on for largely undiscriminating tourist audiences, usually with high prices and dinner included. The quality of the flamenco in *tablaos* can be top-notch, even if the atmosphere lacks the gritty authenticity of the *peñas.*

HISTORY

MICHAEL TAYLOR

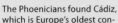

Procession of the Fiesta de Moros y Cristianos (p46)

Spanish history reads like a thriller. The story begins with the great empires of antiquity, moves on to one of the most enlightened civilisations ever to have ruled on European soil, before the rise of Christendom and its powerful kings and queens transformed Spain forever. Jump forward to the turbulent 20th century and you find a nation convulsed by a fratricidal war, whereafter the country disappeared into the long shadows cast by Francisco Franco for four decades. But there's a happy ending: Spain has emerged phoenix-like from dictatorship to become one of Europe's most dynamic and modern countries.

THE PHOENICIANS

To the Ancient Greeks and Romans, the dramatic limestone ridge at Gibraltar, together with Jebel Musa in Morocco, were the Pillars of Hercules and represented the limits of the known world. But the Phoenicians, who came before them, knew differently. From their

8th century BC	218 BC	4th to 7th centuries AD
The Phoenicians found Cádiz, which is Europe's oldest continuously inhabited city.	Roman legions arrive in Spain, initiating the 600-year Roman occupation of Iberia.	Germanic tribes (including the Visigoths) enter the Iberian Peninsula, ending the Pax Romana.

⬃ THE CELTIC NORTH

Around the same time as the Phoenicians brought iron technology to the south, the Celts (originally from Central Europe) brought it – and beer-making – to the north when they crossed the Pyrenees. In contrast to the dark-featured Iberians, the Celts were fair. Celts and Iberians who merged on the *meseta* (plateau; the high tableland of central Spain) are known as Celtiberians. Celts and Celtiberians typically lived in sizable hill-fort towns called *castros*.

base on what is now the southern coast of Lebanon, the seafaring Phoenicians were the first of the ancient civilisations to rule the Mediterranean. Not restricted by the narrow Straits of Gibraltar, they continued on along the Atlantic coast and, in the 8th century BC, established the port of Gadir, the site of modern Cádiz (p280) in southwestern Andalucía. In around 700 BC the colonists introduced iron-making technology, and the Phoenician-influenced culture that developed was very likely the fabled Tartessos, mythologised by later Greek, Roman and biblical writers as a place of unimaginable wealth. Sadly, no traces remain.

One of the Phoenician ports, Carthage (in modern-day Tunisia), grew to be a formidable Mediterranean power in its own right. The Carthaginians unwittingly gave their name to Cartagena (p255), where to this day the Carthaginians and Romans fight mock annual battles in the festival of Carthagineses y Romanos (p238).

GREEKS & ROMANS

In the 7th century BC, Greek traders arrived along the Mediterranean coast and brought with them several things now considered quintessentially Spanish – the olive tree, the grapevine and the donkey – along with writing, coins, the potter's wheel and poultry. But the Romans, who ruled Hispania (as Roman Iberia was known) for 600 years until the 5th century AD, would go on to leave a far more lasting impression. By AD 50, most of Hispania had adopted the Roman way of life. The major exceptions were the Basques who, though defeated, were never Romanised like the rest.

Rome gave the country a road system, aqueducts, temples, theatres, amphitheatres and bathhouses, but they began the process of deforestation as they culled the extensive forests that in their time covered half the *meseta*. Even more than these, their cultural impact was profound. They brought Christianity to Spain, planted olive trees on a massive scale, introduced olive oil production, may even have invented *jamón,* and the basis of most of the languages still spoken here – Castilian, Catalan, Galician and Portuguese – are versions of the vernacular Latin spoken by Roman legionaries and colonists, filtered through 2000 years of linguistic mutation. The Roman era also

711	722	10th century
Muslims invade Iberia from North Africa, overrunning all but Asturias within a few years.	The Christian victory at the Battle of Covadonga (Asturias) sparks the Reconquista (Reconquest) of Spain.	The Cordoban Caliphate reaches its zenith and the city is home to nearly half a million people.

saw the arrival of Jews in Spain who were to play a big part in Spanish life for over 1000 years.

ISLAMIC SPAIN

After the Romans came the Visigoths, but they were a mere historical interlude compared to the great Islamic dynasties that swept them away. In AD 711 Tariq ibn Ziyad, the Muslim governor of Tangier, landed at Gibraltar with around 10,000 men, mostly Berbers (indigenous North Africans). Within a few years the Muslims (often referred to as Moors) had conquered the whole Iberian Peninsula, except small areas in the Asturian mountains in the north. Their advance into Europe was only checked by the Franks at the Battle of Poitiers in 732.

The name given to Muslim territory on the peninsula was Al-Andalus. Political power and cultural developments centred initially on Córdoba (756–1031; p296), then Seville (c 1040–1248; p270) and lastly Granada (1248–1492; p300). It was during the 10th and early 11th centuries, under the independent Caliphate of Córdoba, that Al-Andalus reached the height of its power and lustre and became famous for enlightened scholarship (it was through Al-Andalus that much of the learning of ancient Greece was transmitted to Christian Europe) and religious tolerance. Al-Andalus also developed an extraordinary architectural legacy (see p334) and developed the Hispano-Roman agricultural base by improving irrigation and introducing new fruits and crops, many of which are still widely grown today. Even in language the Muslims left strong traces and Spanish still contains many words of Arabic origin.

➤**THE BEST**

PATRICK SYDER

Teatro Romano, Mérida

ROMAN RUINS

- **Itálica** (p280)
- **Mérida** (p152)
- **Tarragona** (p175)
- **Lugo** (p221)
- **Segovia** (p136)
- **Bolonia** (p288)

SPAIN IN FOCUS

HISTORY

THE CHRISTIAN RECONQUISTA

The Christian Reconquest of Iberia began in about 722 at Covadonga, Asturias, and ended with the fall of Granada in 1492. It was a stuttering affair, conducted by Christian kingdoms that were as often at war with each other as with the Muslims. An essential ingredient in the Reconquista was the cult of Santiago (St James), one of the 12 apostles. In 813, the saint's supposed tomb was discovered in Galicia. The city of Santiago de

1236	1478	1492 (January)
Córdoba falls to Fernando III of Castilla, with Seville following 12 years later.	Isabel and Fernando, the Reyes Católicos (Catholic Monarchs), establish the Spanish Inquisition.	After a long siege, Isabel and Fernando capture Granada and the Reconquista is complete.

SPAIN IN FOCUS

HISTORY

OLIVER STREWE

Tomb of Columbus, Seville Cathedral (p274)

Compostela (p216) grew here, to become the third-most popular medieval Christian pilgrimage goal after Rome and Jerusalem. Santiago became the inspiration and special protector of soldiers in the Reconquista, earning the sobriquet Matamoros (Moor-slayer). Today he is the patron saint of Spain.

By 757, Christians occupied nearly a quarter of the Iberian Peninsula, although progress thereafter was slow. The year 1212, when the combined Christian armies routed a large Muslim force at Las Navas de Tolosa in Andalucía, marked the beginning of the end for Islamic Al-Andalus. The wedding of Isabel (Castilla) and Fernando (Aragón) united two of the most powerful Christian kingdoms, enabling the armies of the Reconquista to make a final push. On 2 January 1492, Isabel and Fernando entered Granada. The surrender terms were fairly generous to Boabdil, the last emir, who got the Alpujarras valleys south of Granada and 30,000 gold coins. The remaining Muslims were promised respect for their religion, culture and property, but this promise was quickly discarded.

THE GOLDEN AGE OF EMPIRE

Isabel and Fernando were never going to be content with Spain alone. In April 1492, the Catholic Monarchs (*Los Reyes Católicos*) granted the Genoese sailor Christopher Columbus (Cristóbal Colón to Spaniards) funds for his long-desired voyage across

1492 (April)	1492 (October)	1556–98
Isabel and Fernando expel around 200,000 Jews who have refused Christian baptism.	Christopher Columbus, funded by Isabel and Fernando, lands in the Bahamas.	The reign of Felipe II marks the zenith of Spanish power.

⚓ THE SPANISH INQUISITION

An ecclesiastical tribunal set up by Fernando and Isabel in 1478, the Spanish Inquisition in Al-Andalus focused first on *conversos* (Jews converted to Christianity), accusing many of continuing to practise Judaism in secret. In April 1492, Isabel and Fernando expelled all Jews who refused Christian baptism. Up to 100,000 converted, but some 200,000 (the first Sephardic Jews) fled into exile. The Inquisitors also carried out forced mass baptisms of Muslims, burnt Islamic books and banned the Arabic language. In 1500, Muslims were ordered to convert to Christianity or leave. Those who converted *(moriscos)* were later expelled between 1609 and 1614.

the Atlantic in search of a new trade route to the Orient. Columbus set off from the Andalucian port of Palos de la Frontera on 3 August 1492, with three small ships and 120 men. After a near mutiny as the crew despaired of sighting land, they finally arrived on the island of Guanahaní, in the Bahamas, and went on to find Cuba and Hispaniola. Columbus returned to a hero's reception from the Catholic Monarchs in Barcelona, eight months after his departure.

Brilliant but ruthless conquistadors followed Columbus' trail, seizing vast tracts of the American mainland for Spain. By 1600, Spain controlled Florida, all the biggest Caribbean islands, nearly all of present-day Mexico and Central America, and a large strip of South America. The new colonies sent huge cargoes of silver, gold and other riches back to Spain. Seville enjoyed a monopoly on this trade and grew into one of Europe's richest cities.

TWO SPAINS

Spain was united for the first time in almost eight centuries after Fernando annexed Navarra in 1512, and in 1519 Carlos I (Fernando's grandson) succeeded to the Habsburg lands in Austria and was elected Holy Roman Emperor (as Charles V). He ruled all of Spain, the Low Countries, Austria, several Italian states, parts of France and Germany, and the expanding Spanish colonies in the Americas. But the storm clouds were brewing. Colonial riches lined the pockets of a series of backward-looking monarchs, a wealthy, highly conservative Church, and idle nobility. Although some of this wealth was used to foster a golden age of art, little was done to improve the lot of ordinary Spaniards and food shortages were rife. At the same time, a succession of monarchs squandered Spain's colonial wealth in ultimately unsuccessful wars down through the centuries.

Early 1600s	1609–14	1808–13
Spain enjoys a cultural golden age with Cervantes and Velázquez at the forefront.	The *moriscos* (converted Muslims) are expelled from Spain in a final purge of non-Christians.	Carlos IV abdicates and French occupation begins, with Napoleon's brother, Joseph, on the throne.

> ## ↘ **WHY MADRID?**
>
> When Felipe II chose Madrid as Spain's capital in 1561, it was hardly the most obvious choice. Madrid (population 30,000) was much smaller and less powerful than Toledo and Seville (each with more than 80,000 people) or Valladolid, the capital of choice for Isabel and Fernando. Unlike other cities, however, Madrid was described by one king as 'very noble and very loyal': Felipe II chose the path of least resistance. Another reason was the location: 'a city fulfilling the function of a heart located in the middle of the body,' as Felipe II was heard to say.

Spain's overseas possessions were ebbing away, but problems at home were even more pressing. In 1812, a national Cortes (parliament) meeting at Cádiz drew up a new liberal constitution for Spain, prompting a backlash from conservatives (the Church, the nobility and others who preferred the earlier status quo) and liberals (who wanted vaguely democratic reforms). Over the next century, Spain alternated between federal republic and monarchy, a liberal-conservative schism that saw the country lurch from one crisis to the next. By the 1930s, Spain was teetering on the brink of war.

THE SPANISH CIVIL WAR

On 17 July 1936, the Spanish army garrison in Melilla, North Africa, rose up against the left-wing government, followed the next day by garrisons on the mainland. The leaders of the plot were five generals, among them Francisco Franco, who on 19 July flew from the Canary Islands to Morocco to take charge of his legionnaires. The civil war had begun.

Wherever the blame lies, the civil war split communities, families and friends, killed an estimated 350,000 Spaniards (some writers put the number as high as 500,000), and caused untold damage and long-lasting misery. Both sides (Franco's Nationalists and the left-wing Republicans) committed atrocious massacres and reprisals, and employed death squads to eliminate opponents. On 26 April 1937, German planes bombed the Basque town of Guernica (called Gernika in Basque), causing terrible casualties. The USSR withdrew from the war in September 1938, and in January 1939 the Nationalists took Barcelona unopposed. The Republican government and hundreds of thousands of supporters fled to France and, on 28 March 1939, Franco's forces entered Madrid.

1872–74	1898	1923–30
The Second Carlist War begins and the First Republic, a federal union of 17 states, collapses.	Spain loses Cuba, Puerto Rico, Guam and the Philippines, its last remaining colonies.	General Miguel Primo de Rivera launches a coup and establishes himself as dictator.

FRANCO'S SPAIN

Francisco Franco would go on to rule Spain with an iron fist for almost four decades until his death in 1975. An estimated 100,000 people were killed or died in prison after the war. The hundreds of thousands imprisoned included many intellectuals and teachers; others fled abroad, depriving Spain of a generation of scientists, artists, writers, educators and more. The army provided many government ministers and enjoyed a most generous budget. Catholic supremacy was fully restored, with secondary schools entrusted to the Jesuits, divorce made illegal and church weddings compulsory.

During WWII Franco flirted with Hitler (although Spain watched the war from the sidelines), but Spain was desperately poor to the extent that the 1940s are known as *los años de hambre* (years of hunger). Despite small-scale rebel activity, ongoing repression and international isolation (Spain was not admitted to the UN until 1955), an economic boom began

MARY EVANS PICTURE LIBRARY/PHOTOLIBRARY

Spanish Civil War poster

SPAIN IN FOCUS

HISTORY

⬎ THE INTERNATIONAL BRIGADES

The International Brigades never numbered more than 20,000 and couldn't turn the tide against the better armed and organised Nationalist forces. Nazi Germany and Fascist Italy supported the Nationalists with planes, weapons and men (75,000 from Italy and 17,000 from Germany), turning the war into a testing ground for WWII. The Republicans had some Soviet planes, tanks, artillery and advisers, but the rest of the international community refused to become involved (although some 25,000 French fought on the Republican side).

1936	1939	1959
The Spanish Civil War begins when General Francisco Franco's rebels rise up against the elected government.	Franco enters Madrid after 350,000 people die during the Civil War; his dictatorship begins.	ETA is founded with the aim of gaining Basque independence.

SPAIN IN FOCUS

HISTORY

Artist's impression of a street battle in Madrid, 1936

MARY EVANS PICTURE LIBRARY/PHOTOLIBRARY

in 1959 and would last through much of the 1960s. The recovery was funded in part by US aid, and remittances from more than a million Spaniards working abroad, but above all by tourism, which was developed initially along Andalucía's Costa del Sol and Catalonia's Costa Brava. By 1965, the number of tourists arriving in Spain was 14 million a year.

But with the jails still full of political prisoners and Spain's restive regions straining under Franco's brutal policies, labour unrest grew and discontent began to rumble in the universities and even in the army and Church. The Basque-nationalist terrorist group Euskadi Ta Askatasuna (ETA; Basque Homeland and Freedom) also appeared in 1959. In the midst of it all, Franco chose as his successor Prince Juan Carlos, the Spanish-educated grandson of Alfonso XIII, the Bourbon king deposed by Republicans in 1931. In 1969, Juan Carlos swore loyalty to Franco and the Movimiento Nacional, Spain's fascist and only legal political party. Franco died on 20 November 1975.

SPAIN'S DEMOCRATIC TRANSITION

Juan Carlos I, aged 37, took the throne two days after Franco died. The new king's links with the dictator inspired little confidence in a Spain now clamouring for democracy, but Juan Carlos had kept his cards close to his chest and can take most

1960s	1975	1977
An economic boom known as the Years of Development brings much-needed prosperity.	Franco dies after ruling Spain for 37 years. King Juan Carlos I succeeds him.	Spaniards vote in the first free elections since the 1930s, cementing Spain's return to democracy.

of the credit for the successful transition to democracy that followed. He appointed Adolfo Suárez, a 43-year-old former Franco apparatchik with film-star looks. To general surprise, Suárez got the Francoist-filled Cortes to approve a new, two-chamber parliamentary system, and in early 1977 political parties, trade unions and strikes were all legalised and the Movimiento Nacional was abolished. After elections in 1977, a centrist government led by Suárez granted a general amnesty for acts committed in the Civil War and under the Franco dictatorship. In 1978, the Cortes passed a new constitution making Spain a parliamentary monarchy with no official religion and granting a large measure of devolution to Spain's regions.

At a social level, Spaniards embraced democracy with all the zeal of an ex-convent schoolgirl. Contraceptives, homosexuality and divorce were legalised, and the Madrid party and arts scene known as *la movida* formed the epicentre of a newly unleashed hedonism that still looms large in Spanish life. Despite challenges such as the brutal campaign by ETA, which killed hundreds in the 1980s, and an unsuccessful coup attempt by renegade Civil Guards in 1981, Spain's democratic, semi-federal constitution and multi-party system have proved at once robust and durable.

❯ ETA – A SNAPSHOT

The first underground cells of ETA appeared in 1952 at the height of Franco's repression. ETA's founders called for independence, but their primary goal was the promotion of the outlawed Basque language, Euskera. In 1967, the old guard of leaders was ousted during an internal crisis over strategy and a younger, more militant leadership emerged. On 7 June 1968, ETA killed a Spanish civil guardsman near San Sebastián. According to the Spanish government, more than 800 people have been killed by ETA terrorism in the decades since, two-thirds of these in the Basque Country.

SPAIN GROWS UP

The 1980s in particular saw Spain pass a succession of milestones along the road to becoming a mature European democracy. That they took these steps so quickly and so successfully after four decades of fascism is one of modern Europe's most remarkable stories.

In 1982, the left-of-centre Partido Socialista Obrero Español (PSOE; Spanish Socialist Worker Party) was elected to power with a big majority, led by a charismatic young lawyer from Seville, Felipe González. During its 14 years in power, the PSOE brought Spain into mainstream Europe, joining the European Community (now the EU) in 1986. They

1981	1982–96	1986
On 23 February, a group of soldiers attempts a military coup by occupying the parliament building.	Spain is governed by the centre-left Partido Socialista Obrero Español (PSOE) led by Felipe González.	Spain joins the European Community (now the EU), having joined NATO in 1982.

↘ THE AZNAR YEARS

Upon coming to power in 1996, José María Aznar promised to make politics dull, and he did, but he also presided over eight years of solid economic progress. Spain's economy grew annually by an average of 3.4%, and unemployment fell from 23% (1996) to 8% (2006). Not surprisingly, the PP won the 2000 election as well, with an absolute parliamentary majority. Aznar's popularity began to wane thanks to his strong support for the US-led invasion of Iraq in 2003 (which was deeply unpopular in Spain) and his decision to send Spanish troops to the conflict.

also oversaw the rise of the Spanish middle class, established a national health system and improved public education, and Spain's women streamed into higher education and jobs, although unemployment was the highest in Europe. But the PSOE finally became mired in scandal and, in the 1996 elections, the centre-right Partido Popular (PP; People's Party), led by José María Aznar, swept the PSOE from power.

ZAPATERO'S SPAIN

As the 2004 general election approached, Aznar handed the PP reins to Mariano Rajoy who came up against the PSOE's José Luis Rodríguez Zapatero, who had successfully managed to distance himself from his party's less than pristine past. The PP looked headed for victory, but early on Thursday 11 March 2004, three days before the general election, bombs exploded on four crowded commuter trains in and near Madrid, killing 191 people and injuring 1800. A quarter of Spain's population, eleven million people, poured onto Spain's streets in demonstrations of peace and solidarity the following day. As the evidence mounted that the bombing was the work of Islamic extremists, the government continued to maintain that ETA was responsible, prompting accusations that the PP was attempting to mislead the public by blaming the bombings on ETA and thereby escape a backlash for its support for the war in Iraq. Three days after the bombing, the PSOE won the election. Subsequent court cases have established that the bombings were carried out by a local group of North Africans settled in Spain.

Spain's new PSOE government hit the ground running. The Zapatero government quickly pulled Spanish troops out of Iraq. It also legalised gay marriages, made divorce easier, took religion out of the compulsory school curriculum, gave dissatisfied Catalonia an expanded autonomy charter, and declared an amnesty for illegal immigrants. In March 2006, ETA, which wants an independent state covering the

1996	2004 (11 March)	2004 (14 March)
The centre-right Partido Popular (PP), led by José María Aznar, wins national elections.	Islamic terrorists bomb four commuter trains in Madrid, killing 191 people.	PSOE, led by José Luis Rodríguez Zapatero, wins a surprise election victory.

Spanish and French Basque Country and Navarra, declared a 'permanent cease-fire', but resumed violence with a bomb that killed two people at Madrid airport nine months later. Zapatero then called off any moves towards dialogue with the ETA. A year later, parliament also passed the 'Historical Memory Law', designed to officially honour the Republican victims of the Civil War and the Franco dictatorship.

Although the government's social and regional reforms prompted a fierce (though peaceful) response from the PP and Catholic Church, the PSOE won national elections in 2008. Soon after the victory, however, the world economic crisis swept through Spain. Zapatero's second term of office looked likely to be a lot harder going than the first.

⬊ TALKING POINTS IN MODERN SPAIN

- **Economic crisis** – Unemployment has soared to almost 20% and all indicators suggest the slump will last longer than elsewhere in Europe.
- **Immigration** – Spain absorbed as many immigrants in 10 years (1996–2006) as France did in the previous 40.
- **ETA** – Although seriously weakened, ETA just won't go away.
- **The Franco years** – The PSOE's Historical Memory Law has controversially overturned the 1970s *pacto de olvido* (pact of forgetting).

2004–06	2006	2008
Zapatero introduces a raft of social reforms and withdraws Spanish troops from Iraq.	ETA declares a permanent ceasefire in March, which lasts until December.	Prime Minister Zapatero wins the general election with an increased majority.

MASTER PAINTERS

Las Meninas by Velázquez, Museo del Prado (p63), Madrid

PETER HORREE/ALAMY

Spain's artistic tradition is arguably Europe's most distinguished, and its big names read like a roll-call of Western art history's elite. Although many Spanish artists deserve the term of 'master', we have restricted ourselves to Spain's Big Four. The story begins with Diego Rodríguez de Silva Velázquez and Francisco José de Goya y Lucientes, and 'ends' with two of the towering artistic figures of the 20th century: Pablo Picasso and Salvador Dalí.

VELÁZQUEZ

No painter has come to symbolise Spain's golden age of the arts in the 17th century quite like Diego Rodríguez de Silva Velázquez (1599–1660). Born in Seville, Velázquez moved to Madrid as court painter and composed scenes (landscapes, royal portraits, religious subjects, snapshots of everyday life) that owe their vitality not only to his photographic eye for light and contrast but also to a compulsive interest in the humanity of his subjects so that they seem to breathe on the canvas. His masterpieces include *Las Meninas* (Maids of Honour) and *La Rendición de Breda* (The Surrender of Breda), both on view in the Museo del Prado (p63). The former painting shows just how enamoured Velázquez was with royal life: he so much wanted to be made a Knight of Santiago that in *Las Meninas* he cheekily portrayed himself with the cross of Santiago on his vest, long before his wish was granted.

GOYA

Born into a modest provincial family in the village of Fuentetodos in Aragón, Francisco José de Goya y Lucientes (1746–1828) began designing for Madrid's Real Fábrica de Tapices (Royal Tapestry Workshop) in Madrid in 1776, but illness in 1792 left him deaf. Many critics speculate that his condition was largely responsible for his wild, often merciless style that would become increasingly unshackled from convention. By 1799, Goya was appointed Carlos IV's court painter.

In the last years of the 18th century he painted enigmatic masterpieces such as *La Maja Vestida* (The Young Lady Dressed) and *La Maja Desnuda* (The Young Lady Undressed). The Inquisition was not amused, and covered up the paintings. Nowadays all is bared in Museo del Prado (p63) alongside many of his other works. At about the same time as his enigmatic *Majas,* the prolific Goya executed the playful frescoes in Madrid's Ermita de San Antonio de la Florida (p67) where the painter is buried. He also produced *Los Caprichos* (The Caprices), a biting series of 80 etchings lambasting

↘ GOYA'S BLACK PAINTINGS

Goya saved his most confronting paintings to the end. After he retired to the Quinta del Sordo (Deaf Man's House) in Madrid, he created his nightmarish *Pinturas Negras* (Black Paintings), which now hang in the Museo del Prado (p63). The *Saturno Devorando a Su Hijo (Saturn Devouring His Son)* captures the essence of Goya's genius and *La Romería de San Isidro* and *El Akelarre (El gran cabrón)* are profoundly unsettling. The former evokes a writhing mass of tortured humanity, while the latter are dominated by the compelling individual faces of the condemned souls of Goya's creation.

SPAIN IN FOCUS

MASTER PAINTERS

KRZYSZTOF DYDYNSKI

La Maja Desnuda by Goya, Museo del Prado (p63), Madrid

the follies of court life and ignorant clergy. The arrival of the French and war in 1808 had a profound impact on Goya. Unforgiving portrayals of the brutality of war are *El Dos de Mayo* (The Second of May) and, more dramatically, *El Tres de Mayo* (The Third of May).

Goya's masterpieces are legacy enough, but he also marked a transition from art being made in the service of the State or Church to art as a pure expression of its creator's feeling and whim.

PABLO PICASSO

Considered by many to be the finest and most influential artist of the 20th century, Pablo Ruiz Picasso (1881–1973) stormed onto the Spanish artistic scene like a thunderclap. Born in Málaga in Andalucía, he moved with his family when still a child to Barcelona. Although he later studied in Madrid's staid Real Academia de Bellas Artes de San Fernando (p67), it was amid the avant-garde freedom of Barcelona's Modernisme (see the boxed text, p108) that Picasso the artist was formed. He later spent much of his adult life in Paris.

Although best known for his weird and wonderful cubist paintings, Picasso's oeuvre spans an extraordinary breadth of styles as his work underwent repeated revolutions, passing from one creative phase to another. The best place to get an overview is Málaga's Museo Picasso (p289).

His early style began, rather gloomily, with what is known as his Blue Period, then moved on through the brighter Pink Period; Barcelona's Museu Picasso (p104) offers an excellent collection of Picasso's early, pre-cubist years. In 1907, Picasso painted *Les Demoiselles d'Avignon,* which was strongly influenced by the stylised masks and wood carvings of Africa, and from there it was a small step to the cubist style (which involved taking objects apart and analysing their shapes), which he pioneered. By the

LEFT: WITOLD SKRYPCZAK; RIGHT: KRZYSZTOF DYDYNSKI

Left: Teatre-Museu Dalí (p172), Figueres; Right: Museu Picasso (p104), Barcelona

↘ PICASSO'S GUERNICA

In the first year of the Civil War, Picasso was commissioned by the Republican government of Madrid to do the painting for the Paris Exposition Universelle in 1937. As news filtered out about the bombing of Gernika (Guernica) on 26 April 1937 in the Basque Country by Hitler's Legión Condor, at the request of Franco (almost 2000 people died in the attack), Picasso committed his anger to canvas; it was a poignant memorial to the first use of airborne military hardware to devastating effect. You can see *Guernica* in Madrid's Centro de Arte Reina Sofía (p63).

mid-1920s he was even dabbling in surrealism. His most famous painting is *Guernica* (see the boxed text, above), and Picasso consistently cranked out paintings, sculptures, ceramics and etchings until the day he died.

SALVADOR DALÍ

Vying with Pablo Picasso for the title of Spain's most original artist is Salvador Dalí. He did spend time in Madrid, where he decided that the eminent professors of Madrid's Real Academia de Bellas Artes de San Fernando were not fit to judge him and thereafter spent four years romping through the city with poet Federico García Lorca and future film director Luis Buñuel. All that remains in the capital are 20 of his hallucinatory works in the Centro de Arte Reina Sofía (p63).

But Dalí belongs above all to Catalonia. He was born in Figueres, home now to the Teatre-Museu Dalí (p171), which is one of Spain's most memorable museums thanks to its elevation of art to a form of theatre, which seems such an apt legacy for such a charismatic figure. He spent much of his adult life in Port Lligat (p171), near Cadaques, and left his mark on the Castell de Púbol (p166), near Girona; this astonishing former mansion is a suitably otherworldly monument to Dalí's wife, Gala.

Preoccupied with Picasso's fame, Dalí built himself a reputation as an outrageous showman and shameless self-promoter. Dalí was a larger-than-life figure, but he was also unrelentingly brilliant. He started off by dabbling in cubism, but became more readily identified with the surrealists. His 'hand-painted dream photographs', as he called them, are virtuoso executions brimming with fine detail and nightmare images dragged up from a feverish and Freud-fed imagination. So strong and confronting are his images that his work is not to everyone's taste. But no one can deny that he was a genius.

SPANISH ARCHITECTURE

Mudéjar carvings, Seville

DAVID TOMLINSON

Spain's architecture tells the story of the country's past. It is an epic tale that recalls the glories of Al-Andalus and of the sublime Romanesque, Gothic, Renaissance and baroque of Christian Spain, before detouring into the Modernisme of Antoni Gaudí and his Catalan cohorts. But Spanish architecture's secret has always been one of constant revolution, and therein lies the story of the country's creative future.

ISLAMIC SPAIN

Islamic Al-Andalus was, for much of its nearly 800-year history, one of the most civilised places on earth and its architects were worthy contributors to this ideal. In 756, a mere 45 years after Islamic armies first swept across the Strait of Gibraltar and at a time when Islamic rulers controlled three-quarters of Spain, Abd ar-Rahman I founded Córdoba's Mezquita (p297). One of the largest mosques in the world, it was a powerful statement that Islam was in Spain to stay. More than Spain's oldest surviving Islamic building of significance, the Mezquita was (and is) the epitome of Islamic architecture's grace and pleasing unity of form. This sense of harmony – perhaps the Mezquita's most enduring miracle – is all the more remarkable given the significant alterations carried out over the centuries.

Hundreds of years later, with Islamic sovereignty restricted to Granada's Nasrid emirate, the Alhambra (p303) came to symbolise the last-days decadence of Islam's ruler.

↘ MUDÉJAR ARCHITECTURE

After the Christian Reconquista, the term Mudéjar (from Arabic *mudayan*, meaning domesticated), which was given to Muslims who stayed on in areas conquered by the Christians, came to stick as an architectural label. Hallmarks of Mudéjar style include geometric decorative designs, often embellished with tiles, and elaborately carved timber ceilings. *Artesonado* is the word used to describe ceilings with interlaced beams leaving regular spaces for decorative insertions. Another unmistakable Mudéjar feature is the preponderance of brick: castles, churches and mansions all over the country were built of this material. Teruel (p185) has an especially rich concentration of Mudéjar architecture.

The only surviving large medieval Islamic palace complex in the world, the Alhambra is at once a palace city and a fortress, with 2km of walls and 23 towers. Within the Alhambra's walls were seven separate palaces, along with mosques, garrisons, houses, offices, baths, a summer residence (the Generalife) and exquisite gardens, but scale is only one element of the Alhambra's charm: the Nasrid architects also refined existing decorative techniques to new peaks of delicacy, elegance and harmony.

Between these two landmarks lie centuries of compelling history, but together the Mezquita and Alhambra give expression to the enduring characteristics of Al-Andalus: enlightened Islam, the opulence of Islamic rule, the imperative to defend against enemies at the gates, and the importance of gardens as a manifestation of earthly paradise. Other significant places where these elements remain include the Alcázar (p271) and Giralda (p274) in Seville; the Aljafería (p182) in Zaragoza; the Alcázar (p283) in Jerez de la Frontera; and the Alcazaba (p291) and Castillo de Gibralfaro (p291) in Málaga.

NEIL SETCHFIELD

Palau Güell (p106), Barcelona

ROMANESQUE & GOTHIC

As the Reconquista gathered momentum, Spanish architects in Christian-controlled territories turned not to the Middle East but to Europe for inspiration. From the 11th century, churches and monasteries in the Romanesque style mushroomed in the north. Many of the finest existing examples are in Catalonia, especially in

Girona (p167), the monastery in El Port de la Selva (p170) and in the Pyrenean Vall de Boí (p174).

A more elaborate Gothic style, characterised by the use of flying buttresses and other technical innovations, replaced the Romanesque; three of Spain's most important Gothic cathedrals – Burgos (p141), León (p139) and Toledo (p142) – were all begun in the 13th century. Although the first two owe much to French models, Spanish architects soon added the huge decorative altarpieces towering over the high altar, and star-vaulting, a method of weight distribution in the roof in which ribbed vaults project outwards from a series of centre points. After an interlude known as Isabelline style, pure Gothic returned in the 16th century, perhaps best exemplified by Salamanca's Catedral Nueva (p134) and Segovia's cathedral (p137).

RENAISSANCE

The Renaissance in architecture was an Italian-originated return to classical ideals of harmony and proportion, dominated by columns and shapes such as the square, circle and triangle. Many Renaissance buildings feature elegant interior courtyards lined by two tiers of wide, rounded arcades. Whereas the Gothic period left its most striking mark upon public Christian architecture, the Renaissance period was an era in which the gentry built themselves gorgeous urban palaces with delightful patios surrounded by harmonious arched galleries. To visit Salamanca (p134) is to receive a concentrated dose of the most splendid work of plateresque (an early form of Renaissance) style. The university facade (p134), especially, is a virtuoso piece, featuring busts, medallions and a complex floral design. Another fine example of the plateresque is the Capilla de Reyes Nuevos in Toledo's Catedral (p142).

Later, more purist Renaissance styles are on show in the Palacio de Carlos V in Granada's Alhambra (p303) and across the centre of Baeza (p309), also in Andalucía.

MODERNISTA MADNESS

Catalonia, at the end of the 19th century, was the powerhouse of the country. Into this optimistic time stepped a group of architects known as the Modernistas. Leading the way was Antoni Gaudí (1852–1926), who sprinkled Barcelona with exotic creations such

---

⬐ BAROQUE BAUBLES

The heady frills of baroque are a Spanish speciality, although Cádiz's cathedral (p280) is one of only a few almost-complete baroque buildings. The leading exponents of this often overblown style were the Churriguera brothers; Alberto Churriguera designed Salamanca's Plaza Mayor (p134) and had a hand in the city's cathedral. Baroque reached new heights of opulence with the Sagrario in Granada's Monasterio de La Cartuja (p305) and the Transparente in Toledo's cathedral (p142). Seville is jammed with gems, while the facade superimposed over the Romanesque original in the cathedral of Santiago de Compostela (p217) and the cathedral in Murcia (p253) are notable.

as his immense, and still unfinished, La Sagrada Família (p105), Casa Batlló (p105) and La Pedrera (p105).

Gaudí was by no means the only Catalan Modernista master to leave his mark on Barcelona. Lluís Domènech i Montaner (1850–1923), for example, was behind the stunning Palau de la Música Catalana (p104) and the Hospital de la Santa Creu i de Sant Pau (p107). For more Modernista masterpieces, see the boxed text, p106. For historical context on Modernisme in Barcelona, see the boxed, p108.

CONTEMPORARY CREATIONS

International experts are buzzing with the energy and creativity surrounding Spanish architecture. At one level, Spanish architects such as Santiago Calatrava (who transformed Valencia and built the Olympic stadium in Athens) are taking the world by storm. At the same time, architects from all over the world are clamouring for Spanish contracts – in part because the projects for urban renewal currently underway in Spain are some of the most innovative in Europe, and municipal governments are funding this extraordinary explosion of architectural ambition. There are hundreds of examples springing up all over Spain, but for our pick of the highlights, see the boxed text, above.

One to watch for the future is Sir Norman Foster's new-look Camp Nou stadium (p107), the home ground of FC Barcelona. The overhaul will create a kind of glow-in-the-dark sponge-cake affair and is planned for completion in 2012.

➤ **THE BEST**

KRZYSZTOF DYDYNSKI

Torre Agbar (p107), Barcelona

MODERN TEMPLES TO SPANISH ARCHITECTURE

- **Ciudad de las Artes y las Ciencias, Valencia** (p234)
- **Museo Guggenheim, Bilbao** (p203)
- **Bodegas Marqués de Riscal, La Rioja** (p211)
- **Torre Agbar, Barcelona** (p107)
- **Barajas Airport Terminal 4, Madrid** (p83)
- **Hotel Puerta América, Madrid** (p73)

SPANISH WINE

DIANA MAYFIELD

Sherry barrels, Jerez de la Frontera (p283)

Despite Spain having the largest area of wine cultivation in the world (1.2 million hectares and growing), it's only recently that the rest of the world has given Spanish wines the recognition that Spaniards feel they deserve. From the distinguished reds of La Rioja to the fortified wines and sherries of the south, Spain's wine is one of the most accessible of all Spanish pleasures. All of Spain's autonomous communities, with the small exceptions of Asturias and Cantabria, are home to recognised wine-growing areas.

THE MARKS OF QUALITY

Spanish wine is subject to a complicated system of wine classification with a range of designations marked on the bottle. Although there are lesser varieties, if a recognised wine-making area meets certain strict standards for a given period and covering all aspects of planting, cultivating and ageing, it receives Denominación de Origen (DO; Denomination of Origin) status; there are 65 such regions in Spain. An outstanding wine region gets the Denominación de Origen Calificada (DOC); some in the industry argue that the classification should apply only to specific wines, rather than every wine from within a region. At present, the only DOC wines come from La Rioja (p210) in northern Spain and the small Priorat area in Catalonia.

Other important indications of quality depend on the length of time a wine has been aged, especially if in oak barrels. The best wines are often, therefore, marked with the

SPAIN IN FOCUS

designation 'crianza' (aged for one year in oak barrels), 'reserva' (two years ageing, at least one of which is in oak barrels) and 'gran reserva' (two years in oak and three in the bottle).

For an overview of Spanish wines, check out www.winesfromspain.com.

A REGIONAL SNAPSHOT

Probably the most common premium red table wine you'll encounter will be from La Rioja, in the north. The principal grape of La Rioja is Tempranillo, widely believed to be a mutant form of Pinot Noir. Not far behind are the wine-producing regions of Ribera del Duero (Castilla y León, in Central Spain), Navarra and Aragón.

For white wines, the Ribeiro wines of Galicia are well regarded, including one of Spain's most charming whites: Albariño. This crisp, dry and refreshing drop is an unusual wine as it's designated by grape rather than region. The Penedès area in Catalonia produces whites and sparkling wine such as cava, the traditional champagne-like toasting drink of choice for Spaniards at Christmas.

◥ THE BEST

Local Spanish wines

PCL/ALAMY

PLACES TO LEARN ABOUT SPANISH WINES

- **Dinastía Vivanco, Briones** (p210)
- **Laguardia, La Rioja** (p210)
- **Museo del Vino, Olite, Navarra** (p211)
- **Sherry Bodegas, Jerez de la Frontera** (p283)

SPANISH WINE

SHERRY & MANZANILLA

Sherry, the unique wine of Andalucía (especially around Jerez de la Frontera and El Puerto de Santa María), is Spain's national dram and is found in every bar and restaurant in the land. Dry sherry, called fino, begins as a fairly ordinary white wine of the Palomino grape, but it's 'fortified' with grape brandy. This stops fermentation and gives the wine taste and smell constituents that enable it to age into something sublime. It's taken as an aperitivo (aperitif) or as a table wine with seafood. Manzanilla is grown only in Sanlúcar de Barrameda (p285) near the coast in southwestern Andalucía. When ordering it, be sure to say 'vino de Manzanilla', since manzanilla alone means chamomile tea.

SUSTAINABLE TRAVEL

DAMIEN SIMONIS

Parque Nacional D'Aigüestortes i Estany de Sant Maurici (p173)

Spain is an easy country to explore in a manner that minimises your impact upon the environment without compromising comfort. That doesn't mean the country is overflowing with ecofriendly resorts and enlightened environmental policies – it isn't. But Spain's outstanding public transport, vast wilderness areas and national parks, and its ample opportunities to lose yourself in local villages (a short-term taste of slow travel) make sustainable travel a viable and thoroughly enjoyable option.

WILDERNESS AREAS & NATIONAL PARKS

Spain has a poor environmental record, and the overdevelopment of the Spanish coast is one of Europe's most pressing environmental issues. But one area where it excels is in setting aside wilderness areas: about 40,000 sq km, or almost 8% of the entire country, is under some kind of official protection. The undoubted star is Andalucía, which has more than 90 protected areas covering some 17,000 sq km (almost 20% of Andalucía).

Although there are numerous designations for protected areas, two main types predominate. The most common are *parques naturales* (natural parks), where public access varies from unlimited to just a few walking trails. More strict in their levels of protection, Spain's 14 *parques nacionales* (national parks) are areas of exceptional importance for their fauna, flora, geomorphology or landscape, and are the country's most strictly controlled protected areas.

For official information and some pictures of national parks, visit the website of Spain's environment ministry at www.marm.es (click on 'Red de Parques Nacionales').

SLOW TRAVEL

The concept of slow travel may seem a misnomer when you've only two weeks in Spain, but slow travel is about far more than just how you get from A to B. It's about lingering in places after other travellers have moved on, slowing down to the pace of village or rural life, and leaving with more than a fleeting understanding of the places you've visited. The philosophy of slow travel may make for environmentally sustainable trips, but above all it's a re-imagining of your journey, a recognition that the depth to which you explore and engage with the places you visit is ultimately more important than how many places you can cover in a short period of time. Fast travel ticks the boxes. Slow travel produces memories that last a lifetime.

❯**THE BEST**

DAVID TOMLINSON

Parque Nacional de Ordesa y Monte Perdido (p174)

NATIONAL PARKS

- **Parque Nacional Sierra Nevada, Andalucía** (p308)
- **Parc Nacional D'Aigüestortes i Estany de Sant Maurici, Catalonia** (p173)
- **Parque Nacional de Ordesa y Monte Perdido, Aragón** (p174)
- **Parque Nacional de los Picos de Europa, Cantabria and Asturias** (p215)
- **Parque Nacional de Doñana, Andalucía** (p308)

The quiet appeal of Spain's villages is not the only consideration. Every euro you spend in a village supports the local economy and slows the inexorable migration of Spaniards towards the cities. The process of urbanisation has placed countless (some estimates suggest as many as 2000) villages under threat. In Castilla y León, for example, award-winning documentary film-maker Mercedes Alvarez is one of just 43 inhabitants in the village of Aldealsenor and, in an interview with *El País* newspaper in 2005, warned of 'the dying without sound of a culture with over a thousand years of history'.

THE SPANISH KITCHEN

GREG ELMS

Delicatessen, Mercado Central (p236), Valencia City

Spanish cuisine is all the rage around the world and no wonder. Uniquely Spanish ways of eating (such as tapas), the enduring appeal of Spanish staples (including *jamón*, paella and olive oil), and the astonishing regional varieties partly explain the phenomenon. But sheer culinary excellence, wedded to the new wave of innovation that has taken hold in the Basque Country, Catalonia and elsewhere, has taken Spanish cuisine to a whole new level. Spaniards spend more on food per capita than anyone else in Europe, and finding out why is one of Spain's star attractions.

EATING LIKE A LOCAL

Spanish cuisine is one of Europe's most accessible. But sometimes the first-time visitor can feel like Alain de Botton in *The Art of Travel* when he ends up eating from the mini-bar in his Madrid hotel room, so eager was he to avoid entering a bar and becoming the object of pity and curiosity. It *can* be like this, at least at first, but there's no reason why it should be.

Spaniards are usually so utterly absorbed in having a good time that you're unlikely to stand out if you're unsure what to do. And knowing what to do is easy. For a start, take your time to look around at what other people are eating, and don't hesitate to point to someone else's plate when ordering – Spaniards do this all the time. Another important weapon in your armoury is to repeat that well-worn Spanish mantra when entering a bar: '*¿Cuál es la especialidad de la casa?*' (What's the house speciality?). Most bars do most things well, but the chances are that locals come here for one or two dishes in particular. Even if you don't understand what the dish is, order it.

WAYS OF EATING

Most visitors complain not about the quality of Spanish food but its timing; you'll find the standard opening hours for restaurants inside the front cover of this book. Outside these hours, many bars serve tapas throughout the day. *Bocadillos* (filled rolls) are another option. Once you do find a bar or restaurant that's open when you're hungry, the typical *carta* (menu) begins with starters such as *ensaladas* (salads), *sopas* (soups) and *entremeses* (hors d'oeuvres). If you can't face a full menu, the *plato combinado* is a meat-and-three-veg dish.

To cap prices at lunchtime Monday to Friday, order the *menú del día,* a three-course set menu, including water, bread and a drink (usually around €10 and up). You'll be given a menu with five or six starters, the same number of mains and a handful of desserts – choose one from each category. Few working Spaniards have time to go home for lunch and taking a packed lunch is just not the done thing. The *menú del día* allows them to eat home-style food without breaking the bank.

When it comes to tapas – bite-sized morsels whose premise is so simple as to have all the hallmarks of genius – some bars, especially in Granada (p306), put a tiny plate of food with every drink you order. Otherwise, tapas varieties are sometimes lined up along the bar and ordering tapas couldn't be easier – you either take a small plate and help yourself or point to the morsel you want. More commonly, they'll have a list of tapas, either on a menu or posted up behind the bar – *raciones* (rations; large tapas serving) or *media raciones* (half-rations; smaller tapas serving) are ideal if you particularly like something and want more than a mere tapa. The best tapas in Spain are the *pintxos* (Basque for tapas) in San Sebastián (p208).

THE LAWS OF SPANISH COOKING

The laws of traditional Spanish cooking are deceptively simple: take the freshest ingredients and interfere with them as little as possible. While the rest of the world was developing sophisticated sauces, Spanish chefs were experimenting with subtlety, creating a combination of tastes in which the flavour of the food itself was paramount. Nowhere is this more evident than with tapas, where carefully selected meats, seafood or vegetables are given centre stage and allowed to speak for themselves. Such are the foundations on which Spanish cooking is built.

If simplicity is the cornerstone of Spanish cooking, it's the innovation and nou-velle cuisine emerging from Spanish kitchens that has truly taken the world by storm. Celebrity chefs such as Ferran Adrià

> ### ⬦ COOKING COURSES
>
> Even if you're only in Spain for a short time, the following places organise full- or half-day cooking courses:
> - **Alambique, Madrid** (p70)
> - **Cooking Club, Madrid** (p70)
> - **Cook and Taste, Barcelona** (p109)
> - **Escuela de Cocina Eneldo, Valencia** (p237)

and Mari Arzak have developed their own culinary laboratories, experimenting with all that's new, but always with a base rooted in traditional Spanish cuisine.

This blend of strong tradition and cutting-edge cuisine is illustrated by a simple fact: Spain is home to both the world's oldest restaurant, Restaurante Sobrino de Botín (p74) in Madrid, and El Bulli (see the boxed text, p177) in Catalonia, a temple of gastronomic experimentation that's consistently voted the world's best restaurant by the respected *Restaurant* magazine.

ICONS OF THE SPANISH KITCHEN

The list of signature Spanish dishes and ingredients, not to mention their regional variations, could fill encyclopedias. But if we had to choose just three culinary icons, they would be olive oil, *jamón* and paella.

OLIVE OIL

Andalucía is the olive oil capital of the world. There are over 100 million olive trees in Andalucía and a remarkable 20% of the world's olive oil originates in Jaén Province. *Aceite de oliva* (olive oil) will appear in just about every dish you order while in Spain – it's a standard base for cooking, is used to dress all manner of salads, and breakfast for many Spaniards includes toasted bread drizzled with olive oil and rubbed with tomato and garlic.

But not all olive oils were created equal. Olive oil production is almost as complicated as that of wine, with a range of designations designed to indicate quality. Reduced to its simplest form, the best olive oils are those classified as 'virgin' (which must meet 40 criteria for quality and purity) and 'extra virgin' (the best olive oil, whose acidity levels can be no higher than 1%); some extra-virgin oils have nearly zero acidity.

GREG ELMS

Seafood paella

JAMÓN

Spaniards are devoted to their cured meats (such as chorizo, *salchichón* and *lomo*), but *jamón* (ham) is Spain's true culinary constant and one of the few things that unites the country. If there is a national dish, this is it. Nearly every bar and restaurant in Spain has at least one *jamón* on the go at any one time, strapped into a cradlelike frame called a *jamónera*. The best *jamón* comes from Andalucía (especially around Jabugo in Huelva Province), around Salamanca, and Aragón.

Spanish *jamón* is, unlike Italian prosciutto, a bold, deep red and well marbled with buttery fat. *Jamón serrano* (which accounts for approximately 90% of cured ham in Spain) refers to *jamón* made from white-coated pigs introduced to Spain in the 1950s. *Jamón ibérico* – more expensive and the elite of Spanish hams – comes from a black-coated pig indigenous to the Iberian Peninsula and a descendant of the wild boar. Gastronomically, its star appeal is its ability to infiltrate fat into the muscle tissue, thus producing an especially well-marbled meat. If the pig gains at least 50% of its body weight during the acorn-eating season, it can be classified as *jamón ibérico de bellota*, the most sought-after designation for *jamón*.

⬊ THE ORIGIN OF TAPAS

There are many stories concerning the origins of tapas. One holds that in the 13th century, doctors to King Alfonso X advised him to accompany his wine between meals with small morsels of food. He enjoyed it so much that he passed a law requiring all bars to follow suit. As for the name, 'tapa' (lid), in the early 20th century a strong gust of wind blew sand in the direction of King Alfonso XIII at a beachside bar near Cádiz. When a quick-witted waiter rushed to place a slice of *jamón* atop the king's sherry, the king ordered another and the name stuck.

PAELLA

Easily Spain's best-known culinary export, paella well deserves its fame. The base of a good paella always includes short-grain rice, garlic, parsley, olive oil and saffron. The best rice is the *bomba* variety, which opens out accordion fashion when cooked, allowing for maximum absorption while remaining firm. Paella should be cooked in a large shallow pan to enable maximum contact with the bottom of the pan where most of the flavour resides. The main paella staples are *paella valenciana* (from Valencia, where paella has its roots), which is cooked with chicken, white beans and sometimes rabbit, and the more widespread *paella de mariscos* (seafood paella), which should be bursting with shellfish. In most restaurants, ordering a paella requires a minimum of two people.

For all paella's fame, a *really* good paella can be surprisingly hard to come by in Spanish restaurants. This is partly because saffron is extremely expensive, prompting many restaurants to cut corners by using yellow dye number 2. It's also because many restaurants play on the fact that every second foreign visitor to Spain will order a paella while in the country, but few will have any idea about what a good paella should taste like. Spaniards are much more discerning when it comes to their national dish, so check out the clientele before sitting down. To get the best paella, you have to go to Valencia (p238), followed by the Balearic Islands (p243) and Barcelona (p112).

SPAIN IN FOCUS

↘ VEGETARIANS & VEGANS

While vegetarians can have a hard time in Spain, most major cities have vegetarian restaurants. Otherwise, salads are a Spanish staple and, in many restaurants, are a meal in themselves. You'll also come across the odd vegetarian paella, as well as *verduras a la plancha* (grilled vegetables); *garbanzos con espinacas* (chickpeas and spinach); and numerous potato-based dishes. *Tascas* usually offer more vegetarian choices than do sit-down restaurants. Vegans will need to ask if dishes contain *huevos* (eggs) or *productos lácteos* (dairy). Restaurants offering a good veg selection are easy to find throughout this book – they're marked with a Ⓥ symbol.

REGIONAL VARIATIONS

THE SPANISH KITCHEN

The Basque Country and Catalonia are Spain's undoubted culinary superstars. Partly because of the area's gastronomic innovation – its avant-garde chefs are world famous for their food laboratories, their commitment to food as art and their crazy riffs on the themes of traditional local cooking. If Spaniards elsewhere in the country love their food, the Basques and Catalans are obsessed with it. Elsewhere, Andalucía, Aragón, Galicia and much of the Spanish interior are considered the bastions of tradition, while Madrid has risen above the mediocrity of its home-grown culinary traditions to be the place where you can get the best of regional specialities from around Spain.

In the Spanish interior, meat is a much-loved mainstay, including *cochinillo asado* (roast suckling pig) in Segovia (p138), *cordero asado* (roast lamb) in most of Castilla y León, and the steaks of Ávila (p133), inland Andalucía or the Basque Country. Around the coast, there are few sea creatures that Spaniards don't eat, from the Atlantic seafood of Galicia (*pulpo gallego*, or spicy boiled octopus is its most famous dish) to the fried fish of Andalucía, or the seafood-based rice dishes of Catalonia or the Balearic Islands. Andalucía is also known for its perfect-in-summer cold soups; the best known is the tomato-and-cucumber-based *gazpacho andaluz*. Cheese, too, is a much-loved Spanish staple, with those from Asturias, Galicia, Castilla-La Mancha and the Pyrenean foothills of Navarra enjoying particular fame.

DALLAS STRIBLEY

Spanish cheeses

DIRECTORY & TRANSPORT

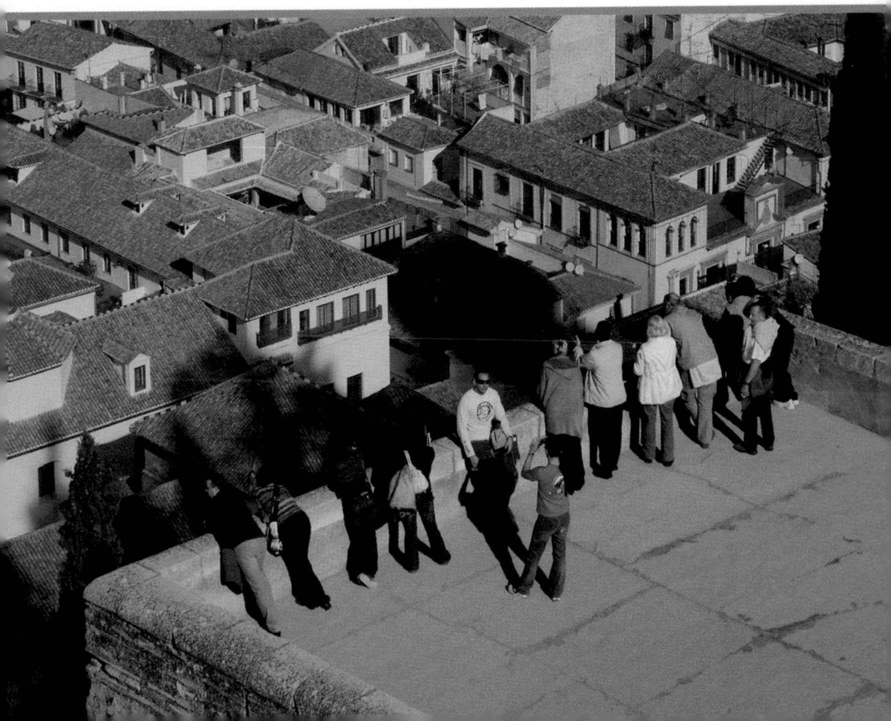

DIRECTORY

ACCOMMODATION

Prices throughout this guidebook are high-season maximums. You may be pleasantly surprised if you travel at other times. What constitutes low or high season depends on where and when. Most of the year is high season in Barcelona, especially during trade fairs. August can be dead in the cities. Winter is high season in the Pyrenees and low season in the Balearic Islands (indeed, the islands seem to shut down between November and Easter). July and August in the Balearics offer sun and fun, but finding a place to stay without booking ahead can be a pain. Weekends are high season for boutique hotels and *casas rurales* (country home, village or farmstead accommodation; see below), but bad for business hotels (which often offer generous specials then) in Madrid and Barcelona.

In places such as Barcelona and Madrid, and other popular tourist locations, a budget place can mean anything up to €40/60 for an *individual/doble* (single/double). At the higher end of this range you can generally expect to find good, comfortable rooms with private bathrooms. Shave a few euros off and you may find the place only has shared bathrooms in the corridor. In less-travelled regions, such as Extremadura, Murcia and Castilla-La Mancha, it can be relatively easy to find perfectly acceptable single/double rooms (usually with shared bathroom) for around €30/45.

Midrange places in the big cities can cost up to about €200 for a fine double, and there are plenty of good and on occasion outright charming options for less. Anything above that price takes you into luxury level. Again, though, much depends on the location and time of year. Cities like Madrid and Barcelona, with busy trade fair calendars, can become more expensive still during such fairs. In many other parts of Spain you'd be hard-pressed to pay more than €150 for the best double in town.

A *habitación doble* (double room) is frequently just that: a room with two beds (which you can often shove together). If you want to be sure of a double bed *(cama matrimonial),* ask for it!

APARTMENTS, VILLAS & CASAS RURALES

Throughout Spain you can rent self-catering apartments and houses from one night upwards. Villas and houses are widely available on the main holiday coasts and in popular country areas.

A simple one-bedroom apartment in a coastal resort for two or three people might cost as little as €30 per night, although more often you'll be looking at nearly twice that much, and prices can jump even further in high season. More luxurious options with a swimming pool might come in at anything between €200 and €400 for four people.

Rural tourism has become immensely popular, with accommodation available in many new and often charming *casas rurales*. These are usually comfortably

---

⇘ BOOK YOUR STAY ONLINE

For more accommodation reviews and recommendations by Lonely Planet authors, check out the online booking service at www.lonelyplanet.com. You'll find the true, insider lowdown on the best places to stay. Reviews are thorough and independent. Best of all, you can book online.

renovated village houses or farmhouses with a handful of rooms. They often go by other names, such as *cases de pagès* in Catalonia, *casas de aldea* in Asturias, *posadas* and *casonas* in Cantabria and so on. Some just provide rooms, while others offer meals or self-catering accommodation. Lower-end prices typically hover around €30/50 (single/double) per night, but classy boutique establishments can easily charge €100 or more for a double. Many are rented out by the week.

Try the following agencies:

Apartments-Spain (www.apartments-spain .com)

Associació Agroturisme Balear (☎ 971 721508; www.agroturismo-balear.com)

Atlas Rural (www.atlasrural.com)

Casas Cantabricas (☎ in UK 01223 328 721; www.casas.co.uk)

Cases Rurals de Catalunya (www.cases rurals.com)

Fincas 4 You (www.fincas4you.com)

Guías Casas Rurales (www.guiascasas rurales.com in Spanish)

Holiday Serviced Apartments (☎ in UK 0845 470 4477; www.holidayapartments.co.uk)

Rustic Rent (☎ 971 768040; www.rusticrent .com)

Secret Destinations (☎ in UK 0845 612 9000; www.secretdestinations.com)

Secret Places (www.secretplaces.com)

Simply Travel (☎ 0871 231 4050; www.simply travel.co.uk)

Top Rural (www.toprural.com)

Traum Ferienwohnungen (www.traum -ferienwohnungen.de)

Vintage (☎ in UK 0845 344 0460; www.vin tagetravel.co.uk)

HOTELS, HOSTALES, PENSIONES & HOSPEDAJES

Officially, places to stay are classified into *hoteles* (hotels; one to five stars), *hostales* (one to three stars) and *pensiones* (basically small private hotels, often family businesses in rambling apartments; one or two stars). These are the categories used by the annual *Guía Oficial de Hoteles,* sold in bookshops, which lists almost every such establishment in Spain, except for one-star *pensiones,* with approximate prices.

In practice, places listing accommodation use all sorts of overlapping names to describe themselves, especially at the budget end of the market. In broad terms, the cheapest are usually places just advertising *camas* (beds), *fondas* (traditionally a basic eatery and inn combined, though one of these functions is now often missing) and *casas de huéspedes* or *hospedajes* (guesthouses). Most such places will be bare and basic. Singles/doubles in these places generally cost from around €15/25 to €25/40.

A *pensión* is usually a small step up from the above types in standard and price. Some cheap establishments forget to provide soap, toilet paper or towels. Don't hesitate to ask for these necessities. *Hostales* are in much the same category. In both cases the better ones can be bright and spotless, with rooms boasting full en suite bathroom. Prices can range up to €40/60 for singles/doubles in more popular or expensive locations.

The remainder of establishments call themselves *hoteles* and run the gamut of quality, from straightforward roadside places, bland but clean, through charming boutique jobbies and on to superluxury hotels. Even in the cheapest hotels, rooms are likely to have an attached bathroom and there'll probably be a restaurant. Among the more tempting hotels for those with a little fiscal room to manoeuvre are the 90 or so **Paradores** (☎ in Spain 902 547979; www.parador.es), a state-funded chain of hotels in often stunning locations, among them towering castles

DIRECTORY

ACCOMMODATION

and former medieval convents. Similarly, you can find beautiful hotels in restored country homes and old city mansions, and these are not always particularly expensive. A raft of cutting-edge, hip design hotels with androgynous staff and a feel à la New York can be found in the big cities and major resort areas.

Many places to stay of all types have a range of rooms at different prices. At the budget end, prices will vary according to whether the room has only a *lavabo* (washbasin), *ducha* (shower) or *baño completo* (full bathroom – that is, bath/shower, basin and loo). At the top end you may pay more for a room with a view – especially sea views or with a *balcón* (balcony) – and will often have the option of a suite. Many places have rooms for three, four or more people where the per-person cost is lower than in a single or double, which is good news for families.

Checkout time is generally between 11am and noon.

REFUGIOS

Mountain shelters *(refugios)* for walkers and climbers are liberally scattered around most of the popular mountain areas (mainly the Pyrenees), except in Andalucía, which has only a handful. They're mostly run by mountaineering and walking organisations. Accommodation – usually bunks squeezed into a dorm – is often on a first-come, first-served basis, although for some *refugios* you can book ahead. In busy seasons (July and August in most areas) they can fill up quickly, and you should try to book in advance or arrive by mid-afternoon to be sure of a place. Prices per person range from nothing to €12.50 a night. Many *refugios* have a bar and offer meals (dinner typically costs around €8 to €10), as well as a cooking area (but not cooking equip-

ment). Blankets are usually provided, but you'll have to bring any other bedding yourself. Bring a torch too.

CLIMATE CHARTS

The *meseta* (high tableland of central Spain) and Ebro basin have a continental climate: scorching in summer, cold in winter, and dry. Madrid regularly freezes in December, January and February, and temperatures climb above 30°C in July and August. Valladolid on the northern *meseta* and Zaragoza in the Ebro basin are even drier, with only around 300mm of rain a year (little more than Alice Springs in Australia). The Guadalquivir basin in Andalucía is only a little wetter and positively broils in high summer, with temperatures of 35°C–plus in Seville that kill people every year.

The Pyrenees and the Cordillera Cantábrica, backing the Bay of Biscay, bear the brunt of cold northern and northwestern airstreams, which bring moderate temperatures and heavy rainfall (three or four times as much as Madrid's) to the north coast. Even in high summer you never know when you might get a shower.

The Mediterranean coast and Balearic Islands get a little more rain than Madrid, and the south can be even hotter in summer. The Mediterranean, particularly around Alicante, also provides Spain's warmest waters (reaching 27°C or so in August). Barcelona's weather is typical of the coast – milder than in inland cities but more humid.

In general you can usually rely on pleasant or hot temperatures just about everywhere from April to early November. In Andalucía there are plenty of warm, sunny days right through winter. In July and August, temperatures can get unpleasantly hot inland.

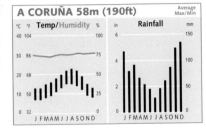

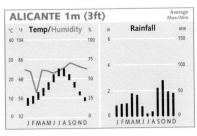

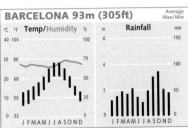

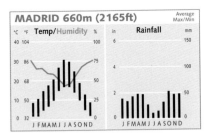

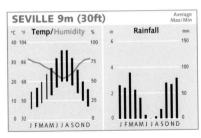

Snowfalls in the mountains can start as early as October and some snow cover lasts all year on the highest peaks.

CUSTOMS

Duty-free allowances for travellers entering Spain from outside the EU include 2L of wine (or 1L of wine and 1L of spirits), and 200 cigarettes or 50 cigars or 250g of tobacco.

There are no duty-free allowances for travel between EU countries but equally no restrictions on the import of duty-paid items into Spain from other EU countries for personal use. You *can* buy VAT-free articles at airport shops when travelling between EU countries.

DANGERS & ANNOYANCES

Spain is generally a pretty safe country. The main thing to be wary of is petty theft (which may of course not seem so petty if your passport, cash, travellers cheques, credit card and camera go missing). Most visitors to Spain never feel remotely threatened, but a sufficient number have unpleasant experiences to warrant an alert. What follows is intended as a strong warning rather than alarmism.

SCAMS

As a rule, talented petty thieves work in groups and capitalise on distraction.

Beware: not all thieves look like thieves. Watch out for an old classic: the ladies offering flowers for good luck. We don't know how they do it, but if you get too involved in a friendly chat with these people, your pockets always wind up empty.

On some highways, especially the AP7 from the French border to Barcelona, bands of delinquents occasionally operate. Beware of men trying to distract you in rest areas, and don't stop along the highway if people driving alongside indicate you have a problem with the car. While one inspects the rear of the car with you, his pals will empty your vehicle. When you do call in at highway rest stops, try to park close to the buildings and leave nothing of value in view.

Even parking your car can be fraught. In some towns fairly dodgy self-appointed parking attendants operate in central areas where you may want to park. If possible, ignore them and find your own. If unavoidable, you may well want to pay them some token not to scratch or otherwise damage your vehicle after you've walked away.

THEFT & LOSS

Theft is mostly a risk in tourist resorts, big cities and when you first arrive in the country or at a new city and may be off your guard. You are at your most vulnerable when dragging around luggage to or from your hotel. Barcelona, Madrid and Seville have the worst reputations for theft and, on isolated occasions, muggings.

The main things to guard against are pickpockets, bag snatchers and theft from cars. Theft can occur around the sights and areas frequented by tourists and on the metro (trains and stations).

Carry valuables under your clothes if possible – not in a back pocket, a daypack or anything that can easily be snatched away. Don't leave baggage unattended and avoid crushes (eg on public transport). Be cautious with people who start talking to you for no obviously good reason. This could be an attempt to distract you and make you an easier victim. Ignore demands to see your passport unless they come from a uniformed police officer (thieves posing as police have been a problem recently); some gangs recycle stolen passports.

Always remove the radio or CD player and GPS unit from your car and never leave any belongings visible when you leave the car.

Anything left lying on the beach can disappear in a flash when your back is turned. Avoid dingy, empty city alleys and backstreets, or anywhere that just doesn't feel 100% safe, at night.

You can also help yourself by not leaving anything valuable lying around your room, above all in any hostel-type place. Use a safe if one is available.

Report thefts to the national police. You are unlikely to recover your goods but you need to make this formal *denuncia* for insurance purposes. To avoid endless queues at the *comisaría* (police station), you can make the report by phone (☎ 902 102112) in various languages or on the web at www.policia.es (click on Denuncias). The following day you go to the station of your choice to pick up and sign the report, without queuing.

If your passport has gone, contact your embassy or consulate for help in issuing a replacement. Embassies and consulates can also give help of various kinds in other emergencies, but as a rule cannot advance you money to get home. Many countries have consulates in cities around Spain (such as Alicante, Barcelona, Málaga, Palma de Mallorca, Seville and Valencia), and your embassy can tell you where the nearest one is (see p354).

DISCOUNT CARDS

At museums, never hesitate to ask if there are discounts for students, young people, children, families or seniors.

SENIOR CARDS

There are reduced prices for people over 60, 63 or 65 (depending on the place) at various museums and attractions (sometimes restricted to EU citizens only) and occasionally on transport. You should also seek information in your own country on travel packages and discounts for senior travellers, through senior citizens' organisations and travel agents.

STUDENT & YOUTH CARDS

At some sights, discounts (usually half the normal fee) are available to students and people under 18. You will need some kind of identification to prove age or student status. An ISIC (International Student Identity Card; www.isic.org) may come in handy for travel discounts but is not accepted at many sights. There is also a teachers' version, ITIC (International Teacher Identity Card).

You'll have more luck with a Euro<26 (www.euro26.org) card (known as Carnet Joven in Spain), which is useful for those under 26. For instance, Euro<26 card holders enjoy 20% or 25% off most 2nd-class train fares; 10% or 20% off many ferries and some bus fares; good discounts at some museums; and discounts of up to 20% at some youth hostels.

For nonstudent travellers under 25 there is also the International Youth Travel Card (IYTC; www.istc.org), which offers similar benefits.

Student cards are issued by hostelling organisations, student unions and some youth travel agencies worldwide.

EMBASSIES & CONSULATES

SPANISH EMBASSIES & CONSULATES

To find the details of any Spanish embassy or consulate, check out the Ministry of Foreign Affairs web page (www.maec.es), click on Servicios Consulares and then choose the country you want. Among those with representation are:

Australia Canberra (☎ 02-6273 3555; www.maec.es/en/Home; 15 Arkana St, Yarralumla ACT 2600); Melbourne (☎ 03-9347 1966; 146 Elgin St, Carlton, Vic 3053); Sydney (☎ 02-9261 2433; Level 24, St Martin's Tower, 31 Market St, NSW 2000)

Canada Ottawa (☎ 613-747 2252; http://spain.embassyincanada.com; 74 Stanley Ave, Ontario K1M 1P4); Montreal (☎ 514-935 5235; Ste 1456, 1 Westmount Sq, Québec H3Z 2P9); Toronto (☎ 416-977 1661; 2 Bloor St East, Ste 1201, Ontario M4W 1A8)

France (☎ 01 44 43 18 00; www.amb-espagne.fr; 22 Ave Marceau, 75008 Paris)

Germany Berlin (☎ 030-254 00 70; www.info-spanischebotschaft.de; Lichtensteinallee 1, 10787); Düsseldorf (☎ 0211-43 90 80; Hombergerstr 16, 40474); Frankfurt am Main (☎ 069-959 16 60; Niebelungenplatz 3, 60318); Munich (☎ 089-998 47 90; Oberföhringerstr 45, 81925)

Ireland (☎ 01-269 1640; emb.dublin.info@mace.es; 17A Merlyn Park, Ballsbridge, Dublin 4)

Japan (☎ 03-3583 8531; emb.tokio@maec.es; 1-3-29 Roppongi Minato-ku, Tokyo 106-0032)

Netherlands (☎ 070-302 49 99; www.claboral.nl; Lange Voorhout 50, The Hague 2514 EG)

New Zealand (☎ 913 11 67; emb.wellington@maec.es; 56 Victoria St, Wellington 6142)

UK London (☎ 020-7235 5555; http://spain.embassyhomepage.com; 39 Chesham Pl, SW1X 8SB); Edinburgh (☎ 0131-220 1843; 63 North Castle St, EH2 3LJ); London consulate (☎ 020-7589 8989; 20 Draycott Pl, SW3 2RZ); Manchester (☎ 0161-236 1262; 1a Brook House, 70 Spring Gardens, M2 2BQ)

USA Washington DC (☎ 202-728 2340; embespus@mail.mae.es; 2375 Pennsylvania Ave NW, 20037); Boston (☎ 617-536 2506); Chicago (☎ 312-782 4588); Houston (☎ 713-783 6200); Los Angeles (☎ 213-938 0158); Miami (☎ 305-446 5511); New York (☎ 212-355 4080); San Francisco (☎ 415-922 2995)

DIRECTORY

EMBASSIES & CONSULATES

PRACTICALITIES

- Use the metric system for weights and measures.
- Bring an international adaptor because plugs have two round pins; the electric current is 220V, 50Hz.
- If your Spanish is up to it, try the following newspapers: *El País* (or the free, constantly updated, downloadable version, *24 Horas,* on www.elpais.es), the country's leading daily and left-of-centre oriented; *ABC,* for a right-wing view of life; Barcelona-based *La Vanguardia,* which on Friday has a great listings magazine for that city; and *Marca,* an all-sports (especially football) paper.
- Tune into: Radio Nacional de España (RNE)'s Radio 1, with general interest and current affairs programs; Radio 5, with sport and entertainment; and Radio 3 (Radio d'Espop), with admirably varied pop and rock music. The most popular commercial pop and rock stations are 40 Principales, Cadena 100 and Onda Cero.
- Switch on the box to watch Spain's state-run Televisión Española (TVE1 and La 2) or the independent commercial stations (Antena 3, Tele 5, Cuatro, La Sexta and Canal Plus). Regional governments run local stations, such as Madrid's Telemadrid, Catalonia's TV-3 and Canal 33 (both in Catalan), Galicia's TVG, the Basque Country's ETB-1 and ETB-2, Valencia's Canal 9 and Andalucía's Canal Sur. Cable and satellite TV is becoming more widespread.

EMBASSIES & CONSULATES IN SPAIN

The embassies are in Madrid. Some countries also maintain consulates in major cities, particularly in Barcelona. Embassies and consulates include the following:

Australia Madrid (Map p53; ☎ 91 353 66 00; www.spain.embassy.gov.au; Torre Espacio, Paseo de la Castellana); Barcelona (Map pp86-7; ☎ 93 490 90 13; Plaça de Galla Placidia 1)

Canada Madrid (Map pp64-5; ☎ 91 423 32 50; www.canada-es.org; Calle de Núñez de Balboa 35); Barcelona (Map pp86-7; ☎ 93 204 27 00; Carrer d'Elisenda de Pinós 10; FGC Reina Elisenda)

France Madrid (Map pp64-5; ☎ 91 423 89 00; www.ambafrance-es.org; Calle de Salustiano Olózaga 9); Barcelona (Map pp98-9; ☎ 93 270 30 00; Ronda de l'Universitat 22B)

Germany Madrid (Map pp64-5; ☎ 91 557 90 00; www.madrid.diplo.de; Calle de Fortuny 8); Barcelona (Map pp86-7; ☎ 93 292 10 00; Passeig de Gràcia 111)

Ireland Madrid (Map pp64-5; ☎ 91 436 40 93; Paseo de la Castellana 46); Barcelona (Map pp86-7; ☎ 93 491 50 21; Gran Via de Carles III 94)

Japan (Map p53; ☎ 91 590 76 00; www.es.emb-japan.go.jp; Calle de Serrano 109, Madrid)

Netherlands Madrid (Map p53; ☎ 91 353 75 00; www.embajadapaisesbajos.es; Avenida del Comandante Franco 32); Barcelona (Map pp86-7; ☎ 93 363 54 20; Avinguda Diagonal 601); Palma de Mallorca (Map p245; ☎ 971 71 64 93; Calle de San Miquel 36)

New Zealand Madrid (Map pp64-5; ☎ 91 523 02 26; www.nzembassy.com; Calle del Pinar 7); Barcelona (Map pp86-7; ☎ 93 209 03 99; Travessera de Gràcia 64)

UK Madrid (Map p53; ☎ 91 714 64 00; www
.ukinspain.com; Torre Espacio, Paseo de la Castellana); Barcelona (Map pp86-7; ☎ 93 366 62 00;
Avinguda Diagonal 477); Palma de Mallorca
(Map p245; ☎ 971 71 24 45; Carrer del Convent
dels Caputxins 4, Edifici B)
USA Madrid (Map pp64-5; ☎ 91 587 22 00;
www.embusa.es; Calle de Serrano 75); Barcelona (Map pp86-7; ☎ 93 280 22 27; Passeig de
la Reina Elisenda de Montcada 23-25; FGC Reina
Elisenda) Consular Agencies in A Coruña,
Fuengirola, Palma de Mallorca, Sevilla
and Valencia.

FOOD
Glorious food. There's plenty of it in
Spain and the regional variety is remarkable. From myriad seafood curiosities in
Galicia to the venison of Castilla and the
avant-garde *nueva cocina* that's cooking in Barcelona, Madrid and the Basque
Country, Spain offers no shortage of surprises. For an overview of what's in store
in Spain's kitchens, see Spain in Focus
(p342).

GAY & LESBIAN TRAVELLERS
Homosexuality is legal in Spain and the
age of consent is 13, as for heterosexu-
als. In 2005 the Socialist president, José
Luis Rodríguez Zapatero, gave the country's conservative Catholic foundations a
shake with the legalisation of same-sex
marriages in Spain.

Lesbians and gay men generally keep
a fairly low profile, but are more open
in the cities. Madrid, Barcelona, Sitges,
Torremolinos and Ibiza have particularly
lively scenes. Sitges is a major destination on the international gay party circuit; gays take a leading role in the wild
Carnaval there in February/March (p46).
As well, there are gay parades, marches
and events in several cities on and around

the last Saturday in June, when Madrid's
gay and lesbian pride march takes place
(p71).

Worth looking for is *Guía Gay de
España,* a countrywide guide published
by Shangay, a gay publishing group; also
check out *El País* for gay and gay-friendly
bars, restaurants, hotels and shops around
the country.

A couple of informative free magazines are in circulation in gay bookshops
and gay and gay-friendly bars. One is
the biweekly *Shanguide.* It is jammed
with listings and contact ads and aimed
principally at readers in Madrid and, to a
lesser extent, in Barcelona. Barcelona's
tourist board also publishes *Barcelona –
The Official Gay and Lesbian Tourist Guide*
bi-annually. The annual, worldwide
Spartacus guide is often on sale at newsstands along La Rambla.

For more information, check out the
following sites on the internet:
Chueca (www.chueca.com in Spanish) You
have to become a member of the site if
you want to access the site's Guía Noc-
turna for bars and clubs.
GayBarcelona (www.gaybarcelona.com)
Includes news and views and an extensive listings section covering bars,
saunas, shops and more in Barcelona
and Sitges.
LesboNet (www.lesbonet.org in Spanish) A
lesbian site with contacts, forums and
listings.
Mensual (www.mensual.com) Click on Guía
de España to search for bars, restaurants
and more.
Shangay (http://shangay.com in Spanish)
For news, art reviews, contacts and
Shanguide listings. You have to register
to get full access.
Voz Gay (www.vozgay.com in Spanish) A
Spanish community website with listings for the whole country.

HEALTH
BEFORE YOU GO

Prevention is the key to staying healthy while abroad. Some predeparture planning will save trouble later. See your dentist before a long trip; carry a spare pair of contact lenses and glasses; and take your optical prescription with you. Bring medications in their original, clearly labelled containers. A signed and dated letter from your physician describing your medical conditions and medications, including generic names, is also a good idea. If carrying syringes or needles, be sure to have a physician's letter documenting their medical necessity.

INSURANCE

If you're an EU citizen, a European Health Insurance Card, available from health centres (in the UK, post offices) covers you for most medical care in public hospitals. It will not cover you for non-emergencies or emergency repatriation. The card is no good for private medical consultations and treatment in Spain; this includes virtually all dentists and some of the better clinics and surgeries. If you do need health insurance, strongly consider a policy that covers you for ambulances and the worst possible scenario, such as an accident requiring an emergency flight home.

Find out in advance if your insurance plan will make payments directly to providers or reimburse you later for overseas health expenditures; if you have to claim later make sure you keep all documentation.

Worldwide travel insurance is available at www.lonelyplanet.com/travel _services.

RECOMMENDED VACCINATIONS

No jabs are necessary for Spain. However, the World Health Organization (WHO) recommends that all travellers should be covered for diphtheria, tetanus, measles, mumps, rubella and polio, regardless of their destination. Since most vaccines don't produce immunity until at least two weeks after they're given, visit a physician at least six weeks before departure.

INTERNET RESOURCES

International Travel and Health, a WHO publication, is revised annually and is available online at www.who.int/ith. Other useful websites:

Age Concern (www.ageconcern.org.uk) Advice on travel for the elderly.

Fit for Travel (www.fitfortravel.scot.nhs.uk) General travel advice for the layperson.

MD Travel Health (www.mdtravelhealth .com) Travel health recommendations for every country; updated daily.

IN SPAIN
AVAILABILITY & COST OF HEALTH CARE

If you need an ambulance, call ☎ 061. For emergency treatment go straight to the *urgencias* (casualty) section of the nearest hospital.

Good health care is readily available, and *farmacias* (pharmacies) offer valuable advice and sell over-the-counter medication. In Spain, a system of *farmacias de guardia* (duty pharmacies) operates so that each district has one open all the time. When a pharmacy is closed, it posts the name of the nearest open one on the door.

ENVIRONMENTAL HAZARDS
ALTITUDE SICKNESS

Lack of oxygen at high altitudes (over 2500m) affects most people to some extent. Symptoms of Acute Mountain Sickness (AMS) usually develop during the first 24 hours at altitude but may be delayed up to three weeks. Mild symptoms include headache, lethargy, dizziness, difficulty sleeping and loss of appetite. AMS may become more severe without warning and can be fatal. Severe symptoms include breathlessness, a dry, irritative cough (which may progress to the production of pink, frothy sputum), severe headache, lack of coordination and balance, confusion, irrational behaviour, vomiting, drowsiness and unconsciousness.

In the UK, fact sheets are available from the **British Mountaineering Council** (☎ 0870 010 4878; www.thebmc.co.uk; 177-179 Burton Rd, Manchester, M20 2BB).

HEAT EXHAUSTION & HEATSTROKE
Heat exhaustion occurs following excessive fluid loss with inadequate replacement of fluids and salt. Symptoms include headache, dizziness and tiredness. Dehydration is happening by the time you feel thirsty – aim to drink sufficient water to produce pale, diluted urine. Replace lost fluids by drinking water and/or fruit juice, and cool the body with cold water and fans. Treat salt loss with salty fluids, such as soup, or add a little more table salt to foods than usual.

Heatstroke is much more serious, resulting in irrational and hyperactive behaviour, and eventually loss of consciousness and death. Rapid cooling by spraying the body with water and fanning is ideal.

BITES & STINGS
Bees and wasps only cause real problems to those with a severe allergy (anaphylaxis).

In forested areas watch out for the hairy reddish-brown caterpillars of the pine processionary moth. They live in silvery nests up in the pine trees and, come spring, leave the nest to march in long lines (hence the name). Touching the caterpillars' hairs sets off a severely irritating allergic skin reaction.

Jellyfish, which have stinging tentacles, generally occur in large numbers or hardly at all, so it's fairly easy to know when not to go in the sea.

Sandflies are found around the Mediterranean beaches. They usually cause only a nasty itchy bite but can carry a rare skin disorder called cutaneous leishmaniasis.

The only venomous snake that is even relatively common in Spain is Lataste's viper. It has a triangular-shaped head, grows up to 75cm long, and is grey with a zigzag pattern. It lives in dry, rocky areas, away from humans. Its bite can be fatal and needs to be treated with a serum, which state clinics in major towns keep in stock.

HYPOTHERMIA
Hypothermia starts with shivering, loss of judgment and clumsiness. Unless rewarming occurs, the sufferer deteriorates into apathy, confusion and coma. Prevent further heat loss by seeking shelter, warm dry clothing, hot sweet drinks and shared body warmth.

WATER
Tap water is generally safe to drink in Spain. If you are in any doubt, ask *¿Es potable el agua (de grifo)?* (Is the (tap) water drinkable?) Do not drink water from rivers or lakes as it may contain bacteria or viruses that can cause diarrhoea or vomiting.

WOMEN'S HEALTH
Travelling during pregnancy is usually possible but always seek a medical check-up before planning your trip. The most risky times for travel are during the first 12 weeks of pregnancy and after 30 weeks.

HOLIDAYS

The two main periods when Spaniards go on holiday are Semana Santa (the week leading up to Easter Sunday) and August. At these times accommodation in resorts can be scarce and transport heavily booked, but other places are often half empty.

There are at least 14 official holidays a year – some observed nationwide, some locally. When a holiday falls close to a weekend, Spaniards like to make a *puente* (bridge), meaning they take the intervening day off too. Occasionally when some holidays fall close, they make an *acueducto* (aqueduct)! National holidays:

Año Nuevo (New Year's Day) 1 January
Viernes Santo (Good Friday) March/April
Fiesta del Trabajo (Labour Day) 1 May
La Asunción (Feast of the Assumption) 15 August
Fiesta Nacional de España (National Day) 12 October
La Inmaculada Concepción (Feast of the Immaculate Conception) 8 December
Navidad (Christmas) 25 December

Regional governments set five holidays and local councils two more. Common dates for widely observed holidays include the following:

Epifanía (Epiphany) or **Día de los Reyes Magos** (Three Kings' Day) 6 January
Día de San José (St Joseph's Day) 19 March
Jueves Santo (Good Thursday) March/April. Not observed in Catalonia and Valencia.
Corpus Christi June. This is the Thursday after the eighth Sunday after Easter Sunday.
Día de San Juan Bautista (Feast of St John the Baptist) 24 June

Día de Santiago Apóstol (Feast of St James the Apostle) 25 July
Día de Todos los Santos (All Saints Day) 1 November
Día de la Constitución (Constitution Day) 6 December

INSURANCE

A travel-insurance policy to cover theft, loss and medical problems is a good idea. It may also cover you for cancellation or delays to your travel arrangements. Paying for your ticket with a credit card can often provide limited travel-accident insurance and you may be able to reclaim the payment if the operator doesn't deliver. Ask your credit card company what it will cover. Worldwide travel insurance is available at www.lonelyplanet.com/travel_services. You can buy, extend and claim online anytime – even if you're on the road.

INTERNET ACCESS

Most laptops now come equipped with wi-fi, meaning you can log on to hotspots where they're available. These are still relatively thin on the ground in Spain, and in some cases (such as in airports and some hotels) you must pay a fee to access the internet this way. Still, a growing number of cafes, bars and restaurants in the bigger cities and tourist resorts offer free wi-fi to customers.

The number of hotels equipped with internet availability (in rooms or in the foyer) is growing rapidly. Hotels in this guide with such services are indicated with an icon ( ).

If you intend to rely on cybercafes (commonly referred to as *cibers*), you'll need three pieces of information: your incoming (POP or IMAP) mail-server name, your account name and your password. Most travellers make constant use of internet cafes and free web-based email such as

Yahoo (www.yahoo.com), Hotmail (www.hotmail.com) or Google's Gmail (www.gmail.com). You typically have to pay about €1.50 to €3 per hour to go online in most cybercafes.

LEGAL MATTERS

If you're arrested you will be allotted the free services of an *abogado de oficio* (duty solicitor), who may speak only Spanish. You're also entitled to make a phone call. If you use this to contact your embassy or consulate, the staff will probably be able to do no more than refer you to a lawyer who speaks your language. If you end up in court, the authorities are obliged to provide a translator.

In theory, you are supposed to have your national ID card or passport with you at all times. If asked for it by the police, you are supposed to be able to produce it on the spot. In practice it is rarely an issue and many people choose to leave passports in hotel safes.

The legal age for voting and for driving is 18 years. The age of consent is 13 years, for both heterosexual and homosexual relations. Travellers should note that they can be prosecuted under the laws of their home country regarding age of consent, even when abroad.

DRUGS

The only legal drug is cannabis and only for personal use, which means very small amounts. Public consumption of any drug is illegal, although in a few bars you may find people smoking joints openly.

POLICE

Spain is well endowed with police forces. The Policía Local or Policía Municipal operates at a local level and deals with such issues as traffic infringements and minor crime.

The **Policía Nacional** (☎ 091) is the state police force, dealing with major crime and operating primarily in the cities. The military-linked Guardia Civil (created in the 19th century to deal with banditry) is largely responsible for highway patrols, borders and security, and often has a presence in more remote areas where there is no *comisaría* (Policía Nacional station).

Just to complicate matters, several regions have their own police forces, such as the Mossos d'Esquadra in Catalonia, the Ertaintxa in the Basque Country and, at some point in the future, a new force in Galicia (a law approving the creation of such a force was established in 2007).

MAPS
CITY MAPS

For finding your way around cities, the free maps handed out by tourist offices are often adequate, although more detailed maps are sold widely in bookshops.

SMALL-SCALE MAPS

Some of the best maps for travellers are by Michelin, which produces the 1:1,000,000 *Spain Portugal* map and six 1:400,000 regional maps covering the whole country. These are all pretty accurate, even down to the state of minor country roads, and are frequently updated and detailed yet easy to read. Also good are the GeoCenter maps published by Germany's RV Verlag.

Probably the best physical map of Spain is *Península Ibérica, Baleares y Canarias* published by the **Centro Nacional de Información Geográfica** (CNIG; www.cnig.es), the publishing arm of the **Instituto Geográfico Nacional** (IGN; www.ign.es).

WALKING MAPS

Useful for hiking and exploring some areas (particularly in the Pyrenees) are

Editorial Alpina's *Guía Cartográfica* and *Guía Excursionista y Turística* series. The series combines information booklets in Spanish (and sometimes Catalan) with detailed maps at scales ranging from 1:25,000 (1cm to 250m) to 1:50,000 (1cm to 500m). The CNIG also covers most of the country in 1:25,000 sheets.

You can often pick up Editorial Alpina publications and CNIG maps at bookshops near trekking areas, and at specialist bookshops such as **Librería Desnivel** (☎ 902 248848; www.libreriadesnivel.com; Plaza de Matute 6), **Altaïr** (☎ 93 342 71 71; www.altair .es; Gran Via de les Corts Catalanes 616) or **Quera** (☎ 93 318 07 43; www.llibreriaquera.com; Carrer de Petritxol 2) in Barcelona. Some map specialists in other countries, such as **Stanfords** (☎ 020-7836 1321; www.stanfords.co.uk; 12-14 Long Acre, London WC2E 9LP) in the UK, also have a good range of Spain maps.

MONEY

As in 14 other EU nations the euro is Spain's currency. You'll find exchange rates on the inside front cover of this book and a guide to costs on p42.

Spain's international airports have bank branches, ATMs and exchange offices. They're less frequent at road crossings now as Spain's neighbours – Andorra, Portugal and France – all use the euro.

Banks and building societies tend to offer the best exchange rates, and are plentiful: even small villages often have at least one. They mostly open from around 8.30am to 2pm Monday to Friday. Some also open Thursday evening (about 4pm to 7pm) or Saturday morning (9am to 2pm). Ask about commissions before changing (especially in exchange bureaux).

Prices in this guidebook are quoted in euros (€), unless otherwise stated.

ATMS

Many credit and debit cards (Visa and MasterCard are the most widely accepted) can be used for withdrawing money from *cajeros automáticos* (automatic telling machines). This is handy because many banks do not offer an over-the-counter cash advance service on foreign cards (and where they do, the process can be wearisome). The exchange rate used for credit and debit card transactions is usually more in your favour than that for cash exchanges. Bear in mind, however, the costs involved. There is usually a charge (hovering around 1.5% to 2%) on ATM cash withdrawals abroad. This charge may appear on your statements.

CREDIT & DEBIT CARDS

You can use plastic to pay for many purchases (including meals and rooms, especially from the middle price-range up). You'll often be asked to show your passport or some other form of identification when using cards. Among the most widely accepted are Visa, MasterCard, American Express (Amex), Cirrus, Maestro, Plus, Diners Club and JCB. Many institutions add 2.5% or more to all transactions (cash advance or purchases) on cards used abroad – this charge does not generally appear on your bank statements.

If your card is lost, stolen or swallowed by an ATM, you can telephone toll free to have an immediate stop put on its use. For MasterCard the number in Spain is ☎ 900 971231, for Visa ☎ 900 991124, for Amex ☎ 900 994426 and for Diners Club ☎ 901 101011.

TAXES & REFUNDS

In Spain, value-added tax (VAT) is known as IVA (*ee*-ba; *impuesto sobre el valor añadido*). On accommodation and restaurant prices, it's 7% and is often included in quoted prices. On retail goods and car hire, IVA is 16%. To ask 'Is IVA included?', say *'¿Está incluido el IVA?'*.

Visitors are entitled to a refund of the 16% IVA on purchases costing more than €90.16 from any shop if they are taking them out of the EU within three months. Ask the shop for a cash back (or similar) refund form showing the price and IVA paid for each item, and identifying the vendor and purchaser. Then present the refund form to the customs booth for IVA refunds at the airport, port or border from which you leave the EU. This works best at airports, where you will need your passport and a boarding card that shows you are leaving the EU. The officer will stamp the invoice and you hand it in at a specified bank at the departure point for immediate reimbursement.

TIPPING

The law requires menu prices to include a service charge; tipping is a matter of choice. Most people leave some small change if they're satisfied: 5% is normally fine and 10% generous. Porters will generally be happy with €1. Taxi drivers don't have to be tipped but a little rounding up won't go amiss.

TRAVELLERS CHEQUES

Travellers cheques usually bring only a slightly better exchange rate than cash, usually offset by the charges for buying them in the first place and the commission you may have to pay to cash them in. Plastic has by now largely supplanted travellers cheques for travel in Spain but the ultracautious may see them as a useful back-up measure in case of something going wrong with their debit and/or credit cards.

Remember to take along your passport when you cash travellers cheques.

Get most of your cheques in fairly large denominations (the equivalent of €100 or more) to save on any per-cheque commission charges.

If you lose your Amex cheques, call a 24-hour freephone number (☎ 900 994426). For Visa cheques, call ☎ 900 948973 and for MasterCard cheques, call ☎ 900 948971. It's vital to keep your initial receipt, and a record of your cheque numbers and the ones you have used, separate from the cheques themselves.

SHOPPING

There are some excellent *mercadillos* and *rastros* (flea markets) around the country, and craft shops can be found in many villages and towns. You may also pick up crafts at weekly or daily markets. The single most likely place you'll find any particular item in most cities is the nationwide department store El Corte Inglés (but not necessarily at bargain basement prices!).

CLOTHES & TEXTILES

Label lovers and fashion victims can keep themselves well occupied in the big cities, such as Madrid and Barcelona, where local and international names present a broad range of options. Ibiza in summer is also a bit of a magnet for clubbing and summer-wear seekers.

Inexpensive rugs, blankets and hangings are made all over the country, notably in Andalucía and Galicia. In Andalucía head for Las Alpujarras and Níjar for colourful items. *Jarapas* (rugs) feature weft threads made of different types of cloth. Other textiles include lace tablecloths and pillowcases (especially from Galicia) and embroidery. Places particularly known for their embroidery include Segovia, La Alberca (Salamanca province), Carbajales (Zamora province), and Lagartera, Oropesa and Talavera (Toledo province).

In Andalucía, every major city centre has a cluster of flamenco shops, selling embroidered shawls, hand-painted fans, flat-top Cordoban hats and, of course, lots of flouncy dresses (*batas de cola*).

LEATHER

Prices of leather goods aren't as low as they used to be, but you can get good deals on jackets, bags, wallets, belts, shoes and boots in many places. Mallorcan shoe brands like Camper and Farrutx have become international beacons – their products are stylish, moderately priced and, especially in the case of Camper, easily found all over Spain. The island of Mallorca is especially known for its leather production – head to the inland town of Inca and you'll find plenty of stores and outlets selling everything from purses to pants.

POTTERY

Crockery, jugs, plant pots, window boxes and tiles are cheap. Islamic influence on design and colour is evident in much of the country. Original techniques include the use of metallic glazes and *cuerda seca* (dry cord), in which lines of manganese or fat are used to separate areas of different colour. Toledo, Talavera de la Reina, Seville, Granada and Úbeda are major centres of production but many other small ceramics centres are sprinkled across the country.

OTHER CRAFTS

Damascene weapons (made of steel encrusted with gold, silver or copper) are still being produced in Toledo. Very pleasing woodwork is available, such as Granada's marquetry boxes, tables and chess sets, some of which are inlaid with bone or mother-of-pearl. Baskets and furniture made from plant fibres are produced throughout Spain but are most common near the coasts.

TELEPHONE

The ubiquitous blue payphones are easy to use for international and domestic calls. They accept coins, phonecards (*tarjetas telefónicas*) issued by the national phone company Telefónica and, in some cases, various credit cards. Phonecards come in €6 and €12 denominations and, like postage stamps, are sold at post offices and tobacconists.

MOBILE PHONES

Spaniards adore *teléfonos móviles* (mobile or cell phones), and shops on every high street sell phones with prepaid cards. The most basic models of cell phones start from around €80 (if you're buying a prepaid SIM card – they are often free for residents taking out a contract).

Spain uses GSM 900/1800, which is compatible with the rest of Europe and Australia but not with the North American GSM 1900 or the system used in Japan. From those countries, you will need to travel with a tri-band or quadric-band phone.

You can rent a mobile phone by calling the Madrid-based **Cellphone Rental** (www.onspanishtime.com/web). It will deliver the phone to a hotel or apartment anywhere in Spain.

PHONE CODES

Dial the international access code (☎ 00 in most countries), followed by the code for Spain (☎ 34) and the full number (including the code, 91, which is an integral part of the number). For example, to call the number ☎ 91 455 67 83 in Madrid, you need to dial the international access code followed by ☎ 34 91 455 67 83.

The access code for international calls from Spain is ☎ 00.

International collect calls are simple. Dial ☎ 99 00 followed by the code for the country you're calling:
Australia ☎ 99 00 61
Canada ☎ 99 00 15
France ☎ 99 00 33
Germany ☎ 99 00 49
Ireland ☎ 99 03 53
Israel ☎ 99 09 72
New Zealand ☎ 99 00 64
UK for BT ☎ 99 00 44
USA for AT&T ☎ 99 00 11, for Sprint and various others ☎ 99 00 13

You'll get straight through to an operator in the country you're calling. The same numbers can be used with direct-dial calling cards.

If for some reason the above information doesn't work for you, in most places you can get an English-speaking Spanish international operator by dialling ☎ 1008 (for calls within Europe) or ☎ 1005 (rest of the world).

Dial ☎ 1009 to speak to a domestic operator, including for a domestic reverse-charge (collect) call *(llamada por cobro revertido)*. For national directory inquiries, dial ☎ 11818.

Mobile phone numbers start with 6. Numbers starting with 900 are national toll-free numbers, while those starting 901 to 905 come with varying conditions. A common one is 902, which is a national standard rate number. In a similar category are numbers starting with 803, 806 and 807.

PHONECARDS

Cut-rate prepaid phonecards can be good value for international calls. They can be bought from *estancos* (tobacconists) and newsstands in the main cities and tourist resorts. If possible, try to compare rates because some are better than

TAKING YOUR MOBILE PHONE

If you plan to take your own mobile phone to Spain, check in advance with your mobile network provider that your phone is enabled for international roaming, which allows you to make and receive calls and messages abroad. Ask what you have to dial in order to use international roaming.

■ Consider buying an alternative SIM card for use on a local network in Spain. If your phone is not blocked (make sure you check this out before leaving home), you can buy any local pay-as-you-go SIM card.
■ Take an international adaptor for the charger plug.
■ Note your phone's number and serial number (IMEI number) and your operator's customer services number. This will help if your phone is stolen.
■ For more advice on using mobile phones abroad go to www.ofcom.org.uk.

others. *Locutorios* (private call centres) that specialise in cut-rate overseas calls have popped up all over the place in the centre of bigger cities.

TIME

Mainland Spain and the Balearic Islands have the same time as most of the rest of Western Europe: GMT/UTC plus one hour during winter and GMT/UTC plus two hours during the daylight-saving period, which runs from the last Sunday in March to the last Sunday in October.

The UK, Ireland, Portugal and the Canary Islands are one hour behind mainland Spain. Morocco is on GMT/UTC year-round. From the last Sunday in March to the last Sunday in October, subtract two hours from Spanish time to get Moroccan time; the rest of the year, subtract one hour.

Spanish time is USA Eastern Time plus six hours and USA Pacific Time plus nine hours.

During the Australian winter (Spanish summer), subtract eight hours from Australian Eastern Standard Time to get Spanish time; during the Australian summer, subtract 10 hours.

TOURIST INFORMATION
LOCAL TOURIST OFFICES

All cities and many smaller towns have an *oficina de turismo* or *oficina de información turística*. In the country's provincial capitals you'll sometimes find more than one tourist office – one specialising in information on the city alone, the other carrying mostly provincial or regional information. National and natural parks also often have visitor centres offering useful information.

Turespaña (www.spain.info, www.tourspain.es), the country's national tourism body, presents a variety of general information and links on the entire country in its web pages.

TOURIST OFFICES ABROAD

Information on Spain is available from the following branches of Turespaña abroad:

Canada (☎ 416-961 3131; www.tourspain.toronto.on.ca; 2 Bloor St W, Ste 3042, Toronto M4W 3E2)

France (☎ 01 45 03 82 50; www.spain.info/TourSpain/?Language=fr; 43 rue Decamps, 75784 Paris)

Germany (☎ 030-882 6543; berlin@tourspain.es; Kurfürstendamm 63, 10707 Berlin) Branches in Düsseldorf, Frankfurt am Main and Munich.

Netherlands (☎ 070-346 59 00; www.spaansverkeersbureau.nl; Laan van Meerdervoort 8a, 2517 The Hague)

Portugal (☎ 21-354 1992; lisboa@tourspain.es; Avenida Sidónio Pais 28 3° Dto, 1050-215 Lisbon)

UK (☎ 020-7486 8077; www.spain.info/uk/tourspain; you may visit the office by appointment only)

USA (☎ 212-265 8822; www.okspain.org; 666 Fifth Ave, 35th fl, New York, NY 10103) Branches in Chicago, Los Angeles and Miami.

TRAVELLERS WITH DISABILITIES

Spain is not overly accommodating for travellers with disabilities but some things are slowly changing. In major cities more is slowly being done to facilitate disabled access to public transport and taxis. A growing number of sights and hotels have made at least some effort to meet the needs of the wheelchair-bound. It is sometimes possible to obtain lists of hotels with wheelchair access from local or regional tourist offices.

ORGANISATIONS

Accessible Barcelona (☎ 93 428 52 27; www.accessiblebarcelona.com) Craig Grimes, a T6 paraplegic and inveterate traveller, created this Barcelona-specific accessible travel site, easily the most useful doorway into the city for the disabled.

Accessible Travel & Leisure (☎ 01452-729739; www.accessibletravel.co.uk; Avionics House, Naas Lane, Gloucester GL2 2SN) Claims to be the biggest UK travel agent dealing with travel for the disabled and encourages the disabled to travel independently.

ONCE (☎ 91 436 53 00; www.once.es; Calle de José Ortega y Gasset 18, Madrid) The Spanish association for the blind. You may be able to get hold of guides in Braille to a handful of cities, including Madrid and Barcelona, although they are not published every year.

Society for Accessible Travel & Hospitality (☎ 212 447 7284; www.sath.org; 347 Fifth Ave, Ste 605, New York, NY 10016) Although largely concentrated on the USA, this organisation can provide general information.

VISAS

Spain is one of 24 member countries of the Schengen Convention, under which 22 EU countries (all but Bulgaria, Cyprus, Ireland, Romania and the UK) plus Iceland and Norway have abolished checks at common borders. Switzerland is in the process of becoming a member and Cyprus was set to join by the end of 2008. For detailed information on the EU, including which countries are member states, visit http://europa.eu.

EU, Norwegian, Swiss and Icelandic nationals need no visa, regardless of the length or purpose of their visit to Spain. If they stay beyond 90 days, they are required to register with the police (although many do not). Legal residents of one Schengen country do not require a visa for another Schengen country.

Nationals of many other countries, including Australia, Canada, Israel, Japan, NZ and the USA, do not need a visa for tourist visits of up to 90 days in Spain, although some of these nationalities may be subject to restrictions in other Schengen countries and should check with consulates of all Schengen countries they plan to visit. If you are a citizen of a country not mentioned in this section, check with a Spanish consulate whether you need a visa.

PHOTOCOPIES

All important documents (passport data page and visa page, credit cards, travel insurance policy, driving licence etc) should be photocopied before you leave home. Leave one copy with someone at home and keep another with you, separate from the originals.

WOMEN TRAVELLERS

Travelling in Spain is as easy as travelling anywhere in the Western world. Spanish men under about 40, who've grown up in the liberated post-Franco era, conform less to old-fashioned sexual stereotypes, although you might notice that sexual stereotyping becomes more pronounced as you move from north to south in Spain, and from city to country. And in terms of equality of the sexes, Spain still has some way to go. The Socialist Zapatero government has introduced measures to promote equality in employment for women and took a lead in 2008 when it appointed a cabinet in which women ministers outnumbered their male counterparts eight to seven. Zapatero also named the country's first ever woman defence minister. Still, few women reach top positions in private enterprise and women's wages remain lower than those of men for the same kind of work.

Women travellers should be ready to ignore stares, catcalls and unnecessary comments. Learn the word for help (socorro) in case you need to draw other people's attention.

By and large, Spanish women have a highly developed sense of style and put considerable effort into looking their best. While topless bathing and skimpy clothes are in fashion in many coastal resorts, people tend to dress more modestly elsewhere.

TRANSPORT

GETTING THERE & AWAY

Spain is one of Europe's top holiday destinations and is well linked to other European countries by air, rail and road.

Flying is generally the fastest and cheapest way of reaching Spain from elsewhere in Europe.

Some good direct flights are available from North America. Those coming from Australasia will usually have to make at least one change of flight.

Flights, tours and rail tickets can be booked online at www.lonelyplanet.com/travel_services.

ENTERING THE COUNTRY

Citizens of the 27 European Union (EU) member states and Switzerland can travel to Spain with their national identity card alone. If such countries do not issue ID cards – as in the UK – travellers must carry a full valid passport. All other nationalities must have a full valid passport.

AIR

AIRPORTS & AIRLINES

The main gateway to Spain is Madrid's **Barajas airport** (Aeropuerto de Barajas; ☎ nationwide flight information 902 40 47 04; www.aena.es), although many European direct flights serve other centres, particularly Barcelona, Málaga, Palma de Mallorca and Valencia. Charter flights and low-cost airlines (mostly from the UK) fly direct to a growing number of regional airports, including A Coruña, Alicante, Almería, Asturias, Bilbao, Girona (for the Costa Brava and Barcelona), Ibiza, Jerez de la Frontera, Murcia, Reus and Seville.

Iberia, Spain's national carrier, flies to most Spanish cities (many via Madrid) from around the world but is generally the expensive way to go.

TICKETS

There is no shortage of online agents:
www.cheaptickets.com
www.ebookers.com
www.expedia.com
www.flightline.co.uk
www.flynow.com
www.lastminute.com
www.openjet.com
www.opodo.com
www.planesimple.co.uk
www.skyscanner.net
www.travelocity.co.uk
www.tripadvisor.com

LAND

You can enter Spain by train, bus and private vehicle along various points of its northern border with France (and Andorra) and the western frontier with Portugal. Bus is generally the cheapest option but the train is more comfortable, especially for long-haul trips.

BUS

Eurolines (www.eurolines.com) and its partner bus companies run an extensive network of international buses across most of Western Europe and Morocco. In Spain they serve many destinations from the rest of Europe, although services often run only a few times a week.

CAR

Prebooking a rental car before leaving home will enable you to find the cheapest deals (for multinational agencies, see p369). No matter where you hire your car, make sure you understand what is included in the price and your liabilities.

TRAIN

The principal rail crossings into Spain pierce the Franco–Spanish frontier along the Mediterranean coast and via

↘ CLIMATE CHANGE & TRAVEL

Travel – especially air travel – is a significant contributor to global climate change. At Lonely Planet, we believe that all who travel have a responsibility to limit their personal impact. As a result, we have teamed with Rough Guides and other concerned industry partners to support Climate Care, which allows people to offset the greenhouse gases they are responsible for with contributions to energy-saving projects and other climate-friendly initiatives in the developing world. Lonely Planet offsets all staff and author travel.

For more information, turn to the responsible travel pages on www.lonely planet.com. For details on offsetting your carbon emissions and a carbon calculator, go to www.climatecare.org.

the Basque Country. Another minor rail route runs inland across the Pyrenees from Latour-de-Carol to Barcelona. From Portugal, the main line runs from Lisbon across Extremadura to Madrid.

Direct trains link Barcelona with Paris, Geneva, Zürich, Turin and Milan at least three times a week. Direct overnight trains also connect Paris with Madrid. Check details on the website of **Renfe** (☎ for international trips 902 24 34 02; www.renfe.es), the Spanish national railway company.

SEA

Ferries run to mainland Spain regularly from the Canary Islands, Italy, North Africa (Algeria, Morocco and the Spanish enclaves of Ceuta and Melilla) and the UK. Most services are run by the Spanish national ferry company, **Acciona Trasmediterránea** (☎ 902 45 46 45; www .trasmediterranea.es).

GETTING AROUND

You can reach almost any destination in Spain by train or bus, and services are efficient and, generally, cheap. Money is being poured into expanding the high-speed train network. Domestic air services are plentiful over longer distances and on routes that are more complicated by land.

While rail prices have climbed considerably in the past few years (along with efficiency, speed and comfort, it should be added!), airfares have become more competitive. However, your own wheels give you the most freedom.

AIR

Iberia and its subsidiary, Iberia Regional-Air Nostrum, have an extensive network covering all of Spain. Competing with Iberia are Spanair and Air Europa, as well as the low-cost companies Clickair (another Iberia subsidiary) and Vueling. Between them they cover a host of Spanish destinations.

The UK low-cost airline EasyJet has a hub in Madrid and offers domestic flights to Oviedo, Ibiza and A Coruña. Ireland's Ryanair also runs a handful of domestic Spanish flights, including Alicante–Zaragoza, Girona–Granada, Girona–Madrid, Madrid–Santander, Reus–Palma de Mallorca, Reus–Santander, Reus–Santiago de Compostela, Reus–Seville and Valencia–Santiago de Compostela.

BICYCLE

Years of highway improvement programs across the country have made cycling a much easier prospect than it once was. There are plenty of options, from mountain biking in the Pyrenees to distance riding along the coast.

If you get tired of pedalling it is often possible to take your bike on the train. All regional trains have space for bikes (usually marked by a bicycle logo on the carriage), where you can simply load the bike. Bikes are also permitted on most *cercanías* (local-area trains around big cities such as Madrid and Barcelona). On long-distance trains there are more restrictions. It's often possible to take your bike on a bus – usually you'll just be asked to remove the front wheel.

Bicycle rental is not as common as you might expect in Spain, although it is becoming more so, especially in the case of mountain bikes *(bici todo terreno)* and in the more popular regions, such as Andalucía and coastal spots like Barcelona. Costs vary considerably, but you can be looking at around €10 per hour, €15 to €20 per day, or €50 to €60 per week.

BOAT

Ferries and hydrofoils link the mainland (La Península) with the Balearic Islands and Spain's North African enclaves of Ceuta and Melilla.

The main national ferry company is **Acciona Trasmediterránea** (☎ 902 45 46 45; www.trasmediterranea.es). It runs a combination of slower car ferries and modern, high-speed, passenger-only fast ferries and hydrofoils. On overnight services between the mainland and the Balearic Islands you can opt for seating or sleeping accommodation in a cabin.

BUS

A plethora of companies provide bus links, from local routes between villages to fast intercity connections. It is often cheaper to travel by bus than by train, particularly on long-haul runs, but also less comfortable.

Local services can get you just about anywhere, but most buses connecting villages and provincial towns are not geared to tourist needs. Frequent weekday services drop off to a trickle on Saturday and Sunday.

For longer trips (such as Madrid to Seville or to the coast), and certainly in peak holiday season, you can (and should) buy your ticket in advance. On some routes you have the choice between express and all-stop services.

In most larger towns and cities, buses leave from a single bus station *(estación de autobuses)*. In smaller places, buses tend to operate from a set street or plaza, often unmarked. Locals will know where to go.

Bus travel within Spain is not overly costly. The trip from Madrid to Barcelona costs around €27 one way. From Barcelona to Seville, one of the longest trips you could do (15 to 16 hours), you pay up to €74 one way.

People under 26 years old should inquire about discounts on long-distance trips. Occasionally a return ticket is cheaper than two singles.

ALSA (☎ 902 42 22 42; www.alsa.es) is by far the biggest bus company operating in Spain. It has routes all over the country, which it operates in association with various other companies.

CAR & MOTORCYCLE
AUTOMOBILE ASSOCIATIONS

The **Real Automóvil Club de España** (RACE; Map pp64–5; ☎ 902 40 45 45; www.race.es; Calle de Eloy Gonzalo 32, Madrid) is the national automobile club. They may well come to assist you in case of breakdown, but in any event you should obtain an emergency telephone number for Spain from your own insurer.

DRIVING LICENCE

All EU member states' driving licences are fully recognised throughout Europe. Those with a non-EU licence are supposed to obtain a 12-month International Driving Permit (IDP) to accompany their national licence, which your national automobile association can issue. If you want to hire a car or motorcycle you will need to produce your driving licence.

FUEL & SPARE PARTS

Petrol (*gasolina*) in Spain is pricey, but generally cheaper than in its major EU neighbours (including France, Germany, Italy and the UK).

Lead-free (*sin plomo*; 95 octane) costs up to €1.21 per litre. A 98-octane variant costs as much as €1.32 per litre. Diesel (*gasóleo*) comes in at €1.25 per litre.

You can pay with major credit cards at most service stations.

HIRE

A selection of multinational car rental agencies is listed below.

Autos Abroad (☎ in the UK 0870 066 7788; www.autosabroad.com)

Avis (☎ 902 24 88 24; www.avis.es)

Budget (☎ in the USA 800 472 3325; www.budget.com)

Europcar (☎ 902 10 50 55; www.europcar.es)

Hertz (☎ 91 372 93 00; www.hertz.es)

National/Atesa (☎ 902 10 01 01; www.atesa.es)

Pepecar (☎ 807 41 42 43; www.pepecar.com) A local low-cost company.

To rent a car in Spain you have to have a licence, be aged 21 or over and, for the major companies at least, have a credit or debit card.

INSURANCE

Third-party motor insurance is a minimum requirement in Spain and throughout Europe.

Car-hire companies also provide this minimum insurance, but be careful to understand what your liabilities and excess are, and what waivers you are entitled to in case of accident or damage to the hire vehicle.

ROAD RULES

Drive on the right. In built-up areas the speed limit is 50km/h (and in some cases, such as inner-city Barcelona, 30km/h), which increases to 100km/h on major roads and up to 120km/h on *autovías* and *autopistas* (toll-free and tolled dual-lane highways, respectively). The minimum driving age is 18 years.

The blood-alcohol limit is 0.05%. Breath tests are common, and if found to be over the limit you can be judged, condemned, fined and deprived of your licence within 24 hours. Fines range up to around €600 for serious offences. Nonresident foreigners will be required to pay up on the spot (at 30% off the full fine).

LOCAL TRANSPORT

All the major cities have good local transport. Madrid and Barcelona have extensive bus and metro systems, and other major cities also benefit from generally efficient public transport.

BICYCLE

Few of the big cities offer much in the way of encouragement to cycle. Barcelona is an exception, where cycling lanes (albeit insufficient) have been laid out along main roads and various hire outlets make it possible for visitors to enjoy them. Barcelona and Seville have introduced public bicycle systems (but in Barcelona it is for residents

TRANSPORT

GETTING AROUND

A MEMORABLE NORTHERN TRAIN JOURNEY

The romantically inclined could opt for an opulent and slow-moving, old-time rail adventure in the colourful north of Spain.

Catch the **Transcantábrico** (www.transcantabrico.feve.es) for a journey on a picturesque narrow-gauge rail route, from Santiago de Compostela (by bus as far as O Ferrol) via Oviedo, Santander and Bilbao along the coast, and then a long inland stretch to finish in León. The eight-day trip costs €3500/5000 per single/double, and can also be done in reverse. There are departures up to four times a month from April to October. The package includes various visits along the way, including the Museo Guggenheim in Bilbao, the Cuevas de Altamira, Santillana del Mar, and the Covadonga lakes in the Picos de Europa. The food is as pleasurable for the palate as the sights are for the eyes, with some meals being eaten on board but most in various locations.

The trains don't travel at night, making sleeping aboard easy and providing the opportunity to stay out at night.

only). Driver attitudes are not always so enlightened, so beware.

BUS

Cities and provincial capitals all have reasonable bus networks. You can buy single tickets (up to €1.30, depending on the city) on the buses or at tobacconists, but in cities such as Madrid and Barcelona you are better off buying combined 10-trip tickets (see Metro, below) that allow the use of a combination of bus and metro, and which work out cheaper per ride. These can be purchased in any metro station.

Regular buses run from about 6am to shortly before midnight. In the big cities a night bus service generally kicks in on a limited number of lines in the wee hours. In Madrid they are known as *búhos* (owls) and in Barcelona more prosaically as *nitbusos* (night buses).

METRO

Madrid has the country's most extensive metro network. Barcelona follows in second place with a reasonable system. Valencia, Bilbao and Palma de Mallorca also have limited metros, and Seville is building one (due to open by the end of 2008). Tickets must be bought in metro stations (from counters or vending machines). Single tickets cost the same as for buses (up to €1.30). The best value for visitors wanting to move around the major cities over a few days are the 10-trip tickets, known in Madrid as Metrobús (€6.70) and in Barcelona as T-10 (€7.20). Monthly and season passes are also available.

TAXI

You can usually find taxi ranks at train and bus stations, or you can telephone for radio taxis. In larger cities taxi ranks are also scattered about the centre, and taxis will stop if you hail them in the street. Look for the green light and/or the *libre* sign on the passenger side of the windscreen. The bigger cities are well populated with taxis, although finding one when you need to get home late on a Friday or Saturday night in places such as Madrid and Barcelona can be tricky. No more than four people are allowed in a taxi.

Daytime flagfall (generally to 10pm) is around €1.30 to €1.95. After 10pm and on weekends and holidays (in some cities, including Madrid and Barcelona), the price can rise to €2.95. You then pay around €0.80 to €1 per kilometre depending on the time of day. There are airport and luggage surcharges. A cross-town ride in a major city will cost about €5 to €8, while a taxi between the city centre and airport in either Madrid or Barcelona will cost €20 to €25 with luggage.

TRAM

Trams were stripped out of Spanish cities decades ago, but they are making a timid comeback in some. Barcelona has a couple of new suburban tram services in addition to its tourist Tramvia Blau run to Tibidabo. Valencia has some useful trams to the beach. Various limited lines, often of little use to visitors, run in places like Bilbao, suburban Madrid and Murcia.

TRAIN

Renfe (☎ 902 24 02 02; www.renfe.es) is the national train system that runs most of the services in Spain. A handful of small private railway lines are noted throughout this book.

Spain has several types of trains. For short hops, bigger cities such as Madrid, Barcelona, Bilbao, Málaga and Valencia have local networks known as *cercanías*. Long-distance (aka *largo recorrido* or Grandes Líneas) trains come in all sorts of different flavours. They range from all-stops *regionales* operating within one region to the high-speed Tren de Alta Velocidad Española (AVE) trains that link Madrid with Barcelona, Burgos, Huesca (via Zaragoza), Málaga,

TRANSPORT

GETTING AROUND

TRAIN ROUTES

TRANSPORT

RAIL PASSES

InterRail (www.interrail.net) passes are available to people who have lived in Europe for six months or more. They can be bought at most major stations and student travel outlets, as well as online.

Eurail (www.eurail.com) passes are for those who have lived in Europe for less than six months and are supposed to be bought outside Europe. They're available from leading travel agencies and online.

Seniors travelling from the UK should ask at the **Rail Europe Travel Centre** (☎ 0844 848 4064; www.raileurope.co.uk) about possible discounts on rail travel in continental Europe.

The InterRail one-country pass for Spain can be used for three, four, six or eight days in one month. For the eight-day pass you pay €309/229/149/154.50/114.50 for adult 1st class/adult 2nd class/youth 2nd class/child 1st class/child 2nd class. Children's passes are for children aged four to 11, youth passes for people aged 12 to 25 and adult passes for those 26 and over. Children aged three and under travel for free. Cardholders get discounts on travel in the country where they purchase the ticket.

Eurail also offers a Spain national pass and several two-country regional passes (Spain-France, Spain-Italy and Spain-Portugal). You can choose from three to 10 days' train travel in a two-month period for any of these passes. The 10-day national pass costs €388/313 for 1st-class adult/2nd-class youth. As with all Eurail passes, you want to be sure you will be covering a lot of ground to make these worthwhile. Check some sample prices in euros for the places you intend to travel on the **Renfe** (www.renfe.es) website to compare.

GETTING AROUND

Seville and Valladolid (and in coming years Madrid–Valencia via Cuenca, and Madrid–Bilbao). Similar to the AVE trains used on conventional Spanish tracks (which differ from the standard European gauge) connect Barcelona with Valencia and Alicante in the Euromed service. A whole host of modern intermediate-speed services (Alaris, Altaria, Alvia, Arco and Avant) offer an increasingly speedy and comfortable service around the country, and have improved services vastly on such shorter-distance runs as Madrid–Toledo and Barcelona–Lleida. Slower long-distance trains include the Talgo and Intercity.

You'll find *consignas* (left-luggage facilities) at all main train stations. They are usually open from about 6am to midnight and charge from €3 to €4.50 per day per piece of luggage.

CLASSES & COSTS

All long-distance trains have 2nd and 1st classes, known as *turista* and *preferente*, respectively. The latter is 20% to 40% more expensive. Some services have a third, superior category, called *club*. Fares vary enormously depending on the service (faster trains cost considerably more) and, in the case of some high-speed services such as the AVE, on the time and day of travel. If you get a return ticket, it is worth checking whether your return journey is by the same kind of train. If you return on a slower train than the outward-bound trip you may be entitled to a modest refund on the return leg. Alternatively, if you return by a faster train you will need to pay more to make your return ticket valid for that train.

Tickets for AVE trains are by far the most expensive. A one-way trip in 2nd class from Madrid to Barcelona (on which route only AVE trains run) could cost as must as €160 (less if booked ahead on the web). Flying is often cheaper (although more of a hassle) and the bus certainly is. By contrast, the trip on the slower but much longer run from Barcelona to Oviedo costs a very reasonable €56.

Children aged between four and 12 years are entitled to a 40% discount; those aged under four travel for free (except on high-speed trains, for which they pay the same as those aged four to 12). Buying a return ticket often gives you a 10% to 20% discount on the return trip. Students and people up to 25 years of age with a Euro<26 Card (Carnet Joven in Spain) are entitled to 20% to 25% off most ticket prices.

Buying tickets in advance on the internet can also bring significant travel discounts (as much as 60% on some AVE services for tickets bought at least 15 days in advance).

On overnight trips within Spain on *trenhoteles* it's worth paying extra for a *litera* (couchette; a sleeping berth in a six- or four-bed compartment) or, if available, single or double cabins in *preferente* or *gran clase* class. The cost depends on the class of accommodation, type of train and length of journey. The lines covered are Madrid–La Coruña, Barcelona–Córdoba–Seville, Barcelona–Madrid (and on to Lisbon) and Barcelona–Málaga.

RESERVATIONS

Reservations are recommended for long-distance trips, and you can make them in train stations, Renfe offices and travel agencies, as well as online (which can be a little complicated). In a growing number of stations you can pick up prebooked tickets from machines scattered about the station concourse.

↘ GLOSSARY

Unless otherwise indicated, these terms are in Castilian Spanish.

ajuntament – Catalan for *ayuntamiento*
alcázar – Muslim-era fortress
AVE – Tren de Alta Velocidad Española; high-speed train
ayuntamiento – city or town hall

barrio – district/quarter (of a town or city)
bodega – cellar (especially wine cellar); also a winery or a traditional wine bar likely to serve wine from the barrel

calle – street
capilla – chapel
Carnaval – traditional festive period that precedes the start of Lent; carnival
castillo – castle
catedral – cathedral
churrigueresco – ornate style of baroque architecture named after the brothers Alberto and José Churriguera
ciudad – city
colegiata – collegiate church
conquistador – conqueror
Cortes – national parliament
costa – coast
cuenta – bill, cheque

ermita – hermitage or chapel
església – Catalan for *iglesia*
estació – Catalan for *estación*
estación – station
estany – lake
extremeño – Extremaduran; a native of Extremadura

feria – fair; can refer to trade fairs as well as to city, town or village fairs that are basically several days of merrymaking; can also mean a bullfight or festival stretching over days or weeks
ferrocarril – railway
festa – Catalan for *fiesta*
FEVE – Ferrocarriles de Vía Estrecha; a private train company in northern Spain
fiesta – festival, public holiday or party

gitanos – the Roma people
Gran Vía – main thoroughfare
GRs – (senderos de) Gran Recorrido; long-distance hiking paths

hospedaje – guesthouse
hostal – cheap hotel
huerta – market garden; orchard

iglesia – church
IVA – *impuesto sobre el valor añadido,* or value-added tax

judería – Jewish *barrio* in medieval Spain

madrileño/a – a person from Madrid
medina – Arabic word for town or city
mercado – market
mercat – Catalan for *mercado*
meseta – plateau; the high tableland of central Spain
mihrab – prayer niche in a mosque indicating the direction of Mecca
mirador – lookout point
Modernisme – literally 'modernism'; the architectural and artistic style, influenced by art nouveau and sometimes known as Catalan Modernism, whose leading practitioner was Antoni Gaudí

Modernista – an exponent of *modernisme*

monasterio – monastery

movida – similar to *marcha*; a *zona de movida* is an area of a town where lively bars and discos are clustered

Mozarab – Christian living under Muslim rule in early medieval Spain

Mozarabic – style of architecture developed by Mozarabs, adopting elements of classic Islamic construction to Christian architecture

Mudéjar – Muslims who remained behind in territory reconquered by Christians; also refers to a decorative style of architecture using elements of Islamic building style applied to buildings constructed in Christian Spain

museo – museum

museu – Catalan for *museo*

parador – luxurious state-owned hotels, many of them in historic buildings

parque nacional – national park; strictly controlled protected area

parque natural – natural park; a protected environmental area

paseo – promenade or boulevard; to stroll

pensión – small private hotel

pintxos – Basque tapas

plaça – Catalan for *plaza*

plateresque – early phase of Renaissance architecture noted for its intricately decorated facades

platja – Catalan for *playa*

playa – beach

plaza – square

port – Catalan for *puerto*

PP – Partido Popular (People's Party)

PSOE – Partido Socialista Obrero Español (Spanish Socialist Workers Party)

pueblo – village

puente – bridge; also means the extra day or two off that many people take when a holiday falls close to a weekend

puerta – gate or door

puerto – port or mountain pass

rastro – flea market; car-boot sale

real – royal

Reconquista – the Christian reconquest of the Iberian Peninsula from the Muslims (8th to 15th centuries)

refugi – Catalan for *refugio*

refugio – mountain shelter, hut or refuge

Renfe – Red Nacional de los Ferrocarriles Españoles; the national rail network

ría – estuary

río – river

riu – Catalan for *río*

Semana Santa – Holy Week, the week leading up to Easter Sunday

Sephardic Jews – Jews of Spanish origin

sierra – mountain range

s/n – sin número (without number), sometimes seen in addresses

tablao – tourist-oriented flamenco performances

tasca – tapas bar

torre – tower

turismo – means both tourism and saloon car; *el turismo* can also mean 'tourist office'

villa – small town

zarzuela – Spanish mix of theatre, music and dance

↘ BEHIND THE SCENES

THE AUTHORS
ANTHONY HAM

Coordinating author, This Is Spain, Spain's Top Itineraries, Planning your Trip, Spain in Focus, Madrid, Castilla y León, Aragón

In 2001, Anthony fell irretrievably in love with Madrid on his first visit to the city. Less than a year later, he arrived there on a one-way ticket, with not a word of Spanish and not knowing a single person in the city. Now, Anthony speaks Spanish with a Madrid accent, is married to Marina, a madrileña, and, together with their daughter Carlota, they live overlooking their favourite plaza in the city. When he's not writing about Spain for Lonely Planet, Anthony is the Madrid stringer for Melbourne's *Age* newspaper and writes about and photographs Madrid, Africa and the Middle East for newspapers and magazines around the world.

Author thanks I'm extremely grateful to the following people who agreed to be interviewed for this book: Leonardo Hernández, Beatriz Castaño, Juan Olazábal, Bego Sanchis, Jordi Faulí, Antoni Pitxot, Gabriella Ranelli, Iñaki Gaztelumendi, Manuel Toharia, María del Mar Villafranca and Sebastián de la Obra. And special thanks to those who helped set up the interviews: Manoli Ramiro (La Sagrada Família), Imma Parada and everyone at the Fundació Gala-Salvador Dalí, Carmen Baz (San Sebastián), Fernando Mujico (Santiago de Compostela), Laura Gatzkiewicz (Valencia), María José García (Ciudad de las Artes y las Ciencias), Ana Fernández (Alhambra) and Rosana de Aza (Casa de Sefarad). Thanks also to my wonderful editor, Lucy Monie, and to my wife and daughter, Marina and Carlota, who endured my absence and late nights as the deadline approached.

DAMIEN SIMONIS
Barcelona, Catalonia, Cantabria & Asturias, Balearic Islands, Calendar, Architecture, Directory, Transport

The spark was lit on a short trip over the Pyrenees to Barcelona during a summer jaunt in southern France. It was Damien's first taste of Spain and he found something irresistible about the place – the way the people moved, talked and enjoyed themselves. Damien came back years later, living in medieval Toledo, frenetic Madrid and, finally, settling in Barcelona. He has ranged across the country, from the Picos de Europa to the Sierra Nevada, from Córdoba to Cáceres, and slurped cider in Asturias and gin in the Balearic Islands. Damien has authored *Barcelona, Madrid, Mallorca,* the *Canary Islands* and the now defunct *Catalunya & the Costa Brava* for Lonely Planet.

SARAH ANDREWS   Galicia

Sarah Andrews has been living in and writing about Spain since 2000, when she moved to Barcelona from North Carolina. Since then, she's worked on many Spain-related titles for Lonely Planet and other publishers, but authoring the Galicia chapter was her first immersion in *gallego* culture. After weeks of soaking in stunning scenery, visiting incredible cities such as Santiago de Compostela, and getting her fill of specialities like *caldo gallego* (Galician soup), she's hooked. Read her recent work online at www .sarahandrews.com.

STUART BUTLER   Basque Country, Navarra & La Rioja, Andalucía

Stuart's first visit to the Basque Country, as a nipper, led to his first taste of surfing. He quickly became addicted to both. When he was older he spent every summer on the beaches in and around both the French and Spanish Basque Country until one day he found himself so hooked on the waves, climate, landscapes and beach 'attractions' that he was unable to leave – he has been there ever since. When not writing for Lonely Planet he drags himself away from home to search for uncharted surf on remote coastlines. The results of these trips appear frequently in the world's surf media. His website is www.oceansurfpublications.co.uk.

JOHN NOBLE   Andalucía, History

In the mid-1990s John, originally from England's Ribble Valley, and his wife, Susan Forsyth, decided to try life in an Andalucian mountain village. A writer specialising in Spain and Latin America, John has travelled throughout Spain and loves its fascinatingly historic cities, wild, empty back country, isolated villages and castles, rugged coasts, and its music, art, tapas, wine and football.

JOSEPHINE QUINTERO   Castilla-La Mancha, Murcia, Extremadura

Josephine started travelling with a backpack and guitar in the late '60s. Further travels took her to Kuwait, where she was held hostage during the Iraq invasion. Josephine moved to the relaxed shores of Andalucía shortly thereafter, from where she has explored most of the country. She loves Castilla-La Mancha for its dramatic landscape and because it is a beautiful, yet largely undiscovered, region where you still need to speak Spanish to order a beer.

MILES RODDIS   Valencia

Miles and his wife Ingrid have lived for more than 15 years in a shoebox-sized apartment in the Barrio del Carmen, Valencia's oldest and most vibrant quarter. Having cut his Lonely Planet teeth on tough African stuff such as Chad, the Central African Republic and Sudan, he nowadays writes about softer Mediterranean lands – Spain, France and Italy. He's the author or co-author of more than 30 Lonely Planet guidebooks, including *Valencia & the Costa Blanca, Best of Valencia, Walking in Spain, Canary Islands* and five editions of *Spain*. He loves Fallas about twice a decade and gets the hell out of town in intervening years.

ARPI ARMENAKIAN SHIVELY   Andalucía

Arpi, her partner Fred Shively and their bearded collie Macduff arrived in the Andalucian spa town of Lanjarón more or less by accident in 2003, via previous writing lives in London and Washington DC. They quickly fell in love with the dramatic Alpujarran landscape, the simplicity of life and the warmth of the community, plus free supplies of Lanjarón's coveted mineral water. As half of a freelance writer and photographer team, Arpi has written many articles about Andalucía's people, places and lifestyles for magazines in Spain and the UK, and plans to write many more as she continues to explore her adopted region in this beautiful country.

THIS BOOK

This 1st edition of *Discover Spain* was coordinated by Anthony Ham, and researched and written by Damien Simonis, Sarah Andrews, Stuart Butler, Anthony Ham, John Noble, Josephine Quintero, Miles Roddis and Arpi Armenakian Shively. This guidebook was commissioned in Lonely Planet's London office, and produced by the following:

Commissioning Editor Lucy Monie
Coordinating Editor Saralinda Turner
Coordinating Cartographer Xavier Di Toro
Coordinating Layout Designer Paul Iacono
Managing Editor Bruce Evans
Managing Cartographers Adrian Persoglia, Herman So
Managing Layout Designer Laura Jane
Assisting Editor Susie Ashworth
Assisting Cartographers Birgit Jordan, Joanne Luke
Cover Naomi Parker, lonelyplanetimages.com
Internal image research Naomi Parker, lonelyplanetimages.com
Project Manager Eoin Dunlevy
Language Content Annelies Mertens

Thanks to Sasha Baskett, Glenn Beanland, Lucy Birchley, Yvonne Bischofberger, Ryan Evans, Suki Gear, Joshua Geoghegan, Mark Germanchis, Chris Girdler, Michelle Glynn, Brice Gosnell, Imogen Hall, James Hardy, Jane Hart, Steve Henderson, Lauren Hunt, Laura Jane, Indra Kilfoyle, Chris Lee Ack, Nic Lehman, Alison Lyall, John Mazzocchi, Jennifer Mullins, Wayne Murphy, Darren O'Connell, Naomi Parker, Piers Pickard, Howard Ralley, Lachlan Ross, Julie Sheridan, Jason Shugg, Caroline Sieg, Naomi Stephens, Geoff Stringer, Jane Thompson, Sam Trafford, Stefanie Di Trocchio, Brian Turnbull, Tashi Wheeler, Clifton Wilkinson, Juan Winata, Emily K Wolman, Nick Wood

SEND US YOUR FEEDBACK

We love to hear from travellers – your comments keep us on our toes and help make our books better. Our well-travelled team reads every word on what you loved or loathed about this book. Although we cannot reply individually to postal submissions, we always guarantee that your feedback goes straight to the appropriate authors, in time for the next edition. Each person who sends us information is thanked in the next edition and the most useful submissions are rewarded with a free book.

To send us your updates – and find out about Lonely Planet events, newsletters and travel news – visit our award-winning website: lonelyplanet.com/contact.

Note: we may edit, reproduce and incorporate your comments in Lonely Planet products such as guidebooks, websites and digital products, so let us know if you don't want your comments reproduced or your name acknowledged. For a copy of our privacy policy visit lonelyplanet.com/privacy.

BEHIND THE SCENES

Internal photographs p4 Bullfighting posters for sale, El Rastro, Madrid, Krzysztof Dydynski; p10 Plaza d'Espana, Seville, Oliver Strewe; p12 Outdoor restaurants, Peñíscola, David Tomlinson; p31 Alcazar, Seville, Bethune Carmichael; p39 Estellencs, Mallorca, Holger Leue; p3, p50 Plaza Mayor, Madrid, David Tomlinson; p3, p85 Casa Batlló, Barcelona, John Banagan; p3, p121 Windmills, Consuegra, Witold Skrypczak; p3, p155 Cadaqués harbour, Costa Brava, Martin Llado; p3, p187 Asturian coastline, Matthew Schoenfelder; p3, p223 Arta Castle wall, Mallorca, Holger Leue; p3, p257 Town hall, Seville, Paul Bernhardt; p312 Seville, Oliver Strewe; p347 Albayzín, Granada, Alfredo Maiquez.

All images are copyright of the photographer unless otherwise indicated. Many of the images in this guide are available for licensing from Lonely Planet Images: www.lonelyplanetimages.com.

ACKNOWLEDGMENTS

Many thanks to the following for the use of their content:
Antoni Pitxot (p158) picture kindly provided by Fundació Gala-Salvador Dalí, Figueres, 2009. Iñaki Gaztelumendi (p190) picture kindly provided by Martin Rendo.

NOTES

NOTES

↘ INDEX

INDEX

B–C

INDEX

C

INDEX

G-L

INDEX

L-M

INDEX

M-O

INDEX

T-Z

MAP LEGEND

ROUTES

Tollway
Freeway
Primary
Secondary
Tertiary
Lane
Under Construction
Unsealed Road

One-Way Street
Mall/Steps
Tunnel
Pedestrian Overpass
Walking Tour
Walking Tour Detour
Walking Path
Track

TRANSPORT

Ferry
Metro
Monorail

Rail/Underground
Tram
Cable Car, Funicular

HYDROGRAPHY

River, Creek
Intermittent River
Swamp/Mangrove
Reef

Canal
Water
Dry Lake/Salt Lake
Glacier

BOUNDARIES

International
State, Provincial
Disputed

Regional, Suburb
Marine Park
Cliff/Ancient Wall

AREA FEATURES

Area of Interest
Beach, Desert
Building/Urban Area
Cemetery, Christian
Cemetery, Other

Forest
Mall/Market
Park
Restricted Area
Sports

POPULATION

⊙ **CAPITAL (NATIONAL)**
● LARGE CITY
● Small City

◉ **CAPITAL (STATE)**
● Medium City
● Town, Village

SYMBOLS

Sights/Activities

Buddhist
Canoeing, Kayaking
Castle, Fortress
Christian
Confucian
Diving
Hindu
Islamic
Jain
Jewish
Monument
Museum, Gallery
Point of Interest
Pool
Ruin
Sento (Public Hot Baths)
Shinto
Sikh
Skiing
Surfing, Surf Beach
Taoist
Trail Head
Winery, Vineyard
Zoo, Bird Sanctuary

Information

Bank, ATM
Embassy/Consulate
Hospital, Medical
Information
Internet Facilities
Police Station
Post Office, GPO
Telephone
Toilets
Wheelchair Access

Eating

Eating

Drinking

Cafe
Drinking

Entertainment

Entertainment

Shopping

Shopping

Sleeping

Camping
Sleeping

Transport

Airport, Airfield
Border Crossing
Bus Station
Bicycle Path/Cycling
FFCC (Barcelona)
Metro (Barcelona)
Parking Area
Petrol Station
S-Bahn
Taxi Rank
Tube Station
U-Bahn

Geographic

Beach
Lighthouse
Lookout
Mountain, Volcano
National Park
Pass, Canyon
Picnic Area
River Flow
Shelter, Hut
Waterfall

LONELY PLANET OFFICES

Australia

Head Office
Locked Bag 1, Footscray, Victoria 3011
☎ 03 8379 8000, fax 03 8379 8111
talk2us@lonelyplanet.com.au

USA

150 Linden St, Oakland, CA 94607
☎ 510 250 6400, toll free 800 275 8555,
fax 510 893 8572
info@lonelyplanet.com

UK

2nd fl, 186 City Rd,
London EC1V 2NT
☎ 020 7106 2100, fax 020 7106 2101
go@lonelyplanet.co.uk

Published by Lonely Planet
ABN 36 005 607 983

Printed by Fabulous Printers Pte Ltd
Printed in Singapore